Emperor of Liberty

The Lewis Walpole Series in Eighteenth-Century
Culture and History

The Lewis Walpole Series, published by Yale University
Press with the aid of the Annie Burr Lewis Fund, is
dedicated to the culture and history of the long eighteenth
century (from the Glorious Revolution to the accession of
Queen Victoria). It welcomes work in a variety of fields,
including literature and history, the visual arts, political
philosophy, music, legal history, and the history of science.
In addition to original scholarly work, the series publishes
new editions and translations of writing from the period, as
well as reprints of major books that are currently unavailable.
Though the majority of books in the series will probably
concentrate on Great Britain and the Continent, the range of
our geographical interests is as wide as Horace Walpole's.

Emperor *of* Liberty

Thomas Jefferson's Foreign Policy

Francis D. Cogliano

Yale

UNIVERSITY PRESS

New Haven and London

Published with assistance from the Annie Burr Lewis Fund.

Yale University Press books may be purchased in quantity for educational, business, or
promotional use. For information, please e-mail sales.press@yale.edu (U.S. office) or
sales@yaleup.co.uk (U.K. office).

Designed by Sonia Shannon.
Set in Bulmer type by Westchester Book Group.
Printed in the United States of America.

Library of Congress Cataloging-in-Publication Data

Cogliano, Francis D.
Emperor of liberty : Thomas Jefferson's foreign policy / Francis D. Cogliano.
pages cm—(The Lewis Walpole series in eighteenth-century culture and history)
Includes bibliographical references and index.
ISBN 978-0-300-17993-4 (cloth : alk. paper)   1. United States—Foreign relations—
1801–1809.   2. Jefferson, Thomas, 1743–1826.   I. Title.
E331.C67 2014
327.73009'034—dc23
2013049557

A catalogue record for this book is available from the British Library.

This paper meets the requirements of ANSI/NISO Z39.48–1992 (Permanence of Paper).

10 9 8 7 6 5 4 3 2 1

For Peter Onuf

Contents

Acknowledgments

It is a pleasure to acknowledge the many debts I have incurred in the course of writing this book.

All research on Jefferson eventually leads to Monticello, Jefferson's home on the outskirts of Charlottesville, Virginia. I am immensely grateful to the Thomas Jefferson Foundation, which owns Monticello and operates it as a museum and research center, for its support while I was writing this book. In particular I am grateful to Leslie Greene Bowman, president of the Thomas Jefferson Foundation, for her encouragement and enthusiasm. Leslie supports research on all aspects of Jefferson and his time. She understands that scholars must follow the evidence wherever it may lead. She seeks neither to "defend" nor "attack" the master of Monticello but promotes scholarship and public engagement through honest dialogue about Jefferson and his legacy. Much of that dialogue at Monticello is conducted under the auspices of the Robert H. Smith International Center for Jefferson Studies. Under the leadership of Andrew Jackson O'Shaughnessy the ICJS has emerged as major scholarly center not only for the study of Jefferson particularly but of revolutionary and early national America generally. During my numerous visits to Charlottesville while writing this book Andrew always offered a warm welcome and generous hospitality. Andrew also afforded me numerous opportunities to present my research and test my ideas at conferences and symposia that he organized in Charlottesville and around the world. While I was writing my manuscript I enjoyed a research fellowship at the ICJS for which I am very grateful. The ICJS campus at Kenwood, within sight of Monticello, is a delightful place to think and write about Jefferson. Among the many good people at Monticello who helped me are: Anna

Berkes, Jeff Looney, Jack Robertson, Mary Scott-Fleming, Cinder Stanton, Susan Stein, Endrina Tay, and Gaye Wilson.

Monticello sits at the center of a large community of scholars who have offered me the benefit of their counsel, support, and friendship. I am especially grateful to Richard Bernstein, Andrew Burstein, Joanne Freeman, Annette Gordon-Reed, Nancy Isenberg, Simon Newman, Hannah Spahn, and Maurizio Valsania. Michael Kranish generously shared his expertise on Jefferson's tenure as governor of Virginia with me. I met Alan Taylor longer ago than either of us cares to remember. He was an exemplary Ph.D. advisor and has remained a good friend ever since. Alan is an historian of extraordinary breadth and imagination. He works harder than any scholar I have ever known setting an example for us all. By pleasant coincidence we each enjoyed fellowships at the International Center for Jefferson Studies while I was writing this book. We had adjoining offices and his presence helped me keep to my writing schedule. As ever, I profited from his advice and good humor.

I am grateful to the School of History, Classics, and Archaeology at the University of Edinburgh for providing me with research leave and funding while I was writing this book. I have the privilege of working with some outstanding colleagues at a university that Jefferson once described as "a place where the best courses upon earth are within your reach." I've discussed this project with many colleagues and friends in Edinburgh including Douglas Cairns, Ewen Cameron, Tom Devine, Fabian Hilfrich, Rhodri Jeffreys-Jones, Robert Mason, Paul Quigley, and Jill Stephenson. Owen Dudley Edwards read my manuscript and provided helpful—and witty—advice. My friend Susan Manning, an outstanding scholar of Scottish and American literature, died suddenly as I was completing this book. Susan was a generous colleague who provided leadership for Edinburgh's community of eighteenth-century scholars. She is missed.

Yale University Press has been a delight to work with. I first discussed this project with Heather McCallum in the London office. Heather introduced me to Chris Rogers, the press's editorial director in New Haven. Chris and I chatted about this book over a lengthy lunch, and he's been encouraging and supportive throughout its writing and production. I'm grateful to Christina Tucker, Margaret Otzel, and Eliza

Childs who've patiently worked with me to see this book through to publication. Bill Nelson drew the maps for this volume.

During my many research trips to the United States I benefited from the kindness and hospitality of friends and family including Beth Cogliano, David and Lisa Cogliano, John and Sally Giangrande, and Alan Swartz. I stayed with Chuck and Andrea Katter for prolonged periods while researching and writing this book. I am grateful to all of them.

This book is dedicated Peter Onuf. Peter took me, like so many others, under his wing when I started writing about Jefferson. He has been extraordinarily generous to me over the years. He always took the time to discuss my project with me and to offer counsel and assistance. He has been so supportive of me that many people in Charlottesville assumed that I was his student. I take that as the highest compliment.

Most important of all is the debt I owe my family: Mimi, Edward, and Sofia. They've patiently waited for the completion of this project and supported me throughout.

A Note on Sources

When he died in 1826, Thomas Jefferson bequeathed to posterity an immense documentary legacy that included private and public correspondence, state papers, and personal records. These are the main sources that I have used in the writing of this book. Since 1950 Princeton University Press has been publishing Jefferson's papers in an ongoing project that is one of the most valuable undertakings in American letters. The Princeton edition of *The Papers of Thomas Jefferson* seeks to publish the entire corpus of Jefferson's papers in a definitive edition. Apart from the inherent value of the project, *The Papers of Thomas Jefferson* has set the standard for scholarly editing in the United States. Since the appearance of the first volume in 1950 the established practices in scholarly editing have changed considerably. As a consequence there has been a transition from editing and correcting documents to literal transcription. Those familiar with Jefferson's writings, either in manuscript or in the latter volumes of the Princeton edition, will know that certain quirks appear. For example Jefferson's use of capital letters, particularly at the beginning of sentences, was inconsistent, and he struggled to distinguish between "its" and "it's." In an effort to make the text flow more smoothly, I have quietly corrected Jefferson's errors—while always citing the original documents. I have retained the spelling in accordance with the volumes of the Princeton edition.

Introduction
Three Emperors

In 1804 the American consul in St. Petersburg, Levett Harris, presented President Thomas Jefferson with a plaster copy of a bust of Tsar Alexander I.[1] Jefferson sent the image to his home, Monticello, on the outskirts of Charlottesville, Virginia, writing, "It will constitute one of the most valued ornaments of the retreat I am preparing for myself at my native home." He displayed the statue in the parlor at Monticello, explaining to Harris that although, as a rule, he did not accept gifts (except books or pamphlets "of minor value"), he made an exception for the bust of the tsar. "My particular esteem for the character of the Emperor," Jefferson wrote, "places his image in my mind above the scope of the law. I receive it, therefore, and shall cherish it with affection. It nourishes the contemplation of all the good placed in his power, and his disposition to do it."[2] Why did Jefferson, who extolled universal equality as the author the Declaration of Independence and who claimed to preside over the spread of democracy in the new American republic, so admire the autocratic tsar of Russia—who ruled an empire that extended from the Baltic to the Pacific?

Jefferson felt that Alexander, with his commitment to enlightened principles of government, was better than most of his royal peers. During his retirement, Jefferson contemplated the apparent ease with which Napoleon had swept aside so many monarchs and conquered Europe. He felt that inherited power led to degeneracy, something Napoleon was able to exploit to good effect. He wrote:

>   While in Europe, I often amused myself with contemplating
> the characters of the then reigning sovereigns of Europe. Louis
> XVI was a fool, of my knowledge. . . . The King of Spain was a
> fool, and of Naples the same. They passed their lives in hunting
> and dispatched two couriers a week, one thousand miles, to let
> each other know what game they had killed the preceding days.
> The King of Sardinia was a fool. All these were Bourbons. The
> Queen of Portugal, a Braganza, was an idiot by nature. And so
> was the King of Denmark. Their sons, as regents, exercised the
> powers of government. The King of Prussia, successor to the
> great Frederick, was a mere hog in body as well as in mind. Gus-
> tavus of Sweden, and Joseph of Austria, were really crazy, and
> George of England you know was in a straight waistcoat. There
> remained, then, none but old Catherine, who had been too lately
> picked up to have lost her common sense. In this state Buon-
> aparte found Europe, and it was this state of its rulers which lost
> it with scarce a struggle. These animals had become without
> mind and powerless; and so will every hereditary monarch be
> after a few generations.

Jefferson exempted the relatively new Russian dynasty from his catalog
of monarchical imbecility and incompetence. "Alexander, the grandson
of Catherine, is as yet an exception. He is able to hold his own. But he is
only of the third generation. His race is not yet worn out."[3]

Alexander acceded to the Russian throne in March 1801, just a few
weeks after Jefferson was inaugurated as the third president of the United
States. After receiving early intelligence about the young tsar, Jefferson
confessed to having "strong spasms of the heart in his favor." In another
letter written the same day, he wrote of the tsar, "The apparition of such
a man on a throne, is one of the phænomena which will distinguish the
present epoch so remarkable in the history of man."[4] Jefferson believed
that Alexander embodied the principles of enlightened monarchy. In
1802 he wrote, "Alexander will doubtless begin at the right end, by taking means for diffusing instruction and a sense of their natural rights
through the mass of his people, and for relieving them in the meantime
from actual oppression." Several years later he wrote to Alexander him-

self, "It will be among the latest and most soothing comforts of my life, to see advanced to the government of so extensive a portion of the earth, and at so early a period of his life, a sovereign whose ruling passion is the advancement of the happiness and prosperity of his people."[5]

Although he believed monarchy to be a flawed system of government which inevitably led to degeneracy and corruption, Jefferson also believed that not all peoples and societies had evolved to the point where they could sustain republican government. For these, enlightened monarchy, of the type that he believed Alexander embodied, was most appropriate. Jefferson believed this was the case in Russia. Alexander's "means of doing good are great," he wrote, "yet the materials on which he is to work are refractory." Jefferson believed Alexander faced "a herculean task to devise and establish the means of securing freedom and happiness to those who are not capable of taking care of themselves. Some preparation seems necessary to qualify the body of a nation for self government."[6] In Jefferson's conception of political and social development, an enlightened monarchy like Alexander's should prepare its subjects to govern themselves before it degenerated, as all monarchies must, into corruption and tyranny.

Jefferson admired Alexander for his geopolitical contributions, as well as for his governance of Russia. When he wrote to Alexander in April 1806, he did so to thank the tsar for offering to mediate the ongoing commercial and diplomatic dispute between the United States and Britain over the issue of neutral trade during wartime. He praised the tsar not only for seeking to advance the happiness and prosperity of his own people but also as a ruler "who can extend his eye and his good will to a distant and infant nation, unoffending in its course, unambitious in its views."[7] As we shall see, the rights of neutrals were a preoccupation for Jefferson during his presidency. Jefferson hoped that Russia might serve as a counterweight to Britain and act as a guarantor of neutral rights, a stance which would benefit the United States as the world's preeminent neutral trader. In 1813 Jefferson wrote of Alexander's offer to mediate in the then ongoing war between Britain and the United States: "I sincerely pray that this mediation may produce a just peace. It will prove that the immortal character, which has first stopped by war the career of the destroyer of mankind, is the friend of peace, of justice, of human happiness, and the patron of unoffending and injured nations."[8]

In the geopolitical realm Jefferson most admired Alexander for his role in the defeat of Napoleon. Jefferson had faith that Alexander would exercise his new global authority responsibly. Such an interpretation required Jefferson to ignore several inconvenient truths: notably that the tsar had come to power after the murder of his father, Paul I; that Alexander and Napoleon had been allies before they became enemies; and that George III's Britain, too, had made a decisive contribution to the defeat of "the destroyer of mankind." Unwilling to acknowledge the role of Britain—which he saw as a regressive force in global affairs only slightly less dangerous than Napoleonic France—in the defeat of Napoleon, Jefferson was inclined to give all the credit to Alexander, whom he idealized as an enlightened and benign ruler.

And so we must return to Monticello. The manner in which Jefferson displayed Alexander's likeness tells us much about why the president found the tsar so appealing. Jefferson placed Alexander's bust in the parlor opposite a bust of Napoleon. The two emperors flanked the doors of the west portico of Jefferson's home. The juxtaposition of Alexander and Napoleon was deliberate. In July 1814 Jefferson wrote to John Adams, contrasting the two emperors: "Bonaparte was a lion in the field only. In civil life a cold-blooded, calculating unprincipled Usurper, without a virtue, no statesman, knowing nothing of commerce, political economy or civil government, and supplying ignorance by bold presumption. . . . To the wonders of his rise and fall, we may add that of a Czar of Muscovy dictating, *in Paris,* the laws and limits to all the successors of the Caesars, and holding even the balance in which the fortunes of this new world are suspended."[9] Jefferson believed that the tsar epitomized the virtues and potential of enlightened monarchy. While the absolutism of the tsar was unfortunate, Alexander had played *the* crucial role in defeating the tyranny of Napoleon. Jefferson intended that the busts of Alexander and Napoleon should underscore the global historical nature of the struggle between liberty and tyranny. Among its many purposes, Monticello stood as a physical monument to Jeffersonian principles. The men and women who visited Jefferson's parlor would be reminded just what was at stake in that struggle when they gazed upon the likenesses of Napoleon and his conqueror, Alexander.

Jefferson presented Alexander and Napoleon not so much as antipodes but as two examples of imperial rule—one enlightened, the other despotic—that characterized the way most of humanity was governed. They were not so much opposites as variants of a type. Both stood in mute contrast to Jefferson, the master of Monticello and president of the United States. Unlike Napoleon, who had seized power and attempted to conquer Europe, and Alexander, who had inherited a vast domain and exercised absolute power, Jefferson had been elected to rule a large and growing republic. His power and authority were derived from the consent of those he governed—at least those who enjoyed full political rights. The real contrast in the Monticello parlor was not between Alexander and Napoleon. The former, representing the best that could be hoped for out of a flawed system of government, and the latter, epitomizing imperial rule at its worst, were two sides of the same debased coin. The important distinction was between Jefferson and his European counterparts. Jefferson represented an alternative form of government and a different future for humanity. He represented the power of an expansive republic that he styled an "empire of liberty." He was a different kind of emperor because his country would be a different kind of empire.[10]

Jefferson's empire, as this book shows, was premised on access to plentiful land and overseas trade. If the United States were to flourish, it would have to expand in order to support its growing population. Jefferson believed that the United States should remain predominantly a nation of small farmers if liberty were to thrive. Because the republic's population grew so rapidly Americans would require additional land. He looked to the west (as well as the south and north) as the home for future generations of Americans. Jefferson did not envision that Americans should be subsistence farmers. In order for them to flourish, they would need to export their produce. This required unfettered access to international markets. The two desiderata for the American republic were land and free trade. The United States would be an empire of liberty because liberty could not thrive without expansion. If liberty were extinguished in the United States, the republican experiment would fail. In Jefferson's mind the growth of the "empire of liberty" and the success of the American republic were one and the same thing. As president, Jefferson sought to realize this vision of an expansionist American republic.

As such, he, more than any other figure, was the father of the first American empire. Acquiring land and guaranteeing access to overseas markets would be the major foreign policy concerns of Jefferson (and his successors James Madison and James Monroe).

Jefferson believed that the American republic was constantly threatened by traditional imperial powers. The wars of the eighteenth century led to important changes in the geopolitical situation in North America. At the conclusion of the Seven Years' War in 1763, France was forced to give up her North American empire. At the Peace of Paris France ceded Canada to Britain. Spain ceded the Floridas to Britain. In recognition of Spanish support during the recent war, France had ceded Louisiana to Spain. As a result of these shifts, Britain ruled all of North America east of the Mississippi River (not including New Orleans), and Spain all of the territory west of the river, except for the far northwest, where Spanish authority was contested by Russia. Twenty years later, at the conclusion of the American War of Independence, Britain returned the Floridas to Spain and conceded generous borders to the United States, which stretched from the Atlantic to the Mississippi and north from the Floridas—whose northern border was then contested by Spain and the United States—to the Great Lakes. Given these dynamics, the republic was threatened from the north by Britain and from the south and west by Spain—and even the by the French, as Napoleon, at the turn of the nineteenth century, sought to revive French imperial ambitions in the West Indies and North America. Jefferson sought to expand the nation's borders and defend its interests, and he did so, he believed, in a world of hostile and predatory empires which sought to destroy the United States.

This book considers Jefferson's efforts to realize his vision of a republican empire. Its emphasis is on the development of Jefferson's thought and actions to achieve the new republic's foreign policy objectives. As such it revisits the subject of Jefferson's statecraft. Statecraft might be defined as the use of the power of the state to achieve its ends.[11] This book examines Jefferson's statecraft through a series of case studies. Although most previous studies have focused on Jefferson's presidency exclusively, in this book I take a longer view, tracing the evolution of Jefferson's statecraft by considering examples chosen from across Jefferson's long public career. Its premise is that we can understand Jefferson's actions as president only if we appreciate how he came to understand power and international relations throughout his career as an office-holder: as governor of Virginia, minister to France, and as secretary of state, vice president, and president of the United States.

The coverage of Jefferson's career is not comprehensive but rather episodic. For example, the chapter on Jefferson's tenure as American minister in Paris focuses on his unsuccessful efforts to negotiate a settlement with the North African Barbary States, rather than on his other activities in Europe. These negotiations are a relatively neglected aspect of Jefferson's years in France, yet they are significant for the purposes of this study because of what they reveal about Jefferson's views on political economy and statecraft. When the Barbary States threatened American trade in the Mediterranean they threatened the well-being of the American republic. Initially Jefferson, along with John Adams, sought to negotiate a settlement with the Barbary States. When this proved impossible, in large part because the Barbary leaders demanded tribute beyond what the Americans were prepared to pay, Jefferson sought to create an international coalition to wage war against the North Africans, thus (he believed) solving the Barbary problem permanently. Despite the relative weakness of the United States, Jefferson was willing to use force to achieve his international objectives. Although this book is not a comprehensive treatment of Jefferson's career as an international statesman, it surveys Jefferson's lengthy career in order to illuminate his understanding of America's place in the world. It focuses on how he defined and promoted the republic's strategic interests, most notably the acquisition of territory and the promotion of free trade.

Historians of American foreign relations tend to divide its practitioners into two broad camps—idealists and realists. The idealists believe that American diplomacy and foreign policy should be guided by moral principles. The realists, by contrast, contend that self-interest and an acceptance of power politics should guide American foreign policy. Although proponents of both schools have claimed Jefferson, he has mainly been identified as an idealist, often by scholars critical of his statecraft.[12] In the most important modern study of Jefferson's statecraft, *Empire of*

Liberty (1990), Robert W. Tucker and David C. Hendrickson argue that Jefferson's approach to international relations rejected traditional eighteenth-century theories of balance of power and raison d'état in favor of a new diplomacy for a revolutionary republic. They write: "The United States, [Jefferson] believed, was the bearer of a new diplomacy, founded on the confidence of a free and virtuous people, that would secure ends based on the natural and universal rights of man, by means that escaped war and its corruptions. This new diplomacy broke radically, Jefferson thought, from the practices and principles of the old European tradition of reason of state, with its settled belief in the primacy of foreign over domestic policy." According to their interpretation, Jefferson sought to pursue American interests as a matter of right, and he eschewed the traditional means of European diplomacy—negotiation, maintenance of the balance of power, and war. "The conflict between an ambitious program in foreign policy and the rejection of the military and financial system characteristic of the Great Powers of Europe went to the core of Jefferson's dilemma in foreign policy." Jefferson resolved this dilemma, write Tucker and Hendrickson, "by placing an inordinate degree of faith in his ability to 'conquer without war'—to secure the objectives of the United States by economic and peaceable means of coercion." As a consequence of his faith in "new diplomacy," they conclude, Jefferson's foreign policy was imbued with a counterproductive moralistic and righteous tone that made it impossible for Jefferson to achieve long-term diplomatic success. Jefferson's success in purchasing Louisiana, they argue, encouraged his moralistic approach to foreign affairs and led to his catastrophic inability to negotiate a solution to the crisis in British-American relations that bedeviled his second term as president. As a consequence Jefferson (and Madison) blundered, leading the United States into an unnecessary war in 1812. As Bradford Perkins, another diplomatic historian who sees Jefferson as an idealist, has written: "Their inept diplomacy produced national disgrace and then a war with England, which, but for good fortune, might well have destroyed the union. Both deservedly left the White House with tarnished reputations."[13]

Some historians have viewed Jefferson as a realist. In an influential 1993 essay Walter LaFeber challenged the interpretation of Tucker and

Hendrickson, arguing that Jefferson managed his foreign policy effectively. He writes:

> The dynamics of Jefferson's foreign policy ran as follows: his early belief in the virtues of, and need for, agrarian expansionism helped lead to a series of conflicts in the international arena that forced him to devise a set of stronger central governmental policies to protect both agrarian and, increasingly, more broadly defined national interests These governmental policies included military action and a dominant presidency. The implementation of Jeffersonian foreign policies helps explain contradictions and paradoxes that turn out more apparent than real.

For LaFeber, Jefferson was consistent in the ends he sought—the extension and protection of the United States as an agrarian republic. What changed were the means he employed, with mixed results, to secure those ends. This view is consonant with the main argument of this book.[14]

The realist/idealist dichotomy isn't all that helpful for understanding Jefferson's statecraft. To be sure Jefferson proclaimed himself an idealist. He articulated a clear, coherent ideological vision for the future of the United States in his various state papers, letters, and other writings. He sought to make this vision come true as a statesman. Further, he was well versed in Enlightenment thinking about international relations. He had read the major theorists of international relations who conceived of a world without war, in which the law of nations mediated disputes between states large and small. Jefferson would have liked to have seen such a world come to pass, and he believed that the spread of republicanism around the globe would make this possible. In 1821, reflecting on the revolutions in the United States and France as well as the current struggles for independence in Latin America, he predicted the triumph of republicanism around the world. "The tyrants of the North have allied against it," he wrote, referring to the European imperial powers, "but it is irresistible. Their opposition will only multiply its millions of human victims; their own satellites will catch it, and the condition of man thro' the whole civilized world will be finally greatly ameliorated."[15]

Despite his faith that republicanism would ultimately prevail, making for a more peaceful world, his acknowledgment that tyrants would continue to offer resistance at great human cost suggests an awareness of the realities of global politics. It might be said that Jefferson was an idealist when writing about the future but a realist when considering the world around him. One of the lessons he derived from his engagement with the Enlightenment project was a belief that reason should be applied to solve problems. He was less committed to fostering an idealized new diplomacy than to insuring that the American republic survived and flourished so that a more peaceful and harmonious republican future might be possible.

The main argument advanced in this book is that although Jefferson was guided by a clear ideological vision for the American republic, he was pragmatic about the means he employed to protect the republic and advance its strategic interests. As he wrote during his presidency, "What is practicable must often controul what is pure theory."[16] While Jefferson's ideological vision for the country was fairly clear, his statecraft, the means by which he sought to realize this vision, was grounded in his experience as a political leader and statesman and his understanding of international power relations. He had faith in the future of the United States and the incipient power of its citizens, but he recognized the relative weakness of the nation in the international realm. Depending on circumstances he deployed a variety a tactics—including negotiation, temporizing, threats, force, and economic coercion—to achieve his ends. Jefferson's ends were consistent, yet he was flexible about the means he employed to achieve them; he was not a doctrinaire ideologue. As one of his most recent biographers, Jon Meacham, has written; "Jefferson had reached the pinnacle by articulating the ideal but acting pragmatically. . . . As president he fully intended to rule in the way he had risen." Meacham explains Jefferson's statecraft: "He was always in favor of whatever means would improve the chances of his cause of the hour. . . . He was not intellectually consistent, but a consistent theme did run through his politics and statecraft: He would do what it took, within reason, to arrange the world as he wanted it to be." In this he was not unlike his contemporaries Napoleon and Alexander I.[17]

One

According to the Judgment of a Good Man

On June 1, 1779, the Virginia House of Delegates met in Williamsburg to elect the commonwealth's new governor. The popular outgoing governor, Patrick Henry, had served three one-year terms and was prohibited by the state's constitution from standing for re-election. The assembly chose among three candidates: Thomas Nelson, Jr., John Page, and Thomas Jefferson. The three men had known each other for years—Page and Jefferson were boyhood friends—and were fervent supporters of the Revolution. On its first ballot the delegates gave Jefferson 55 votes, Page 38 votes, and Nelson 32 votes. A second ballot was necessary—as Jefferson had not achieved an overall majority—and most of Nelson's support went to Page. Jefferson won enough votes, however, to give him a clear majority, and he was elected to a one-year term as governor by a margin of 67 to 61. The defeated Page congratulated his friend wishing him happiness and pledging to do "every thing in my Power to make your Administration easy and agreeable to you." In reply Jefferson reflected, "It had given me much pain that the zeal of our respective friends should ever have placed you and me in the situation of competitors." He continued, "I was comforted however with the reflection that it was their competition, not ours and the difference of the numbers which decided between us, was so insignificant to give you a pain or me a pleasure."[1]

Thomas Jefferson was thirty-six years old when he was elected governor of Virginia. He was more than six feet two inches tall and thin,

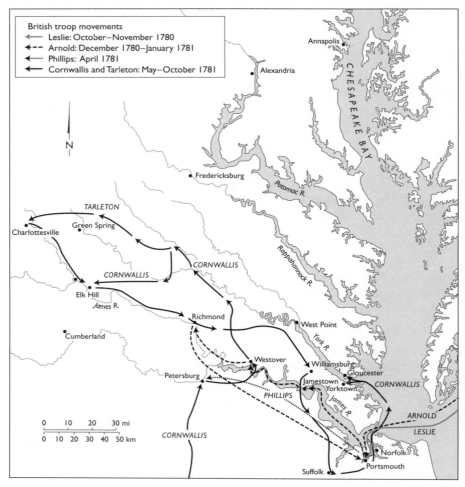

British troop movements
→ Leslie: October–November 1780
◄--- Arnold: December 1780–January 1781
◄······ Phillips: April 1781
◄ Cornwallis and Tarleton: May–October 1781

Annapolis

Alexandria

CHESAPEAKE BAY

N

Fredericksburg

Potomac R.

TARLETON

Green Spring

Charlottesville

CORNWALLIS

CORNWALLIS

Rappahannock R.

Elk Hill

James R.

Richmond

West Point

Cumberland

York R.

Westover

Williamsburg

Gloucester

Petersburg

Jamestown

CORNWALLIS

Yorktown

PHILLIPS

James R.

0   10   20   30 mi
0 10 20 30 40 50 km

ARNOLD

CORNWALLIS

LESLIE

Norfolk

Suffolk

Portsmouth

1. The British Invasions of Virginia, c. 1780–81

with ginger hair. One of his slaves—he owned approximately two hundred when he was elected governor and six hundred over the course of his long life—described Jefferson as "a tall strait-bodied man as ever you see, right square shouldered: nary man . . . walked so straight as my Old Master: neat a built man as ever was seen in Vaginny, I reckon or any place—a straight-up man: long face, high nose." He was a prominent planter from Albermarle County, where he lived on his main estate, Monticello, near Charlottesville. In April 1782 the French nobleman François Jean, Marquis de Chastellux, visited Jefferson at Monticello and described him as "a man not yet forty, tall and thin with a mild pleasing countenance, but whose mind and understanding are ample substitutes for every exterior grace. An American who without ever quitting his country, is at once a musician, skilled in drawing, and astronomer, and natural philosopher, legislator and statesman."[2]

Chastellux also noted that Jefferson had "a mild and amiable wife" and "charming children, of whose education he himself takes charge." In 1772 Jefferson had married Martha Wayles Skelton, a wealthy widow five years his junior. By 1779 Martha Jefferson had given birth to four children, only two of whom—Martha and Maria—survived infancy. Martha, known as Patsy, was several months shy of her seventh birthday and her little sister Maria, nicknamed Polly, was just ten months old when their father was elected governor. Martha Jefferson gave birth to another daughter, Lucy Elizabeth, on November 3, 1780, during her husband's second term as governor. During those two terms, which lasted from June 1779 until June 1781, Jefferson was concerned not only with the defense of Virginia, which he termed his "country," but also his young and growing family, which during the War of Independence would find itself in harm's way.

The thirty-six-year-old governor already had a considerable record of public service. In 1769 he had been elected to represent Albermarle in the House of Burgesses. During the growing dispute between Britain and its colonists in America, Jefferson identified with the radicals in the House of Burgesses. In 1774 he drafted a set of resolutions for Virginia's delegates to the First Continental Congress, articulating the radical position and grounding American resistance to parliamentary authority in British constitutional thinking and history. Admirers of Jefferson's resolutions had them published as a pamphlet, *A Summary View of the Rights of British America.*[3] Although originally published anonymously, this work established Jefferson's reputation as a skilled writer and a dedicated revolutionary. Jefferson was elected to represent Virginia at the Second Continental Congress, which began meeting in Philadelphia in September 1775. Congress named Jefferson to the committee charged with drafting the Declaration of Independence in June 1776. Jefferson was the main author of the Declaration, which Congress amended before adopting it on July 4.

In the autumn of 1776 Jefferson left the Continental Congress and returned to Virginia. He believed that independence would require wholesale legal and constitutional reform and that this must occur within the new states. Soon after his return Jefferson was elected to the House of Delegates (which had replaced the House of Burgesses), and he dedicated much of the subsequent three years to reforming the state's constitution and legal system. He was named to the Committee of Revisors charged with redrafting Virginia's legal code. During this period of ceaseless activity he drafted 126 bills—including bills abolishing primogeniture and entail; disestablishing the Anglican Church; revising the penal code; and proposing a system for universal, state-supported, education. The House of Delegates did not enact all of these bills, but Jefferson believed that such revolutionary reforms were an essential consequence of the Declaration of Independence.

While his record of public service was impressive, Jefferson's contributions had been those of a gifted writer and legislator. He had no executive experience when elected governor. Nor did he possess any significant military experience. In 1770, at the age of twenty-seven, he had been appointed county lieutenant, with the rank of colonel, of the Albemarle County militia. In this position he was responsible for all militia affairs in the county, including insuring that the militia drilled on a regular basis; that the regimental and company muster rolls were maintained; and that militia fines were collected by the sheriff. Jefferson also presided over courts-martial and councils of war. With the start of the Revolutionary War, Jefferson's military duties increased. He reported directly to the governor in preparing the county militia for mobilization. He was also responsible for providing militia soldiers as replacements for the Virginia regiments of the Continental Army. His contributions never extended to service in the field, and he declined to use the title "colonel" although eligible to do so.[4]

A lack of executive experience was not Jefferson's only disadvantage as a wartime governor. In 1776 Virginians adopted a new constitution. Its framers created an executive that was a creature of the state's legislature, the House of Delegates. The House of Delegates elected the state's governor annually. The governor could be re-elected for a maximum of three terms before he had to vacate the office. The governor had to work with an eight-man Council of State, whose members served at the pleasure of the legislature. The constitution vested executive power in the council—as governor Jefferson often felt himself to be the chairman of the council rather than an independent executive. The governor could not call out the militia, make appointments to office, or grant pardons without first seeking the advice of the council. In administrative terms the governor and council should exercise their military authority through the state Board of War appointed by the House of Delegates. (Similarly, commercial decisions should be enacted by the Board of Trade.) The framers of Virginia's constitution deliberately diffused and decentralized executive power. They drafted their constitution in light of their experiences as monarchical subjects who had had their liberties threatened by a powerful monarch. They sought to create an executive office that could govern but not threaten the liberty of the state's citizens. This decentralized constitutional arrangement would hamper Jefferson's efforts when the state was beset by repeated British invasions in 1780 and 1781 (see map 1).[5]

Virginia, despite its size and prominence, had largely been spared during the American War of Independence. There had been some skirmishing between Patriots and Loyalists as British rule deteriorated in 1775, and the Royal Navy shelled the port of Norfolk at the beginning of 1776, but during the early years of the war there had not been major fighting in the Old Dominion. After the rebel victory at Saratoga in October 1777 and the conclusion of the alliance between the United States and France in 1778, the British adopted a new strategy in response to the American rebellion. The government in London prioritized the war with France over suppressing the rebellion throughout the colonies. It would concentrate on attacking the French in the West Indies and reestablishing British rule in the southern rebel colonies. Beginning in late 1778 with an invasion of Georgia, the British concentrated their forces on the south in the last years of the war. In the spring of 1780 a major British army under General Henry Clinton captured Charleston along with 5,500 Continental Army soldiers. Clinton returned to New York in June, leaving his subordinate General Charles Cornwallis in charge of the British forces in South and North Carolina. Cornwallis's forces conducted the main British campaigns in North America in 1780 and 1781. Just as Jefferson became governor, the British focused their attention on the south. The commonwealth, and its governor, would be tested by repeated invasions by British forces.[6]

Just prior to Jefferson's election as governor the British had demonstrated just how vulnerable Virginia was. In early May 1779, a British expedition consisting of 28 ships and approximately 1,800 soldiers under the command Commodore George Collier and Major General Edward Matthew spent two weeks raiding the Virginia coast, occupying the towns of Porstmouth and Norfolk. Governor Patrick Henry, failing to appreciate the gravity of the situation, did not call for a full militia mobilization until May 13, five days after the arrival of British forces. As a consequence the British were able to move along the coast with impunity, occupying ports, plundering homes and plantations, burning shipyards and ships, seizing ordnance, and taking prisoners. Collier felt there was an opportunity for the British to occupy a permanent base in Virginia and thus establish a crucial naval presence between the British headquarters in New York and the main British army in the Carolinas. With regret, he departed after two weeks under orders from Henry Clinton to return to New York. All told the expedition seized or destroyed more than 130 ships and liberated more than 500 slaves who had flocked to the British colors seeking their freedom. The plunder seized by the British filled 17 ships when they departed.[7]

Had Patrick Henry moved quicker, mobilizing the militia as soon as the British appeared, it is unlikely that the Virginians would have fared much better in the face of Collier's expedition. Most of the state's soldiers were serving in the Continental Army in the Carolinas. In September 1780, Jefferson wrote to the president of the Continental Congress deploring his state's vulnerability. The commonwealth was struggling to raise its quota of 3,000 men for the Continental Army and had resorted to offering bounties of cash, land, and slaves to recruits.[8] The governor expressed his hope that the British would not return, but should they choose to invade Virginia again, he felt powerless to stop them. "They would find us in a condition incapable of resistance for want of small arms. Our militia have been long ago disfurnished of their arms for the use of the regulars," wrote Jefferson, and he implored Congress to supply more arms as well as tents. As worrying as the lack of arms and supplies was, Jefferson had a greater concern. He feared that when the hour of trial came, the militia might be found wanting. Jefferson feared that Virginia's citizen-soldiers could not be relied on in a crisis, making the state vulnerable from both without and within. He reported, "A spirit of disaffection which had never been suspected, has lately discovered itself in the counties of Washington, Montgomery, Henry, and Bedford, and had extended so far as that many hundreds has actually enlisted to serve his Britannic majesty, had taken oaths of allegiance to him, and had concerted the time of insurrection. . . . Other counties equally relied on may fail us in the hour of trial."[9] As a precaution Jefferson urged that the capital of the state be moved inland from Williamsburg to Richmond. Just as he hoped the British would not return to Virginia, Jefferson hoped that if they did come back, geography might achieve what he feared the militia would prove unable to do: prevent the capture of the capital by the British. Both hopes would prove illusory.

During the autumn of 1780, General Sir Henry Clinton realized that George Collier had been correct: possessing Norfolk or Portsmouth would be advantageous to the British as they sought to prosecute an increasingly intractable war in the Carolinas. On October 16 Clinton ordered General Alexander Leslie to reestablish a British presence on the Virginia coast. He hoped that occupying the coast would disrupt the flow of supplies to Continental forces in the Carolinas. Leslie's force, consisting of 2,200 soldiers and 6 warships, arrived in Chesapeake Bay on October 21, 1780. Leslie's men easily captured and occupied Portsmouth and Norfolk. Governor Jefferson mobilized the militia, which offered some resistance but could not prevent the British from moving at will on the peninsula between the James and York Rivers. Despite his success, Leslie, like Collier before him, was soon recalled. In the aftermath of the Loyalist defeat at King's Mountain, North Carolina, on October 7, Clinton ordered Leslie to reinforce Cornwallis's army. On November 15, the British again withdrew from Virginia.[10]

Leslie's departure marked a brief respite for Virginia. But as 1780 drew to a close yet another British expedition was sighted in Chesapeake Bay. Commanded by Benedict Arnold, newly commissioned as a brigadier general in the British army after renouncing his allegiance to the rebels, this force consisted of 27 ships and 1,600 men. Arnold's forces were a combination of British regulars, Hessians, and American Loyalists. Arnold undertook the preparations for his expedition during the autumn of 1780. George Washington had kept Governor Jefferson apprised of developments but was only able to surmise that the British forces were "supposed to be destined Southward."[11] The British forces embarked just before Christmas and arrived in Chesapeake Bay on December 30.

Governor Jefferson did not learn of Arnold's arrival until 8:00 a.m. on New Year's Day, 1781. He faced a dilemma when informed that the British again threatened the Virginia coast. In October he had mobilized 6,000 militia to counter Leslie's invasion. Ultimately most of these were not armed and organized in time to be effective. On November 10, Jefferson wrote, "The force called on to oppose the Enemy is as yet in a most Chaotic state, consisting of fragments of 3 Months Militia, 8 Months Men, 18 Months men, Volunteers and new Militia."[12] Two weeks earlier he had commended the spirit of the few soldiers who mustered to meet Leslie's forces but lamented that the "unarmed State of the people leaves it not in our power to say precisely where one hundred horse will be stopped."[13] For most of the militia called up in October to meet Leslie, the mobilization had been a false alarm. The few opposing the British had been brave but unprepared, and Leslie's forces had been able to move at will along Virginia's coast and rivers. When the first reports of Arnold's invasion force reached Jefferson he was loath to call out the militia again for what might be another false alarm, which might alienate the populace. As a consequence (though somewhat inexplicably) Jefferson delayed taking action for twenty-four hours, while awaiting further intelligence. According to a report that Jefferson prepared for the *Virginia Gazette,* it was only when Arnold began plundering plantations around Jamestown on January 2 that "all arrangements were immediately taken for calling in a sufficient body of militia for opposition."[14]

In the short term, at least, these arrangements were ineffective. "Our militia, dispersed over a large tract of country can be called but slowly," Jefferson lamented. Moreover the Virginians expected that Arnold would attack a rebel arms depot in Petersburg and concentrated their few forces there. But on January 4 Jefferson was awakened to the news that Arnold's forces had ascended the James River and occupied Westover, the plantation of William Byrd, just thirty miles from Richmond. Arnold and his men received a warm welcome from Byrd's widow, Mary, a Loyalist. If the governor had dithered on the initial reports of Arnold's arrival, he now acted more decisively. Jefferson dispatched his wife and daughters, including the infant Lucy, to Tuckahoe, a family plantation fourteen miles upriver where he had lived as a child, and turned his attention to defending Richmond, the new state capital.

By January 1781 Richmond had been the capital of Virginia for nine months. It was a rough-hewn village of around 1,800 souls. To Louis H. Girardin, writing of these events a third of a century later (with Jefferson's blessing), "The *fiat* of the Legislature bestowed upon it the magnificent name of city; but it was yet a city in embryo. It scarcely afforded sufficient accommodations for the officers of Government, of which it had but recently been made the seat. The public buildings were temporary and modest. In short, every thing there, except the grand and sublime features of natural beauty impressed by the creator himself on the picturesque site, was in a state of infancy."[15] One visitor "could almost fancy it was an Arabian village swarming of riders in the few and muddy streets,"[16] no doubt particularly on January 4, 1781, as Jefferson oversaw the removal of arms and other stores from the capital, as well as the state's public records. Jefferson ordered that the arms and papers be taken to Westham, six miles up the James from Richmond where the state maintained an arms depot. Fearing the British might attack Westham he sought to have the public records transported across the river to safety. Archibald Blair, a government clerk who was with Jefferson that day recalled, "that Mr. Jefferson was extremely active in removing all the public records from Richmond." Years later James Currie, a Richmond doctor, testified:

> If I recollect any thing, in regard to the circumstances which led to the loss of the Publick records and other valuable papers in the year 1781 during the invasion of the British Army, when Mr. Jefferson was Governor, I do well remember, that he appeared extremely anxious and very active, in having them removd from Richmond and deposited in a place of safety: and if possible entirely out of the reach of the enemy and for that and other duties of his office as chief magistrate did remain in Town fully as long as was either proper or prudent for him so to do; without manifest danger of becoming the prisoner of the invading Army, who were fast approaching the Seat of Government, without any efficient force that could at that time be brought against them, to stop their March, and that his conduct was then perfectly proper and that of a real patriot and friend of his country.[17]

Jefferson spent the day on January 4 overseeing the process. He remembered in old age, "I was never off my horse but to take food or rest, and was everywhere my presence could be of any service."[18] He finally reached his family at Tuckahoe at one o'clock on the morning of January 5.

Later that morning he sent his wife and daughters still farther up river, fearing the British might raid Tuckahoe. He then met with local militia commanders before returning to Westham to oversee the further removal of the public records across the river, disappointed to learn that most of the records remained at the foundry. By 1:00 p.m. he was in Manchester, on the James River opposite Richmond, from where he could observe British troops entering the town, which they captured after their twenty-three-hour nighttime march from Westover. Arnold dispatched his second-in-command, John Graves Simcoe, and a party of rangers to Westham to destroy the munitions there. Simcoe's men burned warehouses and mills, destroyed public records, and threw gunpowder into the James River.[19]

Arnold's men had spent a week at sea before their thirty-mile over-night march to Richmond, where their search for arms and other war matériel quickly degenerated into a more general plundering of the town. They were encouraged in this by their commander, who saw the raid as an opportunity to make money. The British burned public and private buildings and plundered private homes in Richmond. Arnold reported that his men destroyed 503 hogsheads of rum, "two warehouses full of salt and a quantity of grain."[20] To Johann von Ewald (a Hessian officer serving with Arnold), the capture of Richmond "resembled those of the freebooters, who sometimes at sea, sometimes ashore, ravaged and laid waste everything. Terrible things happened on this excursion; churches and holy places were plundered." Ewald estimated that two-thirds of his men "were drunk because large stores of wine and beer had been found in the houses. They were so noisy that one could hear us two hours away."[21] Governor Jefferson viewed the British despoliation of Virginia's humble capital through a spyglass from across the river in Manchester.

The British abandoned Richmond on January 6 after a nearly twenty-four-hour occupation. They returned to Westover and used it as a base to plunder nearby plantations before withdrawing to Portsmouth on January 10. The gathering of thousands of militiamen, a response to Arnold as well as Jefferson's call, threatened to trap the invader upriver. By almost any measure, Arnold's raid had been a success. He had pen-etrated 125 miles into the interior of Virginia, set the government to flight, plundered the capital and neighboring plantations, freed (or cap-tured) hundreds of enslaved Virginians, destroyed rebel supplies, and disrupted the flow of men and supplies to the Continental Army in the Carolinas. He withdrew for the winter in order to secure Portsmouth as a permanent British naval base that would be of use to future operations in the south.

On January 16 Jefferson wrote to his counterpart in North Carolina, Governor Abner Nash, explaining that Arnold's rapidity had made it impossible to organize the defense of Richmond: "The Winds favoring them in a remarkable degree they almost brought the first news them-selves of their movements. They were landed within twenty six miles of this place before we had reason even to suspect they would aim at it." Despite the late notice, Jefferson and the government had done as much as they could to prepare for Arnold's arrival. "The little interval of twenty three hours between that and their actual arrival here was assiduously and successfully employed in withdrawing the public Stores from hence and from Westham, seven miles above this." Their efforts paid off to a limited extent: "This was so far done that our loss did not exceed 300 muskets, about 5 Tons of Powder, some Sulphur, 5 feild [sic] pieces, four pounders, and some inferior articles of no great account. The letters and records of the Executive were the greater part lost. They retired hastily to their shipping after 23 hours possession of this place."[22] Jefferson ignored his own inaction on January 1, inelegantly ascribing the delay to "a fatal inattention to the giving us due notice of the arrival of the hostile force two days were completely lost in calling together the Militia—a time which events proved would have added so much to our collection of Militia as to have rendered doubtful their getting from this place." Jefferson warned his neighbor that "the interruption which they have given to raising men and providing subsistence is likely to be very injurious."[23]

On February 28, Jefferson received a letter from George Washington informing him that Washington was dispatching Continental soldiers under the command of the Marquis de Lafayette to the Chesapeake. Lafayette was charged to act in concert with the French navy in order to dislodge Arnold from Portsmouth.[24] After a forced march, Lafayette arrived at the Head of Elk (modern Elkton) in Maryland on March 3 with 1,200 troops. The young French general wrote to Jefferson, whom he had not yet met, asking him to supply Virginia troops as well as draft horses, boats, ammunition, and maps, "A large Body of Militia Collected in the Shortest time is absolutely essential."[25]

On March 12 Jefferson responded: he had called for the militia to muster in support of Lafayette, but the number of soldiers who reported for duty was negligible. For example, New Kent County was expected to supply 104 men but of the 28 mustered, "one half will desert before they reach the place of destination."[26] "An Idea having unfortunately got abroad that the militia now called on are intended to storm the Enemy's works at Portsmouth," wrote the mortified governor, "the numbers which actually march from the several Counties are so far short of what we ordered as never happened before, and as to have baffled our Calculations on probable Deficiencies." He feared the state did not have enough boats to transport Lafayette's troops and their cannons down Chesapeake Bay. Virginians certainly desired to capture Arnold and liberate Portsmouth: "We have every instrument in motion which can avail us on this most interesting Occasion," he wrote. Unfortunately, "a want of means circumscribes our Exertions. I think it proper therefore to reduce your expectations from what should be ready to what will probably be ready, and even calculating on probabilities I find it necessary to reduce my own expectations at Times." Surprisingly, Jefferson did not seek to excuse his fellow Virginians by telling Lafayette that the state had been invaded and threatened with invasion repeatedly over the previous two years, taking a toll on ordinary Virginians who were repeatedly mobilized, all the while supporting the broader Continental war effort to the south. Rather, Jefferson suggested that Virginians themselves were part of the problem. "I know that you will be satisfied to make the most of an unprepared [people] who have the war now for the first Time seriously fixed in their Country," he continued, "and have therefore all those Habits to acquire which their Northern Brethren had in the year 1776 and which they have purchased at so great an expence."[27] Despite the imperfect efforts of the government, Virginians were unprepared for war and might not be worthy to defend the republic.

Lafayette's bid to liberate Portsmouth and capture Benedict Arnold failed. French naval support for the proposed joint sea and land attack failed to materialize. In late March 2,000 British troops under Major General William Phillips arrived to reinforce Portsmouth. On April 18 the British under Phillips (who had assumed command from Arnold) ascended the James River. Jefferson acted quickly, consulting the council, ordering the removal of public records, and calling the militia to defend Richmond. Virginia's militiamen, reluctant to attack the British in Portsmouth a month earlier, were willing to meet Phillips's army as it threatened the heart of the state. The militia under Baron von Steuben confronted the British at Petersburg on April 25. Although the British won the battle and moved on toward Richmond, the militia performed well. Lafayette brought his Continental soldiers to the capital where they joined forces with the Virginia troops under Steuben in protecting Richmond. The respite was brief. On May 20 Cornwallis joined forces with

Arnold's army. (Phillips had died of disease on May 13.) After having been invaded by four separate British armies since May 1779, Virginia would now be the focus of the British war effort in America.[28]

On May 10, the House of Delegates, having received information concerning "the approach of an hostile army of the enemy" resolved to convene in two weeks' time in Charlottesville, seventy miles to the northwest in the foothills of the Blue Ridge Mountains, county seat of Albemarle.[29] On May 16 Jefferson left Richmond for his home at Monticello, a few miles southeast of Charlottesville. The governor intended the return to Charlottesville to be a permanent homecoming. His unhappy term of office was due to expire on June 2. The repeated invasions of Virginia had required him to manage the state's defenses with limited means. Moreover he had suffered personally. On April 15, on the eve of Phillips's sortie from Portsmouth, Jefferson's infant daughter Lucy died. In a long letter in late May the governor apprised George Washington of the perilous military situation. He concluded, "A few days will bring to me that period of relief which the Constitution has prepared for those oppressed with the labours of my office, and a long declared resolution of relinquishing it to abler hands has prepared my way for retirement to a private station."[30] Although the Virginia constitution would have allowed Jefferson to serve an additional one-year term (his predecessor, Patrick Henry, had served three), Jefferson had no desire to continue in office. He never felt adequately prepared for the continuous military crises that confronted the state. Years later when compiling his notes for this period—the most controversial of his long public career—Jefferson wrote of himself, "His office was now near expiring, the country under invasion by a powerful army, no services but military of any avail, unprepared by his line of life and education for the command of armies, he believed it right not to stand in the way of talents better fitted than his own to the circumstances under which the country was placed."[31]

Upon learning that Virginia's legislature was reconvening in the west, Cornwallis dispatched Lieutenant Colonel Banastre Tarleton, the most effective—and notorious—British cavalry commander of the war, to capture the governor and assemblymen. Tarleton, renowned for speed and ruthlessness, led approximately 250 dragoons and mounted infantry on a dash to Charlottesville to catch the politicians by surprise. As he recalled in his memoirs: "Lieutenant-colonel Tarleton imagined, that a march of seventy miles in twenty-four hours, with the caution he had used, might perhaps give him the advantage of a surprise, and concluded, that an additional celerity to the object of his destination would undoubtedly prevent a formidable resistance: He therefore approached the Rivanna, which runs at the foot of the hill on which the town is situated, with all possible expedition."[32] Tarleton pushed his troops hard in the early summer heat before stopping to rest men and horses at a tavern near Louisa Court House during the evening of Sunday, June 3. Jack Jouett, a captain in the Virginia militia, observed the British soldiers and guessed their intentions. According to Jefferson's account, Jouett knew the "byways of the neighborhood, passed the enemy's encampment, rode all night, and before sunrise of the next day [June 4] called at Monticello."[33] Despite a hazardous night ride of approximately forty miles, Jouett arrived at Monticello and Charlottesville in advance of Tarleton.

Jefferson was at breakfast with several legislators lodging at Monticello when Jack Jouett arrived with the news that Tarleton was headed for Charlottesville. Despite the circumstances, perhaps *because* of the circumstances, Jefferson displayed the hospitality expected of a great planter, allegedly offering Jouett a glass of good Madeira before the captain hastened on to Charlottesville to rouse the assemblymen there. Jefferson then looked after his family, arranging a carriage to take his wife and children to safety at a neighboring plantation. The assemblymen fled after breakfast. Jefferson, however, remained at Monticello—gathering his papers, getting his horse shod, or peering at the British through a telescope, depending on various accounts. He embodied stoicism in the face of danger.[34]

Approaching Charlottesville, Tarleton sent a detachment of dragoons under Captain Kenneth McLeod to Monticello to capture Jefferson. McLeod's men were ascending the mountain road to Jefferson's home when a second militiaman, Christopher Hudson, arrived to warn Jefferson that the British were just minutes away and, finding Jefferson "perfectly tranquil, and undisturbed," urged him to leave immediately. According to Hudson, Monticello was surrounded "in ten minutes at farthest by a troop of light-horse." At that point Jefferson fled Monticello, avoiding the roads and escaping over neighboring Carter's Mountain, leaving his home in the care of his slaves.[35]

According to the traditions of both the Jefferson and Hemings families, the enslaved Martin Hemings hid the Jefferson family silver under the floorboards of one of the Monticello porticos as the British soldiers appeared on the lawn. He acted in such haste that he "slammed down the planks" leaving another enslaved man, Caesar, under the portico. When they reached the house the British demanded Jefferson's whereabouts, and Hemings refused to tell them, defying the British to shoot him. The British occupied Monticello for eighteen hours but left most of Jefferson's belongings, including his slaves, relatively undisturbed (including Caesar who remained beneath the portico for the duration of the occupation).[36] McLeod had reportedly been ordered by Tarleton to respect Jefferson's property. Jefferson reported that the notorious Tarleton "behaved very genteelly with me."[37] Tarleton did not remain long in Charlottesville. He managed to catch seven legislators, but most of the assemblymen escaped across the Blue Ridge Mountains to Staunton. Meanwhile, believing his term as governor had expired, Jefferson escorted his family to safety at his vacation estate Poplar Forest near Lynchburg. Soon after arriving he suffered a fall from his horse and was bedridden for several weeks.

Jefferson's departure gave the impression that he abandoned the governorship, and his subsequent fall from his horse suggested precipitous flight. Betsy Ambler, the teenaged daughter of one of the members of the governor's council, wrote to a friend, "Governor, Council, everybody scampering." She related a story of another fleeing politician, "that is not more laughable than the accounts we have of our illustrious Governor, who, they say, took neither rest nor food for man or horse till reached C[arte]r's Mountain." While Betsy believed that Jefferson's flight was laughable, her father, Jacquelin Ambler, spent the evenings during the movement of the government from Charlottesville to Staunton sleeping in a carriage guarded by an armed slave, constantly on the move to stay ahead of the British. Her mockery of Jefferson may have shielded her father's reputation.[38]

✦

The House of Delegates reconvened in Staunton on June 7, 1781, and debated several measures to strengthen the state's defenses in the face of Cornwallis's invasion.[39] On June 12, with both houses quorate, Thomas Nelson, the popular militia general (and Jefferson's preferred choice), was elected as governor. (In principle the state had been without a governor for ten days after Jefferson's term expired.) The assembly also resolved that the new governor "should present to Captain John Jouett, an elegant sword and a pair of pistols, as a memorial of the high sense which the General Assembly entertain of his activity and enterprise, in watching the motions of the enemy's cavalry on their late incursion to Charlottesville, and conveying to the Assembly timely information of their approach, whereby the designs of the enemy were frustrated, and many valuable stores preserved." While it praised Jack Jouett, the assembly also resolved, "That at the next session of the Assembly an inquiry be made into the conduct of the Executive of this State for the last twelve months."[40]

George Nicholas, a twenty-seven-year-old representative from Jefferson's county of Albermarle, introduced the resolution calling for an inquiry into the executive's conduct. Nicholas was an army veteran and a lawyer from a well-connected family. Jefferson wrote to the younger man in late July. "I am informed," he wrote, "that a resolution on your motion passed the House of Delegates requiring me to render account of some part of my administration without specifying the act to be accounted for." Jefferson continued, "As I suppose that this was done under the impression of some particular instance or instances of ill conduct, and that it could not be intended just to stab a reputation by a general suggestion under a bare expectation that facts might be afterwards hunted up to boulster it, I hope you will not think me improper in asking the favor of you to specify to me the unfortunate passages in my conduct which you mean to adduce against me, that I may be enabled to prepare to yield obedience to the house while facts are fresh in my memory and witnesses and documents are in existence."[41] Nicholas responded immediately, denying that any criticism directed at Jefferson was inherent in his resolution. "You consider me in a wrong point of view when you speak of me as an accuser," he wrote. "As a freeman and the representative of free Men I considered it as both my right and duty to call upon the executive to account for our numberless miscarriages and losses so far as they were concerned in or might have prevented them." Nicholas denied personal animus toward Jefferson. "In doing this I had no private pique to gratify, and if (as I hope it may) it shall appear that they have done everything in their power to prevent our misfortunes I will most readily retract any opinion that I may have formed to their prejudice." He then enumerated five topics related to the preparedness of Virginia that he wanted the inquiry to pursue.[42]

Nicholas referred to the executive in the plural. This wording suggests Nicholas proposed investigating the conduct of Jefferson *and* the council. Jefferson's political allies, however, believed that the inquiry was directed at the former governor alone. Archibald Cary (who had served in the House of Burgesses with Jefferson before the Revolution and was the first Speaker of the Virginia Senate after independence) reported from Staunton that Nicholas had proposed an inquiry "into your Conduct, a Catalogue of omissions, and other Misconduct." None of the members of the council (even those who continued in office under Governor Nelson) were required to answer for their conduct. Nonetheless, Cary sought to reassure Jefferson, noting that his allies had supported the resolution in the belief that the inquiry "would do you honor."[43]

Jefferson prepared to answer a list of charges—eventually expanded to eleven from Nicholas's original five—all related to his conduct during Arnold's invasion the previous winter. On December 12, 1781, the House of Delegates conducted a perfunctory inquiry into Jefferson's conduct. With the surrender of Cornwallis at Yorktown in October, the febrile atmosphere of fear and danger in Virginia had passed. The assembly viewed Jefferson's actions from a more moderate and measured perspective. Although a committee was appointed to conduct the inquiry, none of its members, including George Nicholas, offered information or tabled questions. Jefferson was in attendance—he had accepted election to the House of Delegates for the sole purpose of addressing the charges against him. Louis Girardin wrote of these events after consulting Jefferson: "Mr. Jefferson rose in his seat, addressed the House in general terms upon the subject, and expressed his readiness to meet any accusations that should be preferred against him. Silence ensued—not a word of censure was whispered."[44] In response the House of Delegates and the Senate unanimously adopted the following resolution to vindicate the former governor: "Resolved that the sincere Thanks of the General Assembly be given to our former Governor Thomas Jefferson Esquire for his impartial, upright, and attentive administration whilst in office. The Assembly wish in the strongest manner to declare the high opinion which they entertain of Mr. Jefferson's Ability, Rectitude, and Integrity as cheif [sic] Magistrate of this Commonwealth, and mean by thus publicly avowing their Opinion, to obviate and to remove all unmerited Censure."[45]

Despite the resolution, Jefferson's reputation was damaged by the inquiry. In subsequent years Jefferson's political rivals suggested that he had been guilty of cowardice when he fled from Monticello. It was a charge that he had to address as candidate for president in 1796, 1800, and 1804. He created a careful record of the events in 1781, including collecting depositions to counter the allegation. In 1796 he wrote of his actions in 1781 (satirically assuming that his critics were readers of Cervantes's *Don Quixote*):

> Would it be believed, were it not known, that this flight from a troop of horse, whose whole legion too was within supporting distance, has been the subject, with party writers, of volumes of reproach on me, serious or sarcastic? That it has been sung in verse, and said in humble prose that, forgetting the noble example of the hero of La Mancha, and his windmills, I declined a combat singly against a troop, in which victory would have been so glorious? Forgetting, themselves, at the same time, that I was not provided with the enchanted arms of the knight, nor even the helmet of Mambrino. These closet heroes forsooth would have disdained the shelter of a wood, even singly and unarmed, against a legion of armed enemies.[46]

In 1805, despite having won two presidential elections, his conduct as governor remained a sensitive subject for Jefferson. "This is the famous adventure of Carter's mountain," he wrote, "which has so often resounded through the slanderous chronicles of federalism. But they have taken care never to detail the facts, lest these should shew that this favorite charge amounted to nothing more than that he did not remain in his house, and there singly fight a whole troop of horse, or suffer himself to be taken prisoner."[47]

During his retirement Jefferson encouraged Louis Girardin, a French émigré living near Monticello, to complete John Daly Burk's *History of Virginia* with a volume that included his governorship. Jefferson gave his historian access to all of his papers. Girardin's account, which argued that the governor did all that could reasonably have been expected of him to defend the state, can be read as Jefferson's "official" account of the controversial events in 1781. Jefferson accepted Girardin's version of events when writing his autobiography in 1821: "To write my own history during the two years of my administration, would be to write the public history of that portion of the revolution within this state. This has been done by others, and particularly by Mr. Girardin. . . . For this portion, therefore, of my own life, I refer altogether to his history."[48]

That subsequent political opponents used Jefferson's record as a wartime governor against him in national politics has somewhat obscured the immediate political context for the charges against him. In 1798 George Nicholas, then a substantial political figure in Kentucky and a supporter of Jefferson, sought to repair the damage caused by his original resolution to investigate the former governor in the summer of 1781. "I am happy in having an opportunity of declaring, when it can be attributed to no improper motive," he wrote of Jefferson, "that I have long since, changed the unfavourable opinion, which I once formed of that gentleman's political conduct, and that I consider him one of the most virtuous, as well as one of the ablest, of the American patriots."[49] Notwithstanding Nicholas's subsequent denial of animus against Jefferson, his apology conceded that his original charges *were* politically motivated.

The Virginia assembly was in a state of panic when it reconvened in Staunton in June 1781. One of Jefferson's nineteenth-century biographers described the scene vividly: "Gentlemen, hot from the saddle and grimed with the dust of recent flight, booted and spurred for new flight, and listening momentarily to hear the hoof-clang of pursuing cavalry, undertook to legislate for what seemed to them some radical disorder in the State!"[50] Before decamping from Charlottesville the delegates had decided that during the crisis they required only forty members to be quorate. After gathering in Staunton the assembly adopted a series of measures (first suggested by Governor Jefferson in March and then again in late May) to strengthen the state's defenses. These included bills which gave the governor more power to mobilize and supply the militia, declared martial law within twenty miles of the contending armies, and enabled arms destined for the Continental Army to be kept in the state.[51]

At the same time the assembly debated a measure that would give the governor temporary dictatorial powers in Virginia. None other than George Nicholas introduced this controversial measure to the House of Delegates. Nicholas proposed that in the emergency "a Dictator" was needed "in this Commonwealth who should have the power of disposing of the lives and fortunes of the Citizens thereof without being subject to account." Nicholas "referred to the practice of the Romans on similar occasions" and suggested that George Washington would be appropriate for the role. Nicholas's proposal was seconded by Patrick Henry, Jefferson's predecessor as governor and political rival. Henry "observed it was immaterial to him whether the Officer proposed was called a Dictator or a Governor with enlarged powers or by any other name yet surely an Officer armed with such powers was necessary to restrain the unbridled fury of a licentious enemy and concluded by seconding the Motion." Frightened as the legislators were, they were unwilling to take the step proposed by Nicholas and Henry. "After a lengthy discussion the proposition was negatived."[52] George Nicholas was not alone in advocating that Virginia hand power over to a dictator. At the very moment that the House of Delegates was debating Nicholas's resolution, Richard Henry Lee wrote to Virginia's congressional delegation proposing that Congress send George Washington "immediately to Virginia, and as the head of the Fœderal Union let them possess the General with Dictatorial power until the general Assembly can be convened, and have determined upon his powers, and let it be recommended to the Assembly when met to continue this power for 6, 8, or 10 months as the case may require." Lee assured congressmen who may have been squeamish about subverting the democratic element in republican government that "both antient and modern times furnish precedents to justify this procedure, but if they did not, the present necessity not only justifies but absolutely demands the measure."[53]

Virginians had debated whether to create a dictator once before, during the Revolution. In the autumn of 1776, with Washington's army in retreat across New Jersey and the Continental Congress in flight from Philadelphia to Baltimore, the House of Delegates considered a resolution from George Mason, one of the primary architects of the 1776 Virginia constitution, that declared, "It is become necessary, for the Preservation of the State, that the usual forms of Government shou'd be suspended, during a limitted time, for the more speedy Execution of the most vigorous and effectual Measures, to repel the Invasions of the Enemie."[54] In both 1776 and 1781 the proponents of dictatorship sought to draw on Roman precedents to vest emergency power in the hands of the governor to remedy the deficiency in the Virginia constitution, which created a weak executive in response to the exigencies of the moment.

The proposal to create a dictator was closely related to the effort to impeach Jefferson. Although the supporters of dictatorship claimed that they wanted George Washington (or Nathanael Greene) to wield dictatorial authority, Jefferson and his political allies suspected that the real intention was to give dictatorial power to Patrick Henry. (Nicholas introduced the measure as soon as the government relocated to Staunton, *before* Thomas Nelson was elected to replace Jefferson.)[55] William Wirt, one of Henry's earliest biographers, acknowledged that it was "highly probable, that Mr. Henry was the character who was in view for that office [Dictator]."[56] In order to install Henry as a dictator, it was necessary first to discredit Jefferson, which is why George Nicholas introduced his inquiry into Jefferson's conduct as governor. The inquiry would serve two purposes: it would underscore Virginia's vulnerability, thereby justifying resorting to dictatorship; and it would undermine Jefferson's credibility (as well as that of his supporters in the assembly), making it difficult for them to oppose the proposal. Louis Girardin explained: "An individual, highly conspicuous was necessary to save the country. An individual [Henry], highly conspicuous for his talents and usefulness through the anterior scenes of the great revolutionary drama, was spoken of as the proper person to fill the contemplated office, to introduce which, it was necessary to place Mr. Jefferson *hors de combat.* For this purpose, the misfortunes of the period were ascribed to him; he was impeached in some loose way, and a day for some species of hearing, at the succeeding session of Assembly was appointed." The plot ultimately failed because it lacked enough support in the assembly. Girardin continued, "But the impeachment, sour as was the temper of the Legislature, failed to produce the two ends it had in view, namely, to put down Mr. Jefferson, and to put up the project for a Dictator."[57]

Jefferson reflected on the scheme's significance. Soon after demitting office he received a series of questions from François Barbé-Marbois, the secretary of the French legation in Philadelphia. Jefferson's answers, which he wrote and rewrote between 1781 and 1783, became the *Notes on the State of Virginia,* which Jefferson published in French in 1785 and in English in 1787. In his response to Barbé-Marbois's thirteenth query on the constitution of Virginia Jefferson included a lengthy disquisition on the attempt to create a dictatorship in the state during the war, noting that it "wanted a few votes only of being passed" and lamenting the precarious fate of liberty in Virginia:

> One who entered into this contest from a pure love of liberty, and a sense of injured rights, who determined to make every sacrifice, and to meet every danger, for the re-establishment of those rights on a firm basis, who did not mean to expend his blood and substance for the wretched purpose of changing this master for that, but to place the powers of governing him in a plurality of hands of his own choice, so that the corrupt will of no one man might in future oppress him, must stand confounded and dismayed when he is told, that a considerable portion of that plurality had meditated the surrender of them into a single hand, and, in lieu of a limited monarch, to deliver him over to a despotic one! How must we find his efforts and sacrifices abused and baffled, if he may still by a single vote be laid prostrate at the feet of one man!

Jefferson asserted that the plan for a dictatorship had no basis in the Virginia constitution nor could it be justified out of necessity because extreme necessity would dissolve the government, in which case sovereignty would have reverted to the people of Virginia not "an oligarchy or a monarchy." While there was a precedent for dictatorship in republican Rome, Jefferson noted that Roman government was controlled by a "heavy-handed unfeeling aristocracy, over a people ferocious, and rendered desperate by poverty and wretchedness" (in presumed contrast to Virginia), and temporary dictatorship degenerated ultimately into permanent despotism, a fate Virginia had narrowly avoided. The solution in Virginia, Jefferson argued, was constitutional reform. When peace was restored and independence won, Virginians needed to amend their constitution to correct its defects, not resort to the temporary expedient of vesting power in a dictator who would threaten their liberties.[58] During his tenure as governor, Jefferson had faced a fundamental constitutional question: Given an imperfect constitution, what were the limits on his actions as an executive in the face of external threats to the republic? While he felt that creating a dictatorship went too far—to do so would be to destroy republican government in the name of preserving it—he recognized that an executive might take expedient measures, in the spirit, if not the letter, of the constitution in order to protect the republic. His actions as governor reveal much about his attitude toward the people as citizens and his role as an executive. The lessons he derived from the experience would inform his judgment as a diplomat and president.

Although Jefferson believed that an executive in a republic should be beholden to the people and their legislative representatives, he also came to realize in 1781 that an executive must act decisively in crisis. In so doing he might sometimes have to exceed constitutional limits, provided he did so for the public good and in the spirit of the constitution and, crucially, sought retrospective legislative approval for his actions.[59] Jefferson drew a theoretical distinction between the need to act extra-constitutionally under specific, and limited, circumstances, and a dictator who might act in a capricious and despotic manner. Reflecting on the Roman precedent, Jefferson observed inaccurately, "Their constitution therefore allowed a temporary tyrant to be erected, under the name of a Dictator; and that temporary tyrant, after a few examples, became perpetual."[60] Rather, Jefferson held that while a governor might some-times have to exceed his constitutional authority his actions must be limited. A governor could not be expected to allow the republic to fail owing to punctiliousness and fealty to a flawed constitution, but he must act in accordance with republican principles. The need to act decisively caused Jefferson to exceed his authority several times in 1781. Yet he did so with the intention of protecting, rather than subverting, Virginia's experiment with republican government.

Faced with Arnold's capture of Richmond and the concomitant dis-ruption to the government, Jefferson was compelled to resort to extrale-gal expedients in January 1781. Amid the mayhem wrought by Arnold's forces, the British had destroyed several of the state's printing presses when occupying Richmond. As a result several laws that the assembly had adopted for procuring men and supplies for the state's defense were set to expire before they could be circulated to country magistrates for enforcement. Rather than resort to the assembly for new legislation, which would require it to be printed and circulated, Jefferson instructed the country magistrates to provide supplies and soldiers in accordance with the expiring legislation (which they had not seen). He explained that the assembly would endorse his action. "Could any legal scruples arise as to this," he wrote, "there would be no doubt that the ensuing Assembly influenced by the necessity which induced them to pass the act, would give their sanction to its execution, though at a later date than is prescribed." The British were coming: Virginians had to act now. "However the substance of the act is to procure supplies of beef, cloth-ing, and waggons. The time of doing this is a circumstance only; and the principle is sound both in law and policy, that substance not circum-stance is to be regarded. While we have so many foes in our bowels and environing us on every side, he is but a bad citizen who can entertain a doubt whether the law will justify him in saving his country, or who will scruple to risk himself in support of the spirit of a law where unavoidable accidents have prevented a literal compliance with it." Consistent with his stated position, the governor sought retrospective approval for his action when the assembly met in emergency session in March 1781.[61] The distinction between "substance" and "circumstance" characterized his response to the British invasions of Virginia in 1780 and 1781. Where circumstance demanded that he act beyond the literal demands of the law in order to uphold its substance, Jefferson did not hesitate to act in what he saw as defense of republican government.

Virginia's constitution required the governor to consult his eight-man council, whose "advice and proceedings shall be entered of Record."[62] However, during the winter and spring of 1781 Jefferson managed the war effort with little recourse to the council. The council was rarely quorate (four members were required for a quorum). In early January Jefferson had to make decisions, issue orders, and raise troops in response to Arnold's invasion, without advice of the council, which did not meet until January 19.[63] When the council did meet it endorsed Jefferson's draft proclamation prohibiting Virginians from avoiding military service on a plea of parole by the British earlier in the war.[64] Similarly, during the campaigns of April and May, with the council rarely in attendance Jefferson made military decisions. On May 10 when four members met, they endorsed Jefferson's previous actions declaring, "The foregoing proceedings which have been done (through necessity) without formality of a regular board, being now laid before the board and read, the same are approved."[65]

But Governor Jefferson preferred to take action within the law where possible. In response to Arnold's invasion he called the legislature into emergency session in early March, to suggest creating a standing army for Virginia. "Whether it be practicable to raise and maintain a sufficient number of regulars to carry on the war is a question" he asked the legislators to consider. In the end the assembly demurred, preferring to rely on the militia.[66] On May 28, the government having fled to Charlottesville, Jefferson demanded increased authority to call more militia into the field, to impress supplies, including horses and slaves, and to impose martial law in the war zone. The next day the House of Delegates endorsed these proposals, which were enacted by the whole assembly when it reconvened in Staunton after Tarleton's raid.[67] Far from being timorous and indecisive in the face of danger, Jefferson would marshal the resources of the state. Indeed, in proposing to create a standing army for the state, he was willing to go further than the legislature. Being a political philosopher by nature, he was ready enough to defy such traditional Whig taboos as prohibiting standing armies. His legislature, less original, was therefore more orthodox.

Jefferson's preference for a standing army reflected his growing frustration with the militia. As governor he came to believe that the militia was an imperfect tool to defend the commonwealth. The militia was difficult to raise and slow to mobilize, expensive to arm and equip and proved to be of limited effectiveness against regular British troops. Moreover, Jefferson recognized that militia service was onerous, especially when dwellers along the Tidewater were called out repeatedly to face British invaders in 1780 and 1781. In advocating a Virginia standing army Jefferson observed, "That it would be burthensome is undoubted, yet it is perhaps as certain that no possible mode of carrying it on can be so expensive to the public and so distressing and disgusting to individuals as by the militia."[68]

Jefferson's anxieties betrayed unease about his fellow Virginians. Would they be virtuous enough to sustain republican government? Once independence was declared in 1776, he asked Edmund Pendleton, who had presided over the Virginia constitutional convention, "Should we not have in contemplation and prepare for an event (however deprecated) which may happen in the possibility of things I mean a reacknolegement of the British tyrant as our king, and previously strip him of every prejudicial possession?" He reminded Pendleton "how universally the [English] people run into the idea of recalling Charles the 2 after living many years under a republican government."[69] Jefferson worried that Virginians might similarly backslide into monarchy and tyranny, as surfaced in the debate over the creation of a dictator. In the *Notes on the State of Virginia* Jefferson observed that other states invaded by the British had not resorted to such a solution. "When the proposition was first made [in 1776]," he wrote, "Massachusets had found even the government of committees sufficient to carry them through an invasion. But we at the time of that proposition were under no invasion. When the second was made [in 1781], there had been added to this example those of Rhode-Island, New-York, New-Jersey, and Pennsylvania, in all of which the republican form had been found equal to the task of carrying them through the severest trials." He wondered why Virginians responded differently when confronted by British invaders. "In this state alone did there exist so little virtue, that fear was to be fixed in the hearts of the people, and to become the motive of their exertions and the principle of their government?"[70]

If Virginians gave in to their fear and created a dictatorship, the American experiment with republican government itself might be threatened. Jefferson continued: "The very thought alone was treason against the people; was treason against mankind in general; as rivetting for ever the chains which bow down their necks, by giving to their oppressors a proof, which they would have trumpeted through the universe, of the imbecility of republican government, in times of pressing danger, to shield them from harm."[71] Jefferson first drafted the *Notes on the State of Virginia* in the immediate aftermath of the British invasion and the assembly's challenge to his leadership and courage. But a generation later, Jefferson's amanuensis, Louis Girardin, attributed the rejection of dictatorship to Virginians. According to Girardin, "The pulse of the Assembly was incidentally felt in debates on the state of the Commonwealth, and out of doors by personal conversations. Out of these a ferment gradually arose, which foretold a violent opposition to any species of Dictatorship, and as in a previous instance of a similar attempt, the apprehension of personal danger produced a relinquishment of the scheme."[72]

Whether public opinion had determined the outcome or not, the decision had been a close one. Jefferson was not convinced that public opinion could be relied upon to remedy the defects in the constitution. In 1783 he drafted a proposed new constitution for Virginia (which he included in the *Notes on the State of Virginia*) that would address these. Jefferson noted that the 1776 constitution had been drafted "when we were new and unexperienced in the science of government. It was the first too which was formed in the whole United States. No wonder then that time and trial have discovered very capital defects in it." Chief among these defects was the fact that legislative, executive, and judicial power were vested in the assembly. Jefferson sought to give the executive independence—under his 1783 constitution the assembly could not alter the governor's salary during his term; the governor's term was extended from one to five years; and the governor could act independently of the council. Jefferson's 1783 draft constitution would give the governor far more power than in the dark days of 1780 and 1781. He sought to give the executive enough power to protect the commonwealth without resorting to dictatorship or other endangerment of the republic.[73]

After his presidency Jefferson pondered his tenure as a wartime governor. In January 1812 the then-governor of Virginia, James Barbour, asked Jefferson how he should proceed when the opinion of his eight-man council was evenly divided (something Jefferson rarely faced since his council was infrequently quorate).[74] In response Jefferson reflected on his experience during the invasions of 1780 and 1781. He insisted that he sought to work with the council where possible, "but in the numerous & extraordinary occurrences of an invasion, which could not be foreseen I had to act on my own judgment, and my own responsibility. The vote of general approbation at the session of the succeeding winter, manifested the opinion of the legislature that my proceedings had been correct." Jefferson believed that the constitution was drafted "for the purpose of carrying on that war" and that while the council was meant to control the governor, the executive must be able to govern in its absence. He then provided a full statement on what he conceived the role of the executive during a crisis to be:

> In Executive cases, where promptitude and decision are all-important, an adherence to the letter of a law against its probable intentions, (for every law must intend that itself shall be executed) would be fraught with incalculable danger. judges may await further legislative explanations. But a delay of Executive action might produce irretrievable ruin. The state is invaded, militia to be called out, an army marched, arms & provisions to be issued from the public magazines, the legislature to be convened, and the council is divided. Can it be believed to have been the intention of the framers of the constitution, that the constitution itself & their constituents with it should be destroyed, for want of a will to direct the resources they had provided for its preservation? Before such possible consequences all verbal scruples must vanish, construction must be made *secundum arbitrium boni viri* [according to the judgment

of a good man], and the constitution be rendered a practicable thing.[75]

No government could be expected to commit state suicide. As Jefferson wrote two years earlier, "A strict observance of the written laws is doubtless *one* of the high duties of a good citizen: but it is not *the highest*. The laws of necessity, of self-preservation, of saving our country when in danger, are of higher obligation." The first duty of the executive was to protect the republic, regardless of constitutional strictures, which themselves might be flawed. A governor who adhered strictly to the letter of the law and allowed the republic to be destroyed failed in his primary duty. "To lose our country by a scrupulous adherence to written law, would be to lose the law itself," he wrote, "thus absurdly sacrificing the end to the means."[76]

In a crisis the executive must act quickly and decisively. To interpret the constitution in such a fashion as to leave the state undefended "must be vicious which would leave the nation, under the most dangerous emergencies, without a directing will." But what would prevent Jefferson's "good man" exercising his "directing will" from becoming a dictator who would subvert the republic and threaten liberty in the name of defending it? The executive could only exercise such authority in times of extreme peril when, "an instant of delay in Executive proceedings may be fatal to the whole nation. They must not therefore be laced up in the rules of the judiciary department." The executive must, where possible, "seek the intention of the legislator in all the circumstances which may indicate it, in the history of the day, in the public discussions, in the general opinion & understanding, in reason, & in practice."[77] The "good man" could exercise such authority only for a limited period and must seek retrospective legislative approval.

Thomas Jefferson's tenure as Virginia's governor is generally regarded as a failure. Even his most faithful scholarly admirers seem to accept this. Dumas Malone, Jefferson's most sympathetic and fullest biographer, conceded that the British attacks on Virginia were the lowest point in Jefferson's public life but concluded, "It may be said without much doubt that the most conspicuous failure was that of the government rather than the Governor." According to Julian Boyd, the foremost editor of Jefferson's papers, "Nothing that happened in Jefferson's long public career wounded him so deeply as these charges of negligence, incompetence, and . . . personal cowardice in discharging the duties of his post as governor of Virginia."[78] Nonetheless, Jefferson's lessons from the experience would shape his subsequent career.

In the first place, Jefferson learned just how fragile republics were. It was a commonplace in eighteenth-century thought that republics were ultimately prone to failure. Most were conquered by aggressive predatory powers or collapsed owing to their citizens' lack of the virtue necessary to sustain liberty. In 1780 and 1781 Jefferson had seen these flaws on display as the British overran his state and put its government to flight. More worrying still, the militia—the citizenry in arms—had performed poorly, and the population at large did not seem to support the Revolution with appropriate fervor. In this context the proposal to create a dictatorship in Virginia seemed especially ominous. The military crises that beset Jefferson also exposed the flaws in Virginia's 1776 constitution—particularly the relative weakness of the executive dependent on the assembly whose independent decision making was hampered by the governor's council.

Faced with external threats, internal weakness, and a flawed constitution, Jefferson realized that decisive action was necessary to protect Virginia and that sometimes it was necessary to act outside the law to protect the republic.[79] Such actions, however, had to be carefully qualified. He believed that an executive might act outside of the law only under unusual circumstances—when the fate of the republic itself was at stake, for a limited time, in the spirit of the constitution and in conjunction with popular will, and, crucially, with legislative approval for his actions. The Jefferson who emerged from the War of Independence recognized that the survival of the republic must be the paramount concern of an executive. He was not overly constrained by constitutional scruples or by the means necessary to achieve this end. Throughout the remainder of his career as a diplomat and a member of the executive branch (as secretary of state, vice president, and president) he would apply the conclusions he drew as a wartime governor.

Two

"To Compel the Pyratical States to Perpetual Peace"

On July 24, 1785, the schooner *Maria* out of Boston, bound for Cádiz, was captured by an Algerian xebec, a small three-masted, fourteen-gun vessel, 3 miles off the southwest coast of Portugal. On July 30 the Algerians captured another American vessel, the *Dauphin*, 240 nautical miles northwest of St. Ubes (modern Setúbal), Portugal. The *Dauphin* was bound for Philadelphia, its homeport. The Algerians transported the crew of *Dauphin*, Captain Richard O'Brien, his mate, Alexander Forsyth, and eleven seamen, along with two passengers, to captivity in Algiers. In the two incidents the Algerians had captured twenty-one Americans whom they intended to sell into slavery or hold until ransomed.[1]

The Algerians captured the American vessels in a lucrative practice with deep historic roots. The Barbary States of North Africa—Tunis, Tripoli, Algiers, and Morocco—had engaged in piracy and commerce raiding in the western Mediterranean and the North Atlantic since the sixteenth century. Morocco was an independent state ruled by an emperor. Algiers, Tripoli, and Tunis (whose rulers were the dey, bashaw, and bey, respectively) were nominally part of the Ottoman Empire. The rulers of the North African states derived significant revenue by capturing foreign—normally European—vessels and ransoming their crews or selling them into slavery. The object of the practice was to make money, ideally by forcing the states involved to negotiate peace treaties. Such treaties involved substantial gift giving as well as the payment of annual tribute in exchange for which the sultanates agreed they would not

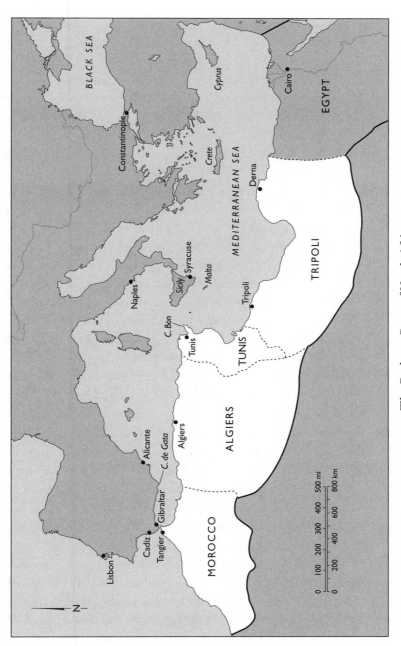

2. The Barbary Coast of North Africa

hamper the tribute payer's shipping.[2] The wealthier and more powerful European states often reckoned that it was cheaper to pay such tribute than to wage war or ransom their subjects, when they bothered about them at all. Prior to independence, American shipping was protected by the Royal Navy and the tribute paid by the British Treasury. With independence those safeguards disappeared. Indeed, the British encouraged the Barbary States to prey on American shipping to demonstrate the weakness of the new republic.[3] A year before the capture of the *Maria* and the *Dauphin,* on October 11, 1784, a Moroccan corsair captured the American brig *Betsey* and its nine-man crew southwest of Cádiz. The Moroccan emperor, Sidi Muhammad ibn Adballah, sought to complete a treaty with the new republic and ordered his men to capture an American vessel to put pressure on the United States. The emperor held the crew of *Betsey* until July 1785 when they were released to the care of the Spanish. The release of the crew of the *Betsey* by the Moroccans just as the crews of the *Maria* and *Dauphin* were captured by the Algerians underscores the complexity of the diplomacy between the United States and the Barbary States.[4]

In 1785 the thirteen American states, bound by the Articles of Confederation, were represented abroad by a handful of diplomats, most notably the ministers in France and Britain—Thomas Jefferson and John Adams, respectively—assisted with varying degrees of competence by consuls, often merchants, scattered around the ports of Europe and the Mediterranean. After the ignominious end to his second term as governor of Virginia, Jefferson briefly retired from public life—save for his return to answer the charges against him before the House of Delegates. At that time he worked on the manuscript of the book that would become *Notes on the State of Virginia.* The tumult in Jefferson's public life was compounded by personal difficulties. On May 8, 1782, Martha Wayles Jefferson gave birth to a daughter, Lucy Elizabeth Jefferson (who bore the same name as the infant daughter who had died during the British invasion of Virginia). Martha Jefferson had borne six children during her ten years of marriage to Thomas Jefferson. She was gravely ill throughout the summer of 1782 and died on September 6. Jefferson was wounded by her death, and his friends, particularly James Madison, sought to entice him back into public life to help overcome his despair.

Madison arranged for Jefferson's appointment by Congress as a representative of the fledgling American republic in Europe. Jefferson departed for Paris with his older daughter, Martha, in July 1784. He was first appointed to serve as one of the commissioners to negotiate commercial treaties in Europe on behalf of the United States. However, in May of 1785 he received notification of his appointment to replace Benjamin Franklin as the American minister to France and two months later confronted the capture of the *Maria* and the *Dauphin* by the Algerians.[5]

Among their responsibilities, Jefferson and Adams were charged with negotiating treaties with the various Barbary States. After the capture of the *Maria* and *Dauphin* that task was greatly complicated by the presence of the American prisoners in Algiers. Securing their release and seeking a long-term solution to the issues arising from their capture became a preoccupation for Jefferson and a source of disagreement between him and Adams. Jefferson believed that the Barbary pirates represented a mortal threat to the American republic and proposed the use of force to counter them. To measure this threat we must consider the role of trade and commerce in Jefferson's thinking about political economy.

In 1780 the secretary of the French legation in the United States, François de Barbé-Marbois, circulated a list of questions about the new republic to the governors of the various states. Jefferson, then governor of Virginia, undertook to answer Marbois's queries in 1781. The result, expanded and edited, particularly after he left office, was eventually published as the *Notes on the State of Virginia* in 1785. The *Notes* is a compendium of natural history, geography, philosophy, and history. In the book Jefferson developed a vision of political economy that elaborated on the eloquent assertion of republicanism he had advanced in 1776 in the Declaration of Independence.[6]

Although generally optimistic about the capacity of his fellow citizens, the failure of Virginians during the British invasions of 1780 and 1781 taught Jefferson just how fragile republics could be.[7] He believed that a republic was only as durable as its citizens were virtuous. For the American experiment with republican government to succeed, Americans must be cognizant of their rights and responsibilities as citizens.

Indeed, the desire to preserve the health of the republic explains Jefferson's devotion to public education throughout his life.[8] In the *Notes on Virginia* Jefferson famously expressed his belief that farmers were the most appropriate citizens for a republic. Owing to their independence and virtue, if properly educated, they were best suited to maintain the moral rectitude necessary to sustain the republic. He wrote:

> Those who labour in the earth are the chosen people of God, if ever he had a chosen people, whose breasts he has made his peculiar deposit for substantial and genuine virtue. It is the focus in which he keeps alive that sacred fire, which otherwise might escape from the face of the earth. Corruption of morals in the mass of cultivators is a phænomenon of which no age nor nation has furnished an example. It is the mark set on those, who not looking up to heaven, to their own soil and industry, as does the husbandman, for their subsistence, depend for it on the casualties and caprice of customers. Dependence begets subservience and venality, suffocates the germ of virtue, and prepares fit tools for the designs of ambition. This, the natural progress and consequence of the arts, has sometimes perhaps been retarded by accidental circumstances: but, generally speaking, the proportion which the aggregate of the other classes of citizens bears in any state to that of its husbandmen, is the proportion of its unsound to its healthy parts, and is a good-enough barometer whereby to measure its degree of corruption. While we have land to labour then, let us never wish to see our citizens occupied at a work-bench, or twirling a distaff.[9]

If the United States remained predominantly a nation of small farmers, its virtuous citizenry would exercise its rights and defend liberty.

Jefferson's agrarian republicanism rested on two related assumptions: first, that republics were ephemeral, and second, that manufacturing would hasten the demise of the American republic. The first was a general lesson he tried to apply to all republics, but the second uniquely challenged Americans at the dawn of the nineteenth century. Jefferson and other republican theorists imagined history testifying that republics eventually succumbed to a variety of perils. A successful republic might enjoy excess wealth which would lead to corruption, decay, and the eventual dissipation of liberty. Alternatively, internal disputes and selfishness and a loss of civic virtue could leave a republic susceptible to aggressive enemies—as had happened in Virginia during the War of Independence. In the American context, Jefferson was aware that the United States stood alone in a world of predatory empires. Nations, like individuals, experienced a life cycle. Jefferson contended that maintaining itself as an agrarian republic would keep the United States youthful, vigorous, and healthy for as long as possible. Nonetheless, hanging over the American republic was the threat of its mortality. By promoting agrarian republicanism Jefferson and his political supporters sought to forestall its inevitable decline.

Jefferson perceived manufacturing as a particular danger to the United States. His famous encomium on the virtues of agriculture appeared in response to a query concerning the state of manufacturing in the *Notes on the State of Virginia*. Within the same response he drew an unfavorable contrast between the circumstances in Europe and the newly independent United States:

> The political œconomists of Europe have established it as a principle that every state should endeavour to manufacture for itself: and this principle, like many others, we transfer to America, without calculating the difference of circumstance which should often produce a different result. In Europe the lands are either cultivated, or locked up against the cultivator. Manufacture must therefore be resorted to of necessity not of choice, to support the surplus of their people. But we have an immensity of land courting the industry of the husbandman. It is best then that all our citizens should be improved in its improvement, or that one half should be called off from that to exercise manufactures and handicraft arts for the other?

In Europe, manufacturing was a necessity because there was not enough accessible land. The result was the creation of a large class of propertyless laborers mired in poverty and ignorance. These were insufficient

material with which to build a lasting republic. "The mobs of great cities," he wrote, "add just so much to the support of pure government, as
sores do to the strength of the human body. It is the manners and spirit
of a people which preserve a republic in vigour. A degeneracy in these is
a canker which soon eats to the heart of its laws and constitution."[10]

In the United States there was ample land available, ensuring that
the majority of Americans would be independent farmers—and proper
republican citizens. Jefferson feared that the program of intensive manufacturing advocated by Alexander Hamilton and other Federalists
during the 1790s would lead to an increase in luxury and corruption,
undermining America's republican institutions and endangering the
republic itself. Manufacturing would accelerate the economic development, wealth stratification, and eventual decline of the republic. Spurn-
ing intensive manufacturing, Jefferson favored a program of extensive
agricultural production across the nation. The spread of farming across
the vast space of the United States would postpone the danger posed by
intensive development.[11]

Although he eschewed manufacturing, Jefferson did not intend
Americans to be subsistence farmers eking out a living from the land.
Some small-scale manufacturing would be necessary to service the agricultural economy—Jefferson himself sought to make nails commercially
at Monticello. This alone would not satiate appetite of Americans for
manufactured goods. As Jefferson wrote to George Washington in 1784:
"All the world is becoming commercial. Was it practicable to keep our
new empire separated from them we might indulge ourselves in specu-
lating whether commerce contributes to the happiness of mankind. But
we cannot separate ourselves from them. Our citizens have had too full a
taste of the comforts furnished by the arts and manufactures to be de-
barred the use of them. We must then in our own defence endeavor to
share as large a portion as we can of this modern source of wealth and
power."[12] Trade was the answer to this dilemma. A year later, in the
Notes on Virginia he explained how the system would work: "Carpen-
ters, masons, smiths, are wanting in husbandry: but, for the general operations of manufacture, let our workshops remain in Europe. It is better
to carry provisions and materials to workmen there, than to bring them
to the provisions and materials, and with them their materials and prin-

ciples. The loss by the transportation of commodities across the Atlantic will be made up in happiness and permanence of government." Americans would export their surplus produce and use the profits to buy goods manufactured in Europe. Thus they could enjoy the benefits of manufacturing without experiencing its deleterious consequences.[13]

During the era of the American Revolution Thomas Jefferson articulated a clear vision of political economy. The United States must be an independent republic, with a government based on the consent of the governed. Republics, however, were fragile entities. In order to ensure that the American republic would flourish and endure, most of its citizens, Jefferson believed, should be independent farmers. Jefferson was optimistic that as long as the majority of American citizens held their own property, the republic would have a stable foundation. They should not be impoverished subsistence farmers, however, but should engage in overseas trade, guaranteeing them wealth and manufactured goods while preserving the United States from the baneful influence of manufacturing. The American republic should be based on commercial agriculture if liberty were to flourish.

Jefferson's vision of political economy rested on two premises—plentiful western land to satisfy the needs of a growing population and secure access to global markets via the Atlantic economy. The American population grew at a prodigious rate during the eighteenth century. In 1743 when Jefferson was born, there were less than a million people in the thirteen British colonies that would rebel to form the United States. When Jefferson was a candidate for president in 1800, there were around 5.3 million Americans.[14] This rate of growth actually increased during the early nineteenth century. With its rapidly growing population, the new republic would need more land if Jefferson's vision were to be realized. An important corollary to Jefferson's republican conception was a commitment to expanding and protecting the overseas trade of the United States.

Jefferson was aware that overseas trade would, inevitably, lead to conflict. Because of the inherent danger of overseas trade, and his belief that "cultivators of the earth are the most valuable citizens," Jefferson preferred that Americans not engage directly in overseas trade themselves but rely on European carriers. Despite this wish he recognized that "our people are decided in the opinion that it is necessary for us to take a share in the occupation of the ocean, and their established habits induce them to require that the sea be kept open to them, and that that line of policy be pursued which will render the use of that element as great as possible to them." Jefferson's personal preference was for the majority of Americans to cultivate the land, but his democratic sensibility was such that he accepted that he and other members of the government should bow before "the decided choice of their constituents," protecting as best they could the right of Americans to trade and fish. "But what will be the consequence?" he asked. "Frequent wars without a doubt. Their property will be violated on the sea, and in foreign ports, their persons will be insulted, emprisoned &c. for pretended debts, contracts, crimes, contrabands &c. &c. These insults must be represented, even if we have no feelings, yet to prevent their eternal repetition. Or in other words, our commerce on the sea must be paid for by frequent war." Jefferson argued that naval strength was the surest protection for American trade: "Weakness provokes insult and injury, while a condition to punish it often prevents it. This reasoning leads to the necessity of some naval force, that being the only weapon with which we can reach an enemy." Contrary to his subsequent reputation as an opponent of sea power reluctant to use force, Jefferson revealed himself to be a militant advocate of naval power. In his thinking naval power was essential to protect American trade, which in turn was vital to the health of the republic. As demonstrated by the Algerian seizures of the *Maria* and the *Dauphin,* American trade in the Mediterranean was threatened by the Barbary States. Jefferson believed that the best way to counter that threat was the use of force. "I think it is to our interest to punis[h] the first insult: because an insult unpunished is the parent to many oth[ers]. We are not at this moment in a condition to do it, but we should put ourselv[es] into it as soon as possible."[15]

All regions of the United States sent their exports to the Mediterranean—rice and lumber from the southern states, wheat and flour from the mid-Atlantic, fish and rum from New England. Jefferson estimated that one-sixth of the wheat and flour and one-fourth of the fish exported from the United States were destined for Mediterranean markets. The most important article that Americans exported was dried salt cod. New Englanders sent their "common fish" to feed slaves in the West

Indies, and they exported "their choice fish to Portugal, Spain and the Mediterranean." The trade, according to Jefferson, employed 1,200 seamen on 80 to 100 vessels annually. John Adams estimated that if a diplomatic settlement could be reached between the United States and the Barbary powers, trade might expand to 200 vessels. Given the importance of overseas trade in Jefferson's vision of political economy, the Barbary States were more than just a nuisance for the United States. The threat they posed to American commerce endangered the republic.[16]

Jefferson believed that war was the best means of achieving a lasting solution to the danger from the Barbary States. Soon after his arrival in France he reported to his neighbor and protégé James Monroe that he and the other American diplomats "have taken some pains to find out the sums which the nations of Europe give to the Barbary States to purchase peace." No European governments would reveal how much they paid for peace, however, and Jefferson estimated that it would cost the United States as much as $300,000 per year. He proposed to enter into negotiations with the Barbary States for reciprocal trade agreements, without tribute. "If they refuse," he asked, "why not go to war with them?" Jefferson was sanguine at the prospect of war with the Barbary powers. He noted that Spain, Portugal, Naples, and Venice were already at war with them, and the Americans would find assistance in their ports. Jefferson declared: "We ought to begin a naval power, if we mean to carry on our own commerce. Can we begin it on a more honourable occasion or with a weaker foe? I am of the opinion [John] Paul Jones with half a dozen frigates would totally destroy their commerce: not by attempting bombardments as the Mediterranean states do wherein they act against the whole Barbary force brought to a point, but by constant cruising and cutting them to peices [sic] by peicemeal [sic]."[17] Jefferson felt that the United States should use the pretext provided by the Barbary States to justify a naval buildup. Although he would later refine his position, Jefferson's letter to Monroe reveals the crucial elements of his future policy toward the Barbary States: the United States should deploy its limited naval power to wage commercial war against the North Africans, in cooperation with regional powers also threatened by the sultanates. American commerce would thus be protected without resort to paying tribute. As minister in France and as secretary of state Jefferson consistently, and unsuccessfully, advocated this policy for the United States.

Despite Jefferson's wishes Congress was unwilling to fund a navy, but in the spring of 1785 it authorized Jefferson and Adams to open negotiations with the Barbary States and allocated $80,000 for the purpose. Congress stipulated that Adams and Jefferson delegate the negotiations to appropriate agents rather than travel to North Africa themselves. In the autumn the American diplomats dispatched Thomas Barclay, an American consul in France, to negotiate in Morocco, and they sent John Lamb, a merchant with experience in the Barbary trade, to Algiers.[18]

Thomas Barclay was an experienced fifty-seven-year-old merchant and diplomat when he was selected to negotiate in Morocco. Barclay had immigrated to Philadelphia in the mid-1760s and established himself as a successful merchant. Initially he concentrated on trading with his native Ireland—his father was a prominent linen merchant in Strabane—but he expanded his business to include the West Indies, England, and the Mediterranean. Barclay was an early supporter of the American resistance to British rule in the colonies. During the War of Independence he worked with Benjamin Franklin on behalf of the Continental Congress in various ports in France and Holland, where he organized supplies for the Continental Army. After the war he was named an American consul in France. With his experience as an international diplomat and merchant, Barclay was well suited for the mission to Morocco. When Jefferson suggested sending Barclay to negotiate with Sidi Muhammad ibn Abdallah, Adams, who had worked with Barclay in Holland and France during the war, responded positively: "We cannot find a Steadier, or more prudent Man."[19]

In early October 1785 Jefferson and Adams instructed Barclay to proceed to Morocco via Madrid. The Spanish had used their good offices to secure the release of the crew of the *Betsey* and its cargo from Sidi Muhammad. The American consul in Madrid, William Carmichael, had acquired extensive knowledge of the Barbary sultanates and the Mediterranean generally and could brief Barclay on the situation in Morocco as well as on the disposition of the Spanish. Jefferson and Adams instructed Barclay to negotiate a treaty of amity and commerce with Sidi Muhammad following, where possible, a draft which Jefferson supplied. He was to transmit the treaty to Jefferson and Adams for their approval. They, then, would send it to Congress for ratification. Mindful that they had to negotiate similar treaties with Algiers, Tripoli, and Tunis and secure the release of the prisoners in Algiers, Jefferson and Adams limited Barclay to a budget of $20,000. Barclay was also charged with gathering as much information as he could regarding the commerce, geography, culture, and government of Morocco. Barclay was to keep the ministers in Paris and London informed of developments at every opportunity.[20]

Barclay was not able to leave Paris until January 15, 1786. He was delayed by difficulties settling his accounts, and business necessitated that he take a circuitous route via Lorient and Bordeaux. Barclay arrived in Madrid by mid-March and he met with William Carmichael, as well as with the conde de Floridablanca, the Spanish foreign minister. Barclay was impressed by Floridablanca, whose manner he described as "frank and easie." Floridablanca treated Barclay "like a man of business" and expressed sympathy for the United States in its dealings with the North Africans. He noted that Sidi Muhammad wanted the Spanish king, Charles III, to act as an intermediary between Morocco and the United States but thought it best if Barclay went to Morocco to negotiate directly, bearing a letter from Charles III expressing his support for Barclay's mission.[21]

Barclay arrived in Marrakech on June 19, six months after leaving Paris. He was presented to Sidi Muhammad at a large public audience. Barclay described Muhammad, who greeted him on horseback: "66 years of age. . . . He is of a middle Stature, inclining to fat, and has a remarkable cast in his right eye which looks blacker than the other; his Complexion is rather dark owing to a small mixture of Negro blood in him." According to Barclay, Sidi Muhammad, an absolute ruler, had taken "the utmost pains to conquer those habits and prejudices in which he was educated" and was a more temperate ruler than his father. The emperor asked Barclay about the causes of the American Revolution and questioned him about the number of American soldiers and whether the United States produced timber suitable for constructing ships. Barclay answered the questions and presented Sidi Muhammad with the letter from Charles

III. The sultan concluded the audience by saying, "Send your Ships and trade with us, and I will do everything you can desire." He then ordered that Barclay and his secretary be given a tour of the royal gardens.[22]

After the public audience the sultan's minister, Taher ben Abdelhack Fennish, opened formal negotiations with Barclay. Sidi Muhammad had suggested that the treaty recently agreed between Morocco and Spain might serve as a model for a treaty with the United States. As the text of the Spanish treaty was not immediately available, Barclay presented Jefferson's draft treaty to the minister as a basis for negotiations. Barclay and Fennish quickly agreed on the terms of a treaty based on the draft. The two sides agreed to respect each other's shipping, and the two nations placed their mutual commerce on most favored nation status. In the event of war between the two nations, prisoners would not be enslaved but would be exchanged within a year of their capture. If hostilities commenced, citizens and subjects of one country resident in the other would have nine months to liquidate their property and depart. The treaty would be binding for fifty years. Crucially, Barclay secured the treaty at a cost of $20,000 and without a commitment to pay annual tribute. When asked about tribute, Barclay replied that he "had to Offer to His Majesty the Friendship of the United States and to receive his in Return, to form a Treaty with him on liberal and equal Terms. But if any engagements for future presents or Tributes were necessary, I must return without any Treaty." Sidi Muhammad, keen to agree a treaty with the United States, was willing to forego annual tribute and accepted most of the terms. The negotiations went smoothly and Sidi Muhammad signed the treaty on June 23, a mere four days after Barclay arrived.[23]

Barclay had a second, private, audience with Sidi Muhammad in the sultan's garden. Sidi Muhammad again met Barclay on horseback. The sultan complained about the treatment he had received at the hands of the British. He then examined the gifts Barclay had brought (particularly a watch and an atlas), asked to be shown a map of the United States, and inquired about its latitude and the location of its major ports. Barclay also "presented him with a book containing the constitutions of America and other public papers, and one of the Interpreters told him it also contained the reasons which induced the Americans to go to war with Great Britain." Sidi Muhammad commanded that the book be translated into Arabic immediately. After that the men discussed "To-bacco, the Day of the Month, and the Sun's Declination" as well as arrangements to appoint an American consul in Morocco after the conclusion of the treaty between the two countries.[24]

The Morocco treaty was a rare success in the history of American relations with the Barbary States. What accounts for Thomas Barclay's diplomatic triumph? In part the credit is due to Barclay himself (and his secretary and translator, David Salisbury Franks). Barclay was well suited by experience and temperament for the mission he was given. Further, France and Spain, particularly the latter, were favorably disposed toward the negotiations. Both of the kingdoms offered support and encouragement that facilitated the negotiations. Most important was the attitude of the Moroccan emperor, Sidi Muhammad. Of the Barbary leaders he had long favored a positive relationship with United States. His seizure of the *Betsey* was not intended as an act of war but rather as the catalyst for a diplomatic settlement. Muhammad sought a commercial treaty with the United States and was willing to make concessions and forego the usual demands for tribute in order to achieve it. As a consequence the threat to American shipping in the Atlantic and Mediterranean diminished somewhat. Unfortunately for the Americans, the circumstances in the other Barbary States were much more problematic, as John Lamb discovered in Algiers.[25]

Captain John Lamb had carried the dispatches from Congress to Jefferson and Adams stipulating that they should open negotiations with the Barbary States. Lamb was a merchant from Norwich, Connecticut, with experience in the Barbary trade. He came recommended to Jefferson by the governor of Connecticut. Although John Jay, then secretary of foreign affairs, had not formally instructed Jefferson to appoint Lamb to negotiate with the Barbary powers, Jefferson assumed this intention. After Lamb arrived in Paris in September 1785, Jefferson suggested to Adams that they appoint Lamb to negotiate with Algiers. Jefferson noted, "He has followed for many years the Barbary trade and seems intimately acquainted with those states." Still he qualified his endorsement of Lamb, who had been rather dilatory in traveling to France: "I have not seen enough of him to judge of his abilities. He seems not deficient as far as I can see, and the footing on which he comes must furnish a presumption for what we do not see. We must say the same as to his integrity, we must rely for this on the recommendations he brings, as it is impossible for us to judge of this for ourselves." To William Carmichael in Madrid, Jefferson wrote of Lamb, "His manner and appearance are not promising." To allay his concerns Jefferson proposed that he and Adams assign a clerk to assist Lamb who, "in case he thought any thing was going amiss, might give us information." Jefferson also recommended that Lamb not be allowed to draw credit on the Dutch banking house that American diplomats used but rather should place his claims through Adams, which would "enable you to check them, if you are sensible of any abuse intended." Jefferson's suspicions of the well-connected Lamb would be borne out during the mission to Algiers.[26]

Jefferson and Adams provided Lamb with the same instructions they had issued to Barclay concerning a commercial treaty. The situation in Algiers was complicated by the twenty-one captive seamen from the *Maria* and the *Dauphin*. Jefferson and Adams authorized Lamb to negotiate for the liberation of the captives, limiting him to a ransom no more than $200 per capita. Because Congress had not authorized the ransom, Jefferson and Adams instructed Lamb to get the consent of the prisoners, each of whom would be "answerable for his own redemption" if Congress did not provide the funding.[27]

Jefferson and Adams took this action without explicit congressional support. They noted that they were empowered to seek only a commercial treaty with Algiers, but confronted by the suffering of the sailors from the *Maria* and the *Dauphin*, they acted, "as we presume strongly that it would be the will of Congress that they [the prisoners] should be redeemed from their present calamitous condition." Early American diplomats, far from home and with limited communication, periodically faced this type of crisis. However there is also a parallel to Jefferson's handling of the affairs during the invasion of Virginia when he acted without reference to his council or the assembly. He and Adams assumed that they must act and sought to do so on behalf of Congress: "We think ourselves bound, in so distant a situation, and where the emergency of the case is so great, to act according to what we think would be the desire of Congress and to trust to their goodness and the purity of their own motives for our justification."[28]

John Lamb arrived in Algiers on March 25, 1786, "after maney little Disappointments." On April 3 Lamb began negotiations with the dey of Algiers, Muhammad V ben Othman. Lamb met with the dey several times. Muhammad refused to negotiate a peace treaty with Lamb and wanted to discuss only the price for ransoming the twenty-one captive Americans. The dey demanded "a most Exorbitent price, far beyond my limits," reported Lamb. At their final meeting Lamb managed to talk the dey down to price of $59,496, far in excess of the $4,200 he had been authorized to pay. Lamb then approached the dey's principal minister, Hassan Bacha El Khaznadji (Pasha Hassan, the treasurer), whom he contacted by making gifts to one of Hassan's confidants, who also acted as interpreter for Lamb (who spoke only English). Pasha Hassan was more accommodating than the dey. Hassan told Lamb that he wanted to see Algiers and the United States conclude a peace treaty and urged him not to be put off by the high price for freeing the captives. Hassan informed Lamb that Algiers would not make a treaty with the United States before it had concluded its ongoing war with Spain. Further, the dey's high price for the release of the captives was dictated by maintaining the value of his Spanish captives while negotiating with Spain. Hassan advised Lamb to go to Spain to await the Algerian-Spanish outcomes before returning to Algiers.[29]

The American prisoners in Algiers provided a slightly different account of the negotiations. According to the captives, Lamb had offered the dey as much as $30,000 for their release, which the dey countered with $48,700. Lamb responded that "the price was great; [and] he would see what he could do in four months time." The Algerians believed that they had struck a deal and that Lamb had left Algiers for Spain to raise the necessary funds. The prisoners, worried that they might be responsible for any price Lamb negotiated and also that if Lamb failed their plight would become more dire, "begged of him to make no further proposition on our account." They feared that Lamb would make it impossible for subsequent American diplomats to negotiate in Algiers and that by offering such a high price Lamb would set a dangerous precedent. "We confess," they wrote, "it would be setting a bad example to pay so great a sum for a few, and other unfortunate captives would feel the ill effects of it." Nonetheless the captives reminded Adams and

Jefferson, "We are not prisoners of war; we are slaves; the consideration of which will induce our country to consider our lamentable misfortune, hoping they will adopt some effectual plan of extricating us from slavery, and not suffer a remnant of their countrymen to die in slavery in this barbarous country." It is difficult to reconcile Lamb's account of the negotiations with the captives'. According to the prisoners, Lamb briefed them after each of his meetings with the dey. "We hope Mr. Lamb has not told us one story, and wrote the Ministers in Europe another," wrote the captives. Nonetheless, they asked, "Why was Mr. Lamb so anxious with his propositions to the Dey, when he declared to us that he had no money appropriated towards our use?"[30]

Whether Lamb believed he had reached an agreement with the Algerians or was simply giving the prisoners false hope, nothing came of his negotiations. Unfortunately for the captives the misgivings that Jefferson and Adams had harbored about Lamb were realized as soon as the Connecticut diplomat arrived in Algiers. Lamb quarreled with his secretary, Paul Randall, whom he sent back to Spain soon after they arrived, with a dispatch for Jefferson and Adams.[31] The American captives were not very impressed by their would-be redeemer. After the collapse of the negotiations Richard O'Brien wrote, "We are much surprised at Mr. Lamb's ungentleman like behaviour whilst he was in Algiers and could hardly believe Congress would [have] sent such a man to negociate so important an affair as the making a peace with the Algerines where it required the most able Statesman and Politician." O'Brien reported that Lamb clashed with the French and Spanish consuls at Algiers, although the Spanish and French governments had provided a measure of diplomatic support to the American efforts with the Barbary States during the period. (The Spanish had been instrumental in helping Thomas Barclay to reach an agreement with Morocco and had received the crew of the *Betsey*.) Lamb browbeat the Spanish consul, the comte d'Expilly, who had provided assistance to the American captives, threatening that if he did not pressure the Algerians to make peace with the Americans, the United States would seize Spanish territory in North America. Lamb shared a "particular intimacy with Mr. Logie, the British Consul, Mr. Lamb's bosom friend," and also a drunkard who was shunned by the diplomatic community in Algiers. When the crews of the *Dauphin* and *Maria* were captured Logie offered them aid and thence used some of the Americans as personal servants whom he humiliated and abused. In September 1786 Lamb's commission was revoked, and he was recalled by Congress.[32]

It is likely that an abler diplomat than John Lamb would have failed as well. John Adams defended the decision to send Lamb to Algiers. "I never saw him nor heard of him," wrote the American minister in London, "He ever was and still is as indifferent to me, as a Mohawk Indian. But as he came from Congress with their Dispatches of such importance, I supposed it was expected We should appoint him." Adams conceded, "There is no harm done.—If Congress had sent the ablest Member of their own Body, at such a Time and under such pecuniary Limitations he would have done no better."[33] Adams noted that when Europeans negotiated in Barbary they normally arrived with naval squadrons as well as treasure and "offer battle at the same time that that they propose treaties and promise presents." Lamb and Barclay, by contrast, were "armed only with innocence and the olive branch."[34] Adams offered his defense of Lamb, such as it was, after he and Jefferson, more able diplomats than John Lamb, had experienced the frustrations of Barbary diplomacy firsthand.

During the winter and spring of 1786, Adams and Jefferson entered into direct negotiations with Tripoli, third of the four Barbary States. In February 1786 an ambassador from Tripoli, Abdurrahman, arrived in London, presenting Adams with a dilemma. Should he attempt to negotiate with Abdurrahman or await the outcome of the ongoing negotiations in Morocco and Algiers? "Feeling his appearance here to be ominous" (Adams believed the Tripolitan would seek to extort tribute from the United States or solicit aid from Britain to wage war against American commerce), the American minister avoided formally meeting Abdurrahman until he learned whether Barclay and Lamb had been successful in Morocco and Algiers. The Tripolitan envoy reported "most of the foreign Ministers have left their cards; but the American has not." Abdurrahman declared, "We will make peace with them, however, for tribute of a hundred thousand dollars a year, not less."[35]

Ultimately Adams concluded "that all the other foreign ministers had made their visits, and he would take amiss a longer inattention." On February 16 the American minister went in the evening with the intention of leaving his card without meeting the ambassador, but a servant announced that Abdurrahman was at home and would be delighted to receive Adams. Adams described the scene to Jefferson:

> I was received in State. Two great Chairs before the Fire, one of which was destined for me, the other for his Excellency. Two Secretaries of Legation, men of no Small Consequence Standing Upright in the middle of the Room, without daring to Sitt, during the whole time I was there, and whether they are not yet upright upon their Legs I know not. Now commenced the Difficulty. His Excellency Speaks Scarcely a Word of any European Language, except Italian and Lingua Franca, in which, you know I have Small Pretensions. He began soon to ask me Questions about America and her Tobacco, and I was Surprized to find that with a pittance of Italian and a few French Words which he understands, We could so well understand each other. "We make Tobacco in Tripoli," said his Excellency "but it is too Strong. Your American Tobacco is better." By this Time one of his secretaries or *upper servants* brought two Pipes ready filled and lighted. The longest was offered me; the other to his Excellency. It is long since I took a Pipe but as it would be unpardonable to be wanting in Politeness in so ceremonious an Interview, I took the Pipe with great Complacency, placed the Bowl upon the Carpet, for the Stem was fit for a Walking Cane, and I believe more than two Yards in length, and Smoaked in aweful Pomp, reciprocating Whiff for Whiff, with his Excellency, untill Coffee was brought in. His Excellency took a Cup, after I had taken one, and alternately Sipped at his Coffee and whiffed at his Tobacco, and I wished he would take a Pinch in turn from his Snuff box for Variety; and I followed the Example with Such Exactness and Solemnity that the two secretaries appeared in Raptures and the superiour of them who speaks a few Words of French cryed out in Extacy, "Monsieur votes etes un Turk."

Having concluded the formalities, Abdurrahman began to question Adams. The Tripolitan asked Adams about the United States. After Adams answered his questions Abdurrahman said that America was a great country but "Tripoli is at War with it." Adams said he was "Sorry to hear that, [and he] Had not heard of any War with Tripoli." Abdurrahman said that there could be no peace without a treaty, and if the Americans sought to trade in the Mediterranean, they must negotiate a treaty with Tripoli just as France, Britain, and all other powers had. Abdurrahman stated that he was empowered to negotiate such a peace treaty with Adams and invited a subsequent session with an interpreter so that they could discuss terms.[36]

The two diplomats met several times during the next week. Abdurrahman returned Adams's visit on February 19, calling on the American at his residence on Grosvenor Square, at noon, accompanied by a Dr. Benamor, probably an English Jew, who had worked as a merchant in Barbary and spoke Arabic, French, and Italian as well as his native English. Abdurrahman chose to use Benamor rather than the translator offered by the British government because he feared that the British were seeking to foster ill will between the Barbary States and the Americans. According to Adams, Abdurrahman "was sorry to say he found here much ill will to the Americans, and a desire to prevent him from seeing the American ministers. For this reason, he would have nothing to do with the Court interpreter." The two men discussed the prospect of war between Tripoli and the United States. The Tripolitan explained that wars between Christian nations were mild, but a war between Muslims and Christians was "horrible" with prisoners "sold into slavery," and he offered to help prevent such a calamity befalling the United States. He provided Adams with a summary of affairs in Barbary. He noted that Algiers was the strongest and most difficult of the sultanates to deal with. (The prospect of the unsavory John Lamb's imminent arrival there must have filled Adams with foreboding.) He suggested that it would be best to reach an agreement first with Tripoli. He claimed that he spoke for Tunis as well as Tripoli and that an agreement with Tripoli would, inevitably, lead to a treaty with Tunis. Agreements with Morocco and Algiers would likely follow. When Adams informed Abdurrahman that Sidi Muhammad had made friendly overtures to the United States and

that Thomas Barclay was en route to Morocco, the Tripolitan "rejoiced
to hear it, and doubted not that this agent would succeed, as the Emperor was a man of extensive views, and much disposed to promote the
commerce of his subjects." The two men did not discuss how much
tribute the United States would have to pay to secure peace with Tripoli,
but Abdurrahman acknowledged that since the United States had a
smaller population than France, Spain, Britain, and Holland and had
just emerged from a lengthy war, it could not be expected to pay as much
tribute as the European nations. The actual figure would have to form
the basis for future negotiations.[37]

Several days later the two diplomats met again, with Abdurrahman
accompanied by Benamor, the translator, "a very decent man." This
time the men discussed specific terms of an agreement. The Tripolitan
ambassador explained to Adams that they might negotiate a perpetual
treaty, "indissoluble and binding forever," or a more limited agreement
for a specific number of years. Abdurrahman advised that a perpetual
treaty would cost more than a limited agreement, £30,000, which could
be paid over a number of years. A short-term treaty would be cheaper
but would require renewal, which would mean that insuring peaceful
relations in the long term would be more costly, particularly as separate
agreements would have to be negotiated with each Barbary power. Adams reported that perpetual treaties with all the Barbary States would
cost £120,000, plus the cost of presents for ambassadors and the gifts
made by consuls in each of the states, and estimated the total cost of the
treaties and gifts at £200,000. This figure did not include the cost of
ransoming the Americans held in Algiers. Nonetheless Adams felt that
the price of completing a treaty would be less costly than war. "If it is not
done," he warned, "this war will cost more millions in sterling money in
a short time, besides the miserable depression of the reputation of the
United States, the cruel embarrassment of all of our commerce, and the
intolerable burthen of insurance, added to the cries of our countrymen
in captivity." By contrast, a perpetual agreement would mean "our commerce, navigation, and fisheries would extend into the Mediterranean,
to Spain, and Portugal, France and England. The additional profits
would richly repay the interest, and our credit would be adequate to all
of our wants."[38]

Adams may have favored paying tribute to the Barbary States from a favorable impression of the Tripolitan ambassador. "This man is either a consummate politician in art and address," he wrote, "or he is a benevolent and wise man. Time will discover whether he disguises an interested character, or is indeed the philosopher he pretends to be. If he is the latter, Providence seems to have opened to us an opportunity of conducting this thorny business to a happy conclusion." Adams believed the talks were promising enough that he dispatched his aide, Colonel William S. Smith (soon to marry Adams's daughter, Abigail) to Paris to brief Jefferson and encourage him to come to London to join the talks, declaring, "There is nothing to be done in Europe, of half the Importance of this, and I dare not communicate to Congress what has passed without your Concurrence. What has been already done and expended will be absolutely thrown away and We shall be involved in a universal and horrible war with these Barbary States, which will continue for many Years unless more is done immediately." Adams saw there was an opportunity for a lasting peace with the Barbary States and needed Jefferson to join the negotiations and support any agreement they might conclude.[39]

Jefferson and William Smith traveled from Paris to London together. Jefferson hired a cabriolet for 72 francs to take them from Paris to Calais and paid another 75 francs for their passage across the channel. After five days' travel, and eighteen days after Adams wrote to him, Jefferson reached London on March 11.[40] Adams had suggested to Jefferson that the object of his journey might be "imputed to Curiosity, to take a Look at England and pay your Respects at Court and to the Corps Diplomatick." Under the cover of sightseeing, during his six-week stay in England, Jefferson participated in negotiations with Abdurrahman as well as the Portuguese ambassador, who was empowered to complete a trade agreement with the United States. Soon after his arrival, Jefferson and Adams met with Abdurrahman, who added little to what he had told Adams, explaining the advantages of completing a perpetual treaty, which would cost £30,000 plus an additional £3,000 commission for him. The American diplomats asked what grounds Tripoli and the other Barbary States had for making war against a nation that had done "them no Injury, and observed that we considered all mankind our friends who had done us no wrong, nor had given us any provocation." Abdurrahman answered, "It was founded on the Laws of their Prophet, that it was written in their Koran, that all nations who should not have acknowledged their authority were sinners, that it was their right and duty to make war upon them wherever they could be found, and to make slaves of all they could take as Prisoners."[41]

Several additional meetings with Abdurrahman could not convince the envoy to lower the price of peace. The conferences became exercises in information gathering by the American envoys who conceded, among themselves, that the $80,000 they were authorized to spend was "but as a drop to a bucket" of what was required to secure a lasting peace. Having experienced the frustrations of Barbary diplomacy firsthand Jefferson concluded, "The U. S. will not buy peace with money."[42] Adams and Jefferson referred the matter to John Jay and Congress, and Jefferson returned to Paris at the end of April. Congress declined to act decisively on the question apart from encouraging Adams and Jefferson to "conclude on the best terms in yr power" treaties with the Barbary States. In January 1787 as Ambassador Abdurrahman prepared to leave London he held a final meeting with John Adams. When Adams told the Tripolitan that Congress had yet to issue new instructions or funds, he responded that "the decree was written in heaven, and, if a peace was pre-ordained between my country and his, it would take place." With this statement the talks between the American commissioners and Tripoli came to an end.[43]

In London Jefferson and Adams discussed the possibility of negotiating directly with the Ottoman emperor, who nominally ruled Tunisia, Tripoli, and Algiers. They agreed that when Jefferson returned to Paris he should discuss such an approach with the comte de Vergennes, the French foreign minister, who had served in Constantinople as the French ambassador to the Sublime Porte earlier in his career. Back in Paris, Jefferson met Vergennes on May 22, 1786, and asked the Frenchman whether the United States might be advised to seek a settlement with the Barbary States through the Ottoman Empire. Vergennes was not encouraging, telling Jefferson the Americans would have to go through the rituals of gift giving and tribute paying at Constantinople, and they would then need to do the same thing in Algiers, Tripoli, and Tunis—and there was no guarantee that a deal made with the Sublime Porte would be binding on the Barbary Coast. "He observed that the Barbary states acknoleged a sort of vassalage to the Porte, and availed themselves of that relation when any thing was to be gained by it; but that whenever it subjected them to a demand from the Porte they totally disregarded it; that money was the sole agent at Algiers, except so far as fear could be induced also."[44]

Apart from the treaty with Morocco, the American negotiations with the Barbary powers had failed. The American prisoners remained in Algiers and Tripoli; Algiers and Tunis still threatened American shipping. The United States was unwilling or unable to meet the financial demands that a diplomatic settlement required. After Jefferson returned to Paris in spring 1786, he and Adams engaged in a thoughtful exchange of ideas about how best to address the problem. The two diplomats disagreed profoundly over the question of how best to protect American interests in the Mediterranean.

Jefferson believed the United States had three options with respect to the "pyratical states": "Buy a peace at their enormous price; force one; or abandon the carriage into the Mediterranean to other powers." He conceded, "All these measures are disagreeable."[45] For his part, John Adams favored paying for a negotiated settlement. Adams explained his position in a letter to Jefferson on July 3, 1786. He felt that four conditions dictated this course of action:

> 1. We may at this Time, have a Peace with them, in Spight of all the Intrigues of the English or others to prevent it, for a Sum of Money.
>
> 2. We never Shall have Peace, though France, Spain, England and Holland Should use all their Influence in our favour without a Sum of Money.
>
> 3. That neither the Benevolence of France nor the Malevolence of England will be ever able materially to diminish or Increase the Sum.
>
> 4. That the longer the Negotiation is delayed, the larger will be the Demand.

For Adams it made sense to negotiate a settlement requiring annual tribute and to do so as soon as possible: "I conclude it to be wisest for Us to
negotiate and pay the necessary Sum without Loss of Time." Delay
would only increase the price of a settlement. The issue came down to a
straight commercial calculation: "At present we are Sacrificing a Million
annually to Save one Gift of two hundred Thousand Pounds. This is not
good Œconomy. We might at this hour have two hundred ships in the
Mediterranean, whose Freight alone would be worth two hundred
Thousand Pounds besides its Influence upon the Price of our Produce.
Our Farmers and Planters will find the Price of their Articles Sink very
low indeed, if this Peace is not made." Adams felt force wasn't worth the
cost. "The Policy of Christendom," he wrote, "has made Cowards of all
their Sailors before the Standard of Mahomet. It would be heroical and
glorious in Us, to restore Courage to ours. I doubt not we could accom-
plish it, if we should set about it in earnest. But the Difficulty of bringing
our People to agree upon it, has ever discouraged me."[46] The United
States could defeat the Barbary powers but at what cost? It would have
to develop a navy and bear the cost of waging war, which would far exceed that of paying tribute. As far as Adams was concerned it made economic sense for the United States to reach a settlement with each of the
Barbary States. As with the major (and many of the minor) European
powers, this would entail paying annual tribute. The cost of tribute,
however, would be far smaller than the profits that the Mediterranean
trade had to offer. Paying tribute might be distasteful, but it was the only
prudent course of action as far as Adams was concerned.

Jefferson wrote a lengthy response to Adams on July 11. He noted,
"Our instructions relative to the Barbary states having required us to
proceed by way of negotiation to obtain their peace, it became our duty
to do this to the best of our power." He continued, "Whatever might be
our private opinions, they were to be suppressed, and the line marked
out to us, was to be followed. It has been so honestly, and zealously." He
acknowledged that he "very early thought it would be best to effect a
peace thro' the medium of war." Although Jefferson agreed with the first
three of Adams's suppositions, "which are in substance that the good
offices of our friends cannot procure us a peace without paying its price,
that they cannot materially lessen that price, and that paying it, we can

have the peace in spight [*sic*] of the intrigues of our enemies," he did not accept the fourth, that a delay in negotiations would increase the cost of a settlement, arguing that the price of peace might rise or fall depending on the number of American ships that were captured. Jefferson then enumerated the reasons why war was preferable to buying peace in North Africa. Among these he believed that justice and honor made war more attractive than negotiating. War with the Barbary States would also serve a larger strategic purpose. "It will procure us respect in Europe," Jefferson declared, "and respect is a safe-guard to interest." In Jefferson's thinking, war would also strengthen the fragile American union. "It will arm the federal head with the safest of all instruments of coercion over their delinquent members and prevent them from using what would be less safe." Although Jefferson believed that Adams would agree in principle with his main arguments in favor of war, he knew that Adams and he differed over the cost and effectiveness of possible military action.[47]

Jefferson estimated that it would cost the United States £450,000 to build and man a fleet of 150 guns, half of which would be used to blockade the Barbary Coast "in constant cruise." Once the fleet was launched, Jefferson estimated that maintaining it would require £45,000 per annum. While war might be costly, and its ultimate cost could be uncertain, so, too, was peace. "If it be admitted however that war, on the fairest prospects, is still exposed to incertainties," Jefferson wrote, "I weigh against this the greater incertainty of the duration of a peace bought with money, from such a people, from a Dey 80. years old, and by a nation who, on the hypothesis of buying peace, is to have no power on the sea to enforce an observance of it." Crucially, Jefferson believed that the cost of war need not be borne by the United States alone. He proposed to create an international confederacy to bring the Barbary States to heel. In his letter to Adams he cited Portugal and Naples as likely members of a coalition, explaining how it might function.

> I suppose then that a Convention might be formed between Portugal, Naples and the U.S. by which the burthen of the war might be quotaed on them according to their respective wealth, and the term of it should be when Algiers should subscribe to a

peace with all three on equal terms. This might be left open for other nations to accede to, and many, if not most of the powers of Europe (except France, England, Holland and Spain if her peace be made) would sooner or later enter into the confederacy, for the sake of having their peace with the Pyratical states guarantied by the whole. I suppose that in this case our proportion of force would not be the half of what I first calculated on.[48]

For Jefferson, war was the best alternative for dealing with the Barbary pirates. War was an honorable choice with benefits internationally and domestically. Crucially, the cost of war would likely be less than that of negotiating a peace agreement and paying tribute, and it could be shared among a coalition of lesser powers, led by the United States, maintaining a perpetual naval blockade of North Africa until the Barbary powers sued for a just peace, without tribute.

Since his return from London in the spring of 1786 Jefferson had pondered the Barbary problem. He developed the ideas that he laid out for Adams into a "Proposed Convention against the Barbary States," which he drafted by early July. The purpose of the convention was "to compel the pyratical states to perpetual peace, without price, and to guarantee that peace to each other." This would be achieved by two or more of the states at war with the Barbary powers adopting the convention and maintaining a naval blockade. Jefferson proposed that the convention first target Algiers, as the most belligerent and difficult of the sultanates. The parties to the convention should agree on their proportionate contribution to the coalition's naval forces, to be met either by ships and men or through a cash contribution. Jefferson recognized that managing a naval coalition of disparate powers would be a challenge and that consultation with individual governments impractical. Instead he optimistically proposed that the ambassadors of each of the signatories to the convention, meeting "at some one court of Europe, . . . shall form a Committee or Council for carrying this convention into effect; wherein the vote of each member shall be computed in proportion to the quota of his sovereign, and the majority so computed shall prevail in all questions within the view of this Convention." He added, "The court of Versailles is proposed, on account of its neighbourhood to the Mediterranean, and because all those powers are represented there, who are likely to become parties to this convention."[49]

The proposal to use naval force to compel the Barbary States to respect the rights of the United States and its maritime allies provides a crucial insight into Jefferson's thinking with respect to international relations. Faced with a crisis—the seizure of the crews of the *Maria* and the *Dauphin,* still held as captives in Algiers—he did not hesitate or scruple about the use of force. He did so with the aim of remaking the diplomacy of the Mediterranean and solving the Barbary problem once and for all. As he recalled in his autobiography, "I was very unwilling that we should acquiesce in the European humiliation of paying a tribute to those lawless pirates and endeavored to form an association of the powers subject to habitual depredations from them."[50] He embraced the opportunity to wage war in defense of international justice and American honor with the end of achieving "perpetual peace" in North Africa. The creation of a confederacy of like-minded nations would minimize the cost of a blockade and give international legitimacy to the endeavor.

Jefferson's "Proposed Convention against the Barbary States" faced significant obstacles—both international and domestic. Looking for allies among the lesser European powers, Jefferson circulated the proposal among the diplomatic community in Paris. He consulted the Neapolitan minister at Versailles, the comte Del Pio, while drafting the proposal, and he later discussed it with the ambassadors from Portugal, Venice, Malta, Denmark, and Sweden, each of whom, he reported, "were favorably disposed to such an association." Jefferson sought to build a coalition among those European maritime nations that had suffered at the hands of the Barbary States but lacked the wealth or naval power to defend their interests. As Jefferson wrote to Adams in July, he had little hope that Britain, France, the Netherlands, or Spain—which "had just concluded a treaty with Algiers"—would join the coalition. The ambassadors at Versailles expressed concern to Jefferson "that France would interfere, and, either openly or secretly support the Barbary powers" and pressed him to discuss the proposed convention with Vergennes. Jefferson reported that he had discussed the matter with Vergennes, who had not expressed opposition to it. He had raised with Vergennes his concern that Britain would seek to subvert the coalition "on behalf of those piratical governments," but the French foreign minister assured him, "She dares not do it." This was hardly a ringing endorsement. Nonetheless Jefferson was optimistic that there was enough European support for his proposal to seek support for it in the United States. He reported, "The other agents were satisfied with this indication of his sentiments, and nothing was now wanting to bring it into direct and formal consideration, but the assent of our government, and their authority to make the formal proposition."[51]

Jefferson faced several challenges in putting his proposal to Congress. First, he was not formally empowered to negotiate such an agreement. He and Adams had been authorized by Congress to conclude trade agreements with the Barbary States, not to create an armed coalition against them. This was not, necessarily, an insurmountable obstacle. Early American diplomats—far from home, facing changing circumstances, and unable to consult their government—often had to demonstrate initiative and exceed their mandates. Jefferson's own representatives would do so during the Louisiana negotiations in 1803. More significant was the opposition of John Adams. Jefferson's fellow commissioner unequivocally favored paying tribute as the surest and cheapest way to achieve peace. Without Adams's support, Jefferson could not represent his proposal as emanating from the American commissioners. Perhaps the most important obstacle was financial. Congress had appropriated $80,000 to negotiate peace with the Barbary powers. During their negotiations with Abdurraham, Adams and Jefferson learned that peace would cost much more than that. Although Jefferson claimed that his proposed convention would cost less than the £200,000 estimated by him and Adams as the cost to negotiate peace treaties, there was no guarantee that Congress would fund the naval buildup required by Jefferson's proposal. Faced with these challenges, Jefferson sought to introduce his plan to Congress through the offices of the Marquis de Lafayette.

Having met Lafayette during the British invasion of Virginia in 1781, Jefferson came to know him better during his tenure in Paris. Jefferson collaborated with him on matters personal, political, and diplomatic, and they discussed creating a coalition to blockade the Barbary Coast during the spring of 1786. By the autumn Jefferson had revised his plan slightly in light of discussions with diplomats at Versailles.[52] On October 22 Lafayette and Jefferson discussed the confederacy. In response Lafayette wrote "to propose myself as a Chief of the Anti-piratical Confederacy. I will ask a Sum of Monney from Naples, Portugal, Rome, Venice, and some German towns, Naval stores and Sea Men from America, a treaty with Maltha, a Harbour in Sicily, and keep up two or three fifties, six large Frigats, and a Number of smaller Vessels filled with Marines to Board the privateers. There will be always two thirds of the squadron out, and one third Refitting, and should a land opportunity offer the King of Naples will lend some Regiments."[53] Lafayette's letter fleshed out the details of the proposed confederacy. The list of potential participants had expanded considerably, with some states providing financial support and others military assistance in the form of men, ships, supplies, and bases. Interestingly, Lafayette's mention of a "land opportunity" suggests that they had pondered invading the Barbary Coast (with Neapolitan troops).

Several days after his conversation with Jefferson, Lafayette wrote to George Washington about the Barbary situation. "There is between Mr. Jefferson and Mr. Adams a diversity of opinion respecting the Algerines," observed the Frenchman. "Adams thinks a peace should be purchased from them, Mr. Jefferson finds it as cheap and more honourable to cruise against them. I incline to the later opinion, and think it possible to form an alliance between the United States, Naples, Rome, Venice, Portugal and some other powers, each giving a sum of money, not very large, whereby a common armement [sic] may distress the Algerines into any terms." Lafayette urged, "Congress ought to give Mr. Jefferson and Adams ample powers to stipulate in their names for such a confederacy." The same day that Lafayette wrote to Washington he also wrote of the confederacy to Congressman James McHenry of Maryland. Two days later he wrote John Jay, the secretary of foreign affairs, to the same effect, proposing that Congress empower Jefferson and Adams to enter into the confederacy.[54]

Because of his disagreement with Adams over the best way to handle the Barbary issue, Jefferson used Lafayette to bring his proposal to Congress.[55] Jay submitted Lafayette's request to Congress without comment on February 15, 1787.[56] Congress neglected to respond to Lafayette's letters until July 27, 1787, when William Grayson, a representative from Virginia, introduced a resolution that the "Minister plenipotentiary of the United States at the Court of France be directed to form a Confederacy with the powers of Europe who are now at War with the piratical states . . . or may be disposed to go to War with them." The resolution was referred to the secretary of foreign affairs by an overwhelming vote of seventeen in favor and three against.[57] But on August 2 Jay responded that he believed it to be "rendered unseasonable by the present State of our Affairs." Jay was interested in promoting the commercial interests of the United States and sympathetic to the American captives, but he did not support the proposal to create a maritime confederacy. He questioned whether it was worthwhile for Americans to engage in the Mediterranean carrying trade rather than allowing others to do so on their behalf. Jay conceded that although he had once supported bolstering the nation's navy, "from Causes originating in the Inefficiency of the national Government our Navigation has since rapidly declined, and the public Revenue, depending on the Effect of Requisitions, has become inadequate to the ordinary Exigencies of the Union." The secretary for foreign affairs doubted that Congress could bear the cost of the enterprise, insisting that Congress lacked the means to build and maintain and supply even three frigates. Under such circumstances Congress should resist adopting such resolutions "until the Means of executing them appear clearly to be within their Reach." Delegates determined to replace the Articles of Confederation were then meeting in Philadelphia to draft a constitution to create a much stronger federal government with the power to tax and exercise power at home and abroad. Jay was a strong supporter of this movement. His claim that Congress lacked the means to defend American interests in Barbary reinforced the case for constitutional change. Jefferson's proposal to create an international coalition to seek redress from the Barbary powers died in Congress.[58]

Having failed to negotiate agreements with Algiers, Tunis, and Tripoli or to create an international coalition to prevent Barbary depredations, Jefferson turned his attention to the fate of the prisoners who continued to languish in Algiers. The number of prisoners from the *Maria* and the *Dauphin* had dwindled somewhat. A couple of captives had been freed when their friends raised the money to ransom them. Several more had died in captivity. While Jefferson awaited a congressional decision on his proposal, he quietly pursued a strategy to secure the release of the remaining captives. Early in 1787 Jefferson approached the general of the Mathurins, a French religious order dedicated to the welfare of prisoners. The Mathurins had long raised funds to ransom captives in Barbary and maintained a diplomatic presence in the sultanates. The general of the order said that the Mathurins would be willing to assist the Americans, though he did not want his members to be perceived as agents for the American government as this would enhance the cost of ransoming the captives and undermine the Mathurins' efforts on behalf of other prisoners. After nine months Jefferson received authorization to use the Mathurins, but it took almost two years to authorize the funding. At that point the Mathurins had been swept up in the French Revolution and were unable to pursue the matter. One consequence of this effort was that while the Mathurins were seeking to ransom the captives, the American government deliberately ignored them. In 1790 Jefferson wrote, "It was necessary . . . to suffer the captives themselves and their Friends to believe, for a while that no Attention was paid to them, no Notice taken of their Letters. . . . It would have been unsafe to trust them with a Secret, the Disclosure of which might forever prevent their Redemption, by raising the Demands of the Captors to Sums, which a due Regard for our Seamen, still in Freedom, would forbid us to give. This was the most trying of all Circumstances, and drew from them the most afflicting Reproaches."[59] The prisoners from the *Maria* and the *Dauphin* were not freed until June 1796, after nearly eleven years in captivity, after the United States and Algiers agreed to a peace settlement. The American negotiators agreed to pay $642,500 to secure the release of the prisoners and to provide $21,600 worth of naval stores annually as tribute.[60]

Jefferson returned to the United States in late 1789. The Barbary question had been the most vexing problem he confronted during his tenure as a diplomat in Europe. Apart from the Moroccan treaty the negotiations between the United States and the Barbary States had failed completely. Frustrated by the negotiations with the Tripolitan ambassador during the spring of 1786, Jefferson despaired of reaching worthwhile agreements with the Barbary States. He believed that the answer was the

use of force and proposed to create an international confederacy to impose a maritime blockade of North Africa. The aim of this proposal was
to foster "perpetual peace" in the Mediterranean without resorting to
paying tribute. By banding together, Jefferson believed, the smaller nations in the North Atlantic world could muster the force necessary to
defend their rights in the face of what they viewed as the depredations of
the Barbary States. In the end nothing came of the scheme. Congress
had been unwilling to support it. Without the support of the great powers it was doubtful that the smaller powers could have created a new
diplomatic settlement in the Mediterranean that was not based on paying tribute.

Jefferson did not give up on the proposal to create a confederacy to
promote and protect maritime rights. As Washington's secretary of state
he revived the scheme. In December 1790 he prepared two reports—on
American trade in the Mediterranean, and on the American captives in
Algiers—for the president and Congress.[61] Jefferson recognized that the
issue of American trade could not be separated from that of the captives.
"The Liberation of our Citizens has an intimate Connection with the
Liberation of our Commerce in the Mediterranean," he wrote. "The
Distresses of both proceed from the same Cause, and the Measures
which shall be adopted for the Relief of the one, may very probably involve the Relief of the other."[62] Jefferson sought to revive his proposal for
an international confederacy to solve the Barbary problem. He reported
that the United States had three options: it could agree to pay ransom for
its seamen when they were captured; it could "obtain Peace by purchasing it"; or it could "repel Force by Force" through "a Concert of Opera-
tion . . . among the Powers at War with the Barbary States."[63] Of the
three options Jefferson preferred employing force to solve the Barbary
problem. He believed that a permanent naval blockade would be more
honorable and, in the long run, less expensive than ransoming captives
or paying annual tribute. Congress did not agree. In response to Jefferson's report the Senate resolved on February 1, 1791, to allocate $40,000
to liberate the captives in Algiers.[64]

For Jefferson, the threat posed by the Barbary corsairs to American
trade was a threat to American liberty. Only through overseas trade
could the United States remain a prosperous agrarian republic whose

citizens were free. By threatening the free trade of the United States, the Barbary States endangered the liberty of American citizens. This threat was literal in the case of the sailors imprisoned in North Africa. Jefferson had concluded during his tenure as governor of Virginia that it was necessary to act decisively and use force, if necessary, to defend the republic. In the case of the Barbary States, he believed that war was the best option when faced with a threat they posed to the republic. As a diplomat in Europe he was reminded repeatedly of the weakness of the United States. One reason the Barbary States preyed on American ships was because the republic was perceived as weak—a view fostered by the British. Jefferson sought to counter this weakness by building a coalition of lesser powers that shared an interest in defeating the Barbary sultanates. In the end nothing came of his proposal. Congress was unwilling to fund American participation in the coalition. It is doubtful whether the smaller European states would have risked alienating the great powers by participating in such a scheme.

Jefferson found his experience as a diplomat immensely frustrating. He achieved relatively little but had acquired a valuable education in great power politics and diplomacy. Daily, at Versailles and elsewhere in Europe, he was reminded that the United States was a marginal power with little ability to influence international affairs. While he believed that the United States had great potential to shape global events by its example as a republic in a world dominated by empires, he could be under no illusions about just how difficult it would be for the new nation to defend its interests. He would reflect on the lessons he learned in Europe after his return. As secretary of state and president, his foreign policy was not based on a desire to create a new diplomacy but on a recognition of the weakness of the United States. He resorted to a combination of tactics—mixing force, threats of force, diplomacy, economic coercion, and, when all else failed, temporizing—to defend and protect vital American interests.

Three

"Mr. Jefferson Is a Decided Republican"

I n August 1789 Thomas Jefferson received permission from Congress to return home on leave. He had been abroad for five years and intended to bring his two daughters to the United States and to attend to his personal affairs at Monticello. The Jefferson party, which included the minister, his daughters Patsy and Polly, and the enslaved siblings James and Sally Hemings, departed from Paris on September 26. Jefferson arranged to ship thirty-eight boxes and trunks filled with clothing, books, personal papers, prints and paintings, busts, and other effects to the United States. The Americans, delayed for ten days at Le Havre by bad weather, finally boarded the packet *Anna* on October 8, crossing the English Channel and landing at Cowes on the Isle of Wight after a rough, twenty-six-hour passage. Jefferson and his entourage were further delayed while they waited for the ship that would take them to Virginia. They finally boarded the *Clermont* on October 22, nearly a month after departing Paris. Fortunately their Atlantic crossing was much easier than their departure from France had been. After a smooth passage they landed in Norfolk, Virginia, on November 23, 1789.[1]

Despite the enormous amount of luggage he brought back to America, Jefferson planned to return to Europe to continue to represent the United States in Paris. After around two months at Monticello, he intended to return to France via New York so that he could formally report to George Washington's new government. Notwithstanding his desire to return to France, Washington wanted Jefferson to join his government. As early as May 1789 James Madison wrote to Jefferson to inquire "whether any appointment at home would be agreeable to you." In response Jefferson reminded his friend of the difficult end to his tenure as governor, which had led to his departure from public office. "My object," he wrote prior to leaving Paris, "is a return to the same retirement. Whenever therefore I quit the present, it will not be to engage in any other office, and most especially any one which would require a constant residence from home."[2] Before his statement of disinterest reached Madison, Washington formally nominated Jefferson as secretary of state on September 25, 1789—the day before the Virginians left Paris. The Senate confirmed the nomination on the same day.[3]

Jefferson learned of his nomination as secretary of state soon after his return to Virginia. On December 15 he wrote to the president-elect expressing his desire to go back to France while conceding, "It is not for an individual to chuse his post. You are to marshal us as may be best for the public good." Jefferson passed the question back to Washington, asking the president to "be so good only as to signify to me by another line your ultimate wish, and I shall conform to it cordially." Over the Christmas holidays Madison made a personal visit to Jefferson and pressed on him the importance of accepting the appointment. The president, undoubtedly exasperated, addressed the subject unequivocally on January 21, "I consider the Office of Secretary for the Department of State as *very* important on many accounts: and I know of no person, who, in my judgement, could better execute the Duties of it than yourself." At last Jefferson formally accepted the appointment on February 14. He arrived in New York on March 21.[4]

For Jefferson, one of the benefits of the recently ratified federal constitution was that it vested substantial authority over foreign affairs in the executive branch. Jefferson's tenure in Paris had made him aware of how difficult it was for Congress to conduct foreign policy. Jefferson firmly believed that a strong executive was necessary to respond to international challenges. Soon after his arrival in New York, President Washington asked Jefferson for his views on the extent of the Senate's power in the realm of foreign relations. Specifically, Washington queried whether the Senate's authority to approve nominations for diplomatic posts extended to approving the office to which diplomats were nominated. In other words, should the Senate approve not only the nominee but also the office he was nominated to fill? Although this seemed a relatively minor matter, Jefferson believed it was essential to assert clearly that while the Senate must approve nominations, it could not determine the office in question. The principle at stake was control over foreign policy. Jefferson stated unequivocally, "The transaction of business with foreign nations is Executive altogether."[5] Jefferson adhered to this principle as Washington's secretary of state (1790–93) and during his two terms as president (1801–9).

Jefferson first expressed his view on executive control over foreign policy in a written opinion on April 24, 1790. A month later he appeared before a Senate committee to testify on the issue. Senator William Maclay of Pennsylvania provided a vivid description of the forty-seven-year-old secretary of state:

> When I came to the Hall Jefferson and the rest of the Committee were there. Jefferson is a slender Man. Has rather the Air of Stiffness in his Manner. His cloaths seem too small for him. He sits in a lounging Manner on one hip, commonly, and with one of his shoulders elevated much above the other. His face has a scrany Aspect. His whole figure has a loose shackling Air. He had a rambling Vacant look and nothing of that firm collected deportment which I expected would dignify the presence of a Secretary or Minister. I looked for Gravity, but a laxity of Manner, seemd shed about him. He spoke almost without ceasing. But even his discourse partook of his personal demeanor. It was loose and rambling and yet he scattered information wherever he went, and some even brilliant Sentiments sparkled from him. The information which he gave us respecting foreign Ministers &ca. was all high Spiced. He has been long enough abroad to catch the tone of European folly. He gave us a sentiment which seemd to savor rather of quaintness.

Maclay may not have realized that Jefferson was suffering from a migraine headache that might have contributed to his rambling air.[6]

Despite Senator Maclay's skepticism, Jefferson's European experience had made him an attractive candidate as the first secretary of state.

He brought invaluable knowledge of European diplomacy to the infant State Department. His experience of Old World diplomacy had taught him to appreciate the relative weakness of the United States in global terms. He was acutely aware that the American republic might easily fall prey to the avaricious and capricious empires that surrounded it. Jefferson sought to exploit circumstances to protect the republic.

The first diplomatic crisis of Washington's presidency originated not in France but along the western coast of the North American continent. The flashpoint was Nootka Sound, a series of inlets along the west coast of Vancouver Island. The Spanish claimed sovereignty over the region according to the terms of their 1493 Treaty of Tordesillas with Portugal, a claim that was challenged by Russia and Britain. During the summer of 1789 ships and fur traders from Britain and even the United States appeared in the region. A British expedition attempted to establish a permanent fur trading post and settlement along Nootka Sound. In response the Spanish navy, anxious about the threat to the region, occupied the settlement, seizing several British ships and imprisoning their crews. News of the seizures reached Europe in January 1790, and the British government issued a protest and demanded the release of its subjects and their vessels. Spain, in turn, wanted the interlopers punished and sought a guarantee that there would be no such incidents in the future.

In April 1790 John Meares, the British merchant who owned the ships in question, arrived in London and testified about the mistreatment of his sailors. The British prime minister, William Pitt the Younger, mobilized the Royal Navy and prepared for war with Spain with full parliamentary support. John Rutledge, Jr., a South Carolina politician visiting Britain, in May wrote to Jefferson that he had dined with several members of Parliament. "I do not remember to have been amongst such insolent bullies," wrote Rutledge. "They were all for war, talked much of *Old England* and the *british Lion,* laughed at the Idea of drubbing the Dons, began to calculate the millions of dollars they would be obliged to pay for having insulted *the first power on Earth.*" Rutledge reported that the MPs were anxious that the Spanish, fearful of British strength, might sue for peace without war.[7]

During the spring and summer of 1790 the Washington administration weighed its response to the emergency. The crisis revealed much about Jefferson's statecraft. During the war crisis of that spring and summer he sought to exploit the possible conflict to the best advantage of the United States. Given the possibility that its northern and southern neighbors might go to war, there was a possibility that the United States could be dragged into the conflict. It was possible that the British or Spanish might seek to attack each other's North American colonies via the United States. Despite the 1783 Peace of Paris, Britain still occupied seven posts in the Old Northwest and in modern Ohio, Indiana, and Michigan. It was not inconceivable that the British could send an expedition down the Mississippi River to attack the Spanish in New Orleans. (This was precisely the route that American farmers west of the Appalachians used to send their grain to market.) A greater threat was that in the event of a British victory in a war with Spain, Britain might regain East and West Florida and take Louisiana, all territories that had been returned to Spain at the end of the American War of Independence. If that happened, Britain would encircle the new American republic in the north, west, and south and dominate the sea to the east.

The British and American governments sought to divine each other's intentions in the event of war during the early stages of the Nootka Sound crisis. Negotiations were hampered because the two nations had not yet achieved a full postwar accord. Ongoing disputes arising from the Peace of Paris, notably the outstanding prewar debts owed by Americans to British merchants, the question of reparations for lost Loyalist property, and the continued British occupation of the forts in the Northwest Territory—justified, according to the British, by the American failure to make good Loyalist losses—bedeviled British-American relations. The United States had sent John Adams as its first minister to the United Kingdom, but the British did not respond until 1791 with the appointment of George Hammond as its minister. The Washington administration sought to normalize diplomatic relations and would have liked to complete a commercial agreement with Britain that would grant Americans access to the lucrative markets of the British Empire, particularly the West Indies. For the time being the British favored the status quo, keeping American traders at bay while occupying the forts in the Northwest.

In order to determine whether these objectives might be achieved President Washington dispatched a representative—Gouverneur Morris—to London in spring 1790. Morris, a one-legged libertine, was a wealthy New Yorker, who had attended the Constitutional Convention in 1787 and was already in Paris on business. He had traveled to France in 1789 and was well connected in the diplomatic and business communities (he would serve as American minister to France between 1792 and 1794). Washington asked Morris to explore the possibility of a commercial treaty and to raise the issue of the western posts and the exchange of ambassadors. In London Morris met with the foreign secretary, the Duke of Leeds, twice before meeting with Leeds and Prime Minister Pitt on May 21. He protested that American sailors had been impressed by the Royal Navy in its mobilization for war with Spain and raised the possibility that the United States and Britain might achieve full diplomatic and commercial relations. Pitt and Leeds cited the ongoing difficulties regarding American debts and Loyalist losses as obstacles to putting British-American relations on a more secure footing. Owing to the growing threat of war, Morris believed that the United States might be in an advantageous position. He predicted that Britain "will give us a good price for our neutrality." The prime minister told Morris that he and the foreign secretary would discuss the matters Morris had raised and get back to him. They never did. The British distrusted Morris because of his close links with the French—he met with French diplomats regularly during his time in London. The American envoy waited in vain for four months during the summer of 1790 before returning to France.[8]

At the same time that Gouverneur Morris was negotiating fruitlessly in London, the British approached the Washington administration. In anticipation of war with Spain, the governor of Quebec, Sir Guy Carleton, Lord Dorchester, sent an aide, Major George Beckwith, to the United States. Beckwith was a thirty-seven-year-old veteran of the American War of Independence. During the war he had specialized in espionage, and he had continued his intelligence-gathering activities after independence. In 1787 and 1788 Governor Carleton had sent him to New York to observe conditions in the United States. In September 1789 Beckwith acted as an unofficial messenger—a role not unlike that of Gouverneur Morris in London in 1790, but fulfilled much more thoroughly—to protest restrictions on British trade which Congress was then considering. While in New York he met with Senator Philip Schuyler and Schuyler's son-in-law, the treasury secretary, Alexander Hamilton. Fearing that the United States might make a move to seize the British forts in the Old Northwest, Carleton sent Beckwith back to New York, where he met secretly with Hamilton in April 1790 and reported that the United States had no immediate plans to move against the posts. Later that spring when the home secretary, William Grenville, informed Carleton that the United States wanted "to cultivate a closer connection" with Great Britain and instructed him to send someone to New York to ascertain how serious the Americans were about a commercial treaty and to gather information about the American threat to the forts in the Northwest or Canada itself in the event of a war between Britain and Spain, Carleton naturally chose Beckwith for the mission.[9]

Carleton gave Beckwith two sets of instructions on June 27. The first, which he was authorized to share American officials, asserted Carleton's goodwill toward the United States and made the case for the United States siding with Britain in the event of a war with Spain. He was also to disavow any British involvement in the violent clashes between Native Americans and American settlers in the Northwest (a charge consistently reiterated by the United States from the time of the Declaration of Independence to James Madison's war message to Congress in 1812). The second set of instructions was secret, not to be shared: Beckwith was to gather information regarding the American position in the looming war. Carleton ordered Beckwith to "take all opportunities of learning the disposition of their Government, and people, towards peace or war, separately, and unconnected with the affairs of Spain, what difference a war with Spain is likely to produce, whether the States are likely to join with that power, what may be the extent of their views and whether they expect any assistance from France in her present situation." Beckwith, as a soldier, should assess the military situation, particularly the threat posed by the Americans (and Spanish) to Canada and the forts in the Northwest.[10]

Beckwith met with Hamilton on the morning of July 8, and they discussed the state of British-American relations. Hamilton optimistically reported to Washington that Beckwith had assured him that "the

Cabinet of Great Britain entertained a disposition not only towards a friendly intercourse but towards an alliance with the United States." Beckwith discussed the potential war between Britain and Spain. The Englishman observed "that it was one in which all Commercial nations must be supposed to favour the views of G. Britain. That it was therefore presumed should a war take place that the U. States would find it to be their interest to take part with Great Britain rather than with Spain." After meeting with Beckwith, Hamilton sought out Jefferson, and the two men went to see President Washington at noon. The president believed that Beckwith was, unofficially, offering the United States a commercial treaty in exchange for its assistance against Spain. Washington asked the members of his cabinet to provide their views on the question within two or three days.[11]

Why did Major Beckwith make his approach to Alexander Hamilton, the secretary of the treasury, rather than to the secretary of state, Thomas Jefferson? Beckwith and Hamilton had known each other for several years. Based on their relationship Beckwith believed correctly that Hamilton would be more favorably disposed toward Britain than Jefferson. One of Beckwith's informants, Dr. William Samuel Johnson, president of King's College and senator from Connecticut, was more explicit, informing him, "Mr. Jefferson is a decided Republican, and perfectly devoted to a French Interest, his language both within and without doors tends to prove it." Senator Johnson continued, "Mr. Jefferson's holding his present office is unfortunate in the idea of forming any close connexion with you as he cannot be confided in." Hamilton, by contrast, had "more favorable sentiments" toward Britain and "possesses a solid understanding, great candor and sincerity in his dealings, and a manly mind, which will not be restrained from a free declaration of his opinions." Hamilton himself believed this, telling Beckwith that Jefferson was, "a gentleman of honor, and zealously desirous of promoting those objects, which the nature of his duty call for, and the interests of his country may require, but from some opinions which he has given respecting Your government, and possible predilections elsewhere, there may be difficulties." Simply put, Beckwith made his approach through Hamilton because he believed the treasury secretary would be more sympathetic (and forthcoming with information), and he believed he could not trust Jefferson.[12]

Why did Hamilton, as treasury secretary, involve himself in foreign policy? In part he simply couldn't help himself. As Andrew Burstein and Nancy Isenberg have written, "Some people are happy to be team players; Alexander Hamilton was not. He did not understand boundaries. He assumed he knew best, and did what he wanted." Since a commercial treaty with Britain was one of Washington's foreign policy objectives, Hamilton felt that this fell within his brief at the Treasury. Hamilton believed that economics was the driving force in international relations. To him, serious diplomacy was, inevitably, Treasury business. Given what he perceived to be Jefferson's bias in favor of France, he felt that Jefferson could not be trusted to oversee negotiations with Britain. Moreover, Washington tended to submit major questions to his cabinet, and secretaries regularly expressed opinions beyond their departments—as Jefferson did regarding Hamilton's fiscal policies. Nonetheless, at best Hamilton blurred the boundaries of his authority when he met with Beckwith, particularly when he gave the Englishman assurances that the United States was not planning military action to acquire the British forts in the Northwest. At worst he exceeded his brief in discussing the foreign policy of the United States with a foreign agent—although Hamilton believed he was trying manipulate Beckwith to the advantage of the United States.[13]

Hamilton's distrust of Jefferson was returned in equal measure. Although the two men managed to work together during the early days of the Washington administration, they gradually became estranged. Jefferson was skeptical about Hamilton's fiscal policies, which he believed were part of a program to consolidate power in the federal government and to promote manufacturing and thus undermine the agricultural economy that Jefferson believed was essential to the American republic. Jefferson came to believe that Hamilton was a closet monarchist who sought to remake the United States in the image of Britain. During his retirement he recalled a dinner that he had had with Hamilton and Vice President John Adams in 1791. Adams, according to Jefferson, said of the British constitution, "Purge that constitution of its corruption and give to its popular branch equality of representation, and it would be the most perfect constitution ever devised by the wit of man." Hamilton countered by saying that such changes would make Britain ungovernable and that the unreformed constitution complete with its corruption was "the most perfect government which ever existed." The dinner convinced Jefferson that Hamilton preferred "an hereditary King with a House of Lords and Commons corrupted to his will, standing between him and the people." A year later, in October 1792, Jefferson warned the president that Hamilton was a closet monarchist who had told him that the Constitution, "was a shilly shally thing, of mere milk and water, which could not last, and was only a step to something better."[14]

When Washington asked members of his cabinet for their opinions on what the United States should do in the event of the British-Spanish war, Jefferson conferred with James Madison, his closest political ally and a member of the House of Representatives. Madison was the leader of the opposition to Hamilton's fiscal program in Congress. On July 12 Jefferson presented "an outline policy contingent on war," which outlined a series of points "in all of which he believes Mr. Madison concurred."[15] In his policy notes Jefferson focused on the possibility that Britain would seek to conquer Louisiana and the Floridas. In his view, if Spain were to lose these territories, Britain would completely encircle the United States and would "seduce" the republic's western states, primarily territory adjoining Virginia, through access to the Gulf of Mexico. Strategically, "Instead of two neighbors balancing each other, we shall have one, with more than the strength of both."[16]

Faced with the threat of encirclement by the British and possible dismemberment of the union, Jefferson asked, "Would the prevention of this be worth a war?" In response he raised several issues, notably the ability of the United States to wage war and pay for the conflict. He highlighted the facts that the United States would lose access to markets if the British occupied Louisiana and would incur "eternal expence and danger from so overgrown a neighbor." He cautioned that a probable war between Britain and the United States was premised on the assumption of a general conflict in which France as well as Spain were arrayed against Britain alongside the United States. "For with Spain alone," he concluded, "the war would be unsuccessful, and our situation rendered worse" than if the United States simply allowed Britain to occupy Louisiana and the Floridas.[17]

Having assessed the threat that Britain might pose to the United States, Jefferson recommended caution, noting that there was "no need

to take part in the war as yet. We may chuse our own time." He counseled delay because Britain might not attack Louisiana and the Floridas.
Even if the British did attempt to conquer Spanish territory in North
America, they might fail, or Spain and France might recover the lost
provinces. Delay would allow the United States to better prepare for the
looming conflict, and it would allow the Americans to exact a higher
price from their would-be allies, France and Spain, for their assistance.[18]

Jefferson recognized that American options were limited by the
weakness of the United States. Nonetheless he believed that the new
republic should do what it could to exploit the situation. He advised
Washington that the United States should seek to maximize its position
by making simultaneous approaches to Spain and Britain. With respect
to Spain he argued that the United States should seek to persuade Madrid that as it could not protect Louisiana and the Floridas, it should
grant these provinces independence. He believed that if they were
granted independence, a coalition of France, the United States, and
Spain could undertake to guarantee their autonomy. If the provinces
were no longer Spanish, Jefferson reasoned, then Britain would have no
grounds to attack them, and a British-American war could be averted. If
Britain went ahead and attacked the newly independent provinces, the
United States could be assured of popular support in going to war to
defend them. Jefferson left unstated his presumption that the United
States might acquire the provinces when Spain relinquished control
over them. The presumption that Spain would simply grant Louisiana
and the Floridas their independence in the face of a potential British
threat was wishful thinking on Jefferson's part.[19]

With respect to Britain, Jefferson provided detailed advice as to how
Washington should respond to Beckwith. The secretary of state argued
that the questions of a commercial treaty and an alliance should be separated. With respect to the former, it would be welcome only if it were
based on complete reciprocity. Regarding a possible alliance, the United
States would need to know more about its purpose, though Jefferson
stipulated that it could not "be inconsistent with existing agreements"—
presumably the existing alliance between the United States and France.
Beckwith should also be informed that in the event of a war between
Spain and Britain, "we are disposed to be strictly neutral," thereby obvi-

ating the need for an alliance. Finally Jefferson advised that Beckwith should be given a clear message regarding Louisiana and the Floridas. He wrote, "We should view with extreme uneasiness any attempts of either power to seize the possessions of the other on our frontier, as we consider our own safety interested in a due balance between our neighbors." He hoped that by sending a clear message the British might be persuaded to attack Spanish possessions in South America or the Caribbean rather than in North America.[20]

Jefferson's recommendations to Washington were consistent with the practice of statecraft that he had come to understand over the previous decade. His tenure as governor of Virginia and as an American diplomat in Europe had taught him how vulnerable the American republic was. Threats could arise quite suddenly and should be prepared for. European powers passed huge territories to one another in peace and war. He was not squeamish about the use of force but felt force should be used only when it could be deployed to good effect—as he proposed to do against the Barbary States. British encirclement of the United States could pose an existential threat to the United States, but, Jefferson believed, the United States was not strong enough to fight Britain without the assistance of France or Spain. While he counseled delay, he advised that the time be used to prepare the nation for war both militarily and diplomatically.

On the diplomatic front, President Washington, at Jefferson's behest, dispatched one of his most trusted aides, David Humphreys, to Europe with letters to key figures in Britain, Portugal, and Spain. Humphreys, thirty-eight years old, was a Continental Army veteran from Connecticut. He had served with distinction during the war and eventually became one of Washington's staff officers (alongside Alexander Hamilton). After the war Humphreys maintained his close relationship with Washington, serving for a time as his private secretary. He accompanied the president-elect to New York when Washington was inaugurated as president in 1789. Washington selected Humphreys for this delicate diplomatic mission, one requiring considerable discretion. Humphreys was to maintain the fiction that he was a private traveler so as to conceal the purpose of his trip. Jefferson instructed Humphreys to travel to London and Lisbon before heading to Madrid to see the American minister in Spain, William Carmichael. Madrid was the most important stop on Humphreys's itinerary. There he was to transmit to Carmichael secret instructions regarding the American position in the looming war between Britain and Spain. Jefferson instructed Carmichael to exploit the crisis to the advantage of the United States by pressing Spain to grant the Americans full access to the Mississippi River.[21]

While Jefferson feared the possibility of British encirclement of the United States, his more immediate concern guaranteed American access to the mouth of the Mississippi River. Access to the Mississippi via the Ohio River was essential to economic well-being of the Americans who lived west of the Appalachian Mountains. In the first half of 1790 forty-one American flatboats carried more than 4,900 barrels of flour, 900 hogsheads of tobacco, and 260 barrels of meat, as well as 100 gallons of whiskey, 500 pounds of butter, 11 tons of iron, and 7 tons of hemp to New Orleans.[22] This trade swelled along with the American population west of the Appalachian Mountains, which Jefferson estimated at 200,000 in 1790. Trade between the Spanish and Americans went upriver as well as down. Over the years an informal, extralegal, and lucrative trade between the growing American settlements upriver and New Orleans had developed. For western Americans, James Madison wrote in 1802, the Mississippi was essential, "It is the Hudson, the Delaware, the Potomac and all the navigable rivers of the atlantic States formed into one stream."[23] As long as the Spanish looked the other way and trade was unimpeded, then the United States need not be excessively worried. Nonetheless, free navigation of the length of the Mississippi was probably the most important strategic concern of the new republic. As a consequence the United States held as an objective obtaining New Orleans or, failing that, completing a commercial agreement with Spain to formalize and guarantee American navigation of the river. Jefferson believed that the United States should take advantage of Spanish vulnerability during the Nootka Sound crisis to consolidate its position on the Mississippi.

Jefferson believed the United States to be in such a strong position that "the immediate and full enjoyment of that [Mississippi] navigation" should be the starting point for Carmichael's negotiations with the Spanish and not an end in itself. Once the American right to navigate the Mississippi had been won the talks could focus on the disposition of East and West Florida, as well as the disputed territory in the southwestern borderland between the United States and Spain. "It may be asked what need of negociation," Jefferson wrote, "if the navigation is to be ceded at all events?" He answered his own question:

> You know that the navigation cannot be practiced without a port where the sea and river vessels may meet and exchange loads, and where those employed about them may be safe and unmolested. The right to use a thing comprehends a right to the means necessary to its use, and without which it would be useless: the fixing on a proper port, and the degree of freedom it is to enjoy in its operations, will require negociation, and be governed by events. There is danger indeed that even the unavoidable delay of sending a negociator here, may render the mission too late for the preservation of the peace: it is impossible to answer for the forbearance of our western citizens. We endeavor to quiet them with the expectation of the attainment of their rights by peaceable means, but should they, in a moment of impatience, hazard others, there is no saying how far we may be led: for neither themselves nor their rights will ever be abandoned by us.

Jefferson urged Carmichael to move quickly, "press these matters warmly and firmly," because the United States was in a temporary position of strength while Spain was threatened by war with Britain, "such a moment must not be lost."[24]

Jefferson provided Carmichael with outline notes that he could deploy in his talks with the Spanish government. The secretary of state began with this premise: "We have a *right* to the navigation of the Missisipi [*sic*]." He asserted that this right was based on nature, treaty, and necessity. More than half of the territory of the United States depended on the Mississippi watershed, and 200,000 American citizens used the river as an outlet for the tobacco, rice, corn, hemp, lumber, and timber. Those citizens produced surpluses of these staples, which they had to export to overseas market. Given the importance of trade to Jefferson's understanding of political economy, he was sympathetic to the need for westerners to market their produce via the Mississippi. Jefferson believed that only through expansion across western lands could the United States survive as a republic. Without access to the Mississippi the union was threatened. Those Americans who lived west of the Appalachian Mountains would demand access to the Mississippi—Jefferson noted ominously that 20,000 western Americans were arms-bearing—with or without the support of the federal government. Faced with such a circumstance the government would have three choices: trying to suppress the rebels, granting them independence, or joining with them in a war against Spain. The first option, Jefferson wrote, "is neither in our principles, nor in our power." Disunion, also, was unacceptable, thus leaving war with Spain the only viable option.[25]

Jefferson deemed acquiring the right to navigate the Mississippi a vital American interest, but how was it to be achieved? According to Jefferson, there were only two choices available to the United States: force or negotiation. It was up to Spain to determine which course it would follow. If armed conflict ensued, the United States might act alone or in an alliance with Britain. If the United States acted alone, it would be able to capture New Orleans. Even if Spain were to recapture the city, the Americans would retake it. The cost of these expeditions would be far greater for Spain than for the United States, which could rely on its well-armed western settlers. As a consequence, New Orleans and its environs would eventually be absorbed into the American union. If the Americans acted in conjunction with the British, Spain would lose all its North American provinces. The Americans would acquire East and West Florida as well as New Orleans, and the British would acquire Louisiana.[26]

By contrast, Jefferson argued, if Spain and the United States entered into negotiations immediately, they would have an opportunity to settle all of their differences. He urged Spain to cede all its territory east of the Mississippi to the United States and to guarantee the republic the right to navigate the length of the river. (This was a more ambitious position than the advice that Jefferson had given Washington a month earlier, when he argued that the United States should urge Spain to grant independence to East and West Florida.) In exchange the United States would guarantee Spain's possessions to the west of the river. The United States would maintain neutrality in any British-Spanish war (while excluding Britain from the Floridas). It would, in Jefferson's words, be a neutrality "very partial" to Spain. If the United States were forced to enter the war, it would be on the side of Spain and, presumably, France. "In fine," Jefferson concluded, "for a narrow slip of barren, detached and expensive country, Spain secures the rest of her territory, and makes an Ally, where she might have a dangerous enemy." Jefferson sought to downplay the size and significance of the Floridas and assure Spain that it could trust the United States. "Conquest [is] not in our principles," he reminded Carmichael, for it is "inconsistent with our government." Further, it would "not [be in] our interest to cross the Missisipi [*sic*] for ages" and "will never be our interest to remain united with those who do." As Jefferson outlined the situation, Spain faced a stark choice: it could lose all of its North American possessions to Britain and the United States, or it could negotiate with the United States, yielding the Floridas and sharing the Mississippi in order to safeguard its possession west of the river.[27]

While David Humphreys was en route to Europe the Washington administration continued its preparations for war. On August 27 the president wrote to the members of his cabinet, asking them how he should respond to Lord Dorchester should the Canadian governor request permission for British troops to cross American territory to attack the Spanish in Louisiana. Washington believed it was likely that the British would attempt to strike New Orleans or other Spanish posts in Louisiana from Detroit, which would necessitate sending their forces through the United States.[28]

The secretary of state answered the president immediately. "I am so deeply impressed with the magnitude of the dangers which will attend our government if Louisiana and the Floridas be added to the British empire," Jefferson wrote, "that in my opinion we ought to make ourselves parties in the *general war* expected to take place, should this be the only means of preventing the calamity." He still counseled patience, as he had advised Washington in early July, suggesting that the United States should preserve "neutrality as long, and entering into the war as late, as possible." Jefferson argued that international law would permit the United States to allow British troops to cross its territory, provided the republic afforded the same privilege to Spain. Alternatively, it could refuse both belligerents to breach its borders. If the United States refused to allow the British permission to enter its territory and they did so anyway—a likely scenario in Jefferson's view—then the United States would be forced into war immediately or would "pocket an acknowledged insult in the face of the world: and one insult pocketed soon produces another." There was, Jefferson argued, a third way, neither defiance nor acquiescence. "That is," he wrote, "to avoid giving any answer." Silence on the matter would allow the United States to protest a British incursion after the fact, "keeping alive an altercation . . . till events should decide whether it is most expedient to accept their apologies, or profit of the aggression as a cause of war."[29]

When Jefferson wrote to Washington he believed that a general war involving Britain, Spain, and France was "almost a certain event."[30] This judgment was incorrect. The French indicated that they would not support Spain in a war over Nootka Sound. Facing a war with Britain without the support of revolutionary France, Spain eventually capitulated and negotiated with Britain. (There is no evidence that American threats to ally with Britain played a role in Spanish thinking.) Under the terms of the Nootka Convention, agreed on October 28, Spain accepted the British occupation of Nootka Sound and the danger of war receded.[31]

For the remainder of his time as secretary of state Jefferson pressured the Spanish over the Mississippi question.[32] Eventually Spanish-American negotiations bore fruit in the Treaty of San Lorenzo (also known as Pinckney's Treaty, after its American negotiator, Thomas Pinckney), which was agreed on October 27, 1795. Under the terms of the treaty Spain agreed to recognize the thirty-first parallel as the border between the United States and the Floridas, and acknowledged the right of citizens of the United States and subjects of Spain to navigate the whole length of the Mississippi. The treaty conferred on Americans the privilege of landing and storing goods for transfer to ocean-going vessels at New Orleans, tax free for three years. This confirmed Jefferson's view that "the right to use a thing comprehends a right to the means necessary to its use." After three years the privilege of entrepôt might continue, or the Spanish might designate another place on the banks of the lower Mississippi for the purpose. Both sides agreed to restrain from encouraging Indians within their territory from interfering with settlers or property in the territory of the other. Although completed after Jefferson had resigned as secretary of state, the Treaty of San Lorenzo fulfilled his objectives and, seemingly, secured the interests of America's western settlers for the foreseeable future.[33]

In the end little came of the Nootka Sound crisis. Nonetheless, the dispute reveals much about Jefferson's approach to foreign policy and statecraft. He had clearly identified the strategic interests of the United States that were at stake: access to the Mississippi River in particular and the security of the south and west more generally. Although the United States was threatened by possible war, Jefferson also saw an opportunity in the crisis. He believed that the United States might exploit the situation and acquire East and West Florida as well as complete navigation rights to the Mississippi. He was willing to go to war to achieve his ends—either in alliance with Spain and France or with Britain or, in extremis, against Britain alone—but in the first instance he relied on diplomacy. Diplomatically he sought to play for time where Britain was concerned, advocating delay in response to possible British requests for an alliance or permission to cross American territory. With respect to Spain he opted for a more aggressive approach. He attempted to cajole the Spanish into giving the United States the Floridas and access to the Mississippi, threatening to ally with Britain if necessary to achieve these ends. He was wildly optimistic and overconfident about Spain's readiness to accede to American pressure. With both Spain and Britain during the summer of 1790 he mixed the threat of war with hints of cooperation, even to the point of forming alliances, in order to achieve his ends. He recognized the weakness of the United States, as he had while trying to build an international coalition against the Barbary States, but sought to exploit the opportunity that the British-Spanish crisis presented. He was not concerned about consistency in his methods so much as expediency in achieving his ends—increasing the present and future security of the American republic.

The Nootka Sound crisis revealed a fault line within the Washington administration. The president's two most able ministers, Jefferson as secretary of state and Hamilton as secretary of the treasury, adhered to fundamentally different approaches on most issues of domestic and foreign policy. As early as 1790 these differences had become apparent. The crack eventually opened into a fissure and then a chasm. During the decade their differences would harden into personal animus and contribute to the emergence of two political parties in the United States. The greatest challenges facing the fledgling United States concerned fiscal policy and international relations. Fiscal and foreign policy were closely related—customs duties were the government's most important source of revenue—and the ministers frequently disagreed over matters of policy. The most significant foreign policy issue confronting the nation was the French Revolution.

During his last months in France Jefferson had observed, and played a small part in, the first stirrings of the French Revolution. He had witnessed the opening of the Estates General in May 1789 and received an early account of the storming of the Bastille on July 14. Jefferson welcomed the adoption of the Declaration of the Rights of Man and the Citizen on August 26. He believed that France was experiencing a republican revolution led by moderate reformers, like the Marquis de Lafayette. In late August, at Lafayette's urging Jefferson hosted a dinner for rival factions from the assembly. The legislators spent six hours at Jefferson's home debating constitutional reform and the future course of the Revolution.[34]

Many Americans initially supported the French Revolution. When the French revolutionary army defeated combined Prussian, Austrian, and French royalist forces who threatened Paris at the Battle of Valmy on September 20, 1792, there were popular celebrations across the United States.[35] On September 21, the monarchy was abolished and France became a republic. Valmy marked the high-water mark for American support of the French Revolution. At the very moment that the revolutionaries were defending Paris, the Revolution took a more radical turn. In early September Parisian mobs massacred more than a thousand prisoners and clerics, fearing that they would aid the invading Prussian forces. The "September massacres," which were frequently conducted in the aftermath of trials before improvised tribunals, anticipated the Reign of Terror of 1793 and 1794, when as many as forty thousand enemies of the Revolution were executed as a result of a power struggle between the Girondins and Jacobins for leadership of the Revolution. On January 21, 1793, the Girondin government executed Louis XVI, and, subsequently, his queen, Marie Antoinette. On February 1 France declared war against Britain, Spain, and the Netherlands, and a general war between the forces of revolution and counterrevolution began.

By 1793 the events in France had divided Americans. Federalist supporters of the Washington administration increasingly saw in France mob rule (which they equated with democracy) and anarchy, which they believed threatened civilization. The opponents of the administration—particularly of Alexander Hamilton's fiscal policies—led in Congress by James Madison (and within the administration by Thomas Jefferson) lamented the violent excesses in France but felt that the advent of the republic was a positive development. They argued that the United States was bound to France legally, by the treaty of 1778, and morally as a sister republic. The secretary of state was especially sympathetic to the French Revolution. Jefferson never gave up on his view that the revolutions in the United States and France were part of a single international republican movement. He saw in the events in France a European counterpart to the American Revolution, which would usher in the spread of liberty around the globe. More than thirty years later he recalled in his autobiography, "The appeal to the rights of man, which had been made in the U.S. was taken up by France, first of the European nations." He believed the spread of liberty around the globe was an inevitable consequence of the republican revolutions in the United States and France. "This is a wonderful instance of great events from small causes. So inscrutable is the arrangement of causes & consequences in this world that a two-penny duty on tea, unjustly imposed in a sequestered part of it, changes the conditions of all its inhabitants."[36]

Jefferson was fairly sanguine about the violence of the French Revolution. In January 1793 he wrote to his former secretary, William Short, then American minister in The Hague, about the violent scenes Short had reported to him from Europe. Writing about the massacres of the previous September, Jefferson conceded, "Many guilty persons fell without the forms of trial, and with them some innocent. These I deplore as much as any body, and shall deplore some of them to the day of my death." Regrettable as the deaths of innocents might be, Jefferson saw them as casualties in a war for liberty. The stakes in the struggle were so high: "The liberty of the whole earth was depending on the issue of the contest, and was ever such a prize won with so little innocent blood?" Jefferson continued with a statement that became notorious: "My own affections have been deeply wounded by some of the martyrs to this cause, but rather than it should have failed, I would have seen half the earth desolated. Were there but an Adam and Eve left in every country, and left free, it would be better than as it now is." Jefferson wrote to Short *before* the Reign of Terror and sought to bolster Short's support for the Revolution, which he feared was wavering. Nonetheless, his insouciance when presented with evidence of the massacre of innocent individuals without trial suggests the degree to which the French Revolution polarized American politics. Because Jefferson believed that the fates of liberty in France and the United States were intertwined he likened the forces of counterrevolution in Europe to those (his Federalist adversaries) in the United States. As such, he was willing to countenance the excesses of the Revolution rather than endanger the fate of liberty at home.[37]

Notwithstanding his personal views, the French Revolution posed an important diplomatic challenge for Jefferson as secretary of state. The Revolution and the wars arising from it dominated the politics and international relations of the Atlantic world. Unconfirmed rumors reached American shores in March 1793 that France and Britain were at war. Jefferson made a general statement of what he believed the American position in the conflict should be in a letter to a Dutch correspondent. "The scene in Europe is becoming very interesting. Amidst the confusions of a general war which seem to be threatening that quarter of the globe, we hope to be permitted to preserve the line of neutrality." Although Jefferson believed that the interests of the United States and France were broadly aligned, and that the defeat of the French Revolution would be a setback for liberty, he did not believe the United States should take sides in the European war. "We wish not to meddle with the internal affairs of any country, nor with the general affairs of Europe. Peace with all nations, and the rights which that gives us with respect to all nations, are our objects." Jefferson held the United States should remain neutral in the European conflict but maintain its treaty obligations to France, provided these did not compromise American neutrality. He sought to maintain this carefully calibrated, slightly contradictory position for the remainder of his tenure as secretary of state.

Confirmation of the European war reached the United States in early April. On April 18 President Washington sent the members of his cabinet a series of thirteen questions regarding how the United States should respond. Washington's queries focused on whether the United States should issue a proclamation of neutrality and what its obligations were to France under the 1778 treaty of alliance between the two nations. The president circulated the questions in anticipation of a cabinet meeting scheduled for the next morning. Jefferson saw the hand of Hamilton behind the questions, which he felt suggested that the United States should repudiate its alliance with France. Jefferson noted that though the questions were written in Washington's hand, "the language was Hamilton's and the doubts his alone."[38]

When the cabinet gathered at the executive mansion at the corner of Sixth and Market Streets in Philadelphia at nine the next morning, discussion focused on the first three questions. The cabinet unanimously agreed that the president should issue a proclamation prohibiting American citizens from taking part in hostilities involving any of the belligerent powers. It also agreed unanimously that the administration should accept a minister from the present French government. The meeting could not reach a decision, however, as to whether the French emissary should be accepted without restrictions. The discussion of this issue proved so prolonged and divisive that the ministers did not have time to discuss the rest of Washington's queries—including the fundamental question: Should the United States continue to honor its treaty with France?[39]

With respect to the first question concerning a proclamation of neutrality, Jefferson differed significantly from his cabinet colleagues. He asserted that such a proclamation would be unconstitutional. Since the constitution granted Congress the authority to declare war, he argued, it implied that only Congress could issue "a declaration that there should be no war." On a pragmatic level, Jefferson opposed the proposal on the grounds "that it would be better to hold back the declaration of neutrality, as a thing worth something to the powers at war, that they would bid for it, and we might reasonably ask as a price, the *broadest privileges* of neutral nations." Here Jefferson demonstrated the expedience and opportunism that had characterized his response to the Nootka Sound crisis. The other members of the cabinet, Hamilton, Secretary of War

Henry Knox, and Attorney General Edmund Randolph (Jefferson doesn't note the presence of Vice President John Adams at the meeting), argued that the president did have the constitutional authority to issue a neutrality proclamation. Unwilling to abrogate the French treaty and seeking support to receive the French minister, Jefferson gave ground on the question of the proclamation. When Attorney General Randolph drafted the proclamation—formally issued on April 22, 1793—on behalf of Washington, he excluded the word "neutrality" from the text in deference to Jefferson's wishes.[40]

The question of whether to accept a French minister with or without restrictions went to the heart of the divisions within the government, and the country at large, over foreign policy. To accept a minister without restrictions could be interpreted as upholding the 1778 treaty of alliance between France and the United States. To accept the minister with restrictions might mean the abrogation or temporary suspension of the treaty. The question divided the cabinet. Jefferson and Randolph favored accepting a French envoy without restrictions, and Hamilton and Knox wanted to impose conditions on the minister. Whereas Jefferson believed in upholding the treaty while maintaining American neutrality, Alexander Hamilton believed the United States should declare itself neutral and repudiate the 1778 treaty. Only in this way, he contended, could the United States avoid a war with Britain. The cabinet could not resolve the issue when it met on April 19 in part because Randolph, the attorney general, wanted to consult with the leading works on international law. Hamilton had cited the Swiss jurist Emmerich de Vattel's *Le droit de gens* (1758) to justify his position that the overthrow of the French monarchy had voided the 1778 treaty, and Randolph wanted to consult the text. The cabinet reconvened to discuss the issue—and the other questions circulated by the president—and still could not reach a decision. In an effort to break the deadlock President Washington asked the members of the cabinet to submit their views on the French treaty to him in writing.

Jefferson submitted a lengthy and learned opinion to the president on April 28. He argued that the treaty of 1778 was a compact between the French and American nations, not their governments or heads of state. He presented evidence drawn from Vattel, Hugo Grotius, Samuel von

Pufendorf, and Christian Wolff to support his contention that a change of government did not abrogate the treaty. Jefferson also sought to separate the question of receiving a French minister from that of whether the 1778 treaty was still binding. He argued "that the receiving a Minister from France at this time is an act of no significance with respect to the treaties, amounting neither to an admission nor denial of them, forasmuch as he comes not under any stipulation in them." He concluded that repudiating the treaty would be, not an act of neutrality, but viewed by the French as tantamount to a declaration of war.[41]

Alexander Hamilton and Henry Knox submitted a joint response to the president on March 2. They argued that the overthrow and execution of Louis XVI nullified the 1778 treaty, and that the treaty was void until France had a stable government. If the United States supported France by adhering to the invalid pact, it would likely provoke a war with Britain. Hamilton sought to counter the pro-French tilt he saw in Jefferson's foreign policy and to clearly align the United States with Britain. According to Jefferson, Hamilton was "panick struck if we refuse our breach to every kick which G. Brit. may chuse to give it. He is for proclaiming at once the most abject principles, such as would invite and merit habitual insults. And indeed every inch of ground must be fought in our councils to desperation in order to hold up the face of even a sneaking neutrality." Hamilton's Anglophilia was so pronounced, according to Jefferson, that "some propositions have come from him which would astonish Mr. Pitt himself with their boldness."[42]

Edmund Randolph submitted his opinion to Washington on May 6. The attorney general addressed all of the president's questions, arguing that the 1778 treaty was still binding and that the United States should accept a French minister without restriction. Randolph reminded the president that France was America's strongest and most steadfast European ally. Further, he warned that repudiating the treaty would be very unpopular in the United States. Notwithstanding the arguments that he and Randolph had submitted, Jefferson feared that the United States would repudiate the 1778 treaty and throw its support behind Britain. "If we preserve even a sneaking neutrality," he wrote on May 5, "we shall be indebted for it to the President, and not to his counsellors." With written representations from the cabinet in hand, Washington decided that the United States would continue to honor the treaty of 1778 and that the government would receive a French envoy without restriction. This represented a victory for Jefferson, who feared Hamilton's influence over the president. Any joy he felt would be short-lived. The envoy in question, Edmond Charles Genet, soon arrived in Philadelphia. He would immediately test the neutrality of the United States and the patience of the secretary of state, not to mention that of the president.[43]

Writing from Paris in late December 1792 the American minister in France, Gouverneur Morris, informed George Washington that the French had appointed a new minister to the United States. Though he had not yet met Edmond Charles Genet, Morris reported that he had heard the envoy was "a Man of good Parts, and very good Education." Several days later Morris dined with Genet and tempered his assessment. "He has," wrote Morris, "I think more of Genius than of Ability and you will see in him at the first Blush the Manner and Look of an Upstart." At dinner Genet had argued with a merchant concerning commercial policy, and "the Merchant was rather an overmatch for the Minister." Morris's assessment of Genet—that he was a passionate man of ability, whose talents did not quite match his opinion of himself—proved accurate. When he reached the United States Genet overstepped his authority, and the result was embarrassment for his government and, ultimately, disgrace for the minister himself.[44]

Edmond Charles Genet was born at Versailles on January 8, 1763. Although he was not a nobleman, his family was well connected. His father, Edmé Jacques Genet, was chief of the Bureau of Interpretation, and his sisters were members of Marie Antoinette's household. Morris described him as "Brother to the Queen's first Woman; from whence his fortune originates."[45] Genet proved to be an adept linguist and was apprenticed in the diplomatic service, notwithstanding his non-noble origins. When his father died in 1781 Edmond was named to succeed him at the Bureau of Interpretation, though he was only eighteen. Genet later served at the court of Catherine the Great in Saint Petersburg from 1788 to 1792. He began as a secretary to the French legation and was promoted to chargé d'affaires. Catherine broke off relations with the French government over its treatment of Louis XVI. Despite his royal connections Genet spoke out in favor of the revolution and was expelled from Russia in July 1792.

Upon his return to France Genet was welcomed by the Girondin government, which appointed him as its minister to the United States in November. At first glance he seemed an ideal candidate to represent France in Philadelphia. He spoke English and was young, charming, and handsome. He was committed to republican principles and favorably disposed toward the United States. Nonetheless his experience in Saint Petersburg suggested that Genet's passion could get the better of him. Gouverneur Morris reported that during his tenure in Saint Petersburg Genet in his enthusiasm for the revolution, "had made some Representations in a much higher Tone than was wish'd or expected. It was not convenient either to approve or disapprove of his Conduct, under the then Circumstances, and his Dispatches lay unnoticed. This to a young Man of ardent Temper, and who feeling Genius and Talents may perhaps have rated himself a little too high, was mortifying in the extreme. He felt himself insulted, and wrote in a Style of petulance to his Chief" when he was expelled. Morris's description of the unhappy end of Genet's tenure in Russia, written in December 1792, might easily have been written a year later to describe Genet's fate in the United States. Morris reported that Genet was allowed to choose his next diplomatic assignment and "He chose America, *as being the best Harbor during the Storm* and if my Informant be right, *he will not put to Sea again untill it is fair Weather,* let what will happen." What Morris and his informant— nor even Genet—did not realize was that storms seemed to follow Genet wherever he went.[46]

Appropriately, Genet was delayed by bad weather and did not arrive in the United States until April 8, 1793. Contrary winds meant that he landed in Charleston, South Carolina, rather than Philadelphia. The envoy bore detailed, wide-ranging instructions from his government. He was instructed to encourage the peoples of Louisiana, the Floridas, and Canada to embrace the principles of the French Revolution and rise up against their imperial masters, overthrowing British and Spanish rule in North America. To achieve this he was authorized to raise armies among the American settlers and Native peoples in Kentucky and other border areas to attack the Spanish. Genet should also negotiate a new commercial treaty with the United States that would bind the two republics much more closely together. Finally, Genet was instructed to seek full payment, ahead of schedule, of America's debt to France, approximately $4.4 million, arising from the War of Independence. Repayment of this debt would allow the hard-pressed French government to supply its West Indian colonies during the war. In the absence of a commercial agreement Genet was to press for observance of the treaty of 1778 in accordance with the French interpretation of that pact. According to the French reading of the treaty, not only should French privateers be allowed to bring their prizes into American ports, but the French should be able to commission and arm new privateers, recruit crews, and establish prize courts in American ports to adjudicate disputes and award prize money. While the existing treaty did allow the French to bring their prizes into American ports, if Genet achieved all the objectives laid out in his instructions, he would effectively enlist the United States as an ally in a war against Spain and Britain.[47]

Genet was greeted by a large and enthusiastic crowd when he arrived in Charleston. He met the governor of the state, William Moultrie, who encouraged him in his plans. Buoyed by his rapturous welcome and the encouragement of the state's political leaders, Genet began issuing letters of marque to commission privateers that would be nominally French but crewed by Americans. He encouraged the French consul in Charleston, Michel-Ange de Mangourit, to arrange expeditions against East Florida. He took these actions before he had been formally received by the United States government (and before Washington had issued his neutrality proclamation on April 22). Genet tarried and schemed in Charleston, celebrated and feted, for ten days before departing for Philadelphia.[48]

The envoy traveled by land from Charleston to Philadelphia. Departing on April 18, he journeyed at a leisurely pace and enjoyed rapturous welcomes en route and did not arrive in the capital until May 16. When he arrived in Philadelphia he boasted of the fraternal feeling that the American people felt for their French counterparts, saying he was confident of their support for his mission.[49] Genet had been traveling when the president issued his neutrality proclamation on April 22. Although Washington had decided that Genet should be received without restriction, his understanding of the 1778 treaty did not conform to the Frenchman's reading of the pact. The position of the United States government was that it should uphold the treaty with France but take no action that would violate its neutrality. Genet failed to recognize this, just as he failed to understand that the executive branch was responsible for foreign policy. His credentials styled him as a minister to the Congress of the United States—as his predecessors had been under the Articles of Confederation. Genet believed that he should negotiate directly with Congress as the body that represented the American people. He did not fully understand the structure of the new American government. With the cheers of Americans of all walks of life still ringing in his ears from his triumphant progress to the capital, he never tried to understand it. He believed that he—and the French Revolution—enjoyed a level of popular support that would enable him to achieve his objectives easily.

President Washington formally received Citizen Genet on May 18. The ambassador presented a letter of credence from his government that read in part, "We have no doubt he [Genet] will employ all his attention to convince you of the desire of the French nation to strengthen more and more the bonds of friendship and fraternity which ought to unite two free peoples, made for reciprocal esteem, and to consolidate between them the most perfect harmony." Jefferson's initial impression was positive "He offers every thing and asks nothing," he confided optimistically to James Madison. Soon, however, Genet began to make requests of the United States government, particularly the secretary of state. The result would be a severe test of the nation's neutrality.[50]

Several days after he presented his credentials to the President, Genet wrote a series of letters to the secretary of state. On May 22 he wrote to propose that the United States liquidate some of its debt to France by providing "the greatest part of the subsistence and stores necessary for the armies, fleets and colonies of the French Republic." The next day Genet wrote to Jefferson again, this time throwing open French ports in Europe and West Indies to Americans, "seeing in them but brothers." He proposed building on the fraternal feeling between the two republics by establishing "a true family compact, that is, in a national compact." Before Jefferson could respond to these two letters the

French minister wrote again: on May 27 he challenged a statement that Jefferson had made on May 15 to Genet's predecessor, Jean Baptiste Ternant, objecting to the capture of the British ship *Grange* by the French frigate *Embuscade* (the vessel that had brought Genet to America) in American territorial waters and to the French commissioning and outfitting of privateers in American ports as well as to the establishment of prize courts by French consuls. In his response Genet agreed to restore the *Grange* but defended the right of the French to operate privateers out of American ports under the treaty of 1778. The man "who asks nothing" had sought within a few days to liquidate much of the American debt to France ahead of schedule; proposed to negotiate a new, closer alliance between France and the United States; and attempted to wage war against Britain from the United States.[51]

The Washington administration was not receptive to Genet's entreaties, which would have subverted its policy of neutrality. On May 20 the administration decided to order all French privateers from American ports.[52] On June 11 Jefferson wrote to Genet to inform him that the United States would not make an advance payment on its debt to France. Armed with a report prepared by Hamilton on the debt, he informed the Frenchman that the schedule of payments on the debt "far exceed the ordinary resources of the U.S." and the country could not afford to liquidate the debt early.[53] Jefferson made no response to Genet's request to open negotiations on a new Franco-American treaty.

Jefferson supported the neutrality policy and he was in broad agreement with the decisions taken in response to Genet. He sought to moderate them somewhat in the interests of protecting relations between the United States and France. Prior to the decision to deny American ports to the French privateers the cabinet had debated whether the British prizes captured by the privateers commissioned by Genet in Charleston, before Washington's neutrality proclamation, should be returned. Predictably, Alexander Hamilton and Henry Knox advocated the return of the prizes; Jefferson and Edmund Randolph opposed making restitution. Jefferson noted that while the twenty-second article of the 1778 treaty prohibited the United States from permitting the enemies of France to outfit privateers in its ports, it allowed France to do so only by implication. The treaty, in Jefferson's reading, permitted the United

States to refuse this privilege to the French. He advocated making such a refusal "to preserve a fair and secure neutrality." On the question of returning the prizes already taken, Jefferson was more sympathetic to the French. Since Genet issued his commissions in good faith prior to the neutrality proclamation, to use force to seize the prizes in question and restore them to the British would be a disproportionate response. Rather, Jefferson advocated letting the privateers keep their prizes and offering "a moderate apology" to Great Britain. Washington sided with Jefferson and Randolph. Future French privateers were to be excluded from American ports, but the prizes were not restored.[54]

Jefferson also adopted a moderate position on the question of the French debt. Yet again opinion within the cabinet was divided. Alexander Hamilton argued that as the United States had no contractual or treaty obligation to repay the debt early it need not do so. That being the case, he argued, it was not necessary to provide Genet with an explanation or justification for the decision to reject his request.[55] Jefferson argued that "to decline the propositions of Mr. Genet on the subject of our debt, without assigning any reasons at all, would have a very dry and unpleasant aspect indeed." He suggested that, as a goodwill gesture, the United States might advance its payments on the debt for 1793. Washington, again, sought a middle course between his divided ministers. He agreed that Genet should be given an explanation but supported the refusal to liquidate any of the debt ahead of schedule.[56]

At this early stage in their relationship, Jefferson believed that he could forge a useful partnership with Genet. Indeed, he confided his opinions about the divisions in the cabinet to Genet. The diplomat reported to his government that Jefferson "gave me useful notions on men in office, and did not at all conceal from me that Senator [Robert] Morris and Secretary of the Treasury Hamilton, attached to the interests of England, have the greatest influence over the President's mind, and that it was only with difficulty that he counterbalanced their efforts."[57] At the same time Jefferson complained to Madison about the likely cabinet response to Genet's proposals, "One person [Hamilton] represents them as a snare into which he hopes we shall not fall. His second [Knox] of the same sentiment of course. He whose vote for most part, or say always, is casting [Randolph], has by two or three private conversations or rather disputes with me, shewn his opinion to be against doing what would be a mark of predilection to one of the parties, tho not a breach of neutrality in form."[58] Jefferson believed that the United States should remain neutral but it should support France if possible—while maintaining the peace. As he wrote to Washington during the debate over the debt repayment, "I think it very material myself to keep alive the friendly sentiments of that country as far as can be done *without risking war* . . ."[59] Early in the summer of 1793 Jefferson believed that his cabinet opponents, particularly Hamilton, were a greater threat to the peace than Genet. As the summer progressed Genet would alienate his most prominent ally in the American government.

Genet, stung by the rebuffs he had received from the Washington administration, was emboldened by the popular support he believed he enjoyed. "I live here in the midst of perpetual fetes," he boasted, "I receive addresses from all parts of the Continent." On June 1 he was honored at a grand public dinner, attended by around two hundred guests, including Thomas Mifflin, the governor of Pennsylvania, state and federal officials, and representatives of the business and expatriate French communities in Philadelphia. During the meal fifteen toasts celebrating the French Revolution and its official representative in the United States were given.[60] Buoyed by such support, Genet complained to Jefferson about the administration's failure to support the French cause. He argued the France had a right by treaty, international law, precedent, and natural justice to fit out privateers in American ports. He questioned whether Washington had the authority to declare neutrality, and he suggested that the president was influenced unduly by the pro-British voices in his cabinet—probably based on Jefferson's revelations to him. Genet, believing he could rely on public support, suggested Congress be recalled to consider the neutrality question. In defiance of the U.S. government, French consuls continued to arm privateers in American ports, prompting a crisis in Franco-American relations.[61]

By mid-June Jefferson had run out of patience with Genet. After consulting the cabinet and the president he wrote a forceful letter to the Frenchman which clearly laid out the American view of its neutrality, particularly as it related to the privateer question. After citing the 1778 treaty and invoking Vattel, Jefferson unambiguously laid out the American position:

> The united States in prohibiting all the belligerent powers from equipping, arming, and manning vessels of war in their ports, have exercised a right, and a duty with justice, and with great moderation. By our treaties with several of the belligerent powers, which are a part of the laws of our land, we have established a State of peace with them. But without appealing to treaties, we are at peace with them all by the law of nature. For by nature's law, man is at peace with man, till some aggression is committed, which, by the same law, authorizes one to destroy another as his enemy. For our citizens then, to commit murders and depredations on the members of nations at peace with us, to combine to do it, appeared to the Executive, and to those whom they consulted, as much against the laws of the land, as to murder or rob, or combine to murder or rob its own citizens, and as much to require punishment, if done within their limits, where they have a territorial jurisdiction, or on the high seas, where they have a personal jurisdiction, that is to say, one which reaches their own citizens only, this being an appropriate part of each nation on an element where all have a common jurisdiction. So say our laws as we understand them ourselves.

Genet's stubborn misreading of the situation had brought about remarkable (and brief) unity in Washington's cabinet. Jefferson had come to believe that Genet was an obstacle to peace. Where Hamilton and Knox feared that he would drag the United States into a war with Britain, Jefferson feared that he might drive the world's two leading republics into a conflict.[62]

Having been stymied over the privateering question and in his attempts to get the American debt repaid early as well as failing to negotiate a new treaty, Genet sought to achieve another of his objectives: fomenting unrest in the borderlands of the new republic. "I excite the Canadians to free themselves from the yoke of England; I arm the

Kentuckians, and I prepare by sea an expedition which will support their descent on New Orleans," he boasted two days after he received his rebuke from Jefferson on the privateering issue.[63] These claims were more aspirations than facts. In mid-June Genet visited Jefferson to discuss his western plans. Genet planned to send a French agent, a botanist named André Michaux, to Kentucky to organize an attack on New Orleans under the guise of a scientific expedition. According to Jefferson's account of the meeting:

> Mr. Genet called on me and read to me very rapidly instructions he had prepared for Michaud who is going to Kentucky, an address to the inhabitants of Louisiana, and another to those of Canada. In these papers it appears that besides encouraging those inhabitants to insurrection, he speaks of two generals at Kentucky who have proposed to him to go and take N. Orleans if he will furnish the expence about £3000. sterl. He declines advancing it, but promises that sum ultimately for their expences, proposes that officers shall be commissioned by himself in Kentuckey and Louisiana, that they shall rendezvous *out of the territories of the US:* suppose in Louisiana, and there making up a battalion to be called [from the] inhabitants of Louisiana and Kentuckey and getting what Indns. they could, to undertake the expedition against N. Orleans, and then Louisiana to be established into an independant state connected in commerce with France and the US. That two frigates shall go into the river Missisipi and cooperate against N. Orleans.—The address to Canada, was to encourage them to shake off English yoke, to call Indians to their assistance, and to assure them of the friendly dispositions of their neighbors of the US.

Genet, undoubtedly aware of Jefferson's interest in securing free navigation of the Mississippi for the United States, probably expected that Jefferson would welcome these plans. Genet went to pains to stress that the expedition would gather outside of American territory. According to Jefferson, Genet "said he communicated these things to me, not as Secy. of state, but as Mr. Jeff." Jefferson gave Genet an ambivalent response. "I told him," he recalled, "that his enticing officers and souldiers from Kentuckey to go against Spain, was really putting a halter about their necks, for that they would assuredly be hung, if they commd. hostilities against a nation at peace with the US." Nontheless, "leaving out that article I did not care what insurrections should be excited in Louisiana." Genet reported that Jefferson told him that the United States was negotiating with Spain for access to New Orleans. Consequently, "the delicacy of the United States did not permit them to take part in our operations; nevertheless he gave me to understand that he thought a little spontaneous irruption of the inhabitants of the Kentucky into New Orleans could advance matters." Jefferson sought to maintain American neutrality, though his willingness to countenance rebellion in Louisiana suggest the opportunism, expedience, and optimism that characterized his response to the Nootka Sound crisis.[64]

In the end nothing came of Genet's western schemes as the minister was removed from his post. The confrontation that led the United States to demand his recall concerned not what the Frenchman might do in Louisiana but his continued defiance over the issue of privateering. The dispute centered on a four-gun British merchant ship, the *Little Sarah*. The *Little Sarah* was captured by the *Embuscade* in early May and brought to Philadelphia. At Genet's urging the vessel was rechristened as the *Little Democrat* and fitted out as a privateer with additional armament, in defiance of the American ban on such activity. President Washington had instructed state governors to use force if necessary to detain French privateers. Thomas Mifflin, the governor of Pennsylvania, appealed to the government for advice as the *Little Democrat* prepared to put to sea during the first week of July. The president was at Mount Vernon, and the cabinet feared that the privateer would depart before Washington returned. Alexander Hamilton and Henry Knox advised Mifflin to use force to detain the ship. Jefferson, fearing that such a step would lead to bloodshed and possible war with France, made a direct appeal to Genet on Sunday, July 7.[65]

Jefferson counseled patience and implored Genet to wait for Washington's return before sending the *Little Democrat* to sea. According to Jefferson, Genet, "took up the subject instantly in a very high tone, and went into an immense feild [*sic*] of declamation and complaint." Genet raged for a considerable period of time, not allowing Jefferson to get a word in. The Frenchman complained about the unfairness and illegality of the American neutrality policy. Earlier he had told Alexander Dallas, the Pennsylvania secretary of state, that he would go above Washington's head, directly to the American people. In speaking to Jefferson he suggested that Congress be called into session to address the question as he believed that the executive had overstepped its authority on the neutrality question. Jefferson, patiently, sought to explain the federal constitution and the separation of powers to Genet. By the end of the stormy session, Jefferson believed that Genet would not send the privateer to sea before Washington's return.[66]

Genet sent the *Little Democrat* downriver, beyond the range of Pennsylvania's guns, but did not, yet, allow the privateer to put to sea. The president was furious when he returned to the capital on July 11 and learned of the contretemps. "Is the Minister of the French Republic to set the Acts of this Government at defiance—*with impunity*?" he fumed, "and then threaten the Executive with an appeal to the People."[67] The president called a meeting of the cabinet on July 12. After that meeting Jefferson wrote to Genet and George Hammond to instruct them that no French privateers nor their prizes should put to sea until the question of what to do about them was addressed once and for all.[68] Several days later Genet ordered the *Little Democrat* to put to sea.

The dispute over the *Little Democrat* had two immediate consequences. In the first instance it compelled the Washington administration to define the limits of its neutrality. During the summer of 1793 the cabinet made a number of decisions that clarified and amplified the neutrality proclamation. The cabinet prohibited the arming of foreign vessels, either military or merchant, in American ports; set the territorial limit of American waters at three miles; and denied foreign diplomats the right to establish prize courts in American ports. American citizens were prohibited from enlisting to fight for foreign belligerents either on land or sea. These principles were enshrined in law when Congress adopted the Neutrality Act in 1794.[69]

The second and more immediate consequence of the *Little Democrat* affair concerned the fate of Genet. Having defied the government and sent the privateer to sea marked the beginning of the end for Genet as French envoy. "What must the World think of such conduct, and of the Government of the U. States in submitting to it?" asked President Washington in exasperation. On July 23 the cabinet met at the president's house to discuss the international situation. Washington raised the question of what should be done with Genet. According to Jefferson, the president expressed the opinion that Genet's correspondence with the members of his government should be sent to Gouverneur Morris in Paris "with a temperate but strong representation of his conduct, drawing a clear line between him and his nation, expressing our friendship to the latter, but insisting on the recall of Genet, and in the mean time that we should desire him either to withdraw or cease his functions." Two days later Washington wrote to Jefferson and instructed the secretary of state to prepare his correspondence and notes of his meetings with Genet as well as his relevant correspondence with the British minister, George Hammond, for presentation to the cabinet.[70]

Jefferson presented the documentation to the cabinet on August 1. The cabinet agreed unanimously with the course of action previously suggested by the president—that is, the correspondence should be sent to the French government with a letter to Morris outlining Genet's behavior and demanding his recall. The cabinet disagreed sharply over whether to issue a public statement on Genet's conduct. They debated the matter over two days. Hamilton proposed that the government should issue a public statement to the effect that Genet had sought to subvert American neutrality and interfered with American domestic politics in an effort to undermine the government. Jefferson strongly opposed the proposal, viewing it as a threat to popular support for the French Revolution in America. It would also call into question the loyalty of his political allies in the emerging Republican party. Diplomatically, such a statement would likely bring about a crisis with France—as the recall of Genet would be seen as a repudiation of the French Revolution if such a statement were issued. Predictably Randolph supported Jefferson's position and Knox supported Hamilton. Washington was sympathetic to Hamilton's proposal but decided to wait to see how the public responded to the recall of Genet to determine whether such a statement was necessary.[71]

Jefferson spent the better part of two weeks drafting his letter to Morris on Genet. He recognized that he needed to address two audiences: the

French government, and the American public. Jefferson stressed Genet's repeated violations of American neutrality, but went to great pains distinguish between Genet's behavior and French policy so as to avoid causing a larger crisis in Franco-American relations. Indeed the letter enumerated Genet's misbehavior while stressing American friendship for France. The cabinet reviewed Jefferson's draft and suggested several changes—tempering the affection for France and the criticism of its enemies—although the substance of Jefferson's letter remained. On August 23 Jefferson sent the letter and his correspondence with Genet to Morris in Paris. He waited two weeks before informing Genet that he had requested his recall. Jefferson delayed informing the minister so that he would be unable to interfere with his letter to Morris.[72]

The Girondin government in Paris had been overthrown by the Jacobins in June 1793. When Gouverneur Morris presented Jefferson's letter and Genet's correspondence to the Jacobin foreign minister, François Deforgues, Deforgues immediately agreed to recall Genet. Several days later the Jacobin government promised to punish Genet for his conduct in the United States. The Jacobins claimed that Genet had deliberately undermined Franco-American relations in an effort to subvert the revolution. As an accused counter-revolutionary, Genet could expect harsh treatment upon his return. The Terror was in full force and Genet would likely be sent to the guillotine. Washington gave the troublesome envoy asylum. He never returned to France. In 1794 he married Cornelia Clinton, the daughter of Governor George Clinton of New York. He spent the rest of his long life in the United States, dying in New York in 1834.[73]

At the height of the Genet imbroglio Jefferson wrote to George Washington expressing his desire to retire from office. Jefferson wrote that he had intended to remain in office only for Washington's first term. Owing to international instability, he had remained for an extra year. He now intended to retire at the end of September, "to scenes of greater tranquility, from those which I am every day more and more convinced that neither my talents, tone of mind, nor time of life fit me."[74] The growing partisan strife in the nation and the persistent divisions within the cabinet had taken their toll on the secretary of state. A week after receiving the letter, Washington visited Jefferson at the country home he rented outside of Philadelphia hoping to persuade him to remain in office. Jefferson explained that the supporters of Hamilton and his fiscal policies had made life unbearable for him:

> I expressed to him my excessive repugnance to public life, the particular uneasiness of my situation in this place where the laws of society oblige me to move always exactly in the circle which I know to bear me peculiar hatred, that is to say the wealthy Aristocrats, the Merchants connected closely with England, the new created paper fortunes that thus surrounded, my words were caught, multiplied, misconstrued, and even fabricated and spread abroad to my injury, that he saw also that there was such an opposition of views between myself and another part of the administration as to render it peculiarly unpleasing, and to destroy the necessary harmony.

Jefferson assured the president that Republicans would desert Genet as soon as the scope and scale of his behavior became public. When the president sought to assure Jefferson of his fidelity to the Constitution Jefferson interrupted him to say, "No rational man in the US. suspects you of any other disposition, but there does not pass a week in which we cannot prove decl[aratio]ns dropping from the monarchical party that our government is good for nothing, it is a milk and water thing which cannot support itself, we must knock it down and set up something of more energy." The two Virginians had had this conversation several times in the past. Realizing that Jefferson was serious about resigning, Washington turned the conversation to the choice of his successor. After they reviewed possible candidates Washington asked Jefferson to extend his term until Congress reconvened. Jefferson agreed and remained in office until December 31.[75]

During his four-year tenure as secretary of state Jefferson sought to guide the United States through the turbulent international waters created by the French Revolution. The conflicts arising from the revolution in France presented the United States with both opportunities and threats. Jefferson sought to protect the fledgling American republic and advance its interests—as demonstrated during the Nootka Sound crisis when he sought to exploit international discord to consolidate an American claim to the Mississippi River. When a general war broke out in Europe in spring 1793 he agreed with the administration's policy of neutrality. Initially he sought to maintain a neutrality consistent with American treaty commitments to France—he favored a neutrality that would allow the United States to keep itself out of the European war without harming the French Republic, whose interests, he believed, coincided with those of the United States. The arrival of Citizen Genet in the United States in spring 1793 immediately challenged this policy. Genet's actions forced the American administration, including Jefferson, to more clearly define what it meant to be neutral. Despite his belief that France remained and should be the United States' most important international partner, Jefferson accepted that only a strict neutrality could keep America out of a European war that might endanger the republic. This was hardly a revolutionary diplomacy that sought to remake the international order.

The struggles over America's policy toward revolutionary France had revealed that there were potent counterrevolutionary forces at home as well as abroad. Jefferson's constant battles within the cabinet with Alexander Hamilton convinced him that the treasury secretary was at the head of a faction bent on overthrowing the Constitution, instituting monarchy, and consolidating power in the hands of a small cabal of wealthy financiers. This was the main theme of Jefferson's conversation with Washington when he tendered his resignation in the summer of 1793. Just as counterrevolutionary powers had formed a coalition to crush the French Revolution, Hamilton and his followers (Jefferson felt) sought to foment a similar counterrevolution within the United States, all the while throwing American support to Britain. It was clear to Jefferson that the struggle over republicanism had to be fought at home and abroad simultaneously. His retirement would be short-lived. He returned to public life to see his domestic foes use international threats to justify subverting the republic.

Four

The Reign of the Witches

T homas Jefferson left Philadelphia on January 5, 1794, and arrived at Monticello eleven days later. On the day Jefferson departed from the capital Horatio Gates, the former revolutionary general, wrote to express his dismay upon learning of his resignation. Gates deployed a nautical metaphor, writing, "If the best Seamen abandon the Ship in a Storm, she must Founder; and if all Human means are neglected, Providence will not Care for The Vessel; She must Perish!" Gates concluded by inviting Jefferson to visit him at his New York estate. Jefferson responded politely, acknowledging Gates's good wishes and his invitation, which he declined, declaring, "The length of my tether is now fixed for life from Monticello to Richmond." He continued, "My private business can never call me elsewhere, and certainly politics will not, which I have ever hated both in theory and practice. I thought myself conscientiously called from those studies which were my delight by the political crisis of my country and by those events quorum pars magna fuisti [of which you have been a great part]." Jefferson also used a nautical metaphor: "In storms like those all hands must be aloft. But calm is now restored, and I leave the bark with joy to those who love the sea." He disclaimed any interest or expertise in politics asserting, "I am but a landsman."[1]

Jefferson's planned retirement would be relatively brief. He may have been sincerely fed up with politics after four bruising years in Washington's administration, and while he devoted much of his time to his plantations and to reconstructing Monticello, Jefferson never completely gave up on politics. He stayed in touch with James Madison and other political allies, and in 1796 was persuaded by Madison to stand for the presidency. He lost a narrow election but was returned to national office in 1797 as vice president in the Federalist administration of John Adams. By the time Jefferson returned to Philadelphia the partisan differences that had characterized his tenure as secretary of state were more intense than ever. As the unsuccessful standard-bearer of the Republicans, Jefferson was the nominal leader of the opposition—while serving in the administration whose policies he opposed.

In February 1798, after nearly a year as vice president, Jefferson offered a perceptive analysis of the partisan situation in the United States in a letter to a Virginia Federalist, John Wise. Jefferson had been overheard in his Philadelphia boardinghouse referring to Wise, then the Speaker of the Virginia assembly, as a "Tory." Wise wrote Jefferson requesting an explanation. Jefferson responded on February 12:

> It is now well understood that two sects have arisen with the US. the one believeing [sic] that the Executive is the branch of our Government which the most needs support: the other that, like the analogous branch in the English government, it is already too strong for the republican parts of the Constitution, and therefore . . . they incline to the Legislative powers. the former of these are called Federalists, sometimes Aristocrats or monocrats and Sometimes tories, after the corresponding sect in the English government, of exactly the same definition: the latter are Stiled [sic] Republicans, Whigs, Jacobins, Anarchists, Disorganisers &c. these terms are in familiar use with most persons and which of those of the first Class I used on the occasion [sic] alluded to I do not particularly remember. they are all well understood to designate persons who are for Strengthening the Executive rather than the Legislative branches of the government.

Jefferson explained that he called Wise a Tory because there was still some confusion in the public mind regarding the terms "Federalist" and "Republicans," which both parties claimed. He claimed "Tory" was simply a political description, preferable in fact to the alternatives, such as "Aristocrats" or "Monocrats" (both terms that he frequently used in his correspondence with political allies), and not an insult. He assured Wise that his esteem for him was in no way diminished "by any Difference which may happen to exist in our political opinions," and he apologized if he had caused him any pain. Although it seems unlikely that Jefferson could have expected Wise or any other American politician not to be insulted at being described as a Tory, given recent memories of the American Revolution, his analysis of the political situation is perceptive. The Federalists (for we may use the terms by which the two parties came to be known) did favor the centralization of power in the hands of the executive. The Republicans worried more about the threat to liberty that such centralization posed and sought to mitigate the danger by vesting power in the Congress and the individual states. It was awkward that Jefferson was the de facto leader of the Republicans (Madison had left Congress in March 1797) while serving as vice president in a Federalist administration.[2]

Foreign policy remained a fundamental area of conflict between the two parties. As ever, the United States was buffeted by international events. The biggest challenge facing the country during the Adams administration concerned American relations with France, its former ally. It led to an armed conflict at sea between the two republics and nearly resulted in open war. The "Quasi-War" with France, as it came to be known, proved to be the gravest test for the new republic since the Peace of Paris in 1783. The Federalists believed the United States was confronted by enemies from within as well as by France. Some believed that Americans sympathetic to France—and Thomas Jefferson was one of the nation's most famous Francophiles—might not support the United States in the coming conflict. Anticipating a declaration of war in the summer of 1798, Federalists in Congress adopted a series of measures to curtail civil liberties and to mitigate the dangers of internal dissent. For Jefferson these laws, known as the Alien and Sedition Acts, represented a greater danger to American liberty than that posed by French warships. Jefferson recognized that, historically, republics were more likely to collapse than be conquered. He saw the Alien and Sedition Acts as a Federalist attempt to consolidate power in the federal government at the expense of liberty. As a solution he proposed that the individual states should have the authority to declare federal actions unconstitutional. By the latter 1790s international relations and domestic politics had become so intertwined that the existence of the union was endangered by international questions. Despite Jefferson's assurances to Horatio Gates, the sea was hardly calm. The landsman was drawn back to the ship, and he discovered that its crew was divided against itself. It was appropriate that Gates chose a nautical metaphor, for international trade was at the heart of the dispute between Federalists and Republicans about what kind of country the United States should become.

In his letter to Jefferson, Horatio Gates had observed, "Your report to Congress upon the Trade of the US., Has Filled every Patriot Breast with Gratitude; and Admiration; you therefore Retreat covered with Glory; The Public Gratitude may one day Force You from that Retreat so make no rash Promises, lest like other great Men you should be Tempted to break them."[3] Although Jefferson had worked on the paper on American trade, to which Gates referred, throughout his period as secretary of state, he did not submit the report to Congress until December 16, 1793. It was his valedictory message as secretary of state, and in it he presented a summary of the country's overseas trade. He observed that the majority of American trade was with Britain, and since Britain sought to wage economic war on the United States through its mercantile regulations, the well-being of the republic was threatened by its dependence on British trade. The *Report on Commerce* provided statistical data to support his arguments. He demonstrated that the United States exported more to Britain and its colonies ($9.3 million) than to all its other trading partners combined. It imported more than $15.2 million worth of goods from Britain but only slightly more than $2 million worth of goods from France, its second-largest trading partner. Despite its importance, American merchants were largely excluded from British-American trade, Jefferson claimed, by discriminatory regulations. In the year between October 1789 and September 1790 the tonnage of American vessels entering French ports was 116,410. By contrast, American tonnage entering British ports was just 43,580. Jefferson proposed that the United States reorient its trade by adopting customs duties to counter discriminatory British policies and negotiating commercial treaties with France and Spain.[4]

Jefferson's *Report on Commerce* was a statement of his political economy, reflecting his vision that the United States must remain a virtuous agrarian republic if liberty were to flourish and his belief that this could be achieved only through westward expansion and international trade. The report developed the ideas on political economy that Jefferson had articulated in the *Notes on Virginia*. The *Report on Commerce* was a repudiation of Alexander Hamilton's fiscal and economic policies and further evidence that it was impossible to separate domestic and foreign policy during the 1790s.

On January 3, 1794, two days before Jefferson departed for Monticello, James Madison, who led the Republicans in Congress, introduced a series of commercial resolutions to Congress, "measures of moderation, firmness, and decision" he argued, "in order to narrow the sphere of our commerce with those nations who see proper not to meet us on terms of reciprocity." Although Madison did not identify Britain as the nation at which his proposals were aimed, it was clear to members of Congress. Madison proposed that the United States adopt retaliatory customs duties on British imports as well as tonnage duties on British vessels. Although Jefferson and Madison believed that the United States should champion the right of free trade, they were willing to countenance the introduction of neo-mercantilist tactics in response to British trade restrictions. Essentially Madison, acting on Jefferson's report, was proposing that the United States create its own mercantilist system, closed to Britain and favoring France. Federalists in Congress delayed acting on Madison's proposals, and support for them, initially strong, dissipated.[5]

While the United States was considering whether to implement a more robust policy toward Britain, the government in London adopted a more aggressive course of action toward the American republic. On November 6, 1793, the British, now at war with revolutionary France, adopted an Order in Council that authorized the Royal Navy and British privateers to seize "all ships laden with goods the produce of any colony belonging to France, or carrying provisions or other supplies for the use of any such colony." Lord Grenville, the home secretary, outlined the British position for George Hammond, the British minister in Philadelphia: "a War between two Nations ought as little as possible to prejudice the usual and accustomed Commerce of a third not engaged in the Quarrel. But the latter ought not, on the other hand, to desire or claim from the War new rights or pretentions to the prejudices of either belligerent Party."[6] Grenville articulated the so-called Rule of 1756, the consistent British position throughout the French revolutionary and Napoleonic wars—trade that was not legal during peacetime was not legal during wartime. In other words the British sought to prevent the United States from trading with Britain's enemies simply to exploit the unusual circumstances created by the war. The United States, by contrast, claimed that neutral nations as non-belligerents should have the right to trade freely. These contrasting positions bedeviled British-American relations until 1815.

The Order in Council of November 6, 1793 was aimed at restricting American trade with the French West Indies. It was effective, in part, because the British kept the order secret in order to guarantee that British vessels would capture a large number of American prizes before it was publicized. Word of the policy did not reach the United States until early March. On March 25 President Washington submitted letters to Congress from Fulwar Skipwith, the American consul in St. Eustatia. Skipwith reported that the British had seized 250 American merchant ships in the West Indies.[7]

The ship seizures were one of several American grievances against Britain in the spring of 1794. In late 1793 the Algerians resumed their attacks on American commerce in the Mediterranean and North Atlantic, and Americans believed they did so at the behest of the British. More significant was the continued British occupation of seven forts in the Northwest Territory. Americans believed that the British used these posts to foment unrest among the Indians of the region. The United States had waged a costly and largely unsuccessful campaign against the Indians of the Northwest since 1791. Rather than yielding the posts, which they had committed to do by the terms of the 1783 treaty that ended the War of Independence, the British were expanding their presence in the region.[8] On February 10, 1794, Guy Carleton, Lord Dorchester, governor-general of Canada since August 1786, gave a speech in Quebec to Indians from the Great Lakes region. Carleton predicted that Britain and the United States would soon be at war, and he urged the Natives to push back the line of American settlement in Ohio when the conflict came. Carleton was not the only official who believed war was imminent. On February 21 Congress authorized funding to build six frigates.[9] In January 1794, *before* the widespread ship seizures in the West Indies began, James Madison estimated that the cost to the United States of British harassment via loss of trade, insurance, Indian war, and increased insurance was more than \$3.5 million.[10] By late March when Washington informed Congress about the ship seizures, a second British-American war seemed inevitable.

In a last-ditch effort to avoid war—which they believed would be catastrophic for the United States—Alexander Hamilton and a group of Federalist senators besought President Washington to send an envoy to London to negotiate a settlement of the various issues that separated Britain and America. The president agreed and eventually nominated the chief justice of the Supreme Court, John Jay, for the role. Jay was well versed in international affairs having served as a diplomat in Spain during the War of Independence and as Congress's secretary of foreign affairs during the 1780s. Jay's orders, composed largely by Hamilton, instructed the envoy to seek the cession of the posts in the Northwest occupied by the British, reparations for ships seized by the Royal Navy, and compensation for the slaves carried away by the British in 1783. Jay was also instructed to negotiate a commercial treaty with Britain.[11]

Jay received a relatively warm welcome in London and negotiated with Lord Grenville throughout the summer and autumn of 1794. Contrary to American expectations, the men reached an agreement that averted war on November 19. Jay yielded to the British over the key question of neutral shipping during wartime, accepting the Rule of 1756. In exchange for this the British agreed to vacate the Northwest forts by 1796. Questions regarding the border, compensation for the captured slaves, and prewar debts were to be settled by arbitration commissions. Britain's biggest concession was to open its empire to American trade with minimal restrictions. American ships could now trade with Britain and Ireland, India, and, crucially, the British West Indies.[12]

Washington was disappointed when he learned the terms that Jay had negotiated. While Jay had avoided war, he had exchanged the American commitment to free trade for preferential commercial access within the British Empire and the Northwest forts (which Britain had originally agreed to vacate in 1783). Washington, correctly, anticipated that the terms of the treaty would be very unpopular. The president hesitated before submitting the treaty to the Senate for ratification. When he sent it to the upper house he stipulated that its terms should be kept secret while the Senate considered it. The Senate ratified the pact with a minimal two-thirds majority, 20 to 10, on June 24, 1795. When the terms of the treaty became known, James Madison and the Republicans in the House of Representatives opposed appropriating the funds necessary to implement the agreement and demanded that the president submit all the correspondence relating to the negotiations to Congress. This prompted a prolonged political and constitutional struggle. Washington and the Federalists contended that the Constitution granted the Senate the power to ratify treaties and that the House of Representatives must approve the funding. Madison and the Republicans asserted that the House should exercise a degree of control over foreign policy through its budgetary power. In the end, opposition in the House collapsed and the treaty was implemented.[13]

The Jay Treaty aroused passionate response, engendering vitriolic debate both in Congress and among the public at large. Jefferson wrote of the response to the treaty, "So general a burst of dissatisfaction never before appeared against any transaction." The treaty fueled increasing partisanship in the press—even leading to attacks on George Washington, who had largely been immune to the types of press criticism that was commonly directed at Jefferson, Madison, and Hamilton (often encouraged *by* Jefferson, Madison, and Hamilton on their foes). Federalists saw in the treaty an opportunity to forge a closer American relationship with Britain. Republicans viewed the treaty as a betrayal of the principles of the Revolution as the United States had sold its independence in exchange for commercial advantages, advantages that came at the expense of France. According to Jefferson, those who understood the details of the treaty rejected it while the uncomprehending "condemn it generally as wearing a hostile face to France. This last is the most numerous class, comprehending the whole body of the people, who have taken a greater interest in this transaction than they were ever known to do in any other."[14]

From his retirement in Virginia, Jefferson viewed the Jay Treaty with suspicion. "From North to South," he wrote, "this monument of folly and venality is universally execrated." Jefferson believed that only the self-interested merchants in New York and Philadelphia could support the treaty, and they did so in the face of popular opposition. However, Jefferson believed the Federalists had overreached. He contended that the treaty had "completely demolished the monarchical party here." Despite this, the former secretary of state worried about the potential for unrest arising from the opposition to the pact. "The public dissatisfaction too and dissension it is likely to produce, are serious evils," he wrote in mid-September. Just because the public opposed the measure did not mean it would not be forced on the people. In a letter in which he ruminated on the meaning of the treaty he wrote of "rogues" who imposed their will on the honest majority of humanity. "These rogues," he wrote, "set out with stealing the people's good opinion, and then steal from them the right of withdrawing it, by contriving laws and associations against the power of the people themselves." He then resorted to yet another nautical metaphor to explain what the Federalists had attempted: "They say that while all hands were below deck mending sails, splicing ropes, and every one at his own business, and the captain in the cabin attending to his log-book and chart, a rogue of a pilot has run them into an enemy's port." In Jefferson's metaphor the dutiful captain was George Washington and the rogue piloting the ship of state into British water was Alexander Hamilton. Jefferson disclaimed any interest in politics. "For my part, I consider myself now but as a passenger, leaving the world and its government to those who are likely to live longer in it."[15]

The Jay Treaty galvanized the Republicans. Opposing the pact allowed like-minded folk around the country to begin to organize as a party. The agreement itself provided the nascent party with a platform. They stood against everything the treaty promoted, particularly a close trading relationship with Britain. Rather, they favored free trade and support for revolutionary France.[16] With George Washington's decision to retire the 1796 presidential election would be the first contested election in American history. Jefferson was coaxed out of retirement by James Madison and allowed his name to go forward. His opponent was the Federalist vice president, John Adams. Neither Adams nor Jefferson campaigned for the election but allowed surrogates to act on their behalves. When the voting was complete Adams won seventy-one votes in the Electoral College and Jefferson sixty-eight. As a consequence Jefferson found himself in the unenviable position of serving as Adams's vice president. After he was sworn into the office Jefferson averred, "The second office of this government is honorable and easy. The first is but a splendid misery." Jefferson's optimism would prove short-lived. He would soon discover that the second office brought with it miseries of its own.[17]

International questions dominated the Adams presidency. As two of the leading scholars of the period write, "The whole of Adams's single term was absorbed to a degree unequalled in any other American presidency, with a single problem, a crisis in foreign relations."[18] Having completed a treaty that ostensibly settled most of the outstanding grievances between the United States and Britain, the biggest challenge facing the Adams administration concerned its relationship with France. The French government, now in the hands of a five-man Directory, viewed the Jay Treaty as a repudiation of the 1778 Franco-American alliance.

The Directory's representative in the United States was Pierre Auguste Adet. Citizen Adet, a noted chemist, was a more able diplomat than Edmond Charles Genet. Nonetheless he represented France at a difficult moment in the history of Franco-American relations, and, like Genet, his actions made the situation worse. During the debate over the Jay Treaty, Jefferson sought to assure Adet that the long-term interests of the United States lay with France, not Britain. From the comfort of his retirement he wrote to the French minister: "Two people whose interests, whose principles, whose habits of attachment, founded on fellowship in war and mutual kindnesses have so many points of union, cannot but be easily kept together. I hope you have accordingly been sensible, Sir, of the general interest which my countrymen take in all the successes of your republic." Jefferson assured Adet, "In this no one joins with more enthusiasm than myself, an enthusiasm kindled by my love of liberty, by my gratitude to your nation who helped us acquire it, by my wishes to see it extended to all men, and first to those whom we love most." Jefferson believed that the United States and France were united by a common dedication to liberty, and that by supporting each other they could advance republicanism around the world.[19]

Notwithstanding Jefferson's assurances, Adet and his government were skeptical about the intentions of the United States. They viewed what they saw as the pro-British policies of the Washington administration with concern. By the late spring of 1796 Adet had concluded that the Republicans, "our friends," would support Jefferson in the coming election, and the Federalists, "the British faction," would back John Adams. As far as the French were concerned the election of 1796 was a referendum on Franco-American relations. If Americans elected John Adams, they would endorse the misguided, pro-British policy of the Washington administration, whereas a vote for Jefferson would be a repudiation of the Jay Treaty and would restore Franco-American relations to their correct footing.[20]

Citizen Adet sought to intervene in the election to insure that the friends of France prevailed. In September he described a visit he had made to Massachusetts to speak to "our friends." He reported that he had met with the "most influential" Republicans in Boston, and "they have all told me France must adopt measures that will cause the merchants to fear for their property, and to make them see the need to place at the head of the government a man whose known character would inspire confidence in the [French] Republic and thus put him in a position to play the mediator between it and the United States." If Adet is to be believed, Republicans were attempting to prompt an international crisis, such as the French seizing American shipping, to aid Jefferson's electoral chances. Of course it is possible that Adet suggested this to his American friends, rather than vice versa. It is likely that he had similar conversations with political sympathizers elsewhere in the United States during the prolonged election campaign.[21]

Adet tried to intervene more directly to affect the outcome of the election. On October 28, just before Pennsylvania voted to allocate its fifteen electoral votes in November, Adet presented a resolution from the Directory to the secretary of state, Timothy Pickering. The resolution stated that the French would treat all neutral vessels in the same manner as the British did. This was an explicit threat to American commerce. Before Pickering could respond, or communicate with President Washington, Adet had the resolution published in the Philadelphia *Aurora,* the leading Republican newspaper. Although addressed to Pickering, Adet intended to use the resolution (adopted the previous summer) to put pressure on Pennsylvania's voters to support Jefferson. In a very narrow election, decided by fewer than two hundred votes, Jefferson won the votes of fourteen of Pennsylvania's electors.[22]

Two weeks after the Pennsylvania election Adet made another appeal directly to the American people. He released a lengthy and bitter letter to the press accompanied by a series of proclamations that announced the suspension of diplomatic relations between France and the United States as a consequence of the Jay Treaty and a more restrictive French policy toward neutral (that is, American) shipping. Adet took this step after most of the voting in the 1796 election had been completed. Dumas Malone, Jefferson's most thorough biographer, believes he may have sought to influence the deliberations of the Electoral College by publishing his letter. Like Citizen Genet, Adet misread the American public. As James Madison wrote to Jefferson in early December, "Adet's Note which you will have seen, is working all the evil with which it is pregnant. Those who rejoice at its indiscretions & are taking advantage of them, have the impudence to pretend that it is an electioneering manoeuvre, and that the French Govt. have been led to it by the opponents of the British Treaty." Although Adet's letter did not originate with the Republican opponents of the Jay Treaty, it was intended to benefit them. It backfired badly.[23]

Adet's meddling, like that of Genet before him, made life more difficult for Jefferson, America's most famous Francophile. Jefferson entered office as Adams's vice president at a moment of Franco-American crisis and tainted by the suspicion that he and his supporters might be more loyal to France than the United States. For his part, Adet was not so certain that incoming vice president could be relied on. At the end of 1796 he wrote:

I do not know if, as I am assured, we shall always find in him a man wholly devoted to our interests. Mr. Jefferson likes us because he detests England; he seeks to draw near to us because he fears us less than Great Britain; but he might change his opinion tomorrow, if tomorrow Great Britain should cease to inspire his fears. Jefferson, although a friend of liberty and learning, although an admirer of the efforts we have made to break our bonds and dispel the cloud of ignorance which weighs down the human race, Jefferson, I say, is American and as such he cannot be sincerely our friend. An American is the born enemy of all the European peoples.[24]

Adet may have exaggerated his ability to get Jefferson elected president, but his reading of the Virginian was astute. Jefferson admired France and he was sympathetic with what he believed were the ideological objectives of the French Revolution, but he was, first and foremost, a pragmatist in his approach to foreign policy. His main aim was to protect the American republic and its interests, and he would not needlessly risk these on behalf of France.

In May 1797 the recently inaugurated vice president wrote a lengthy letter to Elbridge Gerry (this was the letter in which he described the presidency as a "splendid misery"). Gerry was an independent politician from Massachusetts who prided himself on not belonging to either of the emerging political parties. In his letter, Jefferson reflected at length on the international situation. "I do sincerely wish with you that we could take our stand on a ground perfectly neutral and independant [sic] towards all nations. It has been my constant object through public life; and with respect to the English and French particularly," he declared, pointing to his numerous statements, verbal and written, on the subject as evidence. Having established, at least in his own mind, that he favored neither France nor Britain, he set out to demonstrate that Britain had traduced the independence and economic well-being of the United States. "They have wished a monopoly of commerce and influence with us. And they have in fact obtained it. When we take notice that theirs is the workshop to which we go for all we want, that with them center either immediately or ultimately all the labors of our hands and lands, that

to them belongs either openly or secretly the great mass of our navigation," he wrote. He claimed that British subjects, claiming to be American citizens, "false citizens," dominated trade and "now constitute the
great body of what are called *our merchants,* fill our seaports, are planted
in every little town and district of the interior country, sway every thing
in the former place by their own votes and those of their dependants, in
the latter by their insinuations and the influence of their ledgers, that
they are advancing fast to a monopoly of our banks and public funds,
and thereby placing our public finances under their controul, that they
have in their alliance the most influential characters in and out of office."
In this way the British and their Federalist allies—the reference to out-
of-office influential characters was undoubtedly directed at Hamilton—
shaped a pro-British policy that rendered it "impossible for us to say
we stand on independant ground, impossible for a free mind not to see
and to groan under the bondage in which it is bound." The pro-British
forces exercised their influence through their control of the press
and persuaded Americans that "those who wish merely to recover self-
government" were guilty of seeking to place the United States under
French control. Jefferson's views mirrored those of his Federalist adversaries who believed that Republicans were subject to the undue influence of France. In the wake of the controversy over the Jay Treaty,
and the election of 1796, each of the two major political groups in the
United States maintained that their rivals were creatures of foreign
powers. Each believed that their rivals' foreign allegiance threatened
the republic.[25]

Foreign entanglements threatened not only to drag the United States
into unnecessary wars but also to destroy the union. In his letter to
Gerry, Jefferson observed that the *Hartford Courant* had recently raised
the possibility that the northern and southern states might separate. "After plunging us in all the broils of the European nations, there would remain but one act to close our tragedy," he wrote "that is, to break up our
union: and even this they have ventured seriously and solemnly to propose and maintain by argument, in a Connecticut paper." Jefferson expressed his hope that "whatever follies we may be led into as to foreign
nations, we shall never give up our union, the last anchor of our hope,
and that alone which is to prevent this heavenly country from becoming

an arena of gladiators." Jefferson would prefer war to disunion. "Much as I abhor war, and view it as the greatest scourge of mankind, and anxiously as I wish to keep out of the broils of Europe," he continued, "I would yet go with my brethren into these rather than separate from them. But I hope we may still keep clear of them, notwithstanding our present thraldom, and that time may be given us to reflect on the awful crisis we have passed through, and to find some means of shielding ourselves in future from foreign influence, commercial, political, or in whatever other form it may be attempted." Jefferson concluded by endorsing the wish of the revolutionary diplomat Silas Deane, "that there were an ocean of fire between us and the old world." Despite this wish foreign policy and domestic politics remained intertwined.[26]

The French government interpreted John Adams's victory as a repudiation of the 1778 treaty between France and the United States, and it began to implement the threats that Adet had made during the election. The French refused to receive the new American minister in Paris, Charles Cotesworth Pinckney. In March 1797 the Directory issued a proclamation that any Americans captured serving on British vessels—normally the victims of impressments, one of the unresolved American grievances with Britain—should be hanged. Just as war seemed unavoidable between Britain and the United States in late 1793 and early 1794, now war seemed imminent and inevitable between the United States and France. Congress took steps in the spring of 1797 to prepare for war. It strengthened the regular army and approved funding for a 15,000-man "provisional army" to be raised when war was declared. It also approved the construction of three new frigates. (The six frigates approved in 1794 having been reduced to three after the British war scare had passed; in 1797 Congress approved the funding to build the remaining vessels.)[27]

Vice President Jefferson observed the build up to war with trepidation. "Peace is undoubtedly at present the first object of our nation," he wrote to Elbridge Gerry on June 21. He continued: "Interest and honor are also national considerations. But interest, duly weighed, is in favor of peace even at the expence of spoliations past and future; and honor cannot now be an object." In Jefferson's mind the British and French were equally guilty of interfering with American trade, and waging war against one of them was not the answer. "The insults and injuries committed on us by both the belligerent parties from the beginning of 1793 to this day, and still continuing by both, cannot now be wiped off by engaging in war with one of them." While Jefferson had clearly demonstrated that he did not fear waging war to protect American interests, he felt that war should be resorted to only when Americans could clearly gain from the conflict. When this was not the case, he advocated a cautious approach. During the Nootka Sound crisis he had counseled delay in the hope that the United States might be able to exploit any opportunities that might arise without going to war. In the summer of 1797 he advocated a similar policy. He wrote to Gerry, "As there is great reason to expect this is the last campaign in Europe, it would certainly be better for us to rub thro this year as we have done through the four preceding ones, and hope that on the restoration of peace we may be able to establish some plan for our foreign connections more likely to secure our peace, interest and honor in future." Far greater than the danger posed by the French was the threat to the republic posed by the internal divisions within the United States. "Our countrymen have divided themselves by such strong affections to the French and the English, that nothing will secure us internally but a divorce from both nations," Jefferson counseled. "But for this, peace is necessary. Be assured of this, my dear Sir, that if we engage in a war during our present passions and our present weakness in some quarters, that our union runs the greatest risk of not coming out of that war in the shape in which it enters it."[28]

Jefferson had written Gerry to congratulate him. President Adams had named Gerry to join a commission, along with John Marshall and Charles Cotesworth Pinckney, to travel to France to attempt to reach a negotiated settlement and avert war. (Pinckney had remained in Europe after the French refused to receive him as American minister in Paris in November 1796. Marshall and Gerry met him in The Hague, and the three diplomats traveled to Paris in October 1797.) Adams was seeking to emulate the success of his predecessor George Washington, who had dispatched John Jay to London to avert war with Britain in 1794. Although Jefferson distrusted his distant kinsman, Marshall—a prominent Federalist who was serving as attorney general when he was appointed to the diplomatic mission—he had confidence in Gerry and Pinckney. Although the Directory had refused to receive Pinckney as American

minister, Jefferson believed that he, along with Gerry, wanted to negotiate a settlement. "It gives me certain assurance," Jefferson enthused,
"that there would be a preponderance in the mission sincerely disposed
to be at peace with the French government and nation." The envoys traveled to France in autumn 1797. For the time being the pressure for war
abated.[29]

The American diplomats arrived in Paris in October 1797. Initially
the French foreign minister, Charles Maurice Talleyrand, refused to receive them. They were rebuffed repeatedly. The Americans were preparing to give up their mission and return to the United States when
they were approached by several agents, whom the Americans designated, X, Y, and Z, representing Talleyrand. The French solicited a payment of $250,000 for Talleyrand as well as a guarantee for a $12 million
loan from the United States to France as the preconditions for negotiations. The Americans refused, and the talks (which were really whispers
about the possibility of talks) collapsed.[30]

Dispatches from the envoys describing the impasse arrived in Philadelphia on March 4, 1798. Included with the account of the aborted
negotiations were copies of a pending French law that decreed that the
presence of any British goods in a neutral cargo would condemn the
vessel carrying them and that any neutral vessels that had visited British
ports would be denied entry into French ports. The French, like the
British, were denying the American assertion (compromised by the Jay
Treaty) that neutral nations should be able to trade freely and that free
ships made free goods. President Adams conveyed the French proclamation to Congress on March 5 while the main dispatches were decoded.
On March 19 he informed Congress that the diplomatic mission had
failed and urged the legislators to take steps to protect American commerce and secure the frontiers. The president revoked the prohibition
on the arming of merchant vessels that had been decreed by George
Washington.[31]

The vice president viewed these developments with concern. He
observed that while the French decree had depressed American merchants who feared that the British would take their trade, it had "excited
indignation highly in the war-party." Jefferson described Adams's message of March 19, which he believed was tantamount to a war message, as

"insane." Believing that playing for time was the only option available, he argued that Congress should impose a prohibition on arming merchant vessels and then adjourn, ostensibly so its members could consult their constituents. He hoped that if Congress adjourned the momentum for war could be stopped. He hoped that a planned French invasion of Britain would succeed and bring the European war to a close, thereby eliminating the causes of Franco-American tension. At the end of March Jefferson anxiously told Madison, "The question of war & peace depends now on a toss of cross & pile [heads or tails, from the French *pile ou face*]. If we could but gain the season, we should be saved." On April 2 he noted that opinion in Congress was fairly evenly balanced between those in favor of war and peace. "Should the debate hold many days," he wrote hopefully "we shall derive aid from the delay." Jefferson believed that the country faced its gravest crisis since the outbreak of the Revolutionary War two decades earlier. The stakes could not be higher. "The present period therefore of two or three weeks is the most eventful ever known since that of 1775," he wrote, "and will decide whether the principles established by that contest are to prevail or give way to those they subverted."[32]

President Adams submitted the X Y Z dispatches to Congress on April 3, and the press soon printed them. Jefferson claimed that there was nothing in the papers that justified going to war but feared that even his own party would yield to public pressure. Most worrying from a partisan standpoint was an exchange between the envoys and Pierre Bellamy, one of their French interlocutors. Bellamy had met the Americans on October 30, 1797. He warned them that if the negotiations collapsed the French would enjoy support in the United States. Bellamy boasted, "You ought to know that the diplomatic skill of France, and the means she possesses in your country, are sufficient to enable her, with the French party in America, to throw the blame which will attend the rupture of the negotiations on the federalists . . . and may assure yourselves this will be done."[33] Jefferson dismissed this argument as "unworthy of a great nation" but worried that it would "excite disgust & indignation in Americans generally, and alienation from the republicans particularly." Jefferson feared that Republicans, with their loyalty in question, would support the march to war. He had already seen the opposition in Congress to wartime measure begin to crumble. "Such is their effect on the minds of wavering characters," he lamented, "that I fear to wipe of imputation of being French partisans, they will go over to the war-measures so furiously pushed by the other party." He concluded, "Such a shock on the republican mind has never been seen since our independence."[34]

Jefferson's fears were realized. Public outrage at the perceived insult to American honor, and Republican disloyalty, was so potent that Congress adopted a series of measures to prepare for war. Congress approved funding to build three additional frigates and to purchase twelve smaller vessels to convoy American merchantmen across the Atlantic. In addition, Congress appropriated a further $800,000 to procure cannon, small arms, and munitions. On April 30 President Adams signed a bill creating the Department of the Navy. In May the House of Representatives gave final approval to a bill authorizing funding to raise a provisional army of 10,000 men, which could be called out with a declaration of war or a foreign invasion of the United States.[35]

In summer 1798 France and the United States began a maritime war against each other's commerce. The conflict was prosecuted mainly in the Caribbean and off the coast the United States. Hundreds of French privateers operating out of the West Indies attacked American shipping. The French captured dozens of American merchantmen. Within two months the port of Philadelphia alone had lost more than $500,000 of shipping and cargo. Over the course of the next several years the French seized more than 800 American merchant vessels. During the summer of 1798 the frigates *Constitution, United States,* and *Constellation* were launched, and hundreds of American privateers were commissioned. The American navy, confined to attacking armed vessels only, captured eight French ships.[36] The coastal waters of the United States were cleared by 1799, and the Americans began to apply pressure on the French in the West Indies. The conflict, which came to be known as "the Quasi-War" awaited only a formal declaration of war from Congress before escalating into a more general conflict—possibly involving fighting in the borderlands of the United States. (By 1798 Spain had become an ally of France, and it was feared the Floridas and Louisiana might be used to attack the United States.)[37]

Jefferson observed the march to war with exasperation but could do little to stop it. His closest political ally, James Madison, was no longer in Congress, and Jefferson was a member of a Federalist administration seemingly bent on war. (President Adams had retained Washington's cabinet, which acted as though it were answerable to Alexander Hamilton, as the leader of their party, rather than to Adams as the president.)[38] Jefferson did not accept that there was a need for war with France, nor did he think France posed much a danger to the United States; rather, the gravest danger in 1798 came from within. Indeed, Jefferson believed that the United States faced its gravest threat since the War of Independence. In the summer of 1798, in response to the threat of war, Congress adopted measures that in Jefferson's view had the potential to destroy the United States. In response Jefferson formulated a radical and controversial constitutional proposal to preserve the republic.

In late April, as Congress appropriated funding to expand the navy and raise an army, it also began to consider legislation to curtail civil liberties in the United States. In a letter to Madison describing the preparations for war, Jefferson noted ominously, "One of the war-party in a fit of unguarded passion declared some time ago they would pass a citizen bill, an alien bill, & a sedition bill." In June and July Federalists in Congress passed a series of measures to prepare for war and to curb the power of the Republicans. These were the Naturalization Act, which extended the residency period required for citizenship from five to fourteen years; the Act Concerning Aliens, which allowed for the deportation of immigrants at the president's order in peacetime; the Act Respecting Enemy Aliens, which gave the president power to imprison and deport enemy nationals during wartime; and an Act for the Punishment of Certain Crimes (known as the Sedition Act), which called for fines and imprisonment for writing, speaking, or publishing anything of "a false, scandalous and malicious" nature against the government or its officers.[39]

For congressional Federalists the Alien and Sedition Acts were necessary to prepare the United States for war. They worried that immigrants to the United States might constitute a dangerous fifth column determined to subvert the republic. (Federalist concern about Republican-leaning Irish and French immigrants was mirrored by Jefferson's fear that British merchants pretending to be loyal Americans were the drivers of Federalist foreign policy.) Moreover, since 1793 the boundary between domestic politics and foreign policy had been blurred to such an extent that it was invisible by 1798. As the *Philadelphia Gazette* reported on April 6 after the publication of the X Y Z dispatches, the American envoys had been told "that the French had a strong party in America, warmly attached to their cause. That it would be impossible for the United States, to carry on a war, because the people were divided, and were unwilling to fight the French."[40] When Federalists took measures that would gain them an electoral advantage—immigrants tended to support the Republicans, the newspaper editors arrested under the Sedition Act were Republicans—they could, with some justification, claim that they did so in name of national security. Nonetheless, underlying the measures was intolerance, xenophobia, and a desire to gain political advantage. In the perfervid political cultures of the 1790s every political dispute seemed to have momentous implications. Given that the question at issue in the summer of 1798 was whether the United States would go to war with France, it is, perhaps, unsurprising that the Federalists reacted as they did to counter what they saw as the threat posed by their internal and external enemies. High Federalists believed that the Alien and Sedition Acts were as necessary to prepare for war as expanding the navy or raising the provisional army.

For the vice president the Alien and Sedition Acts represented a serious threat to the United States. One of the reasons the prolonged international crises of the 1790s were so dangerous was that they could force Americans to give up their liberty in exchange for security. One of the lessons of history, Jefferson believed, was that republics more often collapsed from within than were conquered from without. He believed that Americans were overreacting to the X Y Z affair and that war with France was unnecessary. He resorted to a medical metaphor to describe the national mood. "The passions are boiling over," he wrote in early May, "and one who keeps himself cool and clear of the contagion, is so far [behind?] the point of ordinary conversation that he finds himself insulated in every society. however the fever will not last." He lamented

the cost of the military preparations (although as president he would
have reason to be grateful for the naval build-up). He believed that when
Americans were confronted by the taxes necessary to pay for the war
they would come to their senses. "War, landtax, & stamp act, are [pallia]-
tives which must calm its ardor. They will bring on reflection, and that
with information is all which our countrymen need to bring themselves
and their affairs to rights."[41] The greatest danger was neither war nor
taxation but the loss of liberty resulting from the Alien and Sedition
Acts. The Federalists were consolidating power in the central government at the expense of the American people. History taught that when
governments acquired power they were loath to give it up. This, not
French aggression, was the real crisis of 1798 as far as Jefferson was concerned.

Jefferson was not alone. In May, John Taylor of Caroline, a leading
Virginia Republican, wrote to the vice president. Taylor made a connection between the international crisis and "our domestic politicks." Taylor continued, "I see nothing to change the opinions which have long
obtruded themselves upon my mind—namely—that the southern states
must lose their capital and commerce—and that America is destined to
war—standing armies—and oppressive taxation, by which the power of
the few here, as in other countries, will be matured into an irresistible
scourge of human happiness."[42] While Jefferson agreed with Taylor's
assessment of the problem—that a costly, unnecessary war would lead to
taxation and a loss of liberty—he feared the sectionalism implicit in Taylor's analysis. Taylor, who was a leading spokesman for southern Republicanism, implied that the southern states might be better off leaving the
union to safeguard their liberty. For Jefferson disunion was as great a
threat to the American republic as Federalist assault on liberty. In both
cases the result would be the collapse of the United States.

Jefferson took the threat of disunion so seriously that he wrote a
lengthy response to Taylor's letter. In it he began to articulate a position
in response to the multiple crises of 1798. He conceded that there was a
regional dynamic to the current political crisis: "It is true that we are
compleatly under the saddle of Massachusets & Connecticut, and that
they ride us very hard, cruelly insulting our feelings as well as exhaust-
ing our strength and substance. Their natural friends, the three other

Eastern states, join them from a sort of family pride, and they have the art to divide certain other parts of the Union, so as to make use of them to govern the whole." Jefferson continued, acknowledging the historical precedents for such behavior. "It is the old practice of despots to use a part of the people to keep the rest in order. And those who have once got an ascendancy, and possessed themselves of all the resources of the nation, their revenues and offices, have immense means for retaining their advantages." Despite this gloomy assessment, Jefferson offered hope. The principles of 1776 had not been so soon forgotten. New England's was not the ancient despotism of a European monarchy. He placed his faith in the American people.

> The body of our countrymen is substantially republican through every part of the union. It was the irresistable influence & popularity of Genl. Washington played off by the cunning of Hamilton which turned the government over to antirepublican hands, or turned the republican members chosen by the people into anti-republicans. He delivered it over to his successor in this state, and very untoward events since, improved with great artifice, have produced on the public mind the impression we see. But still, I repeat it, this is not the natural state. Time alone would bring round an order of things more correspondent to the sentiments of our constituents.

Jefferson contended that any number of factors might return Americans to their "natural state" as republicans—a successful French invasion of Britain, Federalist subversion of the Constitution, or the realization of the human and financial cost of war. Faced with a serious threat to liberty, Jefferson placed his faith in the American people to protect their own liberties.[43]

In a republic, Jefferson explained, there would be differences of opinion. He wrote, "In every free & deliberating society, there must from the nature of man be opposite parties, & violent dissensions & discords; and one of these for the most part must prevail over the other for a longer or shorter time." Disunion was not the answer to such domination, however. "If on a temporary superiority of the one party, the other is to resort to a scission of the union, no federal government can ever exist. If to rid ourselves of the present rule of Massachusets & Connecticut, we break the union, will the evil stop there? Suppose the N. England states alone cut off, will our natures be changed?" If New England left the union, then the southern states would fall out with Pennsylvania. If a southern confederacy were created, then divisions would emerge between Virginia and North Carolina. "Seeing that we must have somebody to quarrel with," Jefferson continued, "I had rather keep our New-England associates for that purpose, than to see our bickerings transferred to others." Rather than embrace disunion, Republicans should temporize, "A little patience and we shall see the reign of witches pass over, their spells dissolve, and the people recovering their true sight, restore their government to its true principles." In the meantime the United States faced the serious prospect of unnecessary war, oppression, and public debt.[44]

By the summer of 1798 the United States was in a perilous state. The unstable international situation had brought the nation to the brink of war with its most important historic ally. The impending war was unnecessary in Jefferson's mind, and the domestic consequences of the crisis with France were more serious still. The Federalist threat to the rights of Americans via the Alien and Sedition Acts was profound. Republicans saw such tyrannical steps as the inevitable consequence of Hamilton's efforts to consolidate power in the federal government. While it was understandable that some Republicans, such as John Taylor, might find solace at the prospect of leaving the union, disunion was no solution as it would lead, inevitably, to the fragmentation of the union.

As vice president, Jefferson was relatively powerless to address the crisis. He cautioned against rash action, either war or disunion, and placed his faith in the inherent republicanism of the American people. He believed that, eventually, they would recognize the danger to their liberties and act to protect them. As he counseled Taylor, "We must have patience, till luck turns, & then we shall have an opportunity of winning back the *principles* we have lost. For this is a game where principles are the stake."[45] The Alien and Sedition Acts raised an important political and constitutional question for Jefferson: What recourse did citizens have when the federal government threatened their liberties and violated the Constitution? He recognized that in times of crisis political leaders sometimes had to move beyond the letter of the Constitution, but such actions should occur only in exceptional circumstances, they must of be limited duration, and ex post facto legislative approval should be sought. Such was not the case in 1798. In adopting the Alien and Sedition Acts the Congress had taken the initiative and created laws that violated the Constitution in anticipation of an unnecessary foreign war. It was not so much a temporary response to a crisis that threatened the government as a crisis created by the government. During the summer of 1798 Jefferson developed his own response to the crisis. He proposed that the states that formed the union should protect their citizens' liberties when the federal government threatened them.

The record is unclear as to precisely when Jefferson began to draft a set of resolutions in response to the Alien and Sedition Acts. Jefferson's nine lengthy resolutions defined the constitutional relationship between the states and the federal government. Jefferson began with the premise that the Constitution was a "compact" between the individual states that "constituted a general government for special purposes, delegated to that government certain definite powers, reserving, each state to itself, the residuary mass of right to their own self-government; and that whensoever the General government assumes undelegated powers, it's acts are unauthoritative, void, & of no force." It was for the individual states, not the federal government, to determine the extent of the federal government's powers. If the federal government overstepped its authority, the individual states could take steps to preserve their liberties. They should first do so by means allowed by the Constitution. "In cases of an abuse of the delegated powers," Jefferson wrote, "the members of the general government being chosen by the people, a change by the people would be the constitutional remedy." However, when a constitutional remedy, presumably election, was not available, the states might resort to more extreme measures. Jefferson continued, "Where powers are assumed which have not been delegated a nullification of the act is the rightful remedy: that every state has a natural right, in cases not within the compact . . . to nullify of their own authority all assumptions of power by others within their limits: that without this right, they would be under the dominion, absolute and unlimited, of whosoever might exercise this right of judgment for them." By the autumn of 1798 Jefferson had articulated the view that the individual states might nullify federal legislation in order to protect the liberty of their citizens.[46]

Jefferson originally intended that his resolutions should be submitted to the Virginia assembly. However, James Madison had drafted a different set of resolutions for the Virginians. These reserved to the states the right to review the constitutionality of federal actions but not to nullify unconstitutional acts.[47] Rather, the state could protest against the relevant legislation in concert with other states. Jefferson submitted his resolutions to the Kentucky legislature via allies in the state, notably John Breckinridge. The Alien and Sedition Acts were unpopular in Kentucky, which was a hotbed of Republicanism, and Jefferson's resolutions were received favorably. On November 10, 1798, the Kentucky House of Representatives adopted a slightly modified version of Jefferson's resolutions—notably omitting reference to nullification but reserving to the states the right to judge the constitutionality of federal legislation.[48]

Scholars, understandably, have focused their attentions on the constitutional implications of the Kentucky Resolutions. Given that the doctrine of nullification came to be closely linked with the protection of slavery, states' rights, and ultimately secession in the decades before the Civil War, Jefferson's reputation was damaged by his association with the doctrine.[49] Although it may seem unfair to hold Jefferson accountable for events which took place after his death, the Kentucky Resolutions have raised questions about Jefferson's constitutional thinking. Throughout the 1790s Jefferson had advocated "strict construction" as the best perspective to adopt in interpreting the federal Constitution. Essentially, if the Constitution did not explicitly allow an action, it could not be taken by the federal government. This was certainly the position that Jefferson took with respect to Hamilton's fiscal program. In the Kentucky Resolutions Jefferson appears to be taking strict construction to its logical conclusion.[50]

While the constitutional aspects of the Kentucky Resolutions are important—the resolves offered a new interpretation of the relationship between the states and the federal government—in order to fully appreciate their significance we need to consider the resolutions as part of Jefferson's response to the crisis of 1798. As Jefferson had told John Taylor early in the summer, the greatest danger arising from the war crisis was the possibility that the American union would collapse. He sought to forestall this in the belief that the American people would eventually come to their senses. As Jefferson wrote to Taylor in late November, after Kentucky had adopted his resolutions, "There is a most respectable part of our state who have been enveloped in the X.Y.Z. delusion, and who destroy our unanimity for the present moment. This disease of the imagination will pass over, because the patients are essentially republican. Indeed the Doctor is now on his way to cure it, in the guise of a tax-gatherer. But give time for the medicine to work." He sought to create the time and space for the disease to pass. Under such circumstances the states were the bulwark of liberty. He wrote, "Our state governments are the *very best in the world* without exception or comparison, our general government has, in the rapid course of 9 or 10 years, become more arbitrary, and has swallowed more of the public liberty than even that of England." The protection of liberty and the preservation of the republic were Jefferson's desiderata. Faced with a tyrannical federal government, Jefferson believed that the states were best placed to protect liberty until the American people could change the federal government.[51]

Jefferson had demonstrated throughout his long public career that his main objective was to preserve liberty and protect the republic. He was pragmatic about the means he employed to achieve these ends. He countenanced war, opportunistic alliances, and negotiation in different circumstances to protect the vital interests of the American republic. During the 1790s he came to believe that the Federalists had made a strategic error in foreign policy by aligning the United States with Britain. This resulted in an unnecessary and avoidable conflict with France, which was a natural ally of the United States. More serious still was the Federalist attempt to aggrandize power during the crisis of 1798 via the Alien and Sedition Acts. In response to the actions of the Federalists Jefferson resorted to the states to judge and, if necessary, nullify federal law. He advocated this role for the states in the interest of protecting liberty and preserving the republic from disunion. Those who seek consistency in Jefferson's actions will be frustrated. He was pragmatic in his approach to statecraft. His end, republican liberty, was consistent, but the means he employed to achieve it varied according to circumstance.

The Virginia and Kentucky Resolutions did not have the effect that Jefferson had hoped for. Of the sixteen states in the union in 1798, none joined Virginia and Kentucky in condemning the Alien and Sedition Acts. Indeed, ten states explicitly rejected the resolutions. The crisis of 1798 had revealed how vulnerable the republic was in a world of warring empires. For Jefferson, the costly military buildup and the curtailment of civil liberties wrought by the Alien and Sedition Acts threatened liberty in the United States and were, potentially, existential threats to the United States as potent as foreign invasion. From his perch as vice president Jefferson could monitor the threat but could do little to counter it. Rather, he placed his faith in the state governments and the "essentially republican" American people in the belief that they would come to their senses and reclaim their liberty.

Almost a year after drafting the Kentucky Resolutions, Jefferson became frustrated with his countrymen. The costly war at sea continued; Republican newspaper editors had been indicted, fined, and jailed under the Sedition Act; and the possibility of a declaration of war persisted. The vice president wrote to James Madison to express his concern at the lack of progress. He wanted Virginia and Kentucky to demand that the other states act in defense of liberty while at the same time expressing in "affectionate & conciliatory language our warm attachment to union with our sister-states, and to the instrument & principles by which we are united." Still, he worried that "passions & delusions" persisted in the federal government, and he feared that the "good sense of the American people and their attachment to those rights which we are now vindicating" might not manifest itself in time to preserve those rights. Faced with such a loss of liberty Jefferson was willing to countenance the breakup of the union. If Americans could not protect "the true principles of our federal compact," it would be necessary "to sever ourselves from that union we so much value, rather than give up the rights of self government which we have reserved, & in which alone we see liberty, safety & happiness."[52] Forced to choose between liberty and union,

Jefferson would choose liberty. His intention in arguing in favor of nullification was to preserve, not undermine, the union. By 1799 he began doubt whether it was possible to preserve both union and liberty.

Fortunately for Jefferson, he never had to make this choice. John Adams, whose support for the Alien and Sedition Acts was lukewarm at best, resisted pressure from his cabinet and from the public and refused to ask Congress for a formal declaration of war. In 1801 the United States and France negotiated a settlement that proved temporary once Napoleon seized power as first consul and then emperor. The Virginia and Kentucky Resolutions made little impact as constitutional statements, but they were powerful political statements. Their adoption and circulation constituted the beginning of the 1800 presidential campaign, when Jefferson again ran against Adams. In 1800 the main issues were international relations and the Alien and Sedition Acts—the domestic measures arising from Federalist foreign policy. Jefferson's faith in the American people was vindicated when he won the election. After spending the better part of a decade implementing or critiquing the policies of others, he would now have the power to implement his own policy.

Five

"Chastise Their Insolence"

Shortly before noon on March 4, 1801, Thomas Jefferson left Conrad and McMunn's boardinghouse on New Jersey Avenue in Washington, DC, and walked to the Capitol to be sworn in as the third president of the United States. Jefferson, a month shy of his fifty-eighth birthday, was the first president to take the oath in the new capital. Washington was then often referred to as the Federal City, though the term was more an aspiration than a description. Barely three thousand people lived in the fledgling capital, a vast expanse carved out of the wilderness along the Virginia and Maryland border and dotted with boardinghouses and incomplete public buildings. The most prominent structures were the president's house at one end of Pennsylvania Avenue and the unfinished Capitol at the other. The avenue in between was a muddy thoroughfare pocked with tree stumps.

Jefferson, dressed as "a plain citizen, without any distinctive badge of office," proceeded on foot through the streets to the Capitol, accompanied by militia officers from Alexandria, Virginia, as well as a group of friends and political allies. At the Capitol he was welcomed with an artillery salute. Jefferson entered the Senate chamber, the largest public room in the city, and was met by the members of Congress. Margaret Bayard Smith, the doyenne of Washington society (such as it was), described the scene: "The Senate chamber was so crowded that I believe not another creature could enter. On one side of the house the Senate sat, the other was resigned by the representatives to the ladies. The roof is arched, the room half circle, every inch of ground was occupied. . . . It has been conjectured by several gentlemen whom I've asked, that there were near a thousand persons within the walls." The Philadelphia *Aurora* supplied a more precise figure, reporting that there 1,140 people in the chamber, including 154 women.[1]

In the Senate chamber Jefferson was greeted by two political rivals: Aaron Burr, the newly inaugurated vice president, and John Marshall, the chief justice of the United States, who would administer the presidential oath to his fellow Virginian. The outgoing president, John Adams, had already departed for his home in Massachusetts. Before taking the presidential oath Jefferson delivered his inaugural address. Jefferson, who was not an effective public speaker, delivered the speech "in so low a tone that few heard it." Samuel Harrison Smith, Margaret Bayard Smith's husband and the publisher of the *National Intelligencer,* was aware that the significance of the address lay in its content not in its delivery. He published the text, which was circulated throughout the United States. His wife believed that the address contained, "principles the most correct, sentiments the most liberal, and wishes the most benevolent, conveyed in the most appropriate and elegant language and in a manner mild as it was firm." Bayard Smith believed that Jefferson's address would allay the concerns of those anxious about his election. "If doubts of the integrity and talents of Mr. Jefferson ever existed in the minds of any one, methinks this address must forever eradicate them."[2]

Students of Jefferson's first inaugural often stress the conciliatory note that the new president struck after the divisive election of 1800, which witnessed the defeat of the Federalists and also a rancorous struggle among the Republicans after Jefferson and Burr received the same number of votes in the Electoral College. For several weeks the outcome of the election was uncertain. The outgoing House of Representatives required thirty-five ballots in February 1801 before it elected Jefferson president and named Burr as vice president.[3] Reflecting on the electoral contest, Jefferson called on Americans to "unite with one heart and one mind, let us restore to social intercourse that harmony and without which liberty, and even life itself, are but dreary things." He reminded his fellow citizens "that though the will of the majority is in all cases to prevail, that will to be rightful, must be reasonable; that the minority possess their equal rights, which equal laws must protect, and to violate would be oppression." In the most memorable phrase in the address Jefferson proclaimed: "We have called by different names brethren of the same principles. We are all republicans: we are all federalists." He then delineated what he called "our own federal and republican principles." These included:

> Equal and exact justice to all men, of whatever state or persuasion, religious or political:—peace, commerce, and honest friendship with all nations, entangling alliances with none; the support of the State governments in all their rights, as the most competent administrations for our domestic concerns and the surest bulwarks against anti-republican tendencies:—the preservation of the General Government in its whole constitutional vigor, as the sheet anchor of our peace at home and safety abroad:—a jealous care of the right of election by the people—a mild and safe corrective of abuses which are lopped by the sword of revolution where peaceable remedies are unprovided:— absolute acquiescence in the decisions of the majority, the vital principle of republics, from which is no appeal but to force, the vital principle and immediate parent of despotism:—a well disciplined militia, our best reliance in peace and for the first moments of war, till regulars may relieve them; the supremacy of the civil over the military authority:—economy in the public expense, that labor may be lightly burthened:—the honest payment of our debts and sacred preservation of the public faith; encouragement of agriculture, and of commerce as its handmaid; the diffusion of information and arraignment of all abuses at the bar of public reason:—freedom of religion; freedom of the press, and freedom of person under the protection of the Habeas Corpus, and trial by juries impartially selected.[4]

Here was a concise summary Jefferson's republican vision.

Jefferson addressed skeptics, at home and abroad, who felt that the American republic was too weak to survive:

I know indeed that some honest men fear that a republican government cannot be strong; that this government is not strong enough. But would the honest patriot, in the full tide of successful experiment, abandon a government which has so far kept us free and firm, on the theoretic and visionary fear, that this government, the world's best hope, may, by possibility, want energy to preserve itself? I trust not. I believe this, on the contrary, the strongest government on earth. I believe it the only one, where every man, at the call of the law, would fly to the standard of the law, and would meet invasions of the public order as his own personal concern.[5]

Jefferson expressed faith in the strength of the citizenry, a citizenry that would rise in arms to defend liberty. His prior experience belied the optimism that he expressed in his inaugural address. In 1781, Virginia's republican citizens had been found wanting during the British invasion. During his negotiations with the Barbary States Jefferson experienced firsthand the weakness of the early republic. The United States had been unable to protect its trade or its citizens in the Mediterranean. The adoption of the Constitution may have redressed that weakness, but the Quasi-War demonstrated that the new government could abuse its power and bring the nation to the brink of an unnecessary war, while threatening the liberties of its citizens. In his inaugural address Jefferson acknowledged that there were Americans who did not share his republican vision. "If there be any among us who would wish to dissolve this Union, or to change its republican form," he declared, "let them stand undisturbed as monuments of the safety with which error of opinion may be tolerated, where reason is left free to combat it."[6] In a rebuke to his Federalist predecessor, who resorted to draconian laws to curb individual liberties, Jefferson counselled toleration for dissenters in the belief that the force of reason would compel them to change their minds.

Jefferson made only passing reference to the international situation in his inaugural address. He described the place of the United States in the North Atlantic state system: "A rising nation, spread over a wide and fruitful land, traversing all the seas with the rich productions of their industry, engaged in commerce with nations who feel power and forget right," a reference to Britain. He noted that the United States was "kindly separated by nature and a wide ocean from the exterminating havoc of one quarter of the globe" and held it as a fundamental principle that the United States should maintain "peace, commerce, and honest friendship with all nations, entangling alliances with none." Free commerce along with extensive land was essential to realizing the republican vision Jefferson articulated (in stirring rhetoric and muted tones) in his first inaugural. Jefferson recognized that international peace and friendship were illusory in 1801. Most of the major and minor European powers were engaged in wars arising from the French Revolution and the subsequent rise to power of Napoleon Bonaparte. During his presidency Jefferson sought to maintain American neutrality and promote the right of the United States to trade freely around the world. Almost immediately after he took the presidential oath Jefferson was confronted by an international challenge from a familiar source: Tripoli declared war on the United States in an effort to negotiate a favorable and lucrative peace treaty. In response, Jefferson, who had long experience with the ways of Barbary diplomacy, opted to wage war in North Africa.

During the 1790s the administrations of George Washington and John Adams pursued a two-track strategy with respect to the Barbary States. The United States undertook to strengthen its navy in order to provide a credible military deterrent to the North Africans and at the same time entered into negotiations with each of the Barbary powers. By the end of the decade the United States had concluded costly treaties with each of the Barbary States.

After Algiers concluded a peace treaty with Portugal in October 1793, its navy was free to prey on American shipping. By the end of November the Algerians had seized eleven American vessels, capturing 105 prisoners who joined the 15 captives still in Algerian custody. In the face of "the depredations committed by the Algerine corsairs on the commerce of the United States," Congress authorized the funding to build four forty-four-gun frigates and two additional vessels mounting thirty-six guns on March 27, 1794. After a preliminary agreement was reached with the Algerians, Congress cut the number of ships by half (two forty-four-gun frigates and one of thirty-six guns). In 1797 the frigates *United States, Constitution,* and *Constellation* were completed and entered American service. The cost of building, arming, and maintaining the vessels was more than $2.5 million.[7]

At the same time that the United States pursued a naval buildup it sought to reach a diplomatic solution to the Barbary problem and opened negotiations with Algiers. The United States and Algiers agreed a peace treaty in 1795, eventually ratified by the Senate in 1796, under the terms of which the Americans agreed to ransom the captives held in Algiers, to pay annual tribute, and to supply the Algerians with a frigate and naval stores. The total cost of the agreement was just under $1 million. After reaching the agreement with Algiers, the United States concluded agreements with Tripoli in late 1796 and Tunis in August 1797. Under their terms the United States agreed to make gifts, often in the form of a combination of cash and naval supplies. As a consequence of the agreements the United States established consular offices in each of the Barbary States to maintain regular diplomatic relations.[8]

The Barbary treaties came at a considerable cost. In monetary terms, the treaties with the Barbary States cost around $1.25 million, slightly more than 20 percent of the federal budget (to which might be added the cost of the naval expansion).[9] Perhaps more significant, the United States had conformed to the European practice of paying tribute to protect its trade and its mariners. Since that tribute partially took the form of ships, arms, and naval stores, the Americans found themselves in the humiliating position of supplying the North Africans with the means to attack their shipping. When George Washington saw the treaty with Algiers he found the provision to supply the dey with arms "disagreeable" but conceded that "there appeared to be no other alternative but to comply, or submit to the depredations of the Barbary Corsairs on our Citizens and Commerce."[10] Washington's successor, John Adams, had been advocating a similarly pragmatic view since the mid-1780s when he and Jefferson first sought to tackle the Barbary question as diplomats in Europe. History showed that the treaties completed by the Federalists were unlikely to offer a permanent solution to the threat the Barbary States posed to American commerce. When there was a change of ruler in Tunis, Algiers, Tripoli, or Morocco, the new ruler would likely demand a renegotiation of treaties and further payment. Failure to comply with the terms of existing treaties—the United States was frequently tardy in meeting its commitments—might lead to a declaration of war, resulting in more expensive peace negotiations.

After the completion of the Algerian treaty, Tripoli emerged as the foremost threat in the Mediterranean. The pasha of Tripoli, Yusuf Karamanli, had come to power in 1795 after murdering his older brother, Hassan, and exiling another brother, Hamet. Yusuf attempted to strengthen the Tripolitan position in maritime diplomacy by enlarging the Tripolitan navy and restoring the sultanate's coastal fortifications. He then sought to renegotiate existing diplomatic agreements. Spain, France, and Venice provided naval stores and ships and paid additional tribute. Yusuf ordered his navy to attack the shipping of states—such as Sweden, Denmark, Naples, and the Netherlands—that resisted his entreaties. The Tripolitans captured two American vessels, prompting negotiations that culminated in an agreement between the United States and Tripoli in November 1796. Under the terms of the agreement the United States agreed to pay more than $56,000 in cash, naval stores, and consular gifts. The agreement did not call for annual tribute.[11]

Pasha Yusuf Karamanli quickly became dissatisfied with the 1796 Tripolitan-American treaty. When the new American consul, James L. Cathcart, arrived in Tripoli in April 1799, Karamanli refused to receive him.[12] The pasha was upset that the gifts he received were a small fraction of the nearly $1 million that the United States had agreed to pay Algiers, and that the United States did not pay him annual tribute. Although Cathcart placated the pasha with enhanced gifts and cash in lieu of promised naval stores, he could not keep him satisfied for long. Periodically, Yusuf or his officers summoned Cathcart to demand increased tribute. In April 1800, the pasha told Cathcart "that he had concluded peace with the United States for much less than he had received from other nations, and that he knew his friends by what he received from them."[13] A few weeks later Cathcart reported that Yusuf had called together the consuls in Tripoli and declared "that he never made reprisals on any nation, or declared war, but in consequence of their promises not being fulfilled, or for want of due respect being shown him; that he conceived himself entitled to the same respect that was shown to the

Bashaws of Algiers and Tunis, but that some nations gave more to the officers in each of those regencies than they had given to him for their peace." Cathcart believed this comment, while delivered to all the consuls, was directed at the United States. Yusuf found it especially galling that the Americans had negotiated the agreement with Tripoli through the good offices of the Algerians. Under its terms, the dey of Algiers guaranteed the treaty and would adjudicate disputes between the signatories. He complained to the Cathcart that the United States acted "as if they had done every thing against their will . . . they solicited the intereference of the Dey of Algiers in consequence of which I concluded a peace with them for almost nothing in comparison to what I had received from other nations."

On May 6, 1800, Cathcart paid his compliments to the pasha at a public festival. "He treated me with great politeness," the consul reported, "but I could easily discern that it was against his inclination. There was something in his countenance that indicated his smiles were not sincere and ought not to be depended on." Several days later one of Yusuf's ministers informed Cathcart that Yusuf would write directly to President Adams because he suspected Cathcart did not treat his concerns seriously. On May 25, Yusuf wrote directly to the president beseeching him to back American professions of friendship with money. We "wish," he wrote, "that these your expressions were followed by deeds and not by empty words." Cathcart believed that the letter to Adams would buy some time but that "the only conclusion which can be drawn from the Bashaw's proceedings is that he wants a present; and if he does not get one, he will forge pretences to commit depredations, on the property of our fellow citizens."[14]

Yusuf Karamanli's patience had been exhausted by autumn 1800. On September 25 the Tripolitans captured an American brig, the *Catherine,* out of New York. The Tripolitans held the *Catherine* and her crew until October 15. After he released the *Catherine,* Yusuf received Cathcart and informed him that he must have "a sum of money" from the United States. On October 22 Yusuf announced that he would declare war on the United States within six months unless his demands—$250,000 plus $20,000 in annual tribute—were met.[15] Relations between Tripoli and the United States deteriorated during spring 1801. As Washington was gripped by the drama arising from the deadlocked election of 1800, Yusuf Karamanli ordered his fleet to prepare to wage war against American commerce. William Eaton, the American consul in Tunis, reported in April, "The Bashaw's corsaires are . . . fitting out against Americans." On May 14 Yusuf formally declared war on the United States by chopping down the flagstaff outside of the American consulate in Tripoli.[16]

The newly inaugurated president entered office with a clear idea of how to address the Barbary problem. As American minister to France, Jefferson had concluded that the use of force rather than the payment of tribute was necessary to rebuff permanently the threat posed by the Barbary States. As president, Jefferson returned to the use of force to protect American commerce in the Mediterranean. On March 21 the attorney general, Levi Lincoln, reported, "It is not improbable that a part of our naval force may be speedily sent into the Mediterranean to guard against exigenc[i]es or by a demonstration of our power to reduce the capricious Sovereigns of Barbary to a sense of justice, thro' the medium of their fears"[17] American diplomats in the region supported the idea of bolstering the American naval presence in the Mediterranean. In mid-April the American minister in Madrid, David Humphreys, opined, "The circumstances seem more than at any former time to reduce us to the alternative of having a few frigates and light armed vessels in the Mediterranean, or of relinquishing our Trade in it." William Willis, the consul in Barcelona, believed that if the United States were to protect its commerce in the Mediterranean, it should "keep a small naval force in these seas" and "discharge with punctuality all the engagements entered into with them & at times to make them presents," thus denying the Barbary States a reason to wage war against American commerce. Richard O'Brien, longtime prisoner and now American consul at Algiers, was less optimistic. Two days before Yusuf struck down the American flag at Tripoli, the old Barbary hand reported that the pasha was bent on war, noting that the United States was in arrears in supplying Algiers with tribute and naval stores and had not provided its consuls on the Barbary Coast with the money necessary for them to maintain a credible diplomatic presence. "War Sir," he reported to the new secretary of state, James Madison, "will shortly be the result of detention and Neglect."[18]

On May 15 Jefferson called a cabinet meeting to discuss the appropriate response to the Barbary crisis. He had decided that the United States should make its overdue treaty payments to the rulers of Algiers and Tunis. The cabinet unanimously endorsed sending a naval squadron to the Mediterranean to deal with Tripoli.[19] Jefferson and the cabinet made a prospective decision in anticipation of a Tripolitan declaration of war. At Jefferson's behest the cabinet officers took a series of actions in preparation for war. On May 20 Acting Secretary of the Navy Samuel Smith ordered Captain Richard Dale to take a small squadron—the frigates *President, Philadelphia,* and *Essex* and the schooner *Enterprize*—to the Mediterranean. If Dale learned that the United States was at war with the any of the Barbary States when he arrived in the Mediterranean, Smith ordered him to "distribute your force in such manner, such, as your judgment shall direct, so as best to protect our commerce & chastise their insolence—by sinking, burning or destroying their ships & Vessels wherever you shall find them." More specifically, Smith ordered Dale to blockade Tripoli and to convoy American merchantmen in the Mediterranean—a tall order for four vessels.[20] Secretary of State Madison wrote to American diplomats in Europe and the Mediterranean, alerting them to the arrival of Dale's squadron and the likelihood of war with Tripoli.[21] Jefferson himself wrote directly to Yusuf Karamanli, assuring him "of our constant friendship and that our desire cultivate peace & commerce with you continues firm & unabated." The president warned the pasha:

We have found it expedient to detach a squadron of observation into the Mediterranean sea, to superintend the safety of our commerce there & to exercise our seamen in nautical duties. we recommend them to your hospitality and good offices should occasion require their resorting to your harbours. we hope that their appearance will give umbrage to no power for, while we mean to rest the safety of our commerce on the resources of our own strength & bravery in every sea, we have yet given them in strict command to conduct themselves towards all friendly

powers with the most perfect respect & good order it being the
first object of our sollicitude to cherish peace & friendship with
all nations with whom it can be held on terms of equality &
reciprocity.[22]

Despite his protestations of friendship, Jefferson put Karamanli on notice. Faced with Tripoli's challenge, the new president had addressed
the military and diplomatic prerequisites for war. In early June Jefferson
wrote, "The real alternative is whether to abandon the Mediterranean,
or keep up a cruize in it." Tribute was not an option. He was "convinced
it is money thrown away, and that there is no end to the demand of these
powers, nor any security in their promises."[23] Jefferson was determined
to use force to settle the Barbary problem once and for all.

Commodore Dale's small squadron arrived at Gibraltar on June 30,
1801. Learning that Yusuf Karamanli had declared war on the United
States, Dale prevented two Tripolitan corsairs moored at Gibraltar from
putting out to sea. Dale escorted some American merchant ships and
briefly undertook to blockade Tripoli harbor.[24] The most significant
action of the year occurred off the coast of Malta when the smallest of the
American vessels, the schooner *Enterprize,* encountered a Tripolitan
corsair, *Tripoli.* The *Enterprize,* armed with twelve six-pound guns,
was commanded by Lieutenant Andrew Sterret and had a crew of ninety
men. The *Tripoli* also had a crew of ninety commanded by Rais Mohammed Rous and was armed with fourteen six-pound guns. The *Enterprize* flew British colors when it encountered the *Tripoli* at 9:00 a.m.
on August 1. Sterret asked Rais Mohammed Rous about his cruise. The
Tripolitan replied that he sought American vessels but had been frustrated by his inability to locate any. At that point Sterret struck the
Union Jack and raised the Stars and Stripes. The two vessels then engaged in a close, bloody action that lasted for three hours. Three times
the Tripolitans attempted to board the American schooner and three
times they were repulsed. Three times, also, Rais Rous struck his colors
suggesting that he intended to surrender. Each time, when the American
officers exposed themselves, the Tripolitans renewed fighting. After the
third such feint, Sterret gave the order to sink the *Tripoli.* Only when
the Tripolitans begged for mercy and sincerely surrendered did Sterret

relent. The *Tripoli* was badly damaged. Twenty of her crew had been killed and another thirty wounded. By contrast, no American sailors or marines were injured in the battle. Sterret dismasted the badly damaged *Tripoli.* A sail was jury-rigged and the corsair sent limping back to Tripoli. Pasha Karamanli had Rais Mohammed Rous paraded through the streets on a donkey, where he was subjected to public scorn, and whipped.[25]

Jefferson had taken the United States to war without consulting Congress. The preparations for the conflict had been undertaken when the legislature was not in session.[26] When the cabinet met on May 15, 1801, Jefferson had asked whether he had the constitutional authority to undertake overseas military operations without a declaration of war from Congress. Treasury Secretary Albert Gallatin asserted: "To declare war & to make war is synonimous. the Exve cannot put us in a state of war. but if we be put into that state either by decln of Congress or of the other nation, the command & direction of the public force then belongs to the Exve." Acting Secretary of the Navy Samuel Smith concurred, stating that "if a nation commences war, the Exve is bound to apply the public force to defend the country."[27] This view was consonant with Jefferson's understanding of executive power under the Constitution.

In taking military action against Tripoli without formal congressional approval, Jefferson was not seeking to subvert the Constitution. Rather, he followed the lessons he had learned as governor of Virginia during the British invasions of 1780 and 1781. He believed an executive must act decisively in a crisis. When Tripoli declared war Congress was not in session. Jefferson consulted his cabinet, which took the view that a declaration of war on the United States necessitated decisive defensive action. Jefferson formally consulted Congress at the earliest opportunity, seeking its approval for his actions and authorization for future actions. In so doing Jefferson believed that his actions were constitutional. What distinguished Jefferson from his Federalist adversaries, at least in his own mind, was his willingness to subject his decisions and actions to legislative approval after the crisis had passed. As in 1781 when Jefferson sought retrospective legislative approval for the actions he took to defend Virginia, so too in 1801, he sought congressional approval for his actions after he had taken them. In his first annual address delivered on December 8, President Jefferson formally informed Congress about developments in the Mediterranean.

> Tripoli, the least considerable of the Barbary States, had come forward with demands unfounded either in right or in compact, and had permitted itself to denounce war, on our failure to comply before a given day. The style of the demand admitted but one answer. I sent a small squadron of frigates into the Mediterranean, with assurances to that power of our sincere desire to remain in peace, but with orders to protect our commerce against the threatened attack. The measure was seasonable and salutary. The bey had already declared war in form. His cruisers were out. Two had arrived at Gibraltar. Our commerce in the Mediterranean was blockaded, and that of the Atlantic in peril. The arrival of our squadron dispelled the danger. One of the Tripolitan cruisers having fallen in with, and engaged the small schooner Enterprise, commanded by Lieutenant Sterret, which had gone as a tender to our larger vessels, was captured, after a heavy slaughter of her men, without the loss of a single one on our part. The bravery exhibited by our citizens on that element, will, I trust, be a testimony to the world that it is not the want of that virtue which makes us seek their peace, but a conscientious desire to direct the energies of our nation to the multiplication of the human race, and not to its destruction.

Jefferson observed that the steps he had taken were defensive only. He explained that Lieutenant Sterret had acted with restraint because he did not have congressional approval. "Unauthorized by the constitution, without the sanction of Congress, to go out beyond the line of defence, the vessel being disabled from committing further hostilities, was liberated with its crew." This suggested that Sterret rendered a more carefully considered constitutional judgment than the circumstances of combat at sea seem to have allowed. Nonetheless, as Jefferson interpreted the Constitution, he had the authority—and the duty—to take action to defend the United States. He asked Congress to approve more aggressive action. "The legislature will doubtless consider whether, by authorizing measures of offence, also, they will place our force on an equal footing with that of its adversaries."[28]

Congress complied with the president's wishes. On December 14, Representative Samuel Smith of Maryland, who had briefly served as acting secretary of the navy and was the brother of Robert Smith, then secretary of the navy, introduced a resolution stating "that it is expedient that the President be authorized by law, further and more effectually to protect the commerce of the United States against the Barbary Powers." Loyal Republicans William Branch Giles of Virginia and Joseph Nicholson of Maryland opposed the resolution pending further information that Jefferson had promised, and moved to table the resolution.[29] Congress returned to the issue in January. After a brief debate the House of Representatives voted in favor of a bill to grant extensive authority to Jefferson to wage war against Tripoli. The bill went to the Senate and was approved with minor amendments on February 1. On February 6, 1802, Jefferson signed the Act for the Protection of the Commerce and Seamen of the United States, against the Tripolitan Cruisers, which augmented the naval forces available for Jefferson to deploy in the Mediterranean, enabled the president to authorize naval commanders and privateers to make prizes of the ships and property of the pasha of Tripoli, and authorized enlisting seamen for two-year terms if necessary. In so doing Congress had ratified Jefferson's decisions and actions against Tripoli during the spring and summer of 1801.[30]

Jefferson needed congressional support. Despite the success of the *Enterprize,* the naval force dispatched to the Mediterranean was too small to maintain a blockade of Tripoli and to convoy American merchant vessels. Richard O'Brien wrote to James Madison from Algiers on July 22, 1801: "I am convinced that Tripoli should have Money or [cannon] Balls without delay. We want sir 3—or 6—or more of our frigates in this sea . . . We cannot therefore be too guarded in preventing The Citizens & property of the US from falling into the hands of Barbary *Villains.*" With congressional approval Jefferson reinforced the Mediterranean squadron with two frigates and an additional schooner, replacing Commodore Dale with Captain Richard V. Morris.[31]

Despite the increase in American naval power, the blockade of Tripoli was ineffective. Tripolitan corsairs evaded the blockade and threatened American merchantmen in the Mediterranean. When the Tripolitans captured the *Franklin*, a brig out of Philadelphia, in June 1802, Richard O'Brien in Algiers sought to negotiate for the release of the crew of nine men. O'Brien noted, with a cynicism born of nearly two decades' experience on the Barbary Coast as a prisoner and diplomat, "It is asserted that there are at Sea at present 6 sail of Tripoline corsairs & it is asserted that the frigates of the U.S. & those of Sweden are blockading Tripoli."[32] (The Swedes, at the time, were also at war with Tripoli.) Moreover the United States faced the danger that a more general war might ensue as the other Barbary States became restive and requested to renegotiate their treaties with the United States. By September Sweden had made peace with Tripoli, and the United States faced the challenge of maintaining the blockade of Tripoli alone. O'Brien offered a gloomy assessment of the situation:

> Relative to our peace on the present Occasion I have my fears we will not succeed . . . we have but two or Three frigates in this Sea what impression Can they make whilst during The Summer at no one time two of them were not in Sight of tripoli. Add to this They Cruised a Great distance of and neither prevented Corsairs of tripoli of going to Sea or returning and with all They talk of Blockade, Vessels of all nations went in and Came out of tripoli without any molestation. Add to this Theire Whole Valuable Countrys trade was left undisturbed.

O'Brien noted that, despite the increased American naval presence in the region, things were worse in 1802 than they had been the previous year: "But at present The affairs of tripoli is in a different train and they have greater Views. They see and know our feeble Efforts to Cruise and blockade—and that we have a great Commerce and not the means or System to protect it. That their Corsairs is augmented and that as they are at peace with portugal they Can push out of The Streights—where our Commerce has no protection or Convoy That they Stand well with all Europe Algrs. and tunis."[33]

While President Jefferson still believed that war was a more honorable and cost-effective course of action than paying tribute, he recognized that the tactic of blockading Tripoli had been ineffective. In March 1803, nearly two years after the commencement of hostilities, Jefferson wrote in exasperation, "Their system is a war of little expense to them, which must put the great nations to a greater expense than the presents which would buy it off."[34] This was precisely the argument that John Adams had made to Jefferson in 1786. Frustrated by the rising cost of the conflict and the failure of the navy to achieve tangible results, Jefferson pursued two different tracks in handling Tripoli. With unanimous cabinet support Jefferson authorized peace negotiations. On April 9, 1803, Secretary of State Madison wrote to James Cathcart, "it is thought best that you should not be tied down to a refusal of presents whether to be included in the peace, or to be made from time to time during its continuance," and authorized the consul to negotiate with Pasha Yusuf. Cathcart had fallen out of favor with the Tripolitan government and the initial negotiations were carried out by Commodore Morris in June 1803. The talks soon broke down when Yusuf demanded a $200,000 gift, far in excess of the $15,000 that Morris was authorized to spend.[35]

At the same time that the United States undertook to negotiate with Pasha Yusuf it also pursued a more aggressive military strategy. In early 1803 Jefferson asked Congress to provide him with more naval resources. With very little debate Congress approved the Act to Provide an Additional Armament for the Protection of the Seamen and Commerce of the United States. The bill authorized Jefferson to build four additional warships and appropriated $96,000 to that end. It also authorized a further $50,000 for gunboats that could more effectively patrol the Barbary Coast.[36] Captain Edward Preble was appointed as commodore of the Mediterranean squadron, which had been enlarged yet again. Preble arrived in the Mediterranean in August to replace Morris.[37] He discovered that the emperor of Morocco had authorized his navy to seize American ships. After briefly blockading the port of Tangier, Preble induced the emperor to accept the 1786 Moroccan-American treaty. Having dealt with the Moroccan problem, Preble was able to concentrate on Tripoli. With his larger squadron, which included more shallow-draft vessels, he was able to mount a more effective blockade.[38]

The need for shallow-draft vessels was brought home in dramatic fashion at the end of October. On the morning of October 31 the thirty-six-gun frigate U.S.S. *Philadelphia* commanded by Captain William Bainbridge encountered a ship while on blockade about five leagues east of Tripoli. When the unidentified vessels raised the Tripolitan flag, the *Philadelphia* gave chase. The American frigate pursued the Tripolitan for two hours until the Arab vessel moved close to shore, beyond the reach of the *Philadelphia*'s guns. Bainbridge gave the order for the *Philadelphia* to give up the chase and to head back to its station. The *Philadelphia* ran aground, stuck on rocks in twelve feet of water. The American crew labored to free the frigate while under fire from Tripolitan gunboats. After four hours without any success in floating the ship and with the number of Tripolitan gunboats increasing, Bainbridge surrendered in order to save his men. At sunset the Tripolitans boarded the *Philadelphia* and made captives of its crew of 307. The next day when the tide was high, the Tripolitans were able to refloat the *Philadelphia* and sail the frigate into the inner harbor in Tripoli.[39]

The capture of the *Philadelphia* was a grievous and embarrassing blow to the American campaign against Tripoli. Before the Jefferson administration had a chance to respond to the loss of the *Philadelphia*, Commodore Preble took the initiative in a bold effort to restore the navy's pride. On February 3, 1804, Preble ordered Lieutenant Commander Stephen Decatur to sail the U.S.S. *Intrepid* to Tripoli harbor to destroy the *Philadelphia*. The *Intrepid* was a former Tripolitan corsair that Preble had captured in December.[40] With a crew of seventy volunteers and accompanied by the U.S.S. *Syren* which was intended to provide covering fire and support for the *Intrepid*, Decatur crossed the Mediterranean from Syracuse to Tripoli. He was delayed by poor weather and did not launch his attack on the *Philadelphia* until February 16. Under the cover of darkness, and with most of its crew concealed below decks, the *Intrepid* approached the *Philadelphia*. The Americans boarded the *Philadelphia* and fought with her crew, killing twenty and driving the rest to swim ashore. The Americans set fire to the *Philadelphia*, completely destroying the frigate whose guns discharged in the heat. Decatur was the last to leave the burning deck of the former American ship. The *Intrepid* and the *Syren* returned to Syracuse without the loss of a man.[41]

The destruction of the *Philadelphia* helped to restore the navy's pride (and made a hero of Stephen Decatur). More immediately, it denied the Tripolitans the use of a state-of-the-art warship to use to attack American shipping—or that Yusuf might sell to Algiers or Tunis. When news of the raid reached the United States it helped soften the blow of the ship's capture. Nonetheless the Tripolitans still held more than three hundred American prisoners, giving Pasha Yusuf significant leverage in any future negotiations with the United States. It appeared that the war was lost and that the Jefferson administration would have to accept a costly and humiliating peace settlement in order to redeem the captives from the *Philadelphia*. American diplomats in the region underscored the weakness of the American position. At the end of December George Davis, who had recently arrived in Tunis as the new American consul there, provided a gloomy assessment of the broader regional consequences of the loss of the *Philadelphia:* "This unfortunate event has given not only the Bashaw but all of Barbary, an influence over us, which no other possible circumstance could have produced; the little National consequence we possessed with this Regency, is already materially effected by our recent misfortune."[42] From Algiers Richard O'Brien offered familiar refrain, "It must be evident to our govt. that They have but two Courses to steer Money or [cannon] Balls." Although he favored war over negotiations, O'Brien expected the Jefferson administration would negotiate and provided a detailed estimate of the cost of peace. Writing before the destruction of the *Philadelphia,* O'Brien estimated that it would cost $500,800 to redeem the ship and its crew and negotiate a peace treaty. He estimated that it would cost $282,800 to liberate the crew alone.[43] Faced with a diplomatic and humanitarian crisis—Jefferson was aware how the presence of just a dozen American captives had complicated American diplomacy in the 1780s—the president was expected to negotiate for peace despite the cost. Jefferson confounded expectations and significantly escalated the war, even undertaking to overthrow Pasha Yusuf Karamanli.

When news of the loss of the *Philadelphia* reached the United States, Jefferson again sought to augment the American presence in the

Mediterranean. The government did not receive Edward Preble's dispatches confirming the capture of the *Philadelphia* until March 1804. According to Navy Secretary Robert Smith:

> The President immediately determined to put in Commission and to send to the Mediterranean a force which would be able beyond the possibility of a doubt, to coerce the Enemy to a peace upon Terms compatible with our Honor and our Interest. A due regard to our situation with Tripoli and precautionary considerations in relation to the other Barbary Powers, demanded our forces in that quarter should be so far augmented as to leave no doubt of our compelling the existing Enemy to submit to our own terms, and of effectually checking any hostile dispositions that might be entertained towards us by any of the other Barbary Powers.

As a result, five additional frigates—the *President, Congress, Constellation, Essex,* and the *John Adams* (the *Adams* had had most of its guns removed so it could act as a transport)—were dispatched to the Mediterranean under the command of Commodore Samuel Barron (who would supersede Preble). Barron would have eleven ships—six frigates and five schooners and brigs, mounting 260 guns—under his command. This represented most of the United States Navy in 1804.[44] On March 21 Congressman Joseph Nicholson introduced a bill that called for a 2½ percent increase in customs duties, with the moneys raised to be put in a Mediterranean Fund to pay for the war. After debating whether a tax increase was the appropriate way to fund the conflict, the House of Representatives voted in favor of the bill, 98 to 0, on March 22. The bill passed the Senate on the same day, 20 to 5. In addition to raising the tax to create the Mediterranean Fund, the act authorized Jefferson to build two additional warships and as many gunboats as he deemed necessary and appropriated $1 million for the purpose.[45]

Navy Secretary Smith instructed Commodore Barron that President Jefferson expected him to "without intermission maintain during the Season in which it may be safely done, an effectual Blockade of

Tripoli, and that you will by all other means in your power annoy the Enemy so as to force him to a peace honourable to the United States." Barron was ordered to cooperate with Tobias Lear, who had replaced Richard O'Brien as consul general in Algiers and who was invested by Jefferson "with full power and authority to negociate a Treaty of Peace with the Bashaw of Tripoli, and also to adjust the terms of conciliation as may be found necessary with any of the other Barbary Powers."[46] Jefferson acted decisively to put the full military and diplomatic force of the United States behind the campaign against Tripoli.

The most vexing aspect of the Tripoli crisis was the presence of 307 American prisoners in Tripoli. The government was under pressure to ransom the prisoners. When a man named Thomas FitzSimons wrote to James Madison to enquire about the measures the government was taking to offer succor to and seek the release of the crew of the *Philadelphia,* Madison answered in a private letter—a formal response would have become part of the public record. According to Madison, "The sympathy of the Executive for the condition of the captives is limited only by the superior consideration of the public good. This would be injuriously affected by too unbounded a desire to release them, in the double view of pecuniary sacrifices which might spring from it, and the encouragement it might hold out to the other Barbary States, and even to Tripoli, to repeat their aggressions." Jefferson had learned during his efforts to free the crews of the *Maria* and the *Dauphin* almost twenty years earlier that it was sometimes necessary to affect disinterest in the fate of Barbary captives. Nonetheless, Madison sought to reassure FitzSimons that "measures are therefore in active preparation for exhibiting and employing an imposing force to compel the Bashaw to terms which may be admissible. In the mean time it must be a satisfaction to the friends of the prisoners to know that they will be amply supplied with necessaries." He noted that there were no limits on private charitable endeavors to support the captives though he cautioned that "it ought certainly to be well considered, whether their measures, by impressing the Bashaw with an opinion of an undue solicitude to relieve them, and possibly thwarting the negotiations of the Executive, may not have a tendency to protract the sufferings of those unhappy men."[47]

The status of the prisoners was further complicated by the unco-ordinated and clumsy efforts of American diplomats. The American representatives in Paris, Constantinople, and St. Petersburg sought the interposition of the French, Ottoman, and Russian empires, respec-tively, to secure the release of the captives. Jefferson recognized that diplomats far from home sometimes had to use their initiative to solve problems without reference to their governments. He himself had done so during his own involvement with Barbary negotiations in the 1780s. Nonetheless he felt that the diplomats' intervention in the fate of the crew of the *Philadelphia* placed the United States in a humiliating position, which would weaken its international standing. When Levett Harris, the American consul in St. Petersburg, made representations on behalf of the prisoners to the Russian imperial chancellor, Count Alexander Vo-rontsov, Jefferson was exasperated.[48] He complained to Madison about the diplomat's action.

> This sordid disposition to throw upon the charity of others, our losses, altho losses of the same kind are daily happening to them, without their having ever sent a brief to us for relief, is a national stain, which unfortunately the nature of the case does not leave us free to wipe off by a disavowal: because on the part of the First Consul, the Emperor, the Grand Seigneur, the hum-ble petitions of our functionaries are granted, the relief has probably been yielded, & carried into execution. If our prison-ers are given up on the firman of the Grand Seigneur we cannot replace them in captivity. On the contrary every moral principle calls for expressions from us to those powers of our grateful ac-knolegements. To reject their boon after it has been yielded at the request of our own agents, would make them our enemies. Their promptitude to serve us shews they are disposed to culti-vate particular friendship with us, and we ought not to lose the occasion of meeting it. But how to combine the sentiments of gratitude, of dignity & friendly disposition which the occasion I presume requires should be expressed to the Russian minister of foreign relations, is the great difficulty to be encountered, and I am glad it falls into so good hands, as yours.[49]

Madison wrote to Harris to tell him that while his desire to help the prisoners in Tripoli was laudable, "the means of conducting our affairs with Tripoli, are amply sufficient." He warned Harris against taking further steps beyond his grade that might complicate the interests of the United States.[50]

Far more serious for Jefferson than national embarrassment was the threat that Harris's initiative posed to the strategic interests of the United States in the Mediterranean. Jefferson feared that Harris's intervention might endanger the military campaign against Tripoli. "Another difficulty more embarrassing is presented," he wrote.

> In consequence of this interposition, suppose, on the arrival of our squadron, our prisoners shall have been liberated. What is the Commodore to do? To go to beating their town about their ears immediately after their having done us voluntary justice, would be an outrage which would revolt the world against us, & especially the sovereigns at whose request it was done. They would be in honour bound to take the interests of Tripoli under their care, to demand indemnification from us, and perhaps that we should pay a ransom for the prisoners liberated. Our expedition then is disarmed, our expences sunk, and the opportunity of vindicating our honor gone. We were free to beg or to fight. We chose the latter & prepared for it. Unauthorised agents have taken the business out of our hands, have chosen to beg, & executed what they chose. Thus two inconsistent plans are going on at the same time, and will run foul of one another in a region so distant, that we cannot decide for ourselves which shall proceed.[51]

Jefferson needed the crew of the *Philadelphia* to remain imprisoned at least until Commodore Barron arrived with his enhanced squadron. Otherwise the cost of the expedition would be for naught, and the opportunity to vindicate American honor and to negotiate a lasting settlement with Tripoli would be lost. If the prisoners were freed through the intervention of a foreign power, the United States would be weakened internationally and the war against Tripoli would, effectively, be lost.

Robert Smith's orders to Samuel Barron allowed the commodore to use his discretion when he arrived in the Mediterranean. One area in which the commodore was given wide latitude concerned Hamet Karamanli, the older brother of Pasha Yusuf, whom Yusuf had deposed when he came to power in 1796. Barron's orders read: "With respect to the Ex-Bashaw of Tripoli, we have no objection to you availing yourself of his co-operation with you against Tripoli—if you shall upon a full view of the subject after your arrival upon the Station, consider his co-operation expedient. The subject is committed entirely to your discretion."[52] Since 1801, when the war began, William Eaton had promoted a scheme to restore Hamet, who was living in exile in Tunis, in the belief that his gratitude to the United States would result in a more harmonious relationship between Tripoli and the United States.

Eaton, a Revolutionary War veteran from Connecticut, had been a captain in the army before being appointed consul in Tunis by John Adams. While in Tunis Eaton encountered the exiled Hamet Karamanli. When Tripoli declared war on the United States Eaton wrote to James Madison advocating that the United States seek to restore the "rightful Bashaw of Tripoli." According to Eaton, the people of Tripoli were "very discontented and ripe for revolt; they want nothing but confidence in the prospect of success: this confidence may be inspired by assurances of our determination to chastise this Bashaw for his outrage against the U.S." According to Eaton replacing Yusuf with Hamet would have long-term benefits for the United States. "The idea of dethroning our enemy and placing a rightful sovereign in his seat makes a deeper impression on account of the lasting peace it will produce with that regency, and the lesson of caution it will teach the other Barbary States." James L. Cathcart, the consul in Tripoli, agreed with Eaton. "I not only contemplate the obtaining a permanent & honorable peace," he wrote to Madison, "but likewise the dethroning the present Bashaw & effecting a revolution in favor of his Brother Hamet, who is at Tunis & thereby insure the United States the gratitude of him & his Successors."[53] Eaton and Cathcart were proposing an ambitious and risky scheme to revolutionize politics in Tripoli and diplomacy along the Barbary Coast.

James Madison originally gave the plan tepid support. "Altho' it does not accord with the general sentiments or views of the United States to intermeddle in the domestic contests of other countries," Madison wrote to Eaton, "it cannot be unfair, in the prosecution of a just war, or the accomplishment of a reasonable peace, to turn to their advantage the enmity and pretensions of others against a common foe." Madison conceded that it was difficult to assess the situation from afar. He expressed a degree of caution in the face of Eaton's optimism, "The event it is hoped will correspond with your zeal with your calculations."[54] The administration had hoped that it could wage a successful war against Tripoli with the navy alone and would not have to involve itself with Tripoli's internal politics or attempt to wage a land campaign in North Africa. Two years later, the administration was more amenable to working with Hamet. "Of the co-operation of the Elder brother of the Bashaw of Tripoli we are still willing to avail ourselves," Madison wrote to Tobias Lear in June 1804, with an important qualification: "*if* the Commodore should Judge that it may be useful." Barron was authorized to spend $20,000 at his discretion to assist Hamet, "but," cautioned Madison, "the less reliance is to be placed upon his aid, as the force under the orders of the Commodore is deemed sufficient for any exercise of coercion which the obstinacy of the Bashaw may demand." William Eaton was appointed United States navy agent for the Barbary Regencies, under the command of Commodore Barron. Eaton's main role would be to serve as American liaison to Hamet Karamanli, which was a signal that the Jefferson administration supported, in a limited way, the campaign to overthrow Pasha Yusuf. Jefferson would have preferred that Barron's squadron brought the war to a successful conclusion without replacing Yusuf. [55]

Commodore Barron arrived in the Mediterranean in autumn 1804. The navy maintained a closer, stronger blockade of Tripoli. In November Eaton took the brig *Argus* to Egypt to find Hamet, who had left Tunis. Eaton and Hamet raised a force of several hundred Arab and Greek mercenaries supplemented by nine U.S. marines. Eaton named himself the general of the polyglot force and led them across the Libyan desert, intending to restore Hamet as pasha. Commodore Barron expressed skepticism about the expedition and found Hamet to be unreliable. On March 22, 1805, he wrote to Eaton to remind him that the United States was not committed to restoring Hamet to the Tripolitan throne but to winning its war with Tripoli—and that cooperation with Hamet should be limited to that end.[56] Undeterred, Hamet and Eaton persevered. They marched more than 600 miles across the desert. On April 27, Eaton's force, assisted by three navy ships, the *Argus, Hornet,* and *Nautilus,* attacked the coastal city of Derna. While the navy shelled the city, Eaton, the marines, and their mercenary allies stormed the main fortress. Within two hours the garrison had fled and Eaton raised the American flag over Derna—the first time that American forces occupied a city on another continent. Hamet and Eaton reinforced Derna and awaited an expected counterattack by forces loyal to Yusuf. The Tripolitans attacked on May 13, but they were deterred by cannon fire from the fortress and the naval ships in the harbor. After a sharp fight lasting approximately four hours, they retreated. Eaton and Hamet intended to continue west to capture Tripoli itself and restore Hamet as pasha. Yusuf indicated that he was willing to negotiate, and Tobias Lear proceeded to Tripoli. The negotiations went quickly and Lear and Yusuf signed an agreement on June 4. Under the terms of the treaty, peace and amity were declared. The United States refused to pay for peace or annual tribute, but Lear agreed to a one-off payment of $60,000 to ransom the crew of the *Philadelphia.*[57] Hamet Karamanli boarded a U.S. warship at Derna and went into exile.

On December 3, 1805, President Jefferson submitted his fifth annual message to Congress. He reflected on the recent conflict with Tripoli, sharing the success with Congress:

> I congratulate you on the liberation of our fellow-citizens who were stranded on the coast of Tripoli and made prisoners of war. In a government bottomed on the will of all the life and liberty of every individual citizen become interesting to all. In the treaty, therefore, which has concluded our warfare with that State an article for the ransom of our citizens has been agreed to. An operation by land by a small band of our countrymen and others, engaged for the occasion in conjunction with the troops of the ex-Bashaw of that county, gallantly conducted by our late consul, Eaton, and their successful enterprise on the city of Derne, contributed doubtless to the impression

which produced peace, and the conclusion of this prevented opportunities of which the officers and men of our squadron destined for Tripoli would have availed themselves to emulate the acts of valor exhibited by their brethren in the attack of last year.[58]

The president pledged to submit the treaty to the Senate in due course. The ambivalence he expressed in his annual message regarding Hamet Karamanli's role in the conflict anticipated a controversy that arose when the Senate debated the Tripolitan treaty.

Jefferson formally submitted the treaty to the Senate on December 11, 1805, and followed with additional related documents in January and February.[59] Jefferson wrote to both houses of Congress on January 13, 1806, requesting financial and material aid for Hamet Karamanli. The president explained: "During the war with Tripoli, it was suggested that Hamet Caramalli [sic], elder brother of the reigning Bashaw, and driven by him from his throne, meditated the recovery of his inheritance, and that a concert in action with us was desirable to him. We considered that concerted operations by those who have a common enemy were entirely justifiable, and might produce effects favourable to both, without binding either to guaranty the objects of the other." Jefferson contended that the United States had never committed to restore Hamet as pasha but conceded that William Eaton might have given Hamet that impression. "In operations at such a distance, it becomes necessary to leave much to the discretion of the agents employed," as Jefferson well knew. Nonetheless, "events may still turn up beyond the limits of that discretion." Pledging to restore Hamet was beyond the limits of Eaton's discretion. Hamet seemed to have believed that the United States would restore him. In consequence Jefferson believed that the United States should attempt to make some restitution to Hamet and to seek the release of his family, which were being held by Yusuf. "A nation," he wrote, "by establishing a character of liberality and magnanimity, gains, in the friendship and respect of others, more than the worth of mere money."[60] The Senate considered the Tripolitan treaty during the spring of 1806. The senators spent three days debating what should be done for Hamet Karamanli, but they could not reach a decision. Eventually the House of

Representatives voted in April to pay Hamet $2,400.[61] The Senate rati-
fied the treaty by a vote of 21 to 8 on April 12, 1806.[62]

Jefferson's biographers and historians have largely neglected the Tripolitan War.[63] In the foremost study of Jefferson's foreign policy, Robert
W. Tucker and David C. Hendrickson devote a five-page footnote to the
conflict. Tucker and Hendrickson maintain that in the campaign against
Tripoli "Jefferson plainly demonstrated that he had no compunction in
principle against the use of force." Nonetheless they qualify this, arguing that the conflict was more akin to a twentieth-century "police action" than a war. They write, "In its scope and effects, it was not to be
confused with a war fought against one of the European states." They
conclude, "The Barbary War is noteworthy not as an exception to an
otherwise consistent pattern of behaviour respecting force but as an example of the difficulties of adhering to principle even in matters of less
than vital interest to the state."[64] This interpretation is anachronistic
and narrow. It supposes that wars were large-scale conflicts with European powers. During the early republic the state deployed deadly force
in armed conflicts with a variety of non-European actors—notably Native Americans. Jefferson pursued a four-year campaign against Tripoli
that involved most of the United States Navy. It was a war, Jefferson
believed, to defend the vital interests of the United States. Tucker and
Hendrickson fail to recognize how important trade—including trade
with the Mediterranean—was in Jefferson's thinking.

The Tripolitan War was a qualified success for Thomas Jefferson.
Despite Yusuf Karamanli's desire to secure a more lucrative treaty with
the United States, the final peace accord did not include annual tribute
or substantial gifts. To an extent Jefferson's view of international relations was vindicated. He had resorted to force rather than paying tribute, a position he had advocated for two decades. The cost of the war,
however, was substantial, greatly in excess of the cost of paying enhanced
tribute to Yusuf. Moreover, while Jefferson had sought to place Barbary-
American relations on a new footing, the United States continued to pay
annual tribute to the other Barbary States according to the terms of the
treaties completed by the Federalists during the 1790s.

When Yusuf Karamanli struck down the flagstaff at the American consulate in Tripoli Jefferson accepted that action as a declaration of war rather than an invitation to negotiate a more lucrative trade agreement. He consulted his cabinet and deployed the navy in the Mediterranean. The war did not begin well for the United States. In the face of military setbacks, notably the loss of the *Philadelphia* and the capture of its crew, Jefferson escalated the conflict, significantly increasing the American naval presence in the region. The administration gave tacit sanction—in the form of $20,000 and three warships—to the efforts of William Eaton and Hamet Karamanli to overthrow Yusuf Karamanli. In order to pay for the conflict Jefferson raised taxes.

The Tripolitan War seems to fly in the face of the tenets of Jeffersonian republicanism. Jefferson was committed to an agrarian republic, skeptical about naval power, and opposed excessive government spending. However, Jefferson's agrarianism rested on the assumption that Americans must trade freely throughout the world. By the time Jefferson was elected president, American trade in the Mediterranean was worth $10 million per annum. The region was deemed of vital strategic importance. A threat to commerce was a threat to the American republic. Jefferson's response to such a threat was entirely consistent with his prior experience and his understanding of statecraft. Jefferson acted decisively and used force to promote and protect the commercial interests of the United States. During his governorship Jefferson had learned to appreciate the need for republican leaders to act decisively in a crisis, without excessive regard for constitutional scruples—provided he obtained retrospective legislative approval for his actions. As a diplomat he had resolved that force was necessary for dealing with the Barbary States. As president he deployed the United States Navy to protect American commerce, even going so far as to countenance removing Yusuf Karamanli from power. He demonstrated similar determination when confronted by another international crisis over the right to navigate the Mississippi in 1802. The result would be the greatest triumph of Jefferson's presidency.

Six

Empire of Liberty

July 4, 1803, marked the beginning of the twenty-eighth year in the life of the American republic. The president of the United States, Thomas Jefferson, primary author of the document that had declared the nation independent, rose at dawn as usual. Shy by nature, he did not relish public celebrations. This champion of democracy and of the wisdom of the American people was not especially comfortable among the people whose virtues he extolled. Nor did he enjoy public speaking. Throughout his career in public service he had exercised his considerable political skills mainly by means of his pen rather than by his oratory. The Fourth of July (this would be his third as president) was usually difficult for him because Washington tradition—if it could be called tradition in what was still only a four-year-old, rough-hewn village of muddy streets, ramshackle boardinghouses, and incomplete public buildings—called for an open house at the president's residence. Members of the public and government would throng there to meet the chief executive. But despite his bashfulness, Jefferson had good reason to awaken with excitement that day. In many respects it was the culmination of his public career.

The day before, Secretary of State James Madison had received a letter from Rufus King, about to demit office as the United States minister to London. King, writing from New York, informed Madison that American diplomats in Paris had completed negotiations with Napoleon for the purchase of the Louisiana Territory. The acquisition of Louisiana, more than 820,000 square miles, would double the size of the

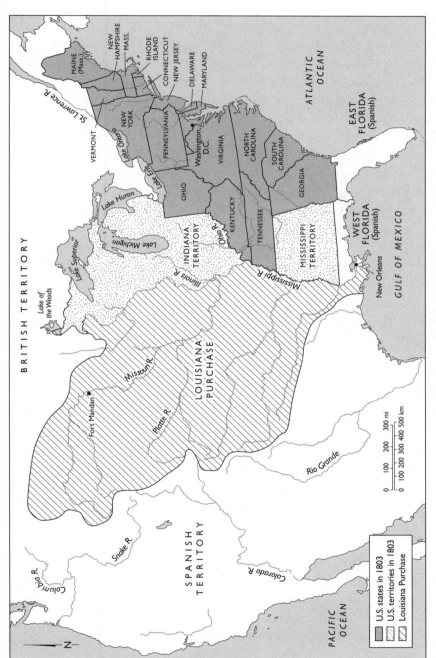

3. The Louisiana Purchase

United States. The United States would also acquire the port of New Orleans and complete control of the Mississippi River, a major strategic objective since independence. Madison sent King's letter to the president. Jefferson, thrilled at the news of this diplomatic coup, sent the letter to the editor of the *National Intelligencer*, a friendly newspaper which served as the administration's mouthpiece. On the morning of the Fourth, copies of the *Intelligencer* carried a brief report of stating, "The Executive have received official information that a Treaty was signed on the 30th of April between the ministers of U.S. and France, by which the U.S. has obtained full right to and sovereignty over New Orleans and the whole of Louisiana." Around noon, Jefferson appeared on the steps of the presidential mansion to greet the crowd and confirm that the United States had, indeed, struck a deal to acquire Louisiana. The purchase of Louisiana was the high point of Jefferson's two terms as president and one of the most notable achievements of his life.[1]

It was entirely appropriate that the nation should learn of the Louisiana Purchase on the Fourth of July. In addition to the news of the Louisiana agreement, Samuel Harrison Smith, the *Intelligencer*'s editor, included in the paper an essay on the significance of the day. Smith reminded Americans that the Fourth of July marked the anniversary of American independence. "While three quarters of the world remain enslaved," he wrote, "and continue a prey to the passions that desolate their fairest regions with human blood, America enjoys solid happiness and unclouded peace." Why were Americans so blessed? According to Smith, it was not because they were physically distinct from other people. Rather, they flourished because they were morally and politically separate: they enjoyed liberty, a liberty guaranteed to them by their republican government:

> The blessings we enjoy all emanate from the right of self-government. This is the pillar of all of our political institutions, to which we are indebted for those numerous and diffusive benefits that tend to every class in society.
>
> Our government is republican;—the only republican government on earth. We may go farther and affirm that it is the only republican government that has ever existed among men.

Other governments have borne the name; ours alone possess the reality.

A republican government is that which alone in the highest degree consults and advances the public good. This can only be accomplished by rulers who truly represent the public will. No other government, in ancient or modern times, has contained all the representative principle applied to all its parts and preserved in constant vigor.

Smith then enumerated the particular benefits that republican government conferred upon the United States. These included: the rule of law; competent and cost-effective administration; low taxes; freedom of expression and conscience; rewards for talent, virtue, and hard work; and peace "in the midst of a warring world." He rehearsed the history of the recent revolution, when Americans defended liberty against tyranny, and called on their descendants to do the same, for only through "an habitual determination to crush every internal or external approach to tyranny" could Americans preserve republican liberty and its benefits.[2]

When Jefferson read the *National Intelligencer* that Fourth of July, he would surely have been pleased. In his mind the republican vision sketched by Smith—with which he wholeheartedly agreed—and the westward expansion of the nation confirmed by the Louisiana Purchase went hand in hand. For the new American republic to succeed, he believed, it must expand. With the acquisition of New Orleans—as well as the vast Louisiana Territory, which would afford future generations of farmers with land—Jefferson had, it seemed, provided for the future health of the United States he had helped to create a generation earlier. At the dawn of the nineteenth century, Jefferson was the leading proponent of a vision of republican empire—what he termed an "empire of liberty"—in the United States. As we have seen, Jefferson, and the political party he led, advanced a view of American republicanism predicated on the geographic expansion of the country. As a consequence Jefferson and his immediate successors pursued a policy of expansion of which the purchase of the Louisiana Territory was the most notable and successful act.

✦

In January 1780 Jefferson, then governor of Virginia, began to plan a western campaign with George Rogers Clark, who commanded the state's forces in the trans-Appalachian west. In the winter of 1778–79 Clark had led a successful campaign in Indiana and Illinois against British posts and Indian villages, culminating in the capture of Vincennes. In 1779 he had attempted unsuccessfully to capture the British fort at Detroit. On January 1, 1780, Governor Jefferson wrote to Clark in anticipation of the 1780 campaign. He advised Clark to choose between attacking the British at Detroit or attacking the Indians of the Northwest, "whom experience has shewn to be incapable of reconciliation." He conceded Clark discretion in the matter but countenanced the use of force, writing: "If against these Indians, the end proposed should be their extermination, or their removal beyond the lakes of Illinois river. The same world will scarcely do for them and us." Eventually Clark captured two Shawnee towns in Ohio. The planning in 1780 demonstrates that Jefferson, who has been portrayed as rather timorous by some historians, was willing to marshal the power of the state to conquer the west.[3]

Although he recognized that it might be necessary to use force to wrest western land from hostile Europeans and recalcitrant Indians, Jefferson's preferred means of expansion was through the colonization of the west (as well as the south and north) by Americans. He believed that as American citizens spread westward, they would bring republican institutions with them, thereby expanding the boundaries of the United States, which would experience organic growth through migration. On January 28, 1780—at the same time that he was planning Clark's western campaign—he informed John Todd (Virginia's county lieutenant in Illinois) that Clark would establish a post near the confluence of the Ohio and Mississippi Rivers. He hoped that the post would allow Virginia to extend its control over the Indians and the French settlers of the Illinois country. Jefferson hoped that Todd would serve in the vanguard of Virginia settlers who would transform the region. He wrote:

> We are in hopes you are endeavouring to introduce our
> Laws and form of Government among the people of Illinois as
> far as their temper and disposition will admit. . . . We wish for
> their own good to give them full participation of the benefits of

our free and mild Government. It is also essentially necessary that all who are parts of the same body politic should be governed by the same laws: and the time to introduce this identity of laws with least inconvenience to themselves, is while they are few. Nothing else can so perfectly incorporate them into the general American body.[4]

At the end of 1780 Jefferson wrote to George Rogers Clark urging him to make another attempt on Detroit in the spring of 1781. If successful, he instructed Clark to "promise protection to the Persons and property of the French and American inhabitants" of the Northwest. By introducing American laws and government, he believed they could assimilate the French settlers into the United States' new republican polity. He hoped "to form to the American union a barrier against the dangerous extension of the British Province of Canada and add to the Empire of liberty an extensive and fertile Country thereby converting dangerous Enemies into valuable friends."[5]

The most effective way to spread republican culture and institutions was through the migration of American settlers beyond the boundaries of the United States. With the spread of American settlement, republicanism and American government were sure to follow. This was a consistent theme in Jefferson's thinking. In 1786 he declared, "Our confederacy must be viewed as the nest from which all of America, North and South is to be peopled."[6] His faith in the "men of the western waters" was such that he believed they would expand the boundaries of the republic at little cost or effort to the United States. Just a decade after he encouraged Virginia settlement of the Illinois country, he encouraged Americans to move into Spanish Florida. As secretary of state, he wrote to George Washington in April 1791:

> Governour Quesada [the Spanish governor of East Florida], by order of his court, is inviting foreigners to go and settle in Florida. This is meant for our people. . . . I wish a hundred thousand of our inhabitants would accept the invitation. It will be the means of delivering to us peaceably, what may otherwise have cost us a war. In the mean time we may complain of this

seduction of our inhabitants just enough to make them believe
we think it very wise policy for them, and confirm them in it.
This is my idea of it.[7]

A decade later still he prophesied that "our rapid multiplication will expand itself . . . & cover the whole Northern, if not Southern continent,
with a people speaking the same language, governed in similar forms,
and by similar laws." Jefferson believed that by carrying the institutions
of republican government with them, Americans could expand the empire of liberty without resort the traditional instruments of conquest—
large standing armies that were costly and ultimately endangered liberty.
Jefferson was willing to use a combination of force, trade, and migration
to bring about the expansive republic that he felt was essential to preserve liberty in the United States. But the spread of liberty would not be
bloodless. While Anglo-American settlers would enjoy the benefits of
republican government and enjoy the rights of citizens, Native Americans would be displaced to make way for American settlements. As they
colonized the west and south, American citizens would bring their slaves
with them to supply the labor that made their economic and political independence possible.[8]

Jefferson sought to promote orderly westward migration and settlement. Unlike many of his peers, he did not engage in speculation in
western lands and so did not have a vested interest in selling land at a
profit or in evicting squatters. Rather, given the importance he ascribed
to western settlement, he sought to develop a plan for the rapid, orderly
growth of the United States by making inexpensive land available to settlers and by drafting legislation that would allow new territories and
states to join the American union. To that end the Virginia assembly,
with Jefferson's strong support, voted in December 1783 to cede to the
United States its claims to the Old Northwest, to which it had maintained a historic claim. At the same time Congress created a committee
to draw up a plan for governing western territory and named Jefferson as
its chair. He prepared a draft, Plan for Government of the Western Territory, which was ready on March 1, 1784, when Congress accepted Virginia's cession creating a national domain in western land.[9]

In his Plan for Government of the Western Territory Jefferson outlined his vision for the west in the future of the American republic and described the mechanisms whereby western territory could be subdivided and governed by the United States until the individual territories acquired enough European-American settlers; then they could draft republican constitutions and, in due course, apply for statehood within the American union. Crucially, according to Jefferson's plan, the new states would enter the American confederation on an equal basis with the thirteen original states. These provisions were testimony to Jefferson's belief that the future of the republic lay in western expansion and settlement.

The Plan for Government of the Western Territory is not as famous as the Declaration of Independence. Nonetheless its significance in American history, though little noted, is immense. Although prompted specifically by the settlement of Ohio, Jefferson's report called for the creation of at least fourteen new states between the Appalachian Mountains and the Mississippi River. In theory new states could be incorporated ad infinitum as the United States acquired new territory. The essence of Jefferson's proposal was incorporated into the Ordinance of 1784, the Land Ordinance of 1785, and the Northwest Ordinance of 1787—although the provisions for territorial self-government were diluted in the latter so as to favor land speculators. He had created a process for the orderly admission of new states to the union, laying the foundation for the rapid geographic expansion of the United States. Historians have not paid sufficient attention to the direct correlation between the republican vision outlined in the Declaration of Independence and the explicitly expansionist program at the heart of the Plan for Government of the Western Territory. The latter provided a colonial policy for a republican empire, which was essential if the grand aspirations of the Declaration were to be realized.[10]

It was a commonplace belief in the eighteenth century, derived from Montesquieu, that republics must be small. Jefferson had articulated a coherent vision of a geographically extensive American empire that would preserve the benefits of republican government. As he wrote to a French correspondent, François d'Ivernois, in 1795:

I suspect that the doctrine, that small States alone are fitted
to be republics, will be exploded by experience, with some
other brilliant fallacies accredited by Montesquieu and other
political writers. Perhaps it will be found that to obtain a just
republic (and it is to secure our just rights that we resort to government at all) it must be so extensive as that local egoisms may
never reach its greater part; that on every particular question a
majority may be found in its councils free from particular interests and giving, therefore, a uniform prevalence to the principles
of justice. The smaller the societies, the more violent and more
convulsive their schisms.[11]

Jefferson, echoing James Madison's argument in the Tenth Federalist,
advanced the view that a larger republic would be more harmonious
than a small one. In America's republican empire political and economic
power would be diffused across a vast territory, thus forestalling dangerous concentrations of power and local schisms. The crucial feature of
Jefferson's imperial vision was that new territories would not be permanent colonies of the older states but ultimately equal partners within the
union. For Jefferson, the American empire would be formed of numerous equal state-republics, each its own locus of power within the federal
union. As he stated in his second inaugural address: "I know that the
acquisition of Louisiana has been disapproved by some, from a candid
apprehension that the enlargement of our territory would endanger its
union. But who can limit the extent to which the federative principle
may operate effectively? The larger our association, the less will it be
shaken by local passions." Because political power would be diffused,
individual rights would be guaranteed, yet the union as a whole would
be strong enough to defend itself in a world of aggressive empires.[12]

The question of citizenship was central to Jefferson's conception of a
republican empire. Jefferson believed that Americans should be bound
by the common political and constitutional principles of the unique
American empire. Subscription to these values would be the test of American identity. He felt that foreign immigrants and people such as the
French settlers of Illinois could assimilate and embrace these values and
become citizens in the American republic. Not all Americans, however,

could meet this standard. In Jefferson's view, his Federalist adversaries, who sought to concentrate power in a strong federal government and to promote manufacturing, embraced policies which were antithetical to the long-term health of the republic. For Jefferson, the tenets of agrarian republicanism became *the* standard for judging fitness for citizenship. He did not accept as valid that his political opponents endorsed a different conception of the future development of the nation. Rather, their views posed a danger to the very survival of the republic.

Federalists were not the only ones excluded from Jefferson's conception of American nationhood. So too were Native Americans and African American slaves. The former were excluded because they were, in cultural and historical terms, not at the same level of development as European Americans. Indians, in Jefferson's view, were not inherently inferior to whites, but their apparent lack of cultural development meant that they could not be easily incorporated into the American republic. Jefferson believed that Native Americans' social and cultural development had been conditioned by their environment, but he felt there was no barrier to Indians' assimilating the republican values and mores of European Americans. In his second inaugural address, Jefferson included a lengthy passage on the state of Native Americans expressing this hope:

> The aboriginal inhabitants of these countries I have regarded with the commiseration their history inspires. Endowed with the faculties and the rights of men, breathing an ardent love of liberty and independence, and occupying a country which left them no desire but to be undisturbed, the stream of overflowing population from other regions directed itself on these shores; without power to divert, or habits to contend against, they have been overwhelmed by the current, or driven before it; now reduced within limits too narrow for the hunter's state, humanity enjoins us to teach them agriculture and the domestic arts; to encourage them to that industry which alone can enable them to maintain their place in existence, and to prepare them in time for that state of society, which to bodily comforts adds the improvement of the mind and morals. We have therefore liberally furnished them with the implements of husbandry and

household use; we have placed among them instructors in the arts of first necessity; and they are covered with the aegis of the law against aggressors from among ourselves.[13]

The problem, as he saw it, was one of timing. It might take Native Americans several generations to become republican farmers. This was time they, and the American republic, did not have. As a consequence, while Jefferson extolled the virtues of Native Americans and lamented their supposed passing into history, he was willing to use force to exterminate or exclude those who were a barrier to the success of the American republic. As president he alternated between policies promoting Indian assimilation and removal in one form or another. Jefferson accepted that Native Americans could be republican citizens in theory, but in practice there was little room for them in his republican empire.[14]

African American slaves presented a different problem in Jefferson's thinking. When Jefferson drafted his plan for western government, he called for the exclusion of slavery from the trans-Appalachian west after 1800. This exclusion was later incorporated into the Northwest Ordinance—thereby sanctioning the practice in the more populous regions south of the Ohio River. Jefferson may have sought the exclusion of slavery from the Northwest because he doubted that Africans and their American descendants were fit to be citizens in the American republic.[15] In the *Notes on the State of Virginia*, Jefferson endorsed a plan of gradual emancipation provided that the former slaves left the state upon acquiring their freedom. "Why not retain and incorporate the blacks into the state, and thus save the expence of supplying, by importation of white settlers, the vacancies they will leave?" he asked. The answer lay in the "deep rooted prejudices entertained by the whites; ten thousand recollections, by the blacks, of the injustices they have sustained; new provocations; the real distinctions which nature has made; and many other circumstances, will divide us into parties, and produce convulsions which will probably never end but in the extermination of one or the other race." Jefferson believed that it was impossible for blacks and whites to live together in freedom. Rather, the only solution to the problem posed by African slavery was emancipation and expatriation. Without this (and Jefferson never pressed for a serious emancipation program), slavery would remain an integral part of the American republic, in both east and west. South of the Ohio River, the empire of liberty would also be an empire of slavery. Although Jefferson conceived of an expansive, egalitarian republic that would serve as a model for human progress, in practice his was to be a republic for white men and their families.[16]

In his words and actions before becoming president in 1801, Thomas Jefferson articulated a clear and coherent vision of an expansive republican empire in the United States. The nation could thrive only as an independent republic—the best and most equitable form of government—if it forestalled the inevitable decline and decay that had beset previous republics. This could best be achieved if the United States expanded so that the majority of its growing population could remain independent farmers. This view was widely shared. "We cannot but anticipate the period," wrote the geographer Jedidiah Morse in 1789, "as not very far distant, when the AMERICAN EMPIRE will comprehend millions of souls, west of the Mississippi." Morse predicted that its political values and culture would guarantee the success of the American empire:

> Here civil and religious liberty are to flourish, unchecked by the cruel hand of civil or ecclesiastical tyranny. Here, Genius aided by all the improvements of former ages, is to be exerted in humanizing mankind—in expanding and inriching their minds with religious and philosophical knowledge, and in the planning and executing a form of government which shall involve all the excellencies of former governments, with as few of their defects as is consistent with the imperfection of human affairs, and which shall be calculated to protect and unite, in a manner consistent with the natural rights of mankind, the largest empire that ever existed.

For the United States to flourish politically, economically, and socially, its citizen farmers needed access to overseas markets for their produce, which would allow them to purchase manufacturing goods without America having to suffer from the dire social and political consequences of manufacturing. Another geographer and surveyor, Thomas Hutchins, made the connection in 1784. He too anticipated that Americans would overspread North America from which they "will have it in their power to the engross the whole commerce of it, and to reign not only lords of America, but to possess, in the utmost security, the dominion of sea throughout the world." Geographers like Morse and Hutchins might make confident predictions, but it fell to political actors like Jefferson and his allies to make them reality.[17]

If Jefferson's empire had a capital, it was New Orleans. That city was where Jefferson's ambitions for western settlement and overseas commerce came together. "There is on the globe one single spot," he wrote in 1802, "the possessor of which is our natural & habitual enemy, New Orleans."[18] Upon becoming president Jefferson was confronted by a crisis over New Orleans, the resolution of which brought the greatest achievement of his presidency. New Orleans was so important because it linked the vast Mississippi valley to the oceans of the world. In his *Notes on the State of Virginia* Jefferson predicted that the Mississippi would be "one of the principal channels of future commerce for the country westward of the Alleghaney [*sic*]" Mountains. In 1786 he declared, "The navigation of the Mississippi we must have."[19] The reasons why New Orleans assumed such importance were demographic and geographic. In the aftermath of the War of Independence large numbers of Americans began to settle in the territories to the west of the Appalachian Mountains. When the war ended in 1783 there were around 8,000 settlers in Kentucky. By 1790, when the first federal census was taken, Kentucky had 73,677 residents, and by 1800 its population was 220,955. Similarly, Tennessee had 105,602 settlers in 1800, and the figure more than doubled, to 261,727, by 1810. Ohio had a population of 42,159 in 1800 but had multiplied by more than five times, to 230,760, when the census of 1810 was taken. In response to this growth Kentucky was admitted as a state in 1792, Tennessee in 1796, and Ohio in 1803. Most of these settlers were farmers and their families (and in the case of Tennessee and Kentucky, their slaves). As such they needed access to markets. It was too difficult and costly to transport meat and agricultural staples like maize, wheat, and tobacco over the mountains. Rather, the farmers of the west relied on the network of rivers in the region, particularly the

Ohio and the Mississippi, which it fed, for their prosperity. In 1802 Jefferson estimated that it was New Orleans "through which the produce of three-eighths our territory must pass to market."[20]

New Orleans was settled in 1718 by French colonists. It represented one end of a massive arc asserting the French empire in North America. At the other end lay Quebec City, founded more than a century earlier. During the seventeenth century French soldiers, explorers, traders, and settlers followed the lakes and rivers through the heart of North America, establishing a chain a settlements that ultimately stretched from Quebec to New Orleans and encompassed claims to much of the territory along the Great Lakes as well as the St. Lawrence, Ohio, and Mississippi Rivers. New Orleans was the largest settlement in Louisiana, a vast and somewhat indeterminate province, almost all of which lay to the west of the Mississippi River. The French were not the only colonists in North America, of course. To the east and south of New France lay the settlements of British North America. Settlers from the populous British colonies along the coast began to push westward during the seventeenth century, a process that continued well after thirteen of the colonies successfully rebelled against British rule. The original colonial power in the New World, Spain, also had significant holdings in North America—claiming East and West Florida—which stretched in an arc around the Gulf of Mexico from the Florida peninsula to the eastern border of Louisiana near New Orleans. To the south and west of Louisiana, Spain claimed much of western North America.

Louisiana was a polyglot province. The largest single group of residents were its various Native American peoples. Among the diverse settlers the dominant group were the French, but these were joined by African slaves; Spanish colonists, soldiers and administrators; and British and American settlers, planters, and merchants. Although not especially populous, by 1800 there were around 50,000 settlers and 30,000 Indians in the Spanish-controlled areas of the lower Mississippi valley (there were more than seven times as many settlers in Ohio, Kentucky, and Tennessee).[21]

Louisiana was of strategic importance to Spain. Most Spanish officials who had considered the situation concluded that Louisiana's greatest value was as a barrier, protecting Spain's valuable Mexican provinces from American encroachment. A year after Jefferson drafted his Plan for Government of the Western Territory, the Spanish intendant in New Orleans, Martin de Navarro, produced a report on the region for his government. "There is none of the provinces of those owned by the king in America which should occupy the attention of the minister so much as that of Louisiana," warned Navarro. He began by reviewing the history of Louisiana. He observed that the colony had not thrived under Spanish rule and contrasted its relative lack of growth with that of the former British colonies in America. He recognized the threat posed by the United States. "We must count upon new enemies," wrote Navarro, "who are regarding our situation and happiness with too great jealousy. The intensity with which they are working to form a city and establish posts, and their immediate neighborhood to our posts of the Illinois may be harmful to us someday." Navarro suggested a relaxation of Spanish mercantile laws as a means of attracting trade and settlers to Louisiana, thus strengthening the colony and thereby protecting Spain's more valuable possessions to the southwest. Navarro suggested that "we shelter ourselves in time by promoting a numerous population in this province in order to observe and even to restrain their intentions. For this purpose, it must not be forgotten that a well-established trade is the chief lever for the increase of a population." The contrast between the reports of Jefferson and Navarro is telling. Whereas Jefferson presented a plan intended to bring order to western settlement while strengthening and enlarging the union, Navarro sought to promote settlement—by liberalizing trade—in order to preserve Spain's imperial holdings. Jefferson's report was the genesis of the expansionist policy of his government, but Navarro's had little impact except as a warning of the potential danger the United States posed to Spain's empire in North America.[22]

Although Americans worried about access to the Mississippi, they were not especially concerned about the Spanish. Indeed, in 1786 Jefferson cautioned against placing the Spanish under too much pressure too soon. "We should take care," he wrote "not to think it for the interest of that great continent to press too soon on the Spaniards. Those countries cannot be in better hands. My fear is that they are too feeble to hold them till our population can be sufficiently advanced to gain it from them peice by peice."[23] The Spanish could not afford to be so sanguine.

The Spanish governor of Louisiana, Baron Francisco Luis Hector de Carondelet, feared the advancing American population. He wrote in 1794:

> This prestigious and restless population, continually forc-
> ing the Indian nations backward and upon us, is attempting to
> get possession of all the vast continent which those nations are
> occupying between the Ohio and Mississippi Rivers and the
> Gulf of Mexico and the Appalachian Mountains, thus becoming
> our neighbor; at the same time they are demanding with threats
> the free navigation of the Mississippi. If they obtain their pur-
> pose, their ambition will not be limited to this part of the Mis-
> sissippi. Their writings, public papers, and speeches, all have as
> their object the navigation to the Gulf by the Mississippi, Mo-
> bile, Pearl, and Appalachicola Rivers which empty into the gulf;
> and the rich fur trade of the Missouri. And in time they will de-
> mand the possession of the rich mines of the interior provinces
> of the very kingdom of Mexico. Their method of spreading
> themselves and their policy are so much to be feared by Spain
> as are their arms. Every new settlement, when it reaches thirty
> thousand souls, forms a state, which is united to the United
> States, so far as regards mutual protection, but which governs
> itself and imposes its own laws. The wandering spirit and the
> ease, with which those people procure their sustenance and shel-
> ter, quickly form new settlements. A carbine and a little maize in
> a sack are enough for an American to wander about in the forests
> alone for a whole month.[24]

Carondelet recognized that the threat posed by the American territorial system was a greater danger to Spain than that of the minuscule American military.

During the 1790s access to the Mississippi was the central issue between Spain and the United States. During his tenure as secretary of state, Jefferson made the Mississippi question one of his top priorities. As we have seen, during the Nootka Sound crisis Jefferson sought to exploit the situation to the advantage of the United States. Secretary of

State Jefferson continued to press Spain on the question. Eventually Spanish-American negotiations bore fruit in the Treaty of San Lorenzo (Pinckney's Treaty), which was signed on October 27, 1795. Under the terms of the treaty Spain agreed to recognize the thirty-first parallel as the border between the United States and the Floridas and acknowledged the right of citizens of the United States and subjects of Spain to navigate the whole length of the Mississippi. The treaty conferred on Americans the privilege of landing and storing goods for transfer to ocean-going vessels at New Orleans, tax-free, for three years. After three years the privilege of entrepôt might continue, or the Spanish might designate another place on the banks of the lower Mississippi for the purpose. Both sides agreed to refrain from encouraging the Indians within their territory from interfering with settlers or property in the territory of the other. Although completed after Jefferson had resigned as secretary of state, the Treaty of San Lorenzo fulfilled his objectives and, seemingly, secured the interests of America's western settlers for the foreseeable future. It seemed to be the diplomatic denouement to the ideological and constitutional program for American expansion that he had implied in the Declaration of Independence and laid out in the Plan for Government of the Western Territory.[25]

The United States was not the only nation with designs on Louisiana. Napoleon Bonaparte, recently named first consul (and returned from his Egyptian campaign) had designs on reviving the French Empire in the New World. The most valuable object in this quest was the island of Saint Domingue. As a center of the sugar trade, Saint Domingue had been one of France's most lucrative colonial possessions. The cultivation of sugar required the brutal exploitation of slave labor, and in 1791 the slaves on Saint Domingue revolted against French rule. A bloody struggle for control of the island ensued. After more than a decade Saint Domingue's slaves prevailed and established the second republic in the Western Hemisphere. In 1800 Napoleon intended to reestablish French rule and slavery in Saint Domingue. The wealth of Saint Domingue would depend on food and other supplies from Louisiana. In anticipation of reestablishing French rule in the New World, Napoleon compelled Spain to agree to the Treaty of San Ildefonso (October 1, 1800), under the terms of which Spain agreed to return Louisiana to France in exchange for the creation in Italy of the kingdom of Etruria, which would be given to the Duke of Parma, son-in-law of Spain's Charles IV. In December 1801, Napoleon dispatched his brother-in-law, Charles Victor Emmanuel Leclerc, to Saint Domingue with an army of 30,000 men to suppress the rebellion, restore slavery, and reassert French authority. Further plans were undertaken to send a second French army to the Americas, this time to New Orleans, to consolidate revived French fortunes in the New World.[26]

Although the provisions of the Treaty of San Ildefonso were secret, rumors of the Spanish retrocession of Louisiana spread around Europe and across the Atlantic. Not long after Jefferson was sworn in as president in March 1801, Rufus King (still U.S. minister), reported from London that Spain had ceded "Louisiana and the Floridas to France." Although this proved to be only partially true, King warned "that this cession is intended to have and may actually produce, Effects injurious to the Union and the consequent happiness of the People of the United States." When Jefferson read the first reports of the treaty he concluded that the retrocession was "was very ominous to us."[27]

Jefferson and his new secretary of state, James Madison, expressed concern at the likelihood of the French resuming control over Louisiana, but they initially placed their faith in diplomacy. The Treaty of San Lorenzo, after all, had guaranteed Americans the right to navigate the Mississippi and to trans-ship their goods at New Orleans. On the face of it, the Americans should have been able to exercise this privilege whether the French or Spanish had ruled Louisiana. In a measured response, Madison instructed the new American ministers in France and Spain, Robert R. Livingston and Charles Pinckney, respectively, to endeavor to learn the terms of the secret treaty and "to prevent a change in our Southern and South Western neighbours" by "the means of peace and persuasion." They should seek confirmation of the American right of deposit at New Orleans.[28] Recent Franco-American relations did not augur well, however. Jefferson and Madison hoped that the change of administration in Washington as well as the peaceful resolution of the crisis might lead to a harmonious settlement of the Mississippi question.

They were to be disappointed. In a series of discouraging dispatches Robert Livingston reported that the French were very enthusiastic about assuming control over Louisiana and had little sympathy for the United States.[29] Increasingly anxious at the prospect of French possession of New Orleans, Jefferson vented his frustration in a private letter to Livingston:

> These circumstances render it impossible that France and U.S. can continue long friends when they meet in so irritable opposition. They as well as we must be very improvident if we do not begin to make arrangements on that hypothesis, The day that France takes possession of N. Orleans fixes the sentence which is to restrain her forever within her low water mark. It seals the union of two nations who in conjunction can maintain exclusive possession of the ocean. From that moment we must marry ourselves to the British fleet and nation. We must turn all our attentions to a maritime force, for which our resources place us on a very high grounds: and having formed and cemented together a power which may render reinforcement of her settlements here impossible to France, make the first cannon, which shall be fired in Europe a signal for tearing up any settlement she may have made, and for holding the two continents in sequestration for the common purposes of the united British and American nations.[30]

It does not seem likely that Jefferson was serious, at this stage, about seeking an alliance with Britain or a war with France to preserve American access to the Mississippi. Nevertheless, he transmitted this letter, with a similarly bellicose cover letter, via a French-born friend, who was well connected to the French government and may have intended to exert some indirect pressure on Napoleon. Further, he took steps to strengthen the American military presence on the northern and southern frontiers, to encourage increased settlement in the Mississippi Territory, and to acquire Indian lands in the southwest, all of which suggest that he took the threat of French control of the Mississippi very seriously and was prepared to use force if diplomacy failed.[31]

The gravity of the situation became apparent in October 1802 when the Spanish intendant in Louisiana (the retrocession was not to take effect until November 1803), Juan Ventura Morales, suspended the American right of deposit at New Orleans. He claimed he did so in response to American smuggling and the fact that the Treaty of San Lorenzo authorized the right of deposit for a three-year period. He ignored the stipulation that the Spanish should provide an alternative site where Americans could deposit and trans-ship their goods if deposit was denied at New Orleans. Morales acted on secret orders, which were unknown to the Spanish governor of Louisiana or the Spanish ambassador in Washington.[32] Spain's motivation—to help or hinder the French acquisition of Louisiana?—is unclear. Regardless of that, Morales's action excited alarm throughout the trans-Appalachian west. At the end of October, William C. C. Claiborne, the American governor of the Mississippi Territory informed James Madison that Morales had "excited considerable agitation in Natchez and its vicinity." In December the Kentucky legislature resolved to support a war to capture New Orleans. The threat of violence seemed very real as 1802 came to a close. Edward Thornton, the head of the British legation in Washington, reported to his government in early January 1803 "that an act of the greatest vigour, such for instance as taking possession of the Island of New Orleans, would be the most popular step the President could take." Thornton feared that if Jefferson opted for diplomacy, westerners might take matters into their own hands. "If a pacific system be that which Mr. Jefferson is determined to adopt at all events," he wrote, "the greatest danger he has to apprehend will be, either from the inhabitants of the Western States, who, if the negociation should go into great length and the right of depot be interdicted, will most probably take upon themselves to vindicate their claims by some act of violence." Several days before the *Gazette of the United States* had warned "that unless the government can give strong assurances of obtaining its rights, the western people will take possession of New Orleans; which will no doubt produce a war."[33]

Jefferson faced growing pressure to act, not only from western settlers but from the Federalist opposition, the press, and members of his own party. On January 11 he nominated James Monroe, a Virginia neighbor and political protégé who was popular in the west, as an extraordinary minister plenipotentiary to France and Spain to negotiate an end to the crisis. The next day Congress appropriated $2 million for the purchase of New Orleans.[34] This did little to placate Jefferson's political opponents who continued to press for war. Ebenezer Mattoon, a Federalist congressman from Massachusetts, wrote in response to Monroe's appointment, "before we were threatened with *war, horrid war;* and only to be avoided by *humble negotiation,* this method might be proper under some circumstances, but at the present time I should prefer a different course." In mid-February 1803 Alexander Hamilton published an essay in a New York newspaper calling for Jefferson to seize the Floridas and New Orleans by force. Meanwhile in Congress, Senator James Ross, a Federalist from Pittsburgh (the only western Federalist in the Senate), introduced a series of resolutions calling for the immediate seizure of New Orleans and authorizing Jefferson to raise an army of 50,000 men from the south and west, and to spend up to $5 million for the purpose. The resolutions sparked a lengthy and passionate debate and were narrowly defeated.[35]

Monroe had a clear objective when he departed for France in early March 1803. He and Robert Livingston were to seek "to procure a cession of New Orleans and the Floridas to the United States and consequently the establishment of the Mississippi as the boundary between the United States and Louisiana."[36] The original American objective in the Louisiana negotiations, therefore, was to secure permanent American navigation of the Mississippi and, if possible, to obtain the Floridas. Neither Livingston, Monroe, nor their political masters expected to obtain land to the west of the Mississippi, and they must have had little hope that Napoleon would abort his American ambition by the sale of his major strategic asset in North America, New Orleans.

As Monroe crossed the Atlantic events transformed the mission and rendered his instructions redundant. During the course of 1802 General Leclerc's campaign to reconquer Saint Domingue had met with intractable resistance from the island's rebels just as his forces were decimated by yellow fever. Several weeks after Juan Morales closed New Orleans to American traffic, causing the diplomatic crisis that threatened war between France and the United States, Leclerc himself succumbed to yellow fever. Leclerc and most of his 30,000-man army were lost. With them died Napoleon's dream of a revived French empire in the New World. During the winter and early spring of 1802–1803 the short-lived

Peace of Amiens between Britain and France broke down, and a European war was in the offing. With waning interest in the New World and a need for the funds to wage war in Europe, Napoleon rethought the Louisiana question and the notion of New Orleans as his capital in the Western Hemisphere.[37]

During the previous two years Robert Livingston had struggled unsuccessfully to secure the American right to navigate the Mississippi and use New Orleans to trans-ship goods. The French foreign minister, Charles-Maurice de Talleyrand-Périgord, had rebuffed Livingston's formal and informal overtures. However, according to Barbé Marbois, Napoleon raised the possibility of selling all of Louisiana to the Americans on April 10. With his schemes for Saint Domingue in ruins and war with Britain threatening, Louisiana would be a liability—easily attacked by the British and difficult for the French to defend. Napoleon would prefer that the Americans acquire it—to his profit—than that the British seized it by force. According to Marbois, on April 11 Napoleon summoned him again to declare:

> Irresolution and deliberation are no longer in season. I renounce Louisiana. It is not only New Orleans that I will cede, it is the whole colony without any reservation. I know the price of what I abandon, and I have sufficiently proved the importance that attach to this province, since my first diplomatic act with Spain had for its object the recovery of it. I renounce it with the greatest regret. To attempt obstinately to retain it would be folly. I direct you to negotiate this affair with the envoys of the United States. Do not even await the arrival of Mr. Monroe: have an interview this very day with Mr. Livingston; but I require a great deal of money for this war, and I would not like to commence it with new contributions. . . . If I should regulate my terms, according to the value of these vast regions to the United States, the indemnity would have no limits. I will be moderate, in consideration of the necessity in which I am making the sale. But keep this to yourself. I want fifty millions, and for less than that sum I will not treat; I would rather make a desperate attempt to keep these two fine countries.

Marbois's account is not wholly reliable. On the eleventh Talleyrand—not Marbois—made the initial approach to Livingston and told him Napoleon was prepared to sell *all* of Louisiana—ultimately 820,000 square miles—and he wanted to know what the United States would pay for the entire province. Livingston was deaf and disbelieving; he did not give an answer, and the next day, April 12—when Monroe arrived in Paris—Marbois went to Livingston's house and made the offer again. Realizing that the French were serious, Livingston and Monroe entered into formal negotiations with Marbois. In a draft treaty dated April 30 they agreed to buy the Louisiana Territory for 60 million *livres* ($11,250,000). The United States further agreed to pay the outstanding claims for French damages owed to Americans as a result of Quasi-War. These totaled another 20 million *livres* ($3,750,000).[38]

The Louisiana Treaty presented Jefferson and his administration with several significant challenges. Perhaps the most significant was whether the United States Constitution authorized the president to acquire territory through the purchase. Jefferson suspected that he did not have such authority. After he learned of the Louisiana Treaty, Jefferson drafted a proposed amendment to the Constitution authorizing the acquisition, which he circulated to Madison, Attorney General Levi Lincoln, and Secretary of the Treasury Albert Gallatin.[39] Jefferson retained doubts about the legality of the treaty, but events, both political and practical, persuaded him not to attempt to amend the Constitution. During the summer Robert Livingston reported that Napoleon was having misgivings about the agreement.[40] If the agreement were not ratified and implemented quickly—the treaty set a six-month deadline—the first consul might repudiate it. Jefferson recognized that it would likely be impossible to amend the Constitution so quickly. Further, attempting to do so might make it difficult to get the treaty ratified. Eventually Jefferson embraced a broad interpretation of the Constitution, particularly its treaty-making provision (Article II, Section 2). Throughout his career as an executive Jefferson had demonstrated a willingness to stretch legal strictures in exceptional circumstances. In each case he believed his actions required subsequent legislative approval. If the Senate, as mandated by the Constitution, ratified the treaty and Congress passed the enabling legislation and appropriated the necessary funds, the treaty would be legally binding and his actions would be vindicated.[41]

The popularity of the Louisiana Treaty facilitated its ratification. Newspapers across the country were generally enthusiastic about it, although Federalists complained about the cost and constitutionality of the treaty. They objected that the Floridas, especially West Florida, were not included in the agreement. The Federalist opposition was somewhat muted, however, because they could not very well object that Livingston and Monroe had secured through negotiation what they were willing to go to war for. Immediately after the agreement became public, Alexander Hamilton complained in the the the *New-York Evening Post* that, apart from New Orleans, the Louisiana Territory was useless except that it might be bartered for the Floridas. Indeed, he feared that the temptations of Louisiana might lure Americans west in such numbers that disunion might result. These were rather weak criticisms and certainly did not resonate with the public, which welcomed the peaceful resolution of the Mississippi crisis and the expansion of the union. From the Federalist stronghold of Massachusetts, Josiah Dwight complained to his brother, Congressman Thomas Dwight (who was en route to Washington to vote on the legislation to fund the purchase), "I am aware that the Jacobins throughout the Country are boasting of their great Diplomatic skill in bargaining for Louisiana—But this is a measure which, when rightly understood, cannot be popular—At present however the people are as completely blinded as were the Sodomites who would have defiled the men of God—A thick film is upon their eyes which it would seem nothing short of miraculous power can remove—When their City shall be on fire they will see the error of their ways—but it will be too late for them to repent."[42] If even the people of Massachusetts were blinded by the splendor of Louisiana, it was unlikely that Congress would fail to ratify the treaty.

On October 20 the Senate ratified the Louisiana Treaty by an overwhelming margin of 24 to 7. On October 28 the House of Representatives passed an act enabling Jefferson to take possession of and govern Louisiana, and it appropriated the money for the purchase. The Senate gave its approval to the treaty on the October 29, and Jefferson signed the bill into law on October 31, 1803.[43] Unthinkable even a few months before, the United States had acquired Louisiana.

Or had it? As soon as the agreement became known the Spanish objected to it—both through the American minister in Madrid and their ambassador in Washington. The Spanish claimed (rightly) that the French were prohibited by the Treaty of San Ildefonso from selling Louisiana to a third power. Since the Spanish still ruled Louisiana, particularly New Orleans, they could, potentially, seek to interfere with the transfer of authority. Spain would have to hand the province to France, which would, in turn, deliver it to the United States. In autumn 1803 war between Spain and the United States once again threatened—although the danger was more remote than it had been the previous year.

Nonetheless, after the ratification of the Louisiana Treaty, Jefferson and Madison made preparations for war should Spain attempted to interfere with the transfer of the territory. On October 31, Madison wrote, on Jefferson's instructions, to the putative American governor of Louisiana, William C. C. Claiborne, who was then the governor of the adjoining Mississippi Territory. He enclosed copies of the treaty ceding Louisiana as well as commissions for Claiborne and General James Wilkinson of the United States Army, authorizing them either jointly or separately to take possession of Louisiana and to exercise civil and military authority in the territory. He ordered Claiborne to proceed to New Orleans immediately with "as many of the Militia of your territory as may be deemed a requisite precaution." Madison noted that the administration feared that Spaniards protesting against the transaction might interfere with the transfer of Louisiana to the United States. Should that be the case, Jefferson authorized Claiborne and Wilkinson to use force.

> Should it be decided that a Coup de Main is immediately proper, it is to be conducted by Genl. Wilkinson. . . . The force will consist of the regular troops near at hand, as many of the Militia as may be requisite and can be drawn from the Mississippi Territory, and as many volunteers from any quarter as can be picked up. To them will be added 500 mounted Militia from Tennessee who it is expected will proceed to Natchez with the least delay possible. . . . In order to add the effect of terror to the

force of arms, it may be given out that measures are in train, which is a truth, for sending on from Kentucky and elsewhere a very great force, such as may be sufficient to overwhelm all possible resistance. Should possession be taken by force, you will proceed to issue your proclamation and exercise the powers vested in you.

Eventually the transfer of Louisiana from Spanish rule to French, and French rule to American occurred without disruption, and these bellicose instructions were never implemented. The Spanish governor, Juan Manuel de Salcedo, turned authority over to Pierre Clément de Laussat on November 30. Laussat, who had arrived in the province the previous March, had originally been sent as the future governor of French Louisiana. As events transpired, his administration lasted only a few weeks; he handed the province over to Claiborne on December 20.[44]

Successful expansion posed its own problems as Jefferson soon learned. For several months after the United States took possession of the territory, American, Spanish, and French officials remained in New Orleans. On January 22, 1804, Claiborne hosted a ball for local dignitaries to encourage harmony among the various groups and to assert his authority as governor. The ball became a brawl when, according to Claiborne and Wilkinson, French officers objected as Claiborne led the crowd in "That Species of Country Dance, which is best known & practised in the United States, passes here by the name of *Contra Danse, Anglaise,* against which (as great Importance is often Attached to mere Words) the Officers and Citizens of France, Strangers & not permanent Residents here, have manifested a decided Disapprobation, and pretended, that the Taste of the Americans, for this Danse, indicated partiality, to the English, their Enemies." The result was "a great Riot and Disturbance . . . much Confusion ensued, Swords were drawn; and it Required, the greatest Exertions, to prevent the Spilling of Blood." After the parties were separated, George Morgan, an American at the ball, reported, "Our countrymen perceiving a disposition for opposition & being desirous to protect their chiefs rallied round them and sang Hail Columbia (a Patriotic Air) which was attempted to be interrupted by some Frenchmen singing the Marseilles Hymn." Several arrests were made, and Claiborne and Wilkinson wrote to Madison to press for the immediate departure of the French under the terms of the Louisiana Treaty.[45]

This trifling incident highlights the political, cultural, and diplomatic challenges that Jeffersonian expansion posed. Isaac Briggs, the chief United States land surveyor for the southern part of the Louisiana Territory, made note of some of these, writing in early January 1804 of the high expectations that some French Louisianans had for the new government. "The people as is usual in all cases of great and sudden change, are unreasonable in their expectations. The reputation of the American Government is so high, that they expect, from it, impossibilities—they expect unbounded licence in many of their vicious, luxurious, and oppressive habits, and at the same time, the full fruition of all those blessings of Republican liberty, which never did, nor never can, long exist, except bottomed on Economy and Virtuous Manners." They were disappointed because Claiborne continued the Spanish system of government, and the American territorial system vested authority in the president and his chosen governor for an indeterminate period before proper representative government could be established. Moreover, Briggs wondered whether the people of Louisiana—an alien place of strategic importance whose languages, history, and culture were little understood by Americans—were suited by culture, temperament, and history for republican government. Briggs continued, "The Divine Author of Nature has indeed made this Country a *Paradise*—but man has converted it into a *Pandemonium*."[46]

Briggs had identified a crucial and immediate challenge for the United States: governance. Claiborne was given temporary, seemingly indefinite authority to govern, but this could not be a permanent solution. Under the scheme of republican empire, which Jefferson had done so much to design, it was possible for territories to make the transition to statehood. Indeed the Northwest Ordinance of 1787 had established a three-stage process for statehood. A territory would first be governed by an appointed governor, secretary, and judges. Once the population of a territory reached 5,000 free white males, it could elect a legislature with limited powers and send a (non-voting) representative to Congress. Having achieved a population of 60,000 free inhabitants, a territory could draft its own constitution and apply for admission to the union as a state. This process had led to Ohio's admission as a state in 1803. Louisiana presented a challenge. Lower Louisiana (i.e., New Orleans and its environs), had a population of around 50,000 free inhabitants, established government structures (albeit not republican), and a tradition of self-rule. The vast expanse to the north and west had fewer inhabitants (particularly since the Constitution excluded Native Americans from citizenship) and might be subject to the territorial system of governance laid down in the Northwest Ordinance, but lower Louisiana seemed too advanced for territorial government.

During the first three months of 1804 Congress debated the "Breckinridge Bill," which originated in a Senate committee chaired by Jefferson's political ally Senator John Breckinridge of Kentucky. The bill was largely the handiwork of Jefferson, who in November 1803 had drafted a proposed government for Louisiana, which Breckinridge largely incorporated into his bill.[47] The Breckinridge Bill called for Louisiana to be administered by a governor appointed by the president. The governor would be assisted by a legislative council, whose members he would select. The government bill was extremely divisive. Many in Congress felt that Louisiana must be given more self-government if the country were to live up to its republican principles. In early March Congress adopted the Breckinridge Bill as well as an act dividing the Louisiana Purchase into two territories. The lower part of Louisiana, south of the thirty-third parallel (more or less the modern state of Louisiana, with the exception of the parishes east of the river then part of Spanish West Florida), was designated the Territory of Orleans to be governed under the terms of the Breckinridge Bill; the remainder, upper Louisiana, was temporarily appended to the Indiana Territory and would be subject to territorial government.[48]

On January 27, 1804, President Jefferson, his vice president, Aaron Burr, his cabinet, including of course James Madison, and numerous congressmen, senators, and government officials gathered at a hotel on Capitol Hill to celebrate the Louisiana Purchase. Toasts were offered for Jefferson and Burr as well as the "tempestuous sea of liberty." Thomas

Dwight, the grumpy Federalist congressman from Massachusetts, was unimpressed. He wrote: "By some these may be considered as the effusions of ardent spirits, but with me when combined with the other sentiments which are too often exhibited by the dominant party they are evidences of that malignancy of mind which will break out eventually in Gallic brutalities. . . . Consider the attachment to Frenchmen & French principles which is evidently growing with rapidity out of the Louisiana acquisition and other recent political events."[49] Dwight misread the situation. The Louisiana Purchase was not the result of Jeffersonian enthusiasm for "French principles." On the contrary it was the fulfillment of Jefferson's ideological vision for an expansive, commercial American republic—a vision that he expressed in the Declaration of Independence, developed in the Plan for Government of the Western Territory, and made a huge stride toward realizing with the acquisition of the Louisiana Territory in 1803. To be sure, Jefferson had not intended to purchase Louisiana when he dispatched Monroe to Paris in March 1803. Nonetheless, the commercial impetus behind Monroe's mission—securing American access to New Orleans, *was* congruent with Jefferson's vision of an "empire of liberty," however new might be his broad construction of the Constitution.

All would not be smooth sailing on the "tempestuous sea of liberty." The Louisiana Purchase raised difficult questions, several of which were unresolved in 1804. One crucial issue concerned the boundaries of the purchase. Just what had the United States bought? Both the eastern and western boundaries were indeterminate. Jefferson and Madison were especially vexed that the United States had not acquired the Floridas. They would argue, unpersuasively, that the eastern boundary of Louisiana included much of what Spain claimed was West Florida. The western boundary, separating Louisiana from Mexico, was also contested. The boundaries of Louisiana would remain an ongoing source of diplomatic wrangling, tension, and potential conflict between Spain and the United States.[50]

More troubling were the human questions that the Louisiana Purchase raised. As we have seen, there was little room for Native Americans or Africans in liberty's empire as conceived by Jefferson. Soon after Congress divided the purchase, Jefferson concluded that upper Louisiana would be a suitable destination for the Indians of the eastern United States. This would solve several problems—it would free up land in the east for settlement by the citizen-farmers of the American republic; it would solve the security problem that supposedly hostile Indians presented to the United States; and it would give those Indians time to assimilate the values and culture of European Americans. Jefferson's proposal underscored the degree to which his was a republic of white men. It also laid the foundation for the subsequent displacement and removal of tribes from the east in the next generation.[51]

Perhaps even more troubling for America's republican empire was the persistence of slavery. Although Isaac Briggs had described Louisiana as a potential paradise in 1804, he was worried that slavery, long practiced in Louisiana and sanctioned by its new governors, might be the serpent in the garden. Briggs saw slavery as a flaw at the heart of the American system, one that threatened the efforts to spread republican government. He wrote:

> When we make, to the world, high professions of Republicanism—hold ourselves up as the boasted Guardians of the Rights of Man—and are reproached for inconsistency—what can we answer, but
> *"Pudet haec opprobria nobis;*
> *Et dici potuisse, et non potuisse refelli."*
> (We are ashamed of these reproaches: both that they can be made and that they cannot be refuted.)[52]

Americans were aware of this difficulty. In 1804 Congress debated seriously several measures to restrict the importation of slaves into the territory acquired in the Louisiana Purchase. These included a successful measure to ban the international slave trade and a failed effort to ban the domestic slave trade. Ultimately slavery was not banned in Louisiana because the right of American citizens to hold slaves had been well established over the previous generation. Indeed, even before Congress began to debate whether to prohibit the import of slaves into Louisiana, South Carolina voted to reopen the Atlantic slave trade in direct response to the Louisiana Purchase. South Carolina's merchants, planters, and

slave traders sought to import more slaves directly from Africa to fulfill
the demands of the new territory. Between 1804 and 1808, when the
Atlantic slave trade was banned by the federal government, 39,075
slaves—10 percent of the total number of slaves imported to North
America—were imported into South Carolina. These men, women, and
children paid for the purchase of Louisiana with their freedom and their
lives. Although the boundaries of Louisiana—and hence Jefferson's
empire—were unclear in 1804, the limits of liberty within that empire
were all too apparent.[53]

Historians disagree as to whether Jefferson deserves credit for the
Louisiana Purchase. Did he have any control over events, or was he simply the lucky beneficiary of the valiant resistance of Saint Domingue's
slaves and Napoleon's genius for reappraisal? To be sure, Jefferson had
no control over yellow fever or the necessities of great-power diplomacy
during his administration. He did recognize the need for the United
States to acquire and settle land in the west and south. As a politician
and statesman he took steps, especially through the creation of the territorial system, to facilitate the expansion of the United States. Further,
he recognized the strategic importance of New Orleans to the American
republic from the mid-1780s. As secretary of state he pursued this as a
matter of urgency culminating in the Treaty of San Lorenzo after he left
office. When that treaty was rendered meaningless by the Treaty of San
Ildefonso, he immediately undertook the diplomatic negotiations that
eventually enabled the Louisiana Purchase.[54]

In their study of Jefferson's statecraft, Robert W. Tucker and David
C. Hendrickson argue that the Louisiana Purchase was the culmination
of Jefferson's moralistic republican vision of international relations that
rejected traditional diplomacy. They write, "The undoubted triumph of
Louisiana is seen to represent something greater than either diplomatic
skill or luck. Instead this acquisition stands out as the justification of a
diplomacy dedicated to the rejection of the necessity allegedly imposed
by a traditional reason of state." Jefferson's good fortune, they argue, led
to a diplomatic success that vindicated his flawed approach to statecraft.
"Louisiana had shown," they write, "that there was no need to arm and
to make sacrifices when vital interests are at stake. Instead it was sufficient to hold up the prospect of alliances that would probably never be

made and to threaten wars that one had no intention of waging. Another lesson was the wisdom of conducting negotiations in which one asks for much while offering little."[55] This interpretation overstates the case somewhat. Jefferson did benefit from very good luck, and circumstances beyond his control induced Napoleon to part with Louisiana. He had, however, placed himself in a position to exploit his good fortune. Jefferson played a weak hand very well, and in the Louisiana negotiations good luck, quick decision making, and the willingness to resort to the methods of traditional statecraft served him well. He demonstrated a willingness to use force and occasional duplicity to complement his diplomacy. During the Louisiana crisis and the subsequent negotiations he achieved a rare, unambiguous, diplomatic triumph for the United States. For a weak state on the periphery of the Atlantic world, it is not surprising that such victories were infrequent. The future travails Jefferson confronted in the international arena were not the result of his learning the wrong lessons from acquisition of Louisiana, but rather that his luck was bad or circumstances less propitious as they had been in 1803. The fundamental international fact that Jefferson faced was that his nation was weaker than most of its rivals. Given that, it's not surprising that the acquisition of Louisiana was the signal diplomatic achievement of his presidency.

The European conflict that created the circumstances that allowed the United States to purchase Louisiana posed a direct challenge to the trade, economic well-being, and independence of the United States. In contrast to the international success in his first term, with the Louisiana Purchase, Jefferson's second term saw a prolonged struggle to protect the political and economic independence of the new nation and was characterized by repeated international trials and failure.

Seven

"They Expect the President to Act"

Romulus Ware was born a slave around 1767 at Pipe Creek near Frederick, Maryland. His mother was a mixed-race woman named Phillis, owned by a man named Norman Bruce. Ware's father was a free white man, Andrew Ware. Andrew Ware and the enslaved woman, Phillis, had two children. These children, while raised by their mother on Bruce's farm, were acknowledged as Ware's children and took their father's name. Upton Bruce, Norman Bruce's son, who was just a few years older than the enslaved Romulus Ware, managed his father's farm and eventually inherited his property, including Phillis and her children. Owing to his mixed parentage, Romulus Ware was light-skinned. Upton Bruce described him as "swarthy or Indian-like, remarkably bright though for a mulatto." William McNair, who worked as Bruce's overseer, described Ware as "of a very bright color, like a very dark white man." According to Bruce, "in consideration of his color, the regard I had for his father (then dead), and the desire expressed by that father to have these children liberated," he allowed Ware to go free when he was twenty years old.[1]

Sometime after acquiring his freedom Ware changed his name to William. William Ware won his freedom at a moment when Chesapeake slaveholders were granting manumissions to their slaves in response to economic and moral pressure in the aftermath of the American Revolution. Between 1790 and 1810 the largest population of free African Americans in the United States emerged in Maryland, despite that state retaining slavery. William Ware, who did not obtain a manumission certificate from Upton Bruce, joined that population. Without a formal certificate of manumission Ware was in a liminal legal position between slavery and freedom. Upton Bruce might have sought to re-enslave Ware, but he seems to have extracted a promise from the younger man that he would pay his master for his freedom. According to Bruce, Ware promised to pay him, "compensation which never has been done." In any event, Ware worked as a wagoner on the road between Hagerstown and Baltimore and lived as a free man. Upton Bruce was aware of Ware's presence for a time but apparently made no effort to re-enslave Ware or to collect what he regarded as his just compensation for Ware's freedom.[2]

William Ware, who was just five feet seven inches tall and slightly built, eventually gave up his work as a teamster and went to sea. During the Napoleonic wars the United States emerged as the foremost neutral carrier in the North Atlantic, and there was plenty of work for merchant seamen. Maritime work was particularly attractive to free African Americans, who welcomed the increased pay, mobility, and freedom that came with life at sea. As the free black population of the new republic increased so too did the number of African Americans and mixed-race Americans working in the maritime trades.[3] Ware served in the United States Navy, aboard the U.S.S. *Chesapeake,* and in the American merchant marine. He was a crewman aboard the American merchant brig *Neptune* in 1805 when it was stopped by H.M.S. *Melampus* in the Bay of Biscay.

The Royal Navy was in desperate need of trained hands, and British officers routinely stopped American vessels to search for deserters. Under the guise of recovering deserters, British naval officers frequently impressed American sailors into the Royal Navy. (They also recovered numerous deserters who had fled British naval service for the safer and more lucrative American merchant service.) Thousands of American sailors were pressed into British service during the first years of the nineteenth century. William Ware was one of them; he was forced to join the crew of the *Melampus* in late 1805. He served aboard the *Melampus* for fifteen months until early 1807. The *Melampus* was then on station with a British squadron off the coast of Virginia searching for French privateers.[4] In February, when the *Melampus* was anchored at Hampton

Roads, "there was an entertainment on board," which occupied all of the ship's officers. Ware and three other sailors—Daniel Martin, John Strachan, and John Little—took advantage of the diversion and stole the captain's gig. They rowed for the shore under a hail of musket fire from the marines on the *Melampus*. When they reached shore they "gave three cheers, and moved up the country." The four runaways made their way to Norfolk where Ware, Martin, and Strachan joined the crew of the U.S.S. *Chesapeake*, which was due to sail to the Mediterranean. John Hamilton, the British consul in Norfolk, issued a formal protest to Captain Stephen Decatur, the commander of the base at Norfolk. (It was Decatur who had led the raid that destroyed the *Philadelphia* in Tripoli harbor in 1804.) Decatur refused to surrender any men "who have voluntarily entered the service of the United States, unless claimed by the magistracy." It was extremely unlikely that an American court would turn American sailors over to British.[5]

The flight of the men from the *Melampus* and their enlistment on the *Chesapeake* was unacceptable as far as the British were concerned. British naval officers were furious that their sailors continued to desert and find succor in the United States. They were affronted when they met on the streets of Norfolk deserters who taunted their former commanders. They appealed to Vice Admiral George Cranfield Berkeley, British commander of the North American station. On June 1 Berkeley issued an order requiring British vessels to stop the *Chesapeake* if they should encounter the frigate in international waters "to show the captain of her this order, and to require to search his ship for deserters." The stage was set for a major international incident when the *Chesapeake* put to sea.[6]

The lives of Thomas Jefferson and William Ware intersected when Ware fled from the Royal Navy and placed himself at the center of a looming international crisis. Jefferson and Ware were born at opposite ends of the Chesapeake social spectrum. When Ware was pressed to the join the crew of the *Melampus*, in a display of coercion that underscored his relative powerlessness in a brutal system of international relations, Jefferson had begun his second term as president of the United States. Ware's life had been bounded by his experiences as a slave and a free man in a world that paid little heed to the rights of a mixed-race man of limited means. He achieved his freedom in post-revolutionary America only to find his liberty taken away from him by the Royal Navy. When he fled the *Melampus* he sought to regain his hard-won independence and autonomy. Jefferson, by contrast, was a beneficiary of the slave system into which Romulus Ware had been born. His entire way of life—his wealth and status—was dependent on slavery. Over the course of his long life Jefferson owned approximately six hundred human beings. He condemned slavery, crucially lamenting the corrosive moral effect of slavery *on slave owners,* but he did little during his lifetime to end it. Indeed, as the strength of his support lay in the south and west, Jefferson owed his political success to the three-fifths clause in the Constitution that gave slaveholders disproportionate political strength as 60 percent of the enslaved population was added to the free population when allocating seats in the House of Representatives and votes in the Electoral College.[7]

Jefferson was much more powerful than William Ware, but during his presidency he was as subject to the caprices of British power as Ware and the thousands of American sailors impressed by the Royal Navy: Jefferson's presidency was held captive by British policies arising from the wars with Napoleonic France. The United States, as the Atlantic world's leading neutral carrier, profited handsomely as a consequence of the European conflict, but it was also buffeted by the major powers as they sought to restrict and control American trade. Jefferson's biggest international challenge as president was protecting and promoting American trade. He did so from a position of relative weakness, as the impressment issue revealed. As a consequence he turned to economic coercion to protect and promote the trade of the United States and to defend American sovereignty. The result was an ineffective embargo that had catastrophic results for the United States. Jefferson's presidency ended in failure because he could not formulate an effective policy to defend American rights and interests.

Shortly after the American and French negotiators reached an agreement on the sale of Louisiana in April 1803, the short-lived Peace of Amiens broke down. Britain declared war on France on May 16, and from then until the ultimate defeat of Napoleon in 1815 Europe was in a constant state of war. During the early years of the nineteenth century Britain built a coalition—which eventually included Austria, Prussia, Russia, and Sweden—to confront Napoleon. The conflict in Europe soon spread, encompassing the overseas colonies of the major protagonists—particularly in the West Indies. The Napoleonic wars presented the United States with both economic opportunity and considerable diplomatic risk. With Britain preoccupied by its struggle with France, the United States supplanted its former colonial master as the world's preeminent merchant carrier. It was a very lucrative trade for the United States: between 1795, when the Jay Treaty was ratified, and 1807, the overall value of American exports increased from $48 million to $108 million. The majority of American trade consisted of staples from the British, French, and Spanish colonies in the West Indies that were briefly landed in the United States, with the payment of nominal customs duties, and then re-exported as American produce. This re-export trade, which was essential to contravene British customs and maritime restrictions, increased in value from $8 million to $60 million between 1795 and 1807. It, along with increased production and exports by American farmers, guaranteed prosperity during Jefferson's first term as president. We have seen that international trade was a crucial corollary to the geographic expansion that was central to Jefferson's understanding of republican political economy. Protecting this trade was the central preoccupation of Jefferson's second term.[8]

In 1804 Secretary of State James Madison offered a perceptive analysis of the international situation. In a letter to Elbridge Gerry, who knew the frustrations of European diplomacy firsthand, Madison wrote that the only threat to American prosperity, "would be a serious collision with some of the Great powers of Europe, which I hope will be avoided." Madison conceded that "we have some points of consequence yet to settle with Spain," in the aftermath of the Louisiana Purchase, but he expressed the hope that "an amicable settlement is at least as convenient to her as to the U. States." Rather, Madison identified relations with Britain as the most likely obstacle to continued American prosperity. "The conduct of G.B. particularly in the case of impressments & blockades is not a little embarrassing." Madison expressed a desire that a comprehensive settlement might be reached (the Jay Treaty had expired in 1803): "We hope therefore that some arrangements may be devised that will prevent not only extremities, but the necessity of measures tending toward them. The Administration in all its branches, is, I am persuaded, sincerely desirous to meet [Britain] on every conciliatory ground, and to make every sacrifice to peace & even to prejudice, which may be consistent with the honor and the essential interests of the nation."[9] While both Britain and France sought to restrict American trade, as Madison suggested, the United States found itself in more frequent and serious conflict with Britain during Jefferson's presidency. With the Battle of Trafalgar on October 21, 1805, Britain gained command of the seas, a position it retained for the next decade. After Trafalgar Britain was better able to enforce blockades and to restrict American trade than France, which became increasingly reliant on American merchant ships to carry its commerce between and among its far-flung colonies. Despite setbacks at sea, France had the upper hand in the military struggle in mainland Europe. Less than two months after Trafalgar Napoleon prevailed at the Battle of Austerlitz (December 2, 1805), dealing the Russians and Austrians a devastating blow.

Faced with the competing demands of Britain and France, the United States confronted a difficult diplomatic challenge. In the wake of British victory at Trafalgar Jefferson wrote, "What an awful spectacle does the world exhibit at this instant, one man bestriding the continent of Europe like a Colossus, and another roaming unbridled on the ocean." Nonetheless, Jefferson conceded "this is better than that one should rule both elements. Our wish ought to be that he who has armies may not have the Dominion of the sea, and that he who has Dominion of the sea may be the one who has no armies. In this way we may be quiet; at home at least."[10] Jefferson's expectation that the United States might find quiet in the balance of power between Britain and France would prove to be unrealistic.

As a neutral country the United States championed the cause of free trade, arguing that it should be able to trade with any of the belligerents—provided it did not attempt to smuggle contraband. France and particularly Britain sought to restrict American trade. The British position was the so-called Rule of 1756, which stipulated that trade that was illegal in peacetime was also illegal during war. In other words, neither the United

States nor any other neutral carrier could trade with Britain's enemies during war unless they had had previous trading agreement with them. This rule had no weight in international law, but the British had adhered to it for more than half a century. The British sought to reap the benefits of trade with the United States while restricting those benefits to their enemies. As a consequence the United States frequently found itself in conflict at sea with its main trading partners. International trade was lucrative, but the danger of war persisted so long as the United States asserted its right to trade and the major belligerents sought to restrict its trade.

As Madison recognized, the issue of impressment was closely linked to that of trade. During the colonial period Royal Navy press gangs occasionally operated in American ports—just as they did in other British ports. During the French revolutionary and Napoleonic wars the Royal Navy struggled to find enough crewmen for its ships. In 1805, when the Battle of Trafalgar was fought, the Royal Navy required 120,000 men, including 10,000 new sailors each year, to maintain its strength. The situation was made worse by the presence of the independent American merchant marine, which offered higher wages and safer working conditions than the British navy. Desertion was a constant problem: British mariners fled the danger of naval service to serve aboard American merchant vessels in British and American ports, in the West Indies, and anywhere else British and American vessels encountered each other. (British warships routinely put in to American ports for water and other supplies.) In 1807 Albert Gallatin, Jefferson's treasury secretary, estimated that as many as 9,000 Britons were serving aboard American merchant ships. According to Gallatin, the growth in American commerce required an additional 4,200 sailors per annum. The United States depended on British sailors to maintain this increase. In response to the constant demand for hands and to recover deserters, the Royal Navy relied on impressment. American merchant vessels were stopped at sea and in ports and their crews were examined. Any likely or suspected deserters or British-born seamen were liable to be forcibly taken and compelled to join the crews of British warships. American-born sailors as well as naturalized American citizens born in Britain were often forced into British service. Indeed, Gallatin claimed that the reason the American merchant marine needed so many British hands was to make up for the Americans lost to impressment. Sometimes impressments took place within American territorial waters or in American ports, which was especially galling to American sensibilities.[11]

As we have seen in the case of William Ware, each episode of impressment involved personal duress for the individuals concerned. For the United States such instances, particularly when they occurred within American territorial waters, represented a challenge to national sovereignty. For example, on June 23, 1804, Secretary of State James Madison summoned the British minister in Washington, Anthony Merry. According to Merry, Madison produced an affidavit which described an incident that had recently taken place in New York harbor. On June 16 an American revenue cutter had approached a British merchant vessel, the *Pitt,* which had just arrived in the harbor. When two American officials—a customs officer and a medical inspector—boarded the *Pitt* with the intention of conducting routine inspections they interrupted a press gang at work. Officers from H.M.S. *Cambrian,* which was moored in New York, were inspecting the crew of the *Pitt* and searching for deserters. The British pressed no fewer than fourteen members of the *Pitt*'s crew. According to the affidavit that Madison produced, the American officials were "prevented, by Menaces and other improper Language . . . from doing the Duty of their respective Departments." According to Merry, "Mr. Madison complained of the Impressment, from its having taken place within the Port, although on board a British Ship, and of the other Acts committed by His Majesty's Officers, . . . as being such a Violation of the American Territory, and an Outrage against the Laws as could not possibly be tolerated, and as requiring a Vindication of the Sovereignty of the United States by the immediate Punishment of the Offenders." Madison also asked for an apology from the British officer in charge of the press gang and the return of all fourteen sailors to the *Pitt.*[12]

Merry consulted with Captain William Bradley of the *Cambrian.* Bradley denied interfering with or mistreating the American officials. According to Merry: "The only Point of Accusation, then, upon which Captain Bradley has not given Satisfaction is that of the Impressment of a Part of the Crew of the Ship *Pitt.* On this Subject he alleges that he has done no more than exercise the Authority with which he is invested of pressing British Subjects on board a British Ship, and that the Circumstance of that Ship having just come within the Jurisdiction of the United States involves a Question upon which he cannot take upon himself to decide, by restoring the Men, without an Instruction from his own Government." Madison was not content to let the matter rest. The crucial issue for Madison was that the incident took place in American territorial waters, not aboard a British vessel. He asserted, "To be within the United States, is to be within their Protection, and to violate that Protection by a foreign armed Force is one of the greatest Indignities that can be offered to any Nation, and one for which ample Satisfaction may most reasonably be required and expected."[13]

Captain Bradley was not through violating the sovereignty of the United States. On July 16 the *Cambrian* stopped the American ship *Diana* off Sandy Hook, New Jersey. The *Diana,* a merchant vessel out of Nantucket, was en route from Liverpool to New York when a press gang from the *Cambrian* boarded it and "forcibly impressed and detained" six passengers, all British subjects. The captain of the *Diana* claimed that the men in question were all civilians and that they had boarded the vessel with the approval of customs officials in Liverpool, thus they should have been allowed to travel to the United States unmolested. With this incident coming so soon after the affair involving the *Pitt,* the secretary of state took the opportunity to repeat his complaint about the actions of Bradley and other British officers in the New York area and to remind Merry "of the respect due both to the Ports of the United States and to the Immunities of their Flag" while calling on the British government to act "in a Manner which may at Once afford the Satisfaction due to the United States and deter Others from similar Acts of Disrespect and Aggression towards friendly Powers." Anthony Merry wrote a lengthy response to Madison in which he explained that it was the Royal Navy's longstanding practice "for His Majesty's Officers to impress British Subjects from British Ships in all foreign Ports, and to demand them out of foreign Ships without any Complaint ever having been made by the foreign Government." Merry averred that he could not discuss the legality of his government's impressment policy "in regard to the pretended Immunity of the Flag of the United States." The government in London,

while not conceding any ground on the question of impressment, adopted a more conciliatory position vis-à-vis the *Cambrian*. In early September, Lord Harrowby, the foreign secretary, met with James Monroe,
the American minister in London, to discuss British-American relations.
Harrowby was interested in negotiating a commercial settlement with
the United States to replace the lapsed Jay Treaty. The two men discussed impressment at some length. Although Harrowby offered no
concessions on the principle of impressment, he said that the government "disapproved & censured" Bradley's conduct "by his removal
from the command [of the *Cambrian*] and ordering him home to account for it."[14]

The incidents involving the *Cambrian* concerned British subjects
who were forced into the Royal Navy in American waters or, as in the
case of the *Diana,* from an American vessel. Much more offensive from
an American perspective were the incidents in which American citizens
were forced to join the British navy. In 1803 the *Superb* out of Philadelphia was fired on by H.M.S. *Galatea,* and six Americans were removed
from the *Superb*. When the captain of the *Superb* protested (one of the
impressed men was his brother), he was forcibly removed from his ship,
"personally abused, and cut with a saber on board the *Galatea*."[15] Sometimes these incidents occurred as a result of honest misunderstand-
ings. Lord Harrowby observed that the "similitude" of Americans and
Britons made them difficult to distinguish from each other. Hard-pressed
British naval officers were not always inclined to make careful distinctions when it came to filling their crews. Indeed, a major American
grievance was that British officers presumed American sailors were British unless they could produce positive proof to the contrary. As Madison wrote early in 1804, "Were it allowable that British subjects should
be taken out of American vessels on the high seas," a concession the
United States was unwilling to make, "it might at least be required that
the proof of their allegiance should lie on the British side. This obvious
and just rule is however reversed; and every seaman on board, tho' going
from an American port, and sailing under the American flag, and sometimes even speaking an idiom proving him not to be a British subject,
is presumed to be such, unless shewn to be an American citizen." The
British, Madison continued, would not allow such an outrage to be

committed against their subjects. Proof of citizenship in the form of testimony and government-issued certificates frequently was not enough to satisfy British naval officers on a rolling deck in the middle of the Atlantic. "Nor is it always against the right presumption alone, which is in favor of the citizenship corresponding with the flag, that the violence is committed," wrote Madison. "Not unfrequently it takes place in defiance of the most positive proof, certified in due form by an american [*sic*] officer."[16]

It is not clear just how many Americans sailors were impressed by the Royal Navy. George W. Erving, the American consul in London who dealt with impressed seamen who claimed to be American citizens, reported that he had received 1,538 such claims between March 11, 1803, and August 1804.[17] On the eve of the War of 1812 then-Secretary of State James Monroe estimated that 6,257 Americans had been impressed since 1803. For the period from 1793 to 1812 the figure is likely at least 10,000.[18] Each case, while an individual tragedy for the souls forced into British service, represented a challenge to American sovereignty and independence. As early as 1801 James Madison, the new secretary of state, noted that impressment undermined British-American relations. "But it is proper to be known that these wrongs have made a deep impression on the American mind, and that if no satisfactory change of conduct be soon apparent, . . . the policy of this Country, can scarcely fail to take some shape more remedial than that hitherto given it." Madison asserted that he and the president were as one on the issue—and in agreement with the American people. "The President wishes it to be understood," he wrote, "that his disposition is in perfect concurrence with that of the Community, and that every proper demonstration of it, will be found in the course of his administration."[19] Given the unwillingness of the British to compromise on the question of impressment, Jefferson and Madison sought to find the appropriate remedial measures to address the problem throughout Jefferson's two terms as president. They failed to do so in large part because the United States was in a relatively weak position with respect to Britain. It could wage war against the Barbary States, but it lacked the military strength to confront Britain. As a consequence, Jefferson resorted to commercial sanctions in order to compel Britain to respect the maritime rights of the United States. He did so not out of excessive idealism, nor out of a misplaced faith in the potency of economic suasion, but because he had few options.

Most of the provisions of the Jay Treaty expired in 1803. Although that pact had never been popular with Republicans, Jefferson believed that a new agreement might be reached to settle the major points of contention in British-American relations. In late December Madison wrote to James Monroe to let him know the cabinet had been discussing a proposal that it hoped would be the basis for British-American negotiations. According to Madison, the main objectives of the plan would be to "get rid of impressments on the high seas, to define blockades and contraband" according to a treaty recently agreed between Britain and Russia, and "to put aside the doctrine that a Colonial trade, not allowed in time of peace, is unlawful in time of war." In exchange, the United States would agree to return British deserters and to adopt legislation to prohibit the export of contraband as defined by mutual agreement between the two countries. The agreement would not be as comprehensive as the Jay Treaty had been, but it would remove the most difficult obstacles to British-American harmony, at least as far as the Jefferson administration was concerned. Madison promised Monroe: "This will be the outline, excepting a few minor propositions. The subject is now before the Cabinet, and it will not be long before it will be forwarded to you in its details."[20]

At the behest of the president, Madison sent Monroe a detailed "plan of a Convention" on January 5, 1804, a draft plan consisting of thirteen articles as well as extensive commentary and notes to guide him in his discussions with the British government. Personal experience and the recent Louisiana negotiations had taught Jefferson and Madison that diplomats far from home needed a degree of autonomy. Nonetheless, Madison stressed to Monroe: "The essential objects for the U. States are the suppression of impressments, and the definition of Blockades. Next to these in importance, are the reduction of the list of contraband and the enlargment [*sic*] of our neutral trade with hostile Colonies. Whilst you keep in view therefore those objects, the two last as highly important and the two first as absolutely indispensable, your discretion in which

the President places great confidence, must guide you in all that relates
to the inferior ones."[21]

Monroe was initially optimistic that a settlement might be reached.
He reported from London in February: "There is a strong motive for
some equitable & amicable arrangement with this government. There
are severally topics of the first importance to both parties and ought to
be adjusted on such fair and liberal principles as to leave no cause of future variance behind."[22] Monroe's optimism was unfounded. He had
several unproductive meetings with government ministers, including an
unpleasant meeting with the new foreign secretary, in late May. According to Monroe: "The conduct of Lord Harrowby thro' the whole of this
conference was calculated to wound and irritate. Not a friendly sentiment towards the UStates or their govt. escaped him." After the meeting
a disconsolate Monroe conceded, "I now consider these concerns as
postponed indefinitely. I do not forsee at what time it will be proper
for me to revive this subject."[23] After the misdeeds of the *Cambrian* in
American waters during the summer of 1804 Harrowby softened his
tone toward Monroe somewhat but did not relax his overall stance. The
British would have welcomed an accommodation with the United States,
but they were unwilling to compromise on the question of impressment
or to make concessions regarding contraband.[24]

The American diplomatic initiative came at a moment when the
British adopted a much more stringent policy toward neutral trade—
particularly the trade of the United States. In May 1805 the British court
of appeals handed down a decision in the case of an American vessel,
Essex. The *Essex* had been carrying a cargo of wine from Barcelona to
Havana via a brief stop in the United States when it was seized by the
British. Since 1800 the British had tolerated "broken voyages" and countenanced the re-export trade. In 1805, however, the court took the view
that as trade between Spain and its colonies had been closed to Americans during peacetime, it was not legal during wartime. The court ruled
that the final destination of the voyage was all-important in determining
the status of a cargo. The court essentially upheld the Rule of 1756,
which opened the way for increased seizures of American ships in the
West Indies. Monroe believed that the *Essex* decision and the resulting
seizures were a part of a concerted British effort to wage commercial

warfare against the United States. He contended that the British felt their commercial hegemony was threatened by the rise of the American carrying trade and were using the war with Napoleon as a pretext to attack American commerce. The British, naturally, saw things differently. In October 1805 James Stephen, an admiralty court judge, published a pamphlet, *War in Disguise; or the Frauds of the Neutral Flags,* in which he argued that the neutral re-export trade benefited Britain's enemies, and that ships bearing neutral goods strengthened Napoleon. Stephen called for the rigorous enforcement of the Rule of 1756 and renewed attacks on neutral trade. This would weaken Napoleon *and* benefit British commerce.[25]

The difference between Monroe's and Stephen's interpretation of the *Essex* decision is really a matter of degree. The decision signaled a more hard-line approach by the British to neutral trade and contraband. The decision was not widely publicized initially, allowing British privateers and naval vessels to capture a large number of unsuspecting American vessels. In London, Monroe complained that 120 American vessels were seized in the immediate aftermath of the decision. All told the British seized 528 American merchant vessels between 1803 and 1807, the majority after 1805. Philadelphia merchants alone claimed to have lost more than 100 ships, valued at $500,000, in the second half of 1805.[26] The crackdown on neutral trade was accompanied by a more robust policy with respect to deserters and impressment. The number of incidents of impressments—on the high seas and in port, in Britain and abroad—increased in 1805 and 1806.

In the wake of Trafalgar, the British seemed determined to press their maritime advantage to the greatest effect. In May 1806 the foreign secretary, Charles James Fox, declared the northern coast of Europe—from Brest to the Elbe—to be under a British blockade. Napoleon responded with the Berlin Decree of November 21, 1806, which declared Britain, its allies, and its colonies under a French blockade. Napoleon's decree created a "paper blockade" because the French lacked the naval resources to place Britain under a blockade. Nonetheless the decree allowed French privateers, particularly those operating in the West Indies, to seize American ships traveling between British colonies and the United States. In November 1807 the British issued Orders in Council that prohibited all neutral trade with France and its allies unless British customs duties were paid. In December 1807 Napoleon issued a further declaration, the Milan Decree, which stipulated that any neutral ships that traded with Britain or allowed themselves to be subjected to British customs regulations forfeited their status as neutrals and would be treated as belligerents. The French seized 307 American ships under the Berlin and Milan Decrees. The United States increasingly found itself squeezed between Britain and France.[27]

With hundreds of their ships seized—Monroe claimed that the Royal Navy seized an American ship every two days between 1805 and 1808[28]—and thousands of their seamen impressed into the Royal Navy, American merchants looked to their government for help. Resolutions and petitions poured into Washington from around the country demanding action. On January 17, 1806, Jefferson submitted the "memorials of several bodies of merchants of the United States" to Congress as evidence of "the most ruinous effects on our lawful commerce and navigation" of the more robust British policies.[29] Also in January, the secretary of state published an anonymous pamphlet with an ungainly title: *An Examination of the British Doctrine, Which Subjects to Capture a Neutral Trade, Not in Time of Peace.* Madison, whose identity as author quickly became known, provided a detailed examination of British maritime policy. The *Examination* did not provide any policy recommendations but outlined the scope and consequences of British interference with American trade.[30]

Congress spent the next several months debating the appropriate course of action to protect America's trade and the liberty of its mariners and to defend American sovereignty. The debate was, at times, acrimonious. Although Republicans dominated both houses of Congress, there was considerable disagreement about how best to proceed. To some extent the debate was so bitter because options were so limited. With diplomacy seemingly having failed, economic coercion appeared to be the only course available to the United States. Jefferson believed that trade restrictions and embargos had worked in the past—particularly in the decade before the American Revolution. These were normally short-term measures, however. Although, as we have seen, Jefferson was not squeamish about using force when necessary to defend American national interests, he hoped that nonviolent methods of national defense could be developed, and he placed a great deal of faith in economic coercion. Given the relative power of American commerce (and the concomitant military weakness of the United States), this was sensible. It remained to be seen, however, whether economic coercion would work, especially during wartime.[31]

The main American grievances concerned British interference with American trade, but a voluntarily disruption of its own trade was not a solution that the United States could consider for the long term as customs duties were a major source of government revenue. Nonetheless, Jefferson, Madison and other Republicans believed that the British and French depended on the American carrying trade to such a degree that even a brief disruption of commerce would bring the Europeans to their senses—and the negotiating table. In spring 1806 congressional debates focused on the manner and degree of commercial pressure that could be brought to bear on the British. In March, Congressman Joseph H. Nicholson of Maryland introduced a bill to prohibit the importation of a relatively narrow list of commodities from Britain—goods made of leather, silk, hemp; window glass; luxury woolens; and items made of tin, brass, and silver. Nicholson's list was limited so as not to deprive Americans of essential goods they could not produce themselves. Moreover the ban on prescribed goods would not take effect until November 15, 1806. Critics of the bill felt it was so mild that it would have no effect at all. The dissident Republican John Randolph famously denounced the legislation as "a milk and water bill, a dose of chicken broth to be taken nine months hence." While Federalists feared the bill would disrupt the still-lucrative trade between the United States and Britain, Republican dissenters like Randolph felt that the bill was too weak to achieve anything. Randolph claimed, "It is too contemptible to be the object of consideration or to excite the feelings of the pettiest state in Europe." The House of Representatives adopted the Non-Importation Act by a vote of 93 to 32 on March 26. The Senate approved the bill on April 15 by a margin of 19 to 9. Jefferson signed the act on April 18.[32]

John Randolph's indictment of the Non-Importation Act was not without merit. It is likely that Congress, and certainly President Jefferson, viewed the act as an invitation to the British to reopen the abortive negotiations that James Monroe had attempted the previous year. The death of the William Pitt, the British prime minister, in January 1806 led to a change in government. William Lord Grenville succeeded Pitt in February. Grenville's foreign secretary, Charles James Fox, was perceived to be more sympathetic to the United States than his immediate predecessors. Jefferson wrote optimistically about the new government, "The late change in the ministry I consider as insuring us a just settlements of our differences and we ask no more." Of the new foreign secretary the president wrote, "In Mr. Fox, personally, I have more confidence than any man in England & it is founded in what, through unquestionable channels, I have had opportunities of knowing of his honesty and & good sense."[33] Two days before Jefferson signed the Non-Importation Act Fox instructed Anthony Merry to "assure the Ministers of the United States of His Majesty's good Will toward said States, and of his earnest wish so to arrange all Matters liable to cause Dispute, that a ground may be laid for permanent Friendship and good Understanding between the Two Nations." Beyond this general expression of goodwill Merry was to give a more specific assurance that "His Majesty's Confidential Servants will very shortly be enabled to enter into Treaty with Mr. Monroe, and will not suffer the Business to be delayed one Day beyond what is absolutely necessary."[34]

The more conciliatory position of the British government combined with the signal of intent from Washington in the form of the Non-Importation Act suggested that the summer of 1806 might be a propitious moment to undertake negotiations. Jefferson would have preferred to delegate the task to Monroe who was already in place in London, had considerable experience of European diplomacy, and was well versed in the relevant issues. But there was an expectation in Congress that Jefferson should appoint a special envoy or commission to undertake the negotiations, as Washington had done when he dispatched John Jay to London to avoid a war in 1794. As a consequence the president nominated William Pinkney, a Maryland Federalist, to join Monroe in London. Pinkney was a successful lawyer and public servant with considerable diplomatic experience. He had served in London on one of the commissions created by the Jay Treaty to adjudicate British-American disputes. He was the author of a memorial adopted by Baltimore merchants in January 1806 condemning the *Essex* ship seizures. Pinkney had written to Jefferson in March to let him know that he was willing to serve if needed. Jefferson formally nominated Pinkney and Monroe as commissioners plenipotentiary to negotiate with the British on April 19. The Senate approved the nominations two days later.[35]

Madison prepared lengthy instructions for Pinkney and Monroe. These closely followed the plan that he and Jefferson had prepared for Monroe the previous year but were slightly more ambitious, seeking a broader agreement between the two countries, including an extension of American territorial waters as far as the Gulf Stream. Nonetheless the main American concerns remained impressment and the restoration of the re-export trade.[36] Jefferson was confident that the negotiations would be more successful than the abortive effort of the previous year. He wrote to Monroe in early May, "No two countries upon earth have so many points of common interest and friendship and their rulers must be great bunglers indeed, if, with such dispositions, they break them asunder."[37] In retrospect, Jefferson's confidence seems misplaced. A few days earlier, H.M.S. *Leander* fired a warning shot at a merchant vessel off Sandy Hook, New Jersey (not far from the spot where the *Cambrian* had stopped the *Diana* in 1804). The shot struck a pilot ship nearby, killing one of its crew, John Pierce. Pierce's death ignited an outburst of anti-British sentiment in New York, which had long suffered from the abuses of the Royal Navy. Thomas Barclay, the British consul in New York, feared for his safety in the aftermath of the incident. Although some newspapers called for a declaration of war in response to the death of Pierce, the president responded in a more measured fashion. He ordered the *Leander,* along with its sister ships, *Cambrian* and *Driver* (which had been at the center of the disputes in New York harbor in 1804), to leave American waters. In order to enforce this order he cut off all supplies to the ships. He also instructed Monroe to seek the court martial of Captain Henry Whitby, the commodore of the British squadron in New York. Jefferson believed that it might be possible to exploit the situation to enhance the American position in the upcoming negotiations. "We concluded therefore that it was best," he wrote, "to make a proper use of the outrage and of our forbearance at St. James's, to obtain better provisions for the future." The *Leander* incident underscored how fragile and perilous British-American relations were by spring 1806.[38]

Pinkney and Monroe began talks with their British counterparts at the end of August. The British commissioners were Henry Vassall-Fox, Lord Holland (Charles James Fox's nephew), and the president of the Board of Trade, William Eden, Baron Auckland. Jefferson was skeptical about Auckland, whom he described as "too wedded to the antient maritime code & navigation principles of England, [and] too much practiced in the tactics of diplomacy." The negotiations suffered a setback when Charles James Fox died on September 13. Jefferson lamented the death of Fox, writing, "His sound judgment saw that political interest could never be separated in the long run from moral right, & his frank & great mind would have made a short business of a just treaty." Fox was succeeded as foreign secretary by Charles Grey, Viscount Howick. Howick was less sympathetic to the United States than his predecessor had been.[39]

The American and British commissioners met from August 27 until December 31. Lord Holland provided a description of the American diplomats:

> We found the two American Commissioners fair, explicit, frank, and intelligent. Mr. Monroe (afterwards President) was a sincere republican, who during the Revolution in France had imbibed a strong predilection for that country, and no slight aversion to this. But he had candour and principle. . . . He was plain in his manners and somewhat slow in his apprehension; but he was a diligent, earnest, sensible, and even profound man. His colleague, who had been partly educated in England and was a lawyer by profession, had more of the forms and readiness of business, and greater knowledge and cultivation of mind ; but perhaps his opinions were neither so firmly rooted nor so deeply considered as those of Mr. Monroe.[40]

Holland recalled that after Fox's death the Americans became more conciliatory, perhaps fearing that they had lost an ally in the British government. They discussed impressment for two and half months. The

Americans stuck to the position that Madison and Jefferson had first outlined in January 1805—that the British should eschew impressment and the United States would do its utmost to return deserters. The prime minister, Lord Grenville, opposed making any concession on the issue "from my strong sense of the impossibility of obtaining anything like a fair execution of the American part of this stipulation."[41] Lord Holland recalled, "The atmosphere of the Admiralty made those who breathed it shudder at everything like concessions to the Americans." According to Holland the two sides could not reach an agreement on the issue:

> My colleague and I took credit to ourselves for having con-vinced them of the extreme difficulty of the subject, arising from the impossibility of our allowing seamen to withdraw them-selves from our service during war, and from the inefficacy of all the regulations which they had been enabled to propose for preventing their entering into American ships. They, on the other hand, persuaded us that they were themselves sincere in wishing to prevent it; and we saw no reason for suspecting that the Government of the United States was less so. But though they professed, and I believe felt, a strong wish to enforce such a provision, they did not convince us that they had the power or means of enforcing it.[42]

The two sides were unable to conclude a formal agreement on the im-pressment question. Nonetheless the American commissioners believed that they had reached an informal understanding that if the Americans made sincere efforts to return British deserters then "no impressment should be made on the high seas . . . except in cases of an extraordinary nature."[43]

Monroe and Pinkney, believing that they had received "most posi-tive assurances" that the British would restrain themselves on the im-pressment question and that this was the best outcome they could achieve, elected to continue the negotiations.[44] Having dispensed with the impressment question—or, more properly, having decided to ignore the impressment question—the negotiations proceeded relatively smoothly in November and December. The Americans won some significant concessions. The British allowed the reintroduction of the re-export trade, provided goods were landed in the United States and subject to modest transit duties. The British also agreed to recognize an extension of American territorial waters to five miles. The negotiators agreed to a rather limited list of contraband items, protection from unannounced blockades, and indemnities in the event British admiralty courts ruled that a vessel was seized unjustly. In exchange for these concessions the American negotiators agreed that British commerce would not be subject to commercial sanctions—such as non-exportation or non-importation—that did not apply to other nations as well. By negotiating over the list of contraband items and accepting the right of the British to seize contraband from American vessels, Monroe and Pinkney conceded the principle that free ships make free goods. The British and American commissioners signed the provisional treaty on December 31, 1806.[45]

In Washington, President Jefferson was encouraged by the early reports concerning the talks in London. In response to a request from Monroe and Pinkney he asked Congress to delay the implementation of the Non-Importation Act as a good-faith gesture and to allow the commissioners time to complete their negotiations. In making the request—which Congress approved, delaying implementation until July 1, 1807—he observed that the negotiations were being carried out "in a spirit of friendship and accommodation, which promises a result of mutual advantage."[46] When the full text of the treaty arrived in January 1807, Jefferson was disappointed. Appended to the text was a note stating that George III would not accept the treaty unless the United States rejected Napoleon's Berlin Decree.[47]

Jefferson faced one of the most important foreign policy decisions of his presidency with the Monroe-Pinkney treaty. In accepting the treaty, the United States would effectively give up its neutrality and enter into a commercial alliance with Britain. It would also have to forgo commercial sanctions as a diplomatic weapon, and the impressment issue would remain unresolved. The advantages were that peace with Britain would be maintained, as would the commercial prosperity that had accrued through the expansion of the American carrying trade during the European war. Monroe and Pinkney believed they might also have secured a British promise not to engage in impressment except in unusual situations (provided the United States returned British deserters), but this was not definitively addressed in the agreement. As the president studied the treaty text he was increasingly unhappy with its provisions—particularly its failure to address the impressment question. He wrote to Madison on February 1, 1807, "I believe the sine qua non we made is that of the nation, and that they would rather go on without a treaty than one which does not settle this article."[48]

Jefferson called a cabinet meeting on the morning of February 2 to discuss the treaty. He put three questions to his cabinet. First he asked, "Shall we agree to any treaty yielding the principle of our non-importn act, and not securing us agt. impressments?" The cabinet unanimously agreed that the treaty should be rejected. According to Jefferson's notes, the cabinet was unwilling to yield "the only peaceable instrument [commercial sanctions] for coercing all our rights." The cabinet concluded, "We had better have no treaty than a bad one. It will not restore friendship, but keep us in a state of constant irritation." Jefferson's second question concerned what the United States should do if it rejected the treaty: "Shall we draw off in hostile attitude, or agree informally that there shall be an understanding between us that we will act in practice on the very principles proposed by the treaty . . . ?" The cabinet unanimously agreed that the United States should seek to promote a more harmonious relationship with Britain in the absence of a formal treaty. In essence, the administration wanted to secure the benefits of the agreement, particularly the revival of the re-export trade, without making onerous concessions. Finally, Jefferson asked the cabinet whether he should submit the treaty to the Senate for its consideration. Since the administration would not be seeking to ratify the treaty the cabinet, again unanimously, agreed that there was no need to submit the treaty to the upper house.[49]

While Jefferson was in the habit of consulting his cabinet on major questions, the decision as to whether to submit the treaty to the Senate for ratification ultimately lay with him. The cabinet deliberations confirmed his own view that without an agreement on impressment the treaty could not be ratified, and he decided not to submit it to the Senate. After the cabinet meeting he requested that Madison write to Monroe and

Pinkney on his behalf to explain his reasoning and to instruct them to pursue further negotiations with the British with an eye toward finding a permanent solution to the impressment question.[50]

Historians have been critical of Jefferson's response to the Monroe-Pinkney treaty. Bradford Perkins invoked the realist/idealist dichotomy, writing: "Monroe and Pinkney not only spoke the traditional accents of American realism; they also opened the door to peace and uneasy friendship. They did these at the cost of important moral considerations, and Jefferson and Madison expressed more nobly the new nation's aspirations. But if the administration rejected compromise in the interest of idealism and psychological equality, by its future course it condemned itself, lacking the will to vindicate these commendable objectives." Perkins later wrote, "No doubt in insisting on the fullness of American rights, Jefferson and Madison spoke for the nation's aspirations, but they devised no effective strategy to redeem them." Donald R. Hickey, a leading historian of the origins of the War of 1812, argued that Jefferson "missed an opportunity to reforge the Anglo-American accord of the 1790s and to substitute peace and prosperity for commercial restrictions and war." Even Dumas Malone, Jefferson's most sympathetic biographer, asked whether "Jefferson was sufficiently aware that diplomacy, like politics, is the art of the possible" and should have accepted the treaty.[51]

The prevailing interpretation suggests that Jefferson made an error when he refused to submit the treaty to the Senate. This view is flawed. It assumes that Jefferson had a wider range of options available to him than he did. Jefferson believed that it was politically and ethically impossible to compromise over the impressment question. Most modern historians treat this as incidental to the larger question of neutral trade, but Jefferson and Madison consistently insisted that it was the sine qua non of any diplomatic settlement. As David Erskine, the new British minister in Washington (Merry had been recalled during the autumn of 1806), advised his government, "All the parties in this country take a warm interest on the point of the non-impressment of sailors (claimed by the British) out of American ships on the high seas, and . . . I am persuaded that no cordiality can be expected from this country whilst it is deemed necessary by His Majesty to enforce that right."[52] Faced with a treaty that did not address the impressment question, Jefferson felt he could not submit the agreement to the Senate. Jefferson did not see his refusal to submit the treaty as the final rejection of the pact and a decision to commit the United States to war. Rather, he believed that withholding the treaty from the Senate and sending it back to Monroe and Pinkney was the means to continue the negotiations, not close them off. Bradford Perkins ascribes Jefferson's failure to a combination of idealism and a lack of will. On the contrary, Jefferson's response to the Monroe-Pinkney treaty was grounded in a realistic assessment of the situation, not excessive idealism. Jefferson appreciated the relative weakness of the United States. When confronted by disproportionate power and relatively limited options Jefferson's instinct was to temporize and play for time. Madison summed up the administration's position, "As long as the negotiation can be honorably protracted, it is a resource to be preferred, under existing circumstances, to the peremptory alternative of improper concessions or inevitable collisions."[53] Jefferson hoped, but did not expect, that the British position on impressment might soften, possibly in response to the changing military situation. Unfortunately events would lead to the rapid deterioration of British-American relations. An "inevitable collision" would lead to a deadly encounter at sea over impressment and prompt the greatest diplomatic crisis of Jefferson's presidency.

On June 22, 1807, the U.S.S. *Chesapeake,* commanded by Captain James Barron, left Norfolk, Virginia, and put to sea. Barron had been appointed commodore of the American fleet in the Mediterranean, and the *Chesapeake* was headed for the Barbary Coast. The *Chesapeake,* a thirty-eight-gun frigate, had a full complement of 370 men, including the 3 deserters from the *Melampus:* William (formerly Romulus) Ware, Daniel Martin, and John Strachan. Although Barron had been appointed commodore on May 15, he made only two visits to his flagship prior to its departure on June 22. According to a later court-martial, on neither of these visits did Barron "examine particularly into her state or condition." The *Chesapeake,* it turns out, was not fully ready for sea: the frigate's guns had not been tested and her crew had been called to quarters only three times. As Commodore Barron himself conceded, the ship was unprepared for action. Barron apparently felt he could prepare the ship for action, drill the crew, and practice the guns during the transatlantic crossing. Unfortunately, he would need the ship's guns within a few hours of leaving port.[54]

As the *Chesapeake* departed Hampton Roads for international waters it passed two British warships, the *Bellona* and the *Melampus* (whose crew no doubt knew that its deserters were aboard the American frigate). A third ship, H.M.S. *Leopard,* a fifty-gun ship commanded by Captain S. P. Humphreys, lay off Cape Henry. The *Leopard* pursued the *Chesapeake.* Captain Humphreys signaled the *Chespeake* at four in the afternoon, and soon thereafter a messenger boarded the ship with a copy of Berkeley's order for the recovery of deserters. After delaying for forty-five minutes, Barron drafted a letter to Humphreys denying that there were any British deserters among the *Chesapeake*'s crew. After receiving Barron's letter Humphreys tried repeatedly to hail the *Chesapeake,* but Barron affected not to hear him. Meanwhile Barron ordered the crew to beat to quarters and the *Chesapeake* cleared for action. Before the crew could clear the decks and prepare the guns, the *Leopard* began firing. "It is distressing to me to acknowledge," Barron later reported, "that I found the advantage they had gained over our unprepared and unsuspicious state, did not warrant a longer opposition; nor should I have exposed this ship and crew to so galling a fire had it not been with a hope of getting the gun-deck clear, so as to have made a more formidable defence; consequently our resistance was but feeble." The *Leopard* delivered two devastating broadsides to the *Chesapeake* at close range. After nearly thirty minutes Barron, having ordered the symbolic firing of one gun so it might be said that he offered resistance, ordered the *Chesapeake* to strike her colors. A third broadside struck the *Chesapeake* while the flag was coming down. The *Leopard* sent a boat over and mustered the American crew. After examining the crew, the British removed the three men from the *Melampus*—Ware, Martin, and Strachan—as well as a fourth man, John Wilson (an alias for Jenkin Ratford). Like the three men from the *Melampus,* Ratford was a deserter from the Royal Navy: he had deserted from H.M.S. *Halifax* in Norfolk and joined the crew of the *Chesapeake.* But unlike Ware, Martin, and Strachan, Ratford was British-born. The *Chesapeake* had suffered grievously before the guns of *Leopard*. Three of her crewmen were killed in the incident and a further eighteen were wounded, eight seriously, one of whom died a few days later. The *Leopard* inflicted extensive damage to the frigate's masts, rigging, and hull; after the incident its officers counted twenty-two British cannonballs in the *Chesapeake*'s hull. Humiliated, the *Chesapeake* struggled back to Hampton Roads with three and a half feet of water in its hold and all able-bodied hands at the ship's pumps to prevent it from sinking. The *Leopard* rejoined the British squadron off the Virginia Capes with Ware, Martin, Strachan, and Ratford aboard. The men faced an uncertain fate. As deserters they faced courts-martial and might be executed.[55]

Word of the attack on the *Chesapeake* spread quickly throughout the Virginia Tidewater. Enraged residents of Norfolk and Portsmouth held a public meeting on June 24 and resolved not to trade or communicate with the British fleet off Virginia. The fleet depended on the ports for supplies and to make repairs. Furious Virginians destroyed two hundred casks of water that were waiting to be delivered to the British vessels. After one of the *Chesapeake*'s wounded sailors, Robert MacDonald, died on June 27, a crowd of four thousand joined his funeral procession. The public demanded that Commodore Decatur prepare to defend the ports from the threat of British attack by manning gunboats in the harbor, strengthening defenses, and enrolling volunteers if necessary.

Outrage at the attack on the *Chesapeake* quickly spread beyond Virginia. Americans across the country, particularly in the coastal cities that had often suffered from the visits of British naval vessels, were furious. There was an expectation that the attack would lead to a declaration of war. The *Chesapeake,* after all, was a United States warship, not a merchantman. Moreover, the attack and the resulting loss of life had been a deliberate response to orders. It was not an accident, like the death resulting from the *Leander*'s errant warning shot. Americans, united as they had not been since the end of the War of Independence, hearkened back to the example of 1776 and demanded retribution in the name of their patriotic forebears. President Jefferson himself reported, "They have often enough, God knows, given us cause of war before; but it has been on points which would not have united the nation. But now they have touched a chord which vibrates in every heart." Senator Samuel

Smith, now a Republican senator from Maryland (and brother of Robert Smith, the secretary of the navy), described a meeting held in Baltimore at the end of June: "Every man, almost, of respectability of whatever party was present. There appeared but one opinion—War—in case satisfaction is not given." Smith held out the possibility that war could be avoided, if the United States could achieve some sort of diplomatic settlement in response to the attack on the *Chesapeake*. But there seemed little hope of such a solution. As the *Virginia Argus* fulminated, "Federalists and Republicans are united in expressing their abhorrence of the conduct of the perfidious nation, and in the resolution of encountering them in War to revenge the unparalleled insults and injuries which they have inflicted on our country."[56]

Back in Norfolk on June 23, Commodore Barron wrote a report on the *Chesapeake-Leopard* incident.[57] The report was delivered to Washington, DC, on June 25 by Captain Charles Gordon, who had served on the *Chesapeake* under Barron on the twenty-second. Gordon was able to answer questions of the president and the secretary of the navy and address any matters arising from Barron's report. (Barron, having suffered a leg wound in the attack, was unable to deliver his report in person.) The attack on the *Chesapeake* presented Jefferson with a dangerous crisis. He was under pressure to take a strong stand in defense of American rights. Senator Samuel Smith warned him that the outraged public demanded action. If Jefferson allowed the moment to pass, Smith claimed, it would damage the national character: "It we temper too much with the martial ardour of the people, . . . we shall moderate it down until we become a pusillanimous race." The current public outrage meant that "our militia will again take to their arms & they expect the President to act."[58] Of course war with Britain presented considerable challenges for the United States. It would be costly in human and financial terms. War against the Barbary States was an undertaking of limited risk. Although that conflict might prove costly, the number of American lives at stake was minimal and the Barbary States would not launch attacks on the United States itself. War with Britain was a considerably different matter.

Congress was not in session when Barron's report reached Washington, and Jefferson's cabinet was dispersing for the summer—the president himself was planning to go to Monticello. The secretary of war, Henry Dearborn, had left for Maine, and Albert Gallatin, the secretary of the treasury, was in New York. Jefferson wrote to both men after receiving Barron's report, summoning them back the capital for an emergency cabinet meeting on July 2. (Dearborn had traveled only as far as Philadelphia.)[59] All the cabinet secretaries—Madison, Dearborn, Gallatin, Secretary of the Navy Robert Smith, and Attorney General Caesar Rodney—attended the meeting. (Vice President George Clinton was in New York.) They agreed unanimously to issue a proclamation ordering all armed British vessels to leave American waters and prohibiting Americans from supplying the ships. They further agreed to recall all American warships from the Mediterranean to remove them from danger. Having addressed the immediate cause of conflict—the presence of British warships in the United States—the cabinet then identified its conditions for a diplomatic settlement. They decided that a fast sloop should depart immediately for London with dispatches for James Monroe "demanding satisfaction for the attack on the *Chesapeake,* in which must be included. 1. A disavowal of the Act & of the principle of searching a public armed vessel. 2. A restoration of the men taken. 3. A recall of Admiral Barclay [*sic*]."[60] Jefferson sought to give the British government the opportunity to repudiate Berkeley's order and make amends for the *Leopard*'s action. Treasury Secretary Gallatin conceded, "Every person not blinded by passion and totally ignorant of the laws and usages of civilized nations knows that, whenever injuries are received from subordinate officers, satisfaction is demanded from the government itself before reprisals are made."[61] Jefferson also sought to revisit the impressment issue, which was at the heart of British-American differences. Seeking a negotiated settlement to the crisis would also allow American naval vessels enough time to return to the United States before hostilities commenced should the negotiations fail. Jefferson and Madison immediately drafted a proclamation outlining the administration's initial response to the attack.[62]

The cabinet met three more times in the next five days to address the crisis. On July 4 it considered whether to call Congress into session. Jefferson recognized that he could not control how the Royal Navy might act during the crisis—and took steps to defend the coast—but he also accepted that only Congress had the authority to declare war. He wrote to William Cabell, the governor of Virginia, on June 29, explaining that the cabinet had to be careful not to take any steps that would undermine Congress by making war inevitable. "Whether the outrage is a proper cause of war, belonging exclusively to Congress," he wrote, "it is our duty not to commit them by doing anything which would have to be retracted. We may, however, exercise the powers entrusted to us for preventing future insults within our harbors, & claim firmly satisfaction for the past. This will leave Congress free to decide whether war is the most efficacious mode of redress in our case." The cabinet agreed to call Congress into early session on October 26. Albert Gallatin and Robert Smith wanted to call Congress into session sooner, but Jefferson favored waiting until October. According to Gallatin, health fears precluded summoning Congress during the hot summer months. Jefferson may also have hoped that, with a delay, Congress would not feel rushed to declare war on Britain. An October recall would signal intent, but not panic, and would allow enough time to receive a reply from Britain to Jefferson's proclamation.[63]

On July 5 the cabinet agreed that the governors of the various states should make preparations to call out 100,000 militia in the event of war. Most of these would be used to defend the coast, but "for those in the North we may look to a winter expedn against Canada." On July 7 the cabinet considered the more pressing question of the defense of Chesapeake Bay. After the residents of Norfolk adopted an ordinance prohibiting all contact with the Royal Navy, John Douglas, commodore of the British fleet off Virginia, threatened to "obstruct the whole trade of the Chesapeake" and shifted his fleet to Hampton Roads. Virginians believed that the British were preparing to invade their state and attack Norfolk. Jefferson, of course, appreciated just how vulnerable the Virginia coast was to amphibious attack by the British. When the cabinet met on the seventh it urged Governor Cabell to call out the militia to defend Norfolk and its environs. It also ordered that Decatur prepare the American gunboats at Hampton Roads for action.[64]

Jefferson felt he had taken appropriate steps to defend the United States, while still allowing for a negotiated settlement to the crisis, yet he believed that the situation was very unstable. He feared that the British naval forces in Chesapeake Bay might compound the crime they had committed against the *Chesapeake* and precipitate a wider British-American conflict. He wrote on July 7, "The British commanders have their foot on the threshold of war. . . . Blows may be hourly possible." Jefferson addressed these remarks to his secretary of war, Henry Dearborn, who was traveling to New York to confer with the vice president, George Clinton, on the defense of that state and to witness a demonstration by Robert Fulton of the destruction of a ship by an underwater torpedo—a device that might be useful to the United States should it need to defend its harbors against the Royal Navy.[65] In the absence of the secretary of war, Jefferson managed the defense of the United States himself. He wrote numerous letters to military officers and elected officials around the country.[66] His most important correspondence was with the governor of Virginia. Jefferson and Governor Cabell exchanged numerous letters during the crisis. He took a close interest in the defense of his home state. The president insured that Henry Dearborn sent arms, artillery, and munitions to Virginia. Jefferson was careful to recognize Cabell's authority as the governor of Virginia—as a member of the House of Delegates in 1798, Cabell had voted for the Virginia Resolutions, so he was well aware of the distinction between federal and state authority—and the two men worked together harmoniously during the war crisis of July 1807.[67]

The initial war crisis in Chesapeake Bay had passed by the end of July. By the middle of the month Commodore Douglas removed his vessels from Hampton Roads, and the immediate threat of blockade of Chesapeake Bay or an attack on Norfolk receded. On July 26 the cabinet met and agreed that the militia guarding Norfolk, which had been mustered for nearly a month, could be dismissed—except for an artillery company to help with the shore batteries and a cavalry patrol to insure that no supplies were sent to the British fleet. The cabinet still expected war and devoted most of its meeting on July 26 to discussing detailed plans for the invasion of Upper and Lower Canada should negotiations with Britain break down and Congress declare war on its return.[68]

In the direct aftermath of the attack on the *Chesapeake* Jefferson demonstrated what he had learned about statecraft, crisis management, and politics in the quarter century since his disastrous tenure as governor of

Virginia. In mid-July Jefferson reflected with satisfaction on the response to the crisis in a letter to his old friend John Page (whom he had defeated in the election for governor in 1779):

> I am much pleased with the ardor displayed by our country-men on the late British outrage. It gives us the more confidence of support in the demand of *reparation* for the past, & *security* for the future, that is to say, an end of impressments. If motives of either justice or interest should produce this from Great Brit-ain, it will save a war; but if they are refused, we shall have gained time for getting in our ships & property, & at least 20,000 seamen now afloat on the ocean, and who may man 250 priva-teers. The loss of these to us would be worth to Great Britain many victories of the Nile & Trafalgar. The meantime may also be importantly employed in preparations to enable us to give quick and deep blows.[69]

In 1807 Jefferson acted promptly and decisively in response to the crisis, marshalling the diplomatic and military resources of the government and providing support for the government of Virginia. He consulted his cabinet, and he decided to recall Congress. He did not, however, give in to the pressure within his cabinet to call Congress back too soon. He did so, in part, to give diplomacy a chance to work. If nothing else, he would buy time for the United States to prepare for war, should a declaration of war be necessary. He had enhanced the nation's defenses without esca-lating the conflict. Not only had Jefferson performed better, but he felt that his countrymen had behaved better in 1807 than they had in 1781. The events of 1807 seem to have borne out the boast that Jefferson made in his first inaugural address, that the United States had "the strongest Government on earth . . . the only one where every man, at the call of the law, would fly to the standard of the law, and would meet invasions of the public order as his own personal concern."

Although Jefferson ably handled the immediate aftermath of the *Chesapeake-Leopard* affair, the larger crisis in British-American relations remained unresolved. The president held out some hope that the dis-pute and its underlying causes—impressment and neutral rights—might be settled peacefully. The immediate crisis having passed, Jefferson left the capital for Monticello on August 1, 1807, and remained away for two months, not returning to Washington until October 3. There was little he or his government could do but wait for the British to respond to the American demand for restitution and reparations for the *Chesapeake* and an end to impressment.

Jefferson never fully appreciated the danger that Napoleonic France posed to Britain. Indeed, one reason James Monroe and William Pinkney were willing to compromise on the impressment question in 1806 had been because they feared the threat that Napoleon posed to Europe and were concerned he might defeat Britain. The lengths the British would go to defeat Napoleon became apparent in September 1807 with the attack on Copenhagen. Denmark, like the United States, was a neutral country, but the British feared that its navy would be captured by Napoleon and used in the Baltic. When the Danes refused to surrender their navy to the British, the Royal Navy bombarded the Danish capital until the Danes capitulated, killing two thousand civilians in the attack. In its death struggle against Napoleon, Britain was not overly concerned about the rights of neutrals. Under such circumstances the British were willing to resort to harsh tactics and would not cavil over the rights of neutrals, be they Danish or American. After the bombing of Copenhagen, George Canning, the British foreign secretary, wrote, "We are hated throughout Europe and that hate must be cured by fear."[70] When set against two thousand dead Danes, the four American sailors killed by the *Leopard* were hardly likely to trouble the British. Those Americans who clamored for war with Britain during the summer of 1807 might have been given pause if they had seen the rubble of Copenhagen.

Notwithstanding Canning's sanguinary approach to foreign relations, Britain was not seeking a war with the United States. On July 7 the French and Russians signed a treaty at Tilsit that ended their war and brought Russia into the conflict against Britain as France's ally. As a consequence, when word of the *Chesapeake-Leopard* incident reached London, the British sought to conciliate the Americans. Canning wrote to Monroe to "assure you that his Majesty neither does nor has at any time maintained the pretension of a right to search ships of war, in the national service of any State, for deserters." In his talks with Monroe,

Canning was willing to acknowledge that Berkeley had overstepped his authority in ordering the search of an American warship and offered to pay reparations to the United States. He was willing to return the three American-born deserters taken from the *Chesapeake* (Jenkin Ratford had been executed for desertion on August 31),[71] but he was unwilling to yield on the principle of impressment, "the right and practice of which," Canning wrote, "have been exercised by Great Britain from the earliest ages of British naval power, even without any qualification or exception in favour of national ships of war." That Britain was willing to concede that it should not stop American warships was as far as Canning was willing to go. There would be no further concession or compromise on the impressment question in response to the *Chesapeake* incident. On October 16, George III issued a proclamation "For Recalling and Prohibiting British Seamen from Serving Foreign Princes and States." It commanded British naval officers to remove all British-born sailors from foreign merchant ships. On November 11 the British government issued a new Order in Council that required all American merchant vessels to stop at British ports and obtain a license before proceeding to Europe. This condition would put them in violation of Napoleon's Berlin Decree and subject them to seizure. Although showing a degree of flexibility and contrition on the specific issues arising from the attack on the *Chesapeake,* the British were unwilling to make any meaningful concessions on what Jefferson believed were the underlying causes of the incident.[72]

When Congress convened on October 26, 1807, it had to decide between war or peace. Jefferson submitted a lengthy annual message on October 27, in which he summarized the difficult state of British-American relations and explained why he had called Congress into session a month early. In his original draft he had catalogued British aggression in a way as seemed to invite a declaration of war. Treasury Secretary Gallatin had urged him to moderate his tone, and Jefferson had done so. The result was a litany of British misdeeds that stopped short of asking for war. Jefferson still felt war might be necessary, and he hinted at it in an oblique fashion: "The love of peace so much cherished in the bosoms of our citizens, which has so long guided the proceedings of their councils and induced forbearance under so many wrongs, may not insure our continuance in the quiet pursuits of industry."[73] The circumlocution of this passage suggests that war was something he accepted rather than sought. Tempers in the United States had cooled considerably since the summer. The patriotic ardor Jefferson had praised in his countrymen and -women after the attack on the *Chesapeake* had dissipated, as had the American appetite for war.

One reason it was difficult to formulate a response to the attack on the *Chesapeake* was because the government had not yet heard from Monroe in London. Jefferson wrote to Governor Cabell on November 1, "Within about a fortnight we think we may expect answer from England which will decide whether this cloud is to issue in a storm or a calm."[74] Yet, as Jefferson conceded, ultimately the decision for war or peace lay in London, not Washington. Nonetheless the administration had to plan for various contingencies, and Jefferson took steps to strengthen the nation for the war. In his letter to Cabell he wrote of Congress, it "will authorise a complete system of defensive works," including augmenting shore defenses and adding "a considerable enlargement of the force in gunboats. A combination of these will, I think, enable us to defend the Chesapeake at its mouth, and save the vast line of preparation which the defence of all its interior waters would otherwise require." As Jefferson predicted, Congress appropriated the funding to increase the nation's fleet of gunboats by 188 vessels.[75]

Word of the failure of the Monroe-Canning talks reached Washington in early December. (Monroe followed soon after, arriving in the capital on December 22.) Jefferson sent a message to Congress on December 7, providing the legislators with all the documentation relating to the attack on the *Chesapeake* and the failed negotiations.[76] On December 14 the administration learned that Napoleon's Berlin Decree would apply to the United States. With the ongoing crisis in British-American relations over impressment and neutral rights unresolved, coupled with the more aggressive French policy aimed at restricting American trade, Jefferson submitted a special message to Congress on December 18 calling for a trade embargo: the United States would call its ships home and cease exporting its produce until its adversaries relaxed their restrictions on American trade. Congress moved rapidly. Senator Smith

introduced an embargo bill, and the Senate passed it that afternoon by a
vote of 22 to 6. On the twenty-second the House approved the bill by a
vote of 82 to 44.[77]

In a letter to William Cabell written after first learning about the
attack on the *Chesapeake*, Jefferson mused "whether, having taught so
many other useful lessons to Europe, we may not add that of showing
them that there are peaceable means of repressing injustice, by making it
the interest of the aggressor to do what is just, and abstain from future
wrong."[78] Jefferson had always believed that economic coercion could be
an effective tool in international relations. It was preferable to war, but
the threat of force had to underlie commercial coercion for the tactic to
be effective. As such, Jefferson conceived of boycotts, non-importation,
and embargos both as peaceable alternatives to war *and* as essential
preparation for war.

The embargo, which was in place from late 1807 until 1809 when
James Madison became president, was a disaster for the American economy. The value of American exports declined from $108 million in 1807
to just $22 million in 1808. Although the intention of the embargo was to
demonstrate to Britain that it could not live without American trade, it
did no such thing. American farmers, particularly in the south and west,
suffered because they could not find a market for their crops. Wholesale
agricultural prices declined by 21 percent between 1807 and 1808. The
average price of a bushel of wheat declined from $1.30 to $1.00 during
the same period. Merchants, particularly in the northeast, as well as all
who depended on the maritime commerce also suffered. The British, in
contrast, were largely untroubled by the embargo. The embargo prohibited Americans from exporting their produce, but it did not prohibit the
British from sending exports to the United States. With the Americans
voluntarily removing themselves from the carrying trade, the British
were able to recover some of their market share and to sell their exports
in the United States. Britain's colonies in the West Indies, which depended to a large extent on American trade, suffered somewhat, but
American smuggling helped to make up for the loss of legal exports.
Smuggling, by coasting vessels and across the northern and southern
borders of the United States, became endemic. Illicit trading was so rife
that the Jefferson administration urged Congress to pass a series of en-

forcement acts in 1808 and 1809 to give the Customs Service greater authority to stop smuggling. As a result the federal government began to exercise greater police powers than it had when the Federalists were in power.[79]

Despite its catastrophic economic impact, the embargo might have been worthwhile if it had proved effective as a diplomatic tool. Unfortunately for Jefferson it did little to compel the British or the French to respect American rights. Given how little the loss of American exports affected Britain, it was considered a small price to pay to retain impressment. Although James Madison had been a strong supporter of the embargo—he and Jefferson were in agreement on the policy—when he was elected president in 1808 he favored its repeal. On February 3, 1809, Congress voted to repeal the embargo, effective from March 4, Madison's first day in office. Congress replaced the embargo with the Non-Intercourse Act, which prohibited trade with Britain and France but permitted it with all other nations, thereby rendering trade restrictions a nullity.[80]

Jefferson had hoped that the embargo might prove sufficient to compel the British and French to relax their restrictions on American trade and, in the case of the British, to give up impressment. He was aware that the embargo alone was unlikely to achieve a change in British or French policy—because it permitted imports to the United States while prohibiting American exports its coercive power was limited. Jefferson viewed the embargo as a crucial antecedent to a war. Its chief accomplishment would be to give American merchant ships time to return to the United States; the navy's frigates had already been called home. As he wrote to Cabell in March 1808, "The great objects of the embargo are keeping our ships and seamen out of harm's way." Two days earlier he had written to Madison, "I take it to be an universal opinion that war will become preferable to a continuance of the embargo after a certain time." Jefferson proposed that American diplomats use the time before the war to communicate to the governments in London and Paris that if they removed their restrictions on American trade, the United States would remain "faithfully neutral," but if the restrictions persisted, war would be inevitable. "When that time arrives," he wrote, "if one has withdrawn [its restrictions] and the other has not, we must declare war against that other; if neither shall have withdrawn, we must take our choice of enemies between them." Jefferson expected that when Congress met in the winter of 1808–9, "they may decide whether war must be declared and against whom."[81]

As policy the embargo failed. It damaged the American economy, failed as a diplomatic tool, and was politically divisive. Historians often ascribe the embargo to misguided Jeffersonian idealism. Gordon Wood has written that the embargo was "perhaps with the exception of Prohibition, the greatest example in American history of ideology brought to bear on a matter of public policy." Robert W. Tucker and David C. Hendrickson have argued that Jefferson's "cardinal error" was his disregard for the balance of power in favor of neutral rights. According to Tucker and Hendrickson, Jefferson's "deepest tendency was to convert questions of interest into matters of right and wrong, which then assumed a kind of independent character and became inseparably annexed to the honor and independence of the country. His tendency to do so is the measure of his moralism; his moralism, in turn, not only constituted the central aspect of his diplomatic outlook but is also identifiable as the primary corrupting factor within it." This interpretation assumes that Jefferson had a range of options available to him but was blinded by his idealism or moralism. On the contrary, Jefferson had relatively few options available to him. He chose economic coercion, preparatory to war, as, he believed, the least bad of these.[82]

In late November 1807, having received James Monroe's dispatches from London, Jefferson reflected on his, and Congress's, options for dealing with Britain. According to Jefferson, there were only three options: "War, Embargo or Nothing." In Jefferson's thinking, "the middle proposition is most likely." Given the military and naval power of Britain with respect to the United States, war was not an attractive prospect. As a sympathetic South Carolina newspaper opined during the embargo, "We are reduced to this situation: submit to pay TRIBUTE to England, and be plundered by France, to go to WAR, or hold to the Embargo . . . France we cannot touch; and England, by her powerful navy could soon sweep us from the ocean." Inaction was not really an option as the British Orders in Council and Napoleon's decrees would have forced the United States to choose between Britain and France—and thus alienate the other. If, as Tucker and Hendrickson suggest, Jefferson accepted impressment, he would, effectively, be choosing to side with Britain. This may have been economically beneficial to the United States, but to compromise the sovereignty of the United States by accepting impressment was politically untenable. To do so would have been to repudiate the republican legacy of the American Revolution. Jefferson would have had to sacrifice the independence of the republic in order to safeguard the United States. Given the reality of power politics, he made a reasonable, if unpalatable, choice in opting for the embargo while preparing the nation for war. In the past Jefferson had opted to temporize not out of indecision but because circumstances might change to benefit the United States. George Herring ably summarized Jefferson's position: "Unwilling to compromise and unable to fight, Jefferson fell back on an embargo of American commerce." By accepting the embargo, he bought the country time and sought to prepare for a war that seemed inevitable. Given his limited options, it was probably the best decision available to him.[83]

If Jefferson's choice of the embargo is understandable and consistent with his previous practice of statecraft, he can be faulted for its execution. The embargo was flawed by design—the continued allowance of British imports was a serious flaw—and enforcement. The use of the coercive power of the state to enforce the embargo did relatively little to stem smuggling, but it alienated Jefferson's supporters. Jefferson believed that the embargo would provide the United States with the time to prepare for war. The deleterious economic consequences of the embargo had the opposite effect: the United States was less prepared as a result of the embargo than it had been at its beginning. Jefferson viewed with disappointment and anger violations of the embargo. More than simple law-breaking, smuggling demonstrated once again that the American republic could be endangered by the weakness of its citizens. What Jefferson failed to see was his own weakness as a leader. He did not adequately make the case for the embargo to the American people. The problem with the embargo was not the decision to adopt the policy but rather its implementation. Jefferson contributed to this failure, and it was his greatest error as president.[84]

For the men who had come to epitomize the fractured and fragile state of British-American relations—William Ware, Daniel Martin, and

John Strachan—the embargo brought little respite. They, along with Jenkin Ratford, had been tried before courts-martial for desertion in August 1807. Ratford was sentenced to hang, and his sentence was carried out quickly. The three American sailors were sentenced to 500 lashes, but their sentences were suspended and they were compelled to return to the Royal Navy. Ironically, the embargo prolonged their service as negotiations for their release did not take place until after its repeal. American and British diplomats reached an agreement to return the American sailors and compensate families of the men killed or wounded in the *Chesapeake* incident. The sailors were not returned until the summer of 1812—a month after the United States declared war on Britain. William Ware was not among the men released. He died in a British naval hospital in 1809.[85]

The first grievance that James Madison cited in his war message to Congress on June 1, 1812, was impressment.[86] The War of 1812 was sometimes referred to as "Mr. Madison's War." As he was the president who called for the declaration of war in 1812 and was the architect of many of the policies that Jefferson advocated as president, this is fitting. Jefferson, too, bears much of the responsibility for the conflict. It might just as well have been dubbed "Mr. Jefferson's War."

Conclusion
"Ne Plus Ultra"

After Jefferson left the White House, the British minister in Washington, David Erskine, opened discussions with the new secretary of state, Robert Smith. Erskine had received instructions from London to reach a settlement with the Americans. The Canning government stipulated several requirements for an agreement: American ports should be open to the British and closed to France; the United States must accept the Rule of 1756; and the Royal Navy should be permitted to seize American vessels trading with France. These conditions were unacceptable to the United States. Erskine quietly ignored these requirements and entered into talks based on the concessions he was empowered to make—notably that the British would offer reparations for the attack on the *Chesapeake* and revoke the most rancorous Orders in Council that restricted American trade. Erskine hoped that by making progress on these issues the way might be open for a more comprehensive settlement of British-American differences. In response to his initiative President Madison issued a proclamation on April 19, 1809, formally suspending the Non-Intercourse Act of March 1 (which Congress had adopted to replace the embargo). Although the immediate crisis in British-American relations seemed to have passed without war—the underlying causes of the crisis, impressment and the Rule of 1756, remained unresolved.[1]

Writing in his retirement at Monticello, Jefferson congratulated his friend and successor in late April on what seemed to be a diplomatic breakthrough. He was loath to concede too much to the British, comparing

their government to that of the Barbary States and claiming the concessions were a vindication of the embargo (and its successor): "The British
ministry has been driven from its Algerine system, not by any remaining
morality in the people but by their unsteadiness under severe trial." Jefferson urged caution regarding the possibility of a wider commercial
treaty with Britain:

> They never made an equal commercial treaty with any na-
> tion, & we have no right to expect to be the first. It will place
> you between the injunctions of true patriotism & the clamors of
> a faction devoted to a foreign interest in preference to that of
> their own country. It will confirm the English too in their prac-
> tice of whipping us into a treaty. They did it in Jay's case; were
> near it in Monroe's, & on failure of that, have applied the scourge
> with tenfold vigour, & now come on to try its effect. But it is the
> moment when we should prove our consistence, by recurring to
> the principles we dictated to Monroe, the departure from which
> occasioned our rejection of his treaty, and by protesting against
> Jay's treaty being ever quoted, or looked at, or even mentioned.
> That form will for ever be a millstone round our necks unless we
> now rid ourselves of it, once for all.

Given Canning's stipulations for any future agreement, it was unlikely
that a permanent settlement could be reached, particularly if the Madison administration stuck to the instructions that Jefferson and Madison
had given to Monroe in 1804. Jefferson's analysis of the situation was
perceptive—to a point. With undue faith in the efficacy of the recently
repealed embargo, he asserted, "The occasion is highly favorable, as we
never can have them more in our power."[2] He completely misread Madison's ability to extract concessions from London. Madison, like Jefferson, was caught between the competing demands and strictures of Britain
and France. Unable to satisfactorily resolve these, the long-anticipated
rupture came in June 1812 when Congress declared war on Britain at
Madison's behest. The war, which went badly for the United States, was
nearly calamitous. Only the end of the broader conflict in Europe in 1814
and 1815 led to its conclusion—and the restoration of the status quo ante

bellum—as well as the relaxation of British restrictions on American trade, including impressment, which were no longer necessary.

After considering the state of British-American relations in his letter, Jefferson turned to Napoleon. Of the French emperor he wrote:

> He ought the more to conciliate our good will, as we can be such an obstacle to the new career opening on him in the Spanish colonies. That he would give us the Floridas to withhold intercourse with the residue of those colonies cannot be doubted. But that is no price, because they are ours in the first moment of the first war, and until a war, they are of no particular necessity to us. But, altho' with difficulty, he will consent to our receiving Cuba into our union to prevent our aid to Mexico and other provinces. That would be a price, and I would immediately erect a column on the Southernmost limit of Cuba and inscribe on it a Ne plus ultra as to us in that direction. We should then have only to include the North in our confederacy, which would be of course in the first war, and should have such an empire for liberty as she has never surveyed since the creation: and I am persuaded no constitution was ever before so well calculated as ours for extensive empire and self government.

This passage gives us an extraordinary insight into Jefferson's statecraft. In an echo of the Nootka Sound crisis the former president is suggesting that the United States should use the pretext of Latin American independence to acquire the Floridas from Spain—though if they could not be bargained for, they might be seized in a war. Having added the Floridas to the union, it would be easy to acquire Cuba in exchange for withholding aid from the Mexican revolutionaries. Cuba's proximity to Florida would be the key to its acquisition because, Jefferson wrote, it "can be defended by us without a navy." After dealing with maritime disputes for almost two decades, he believed the United States should, as principle, avoid overseas possessions. "Nothing should ever be accepted which would require a navy to defend it." Cuba was as far south as Jefferson was willing to go. But he was willing to add Canada to the American confederacy, completing the "empire for liberty."

Jefferson believed that United States was constitutionally suited for such expansion as new states could be added to the union—in a process he himself had conceived almost thirty years previously. According to Jefferson, the American empire could expand and also maintain its liberty. This was a specific plan for American expansion, not an idealized vision of what might be. Of course Jefferson's plan only partially came to pass. The United States annexed West Florida during the War of 1812 and acquired East Florida via treaty in 1819. It unsuccessfully invaded Canada during the War of 1812. By the middle of the century, however, it had added the modern Southwest, Pacific Coast, and Northwest via a combination of war, migration, negotiation, and purchase—all the elements of Jefferson's statecraft.[3] It might be said that Jefferson's vision for a capacious American empire outlived its author. It continues to shape the world we live in today.

Notes

Abbreviations

AHR	*American Historical Review*
ASPFR	*American State Papers: Foreign Relations,* 6 vols. (Washington, DC: Gales and Seaton, 1833)
CFM	Frederick Jackson Turner, ed., *Correspondence of the French Ministers to the United States, 1791–1797, Annual Report of the American Historical Association for 1903* (Washington, DC: Government Printing Office, 1904)
GW	George Washington
IBM	Bernard Mayo, ed., *Instructions to the British Ministers to the United States, 1791–1812* (Washington, DC: Government Printing Office, 1941)
JER	*Journal of the Early Republic*
JM	James Madison
Malone, *Jefferson and His Time*	Dumas Malone, *Jefferson and His Time,* 6 vols. (Boston: Little, Brown, 1948–81)
PGW:PS	Theodore J. Crackel et al., eds., *The Papers of George Washington: Presidential Series,* 16 vols. to date (Charlottesville: University of Virginia Press, 1987–)
PJM:PS	J. C. A. Stagg et al., eds., *Papers of James Madison: Presidential Series,* 7 vols. to date (Charlottesville: University of Virginia Press, 1984–)
PJM:SS	J. C. A. Stagg et al., eds., *Papers of James Madison: Secretary of State Series,* 9 vols. to date (Charlottesville: University of Virginia Press, 1986–)
PTJ	Julian P. Boyd et al., eds., *The Papers of Thomas Jefferson,* 38 vols. to date (Princeton: Princeton University Press, 1950–)
PTJ:RS	J. Jefferson Looney, ed., *The Papers of Thomas Jefferson: Retirement Series,* 8 vols. to date (Princeton: Princeton University Press, 2004–)
TJ	Thomas Jefferson
TJP	Thomas Jefferson Papers, Library of Congress

TJW	Merrill D. Peterson, ed., *Thomas Jefferson: Writings*
	(New York: Library of America, 1984)
WMQ	*William and Mary Quarterly*
WTJ	Paul Leicester Ford, ed., *The Works of Thomas Jefferson,*
	12 vols. (New York: G. P. Putnam's Sons, 1904–5).

Introduction
Three Emperors

1. Levett Harris to TJ, August 7, 1804, TJP.

2. TJ to Levett Harris, Washington, April 18, 1806, TJP.

3. TJ to John Langdon, March 5, 1810, *TJW,* 1221–22.

4. TJ to Thomas Cooper, Nov. 29, 1802, *TJW,* 1109; TJ to Joseph Priestley, Nov. 29, 1802, TJP.

5. TJ to Joseph Priestley, Nov. 29, 1802, TJP; TJ to the Emperor Alexander, April 19, 1806, *TJW,* 1161.

6. TJ to Thomas Cooper, Nov. 29, 1802, *TJW,* 1109; TJ to Joseph Priestley, Nov. 29, 1802, TJP.

7. TJ to the Emperor Alexander, April 19, 1806, *TJW,* 1161.

8. TJ to Madame de Staël, May 24, 1813, *TJW,* 1276.

9. TJ to John Adams, July 5, 1814, *TJW,* 1340.

10. Jefferson's first recorded use of the phrase "empire of liberty" is in a 1780 letter to George Rogers Clark. TJ to George Rogers Clark, Dec. 25, 1780, *PTJ,* 4:237. He used it, as well as the variation "empire for liberty," to describe the expansive American republic. For interpretations of Jefferson's use of the term, see Peter S. Onuf, *Jefferson's Empire: The Language of American Nationhood* (Charlottesville: University Press of Virginia, 2000), ch. 2, and Julian P. Boyd, "Thomas Jefferson's 'Empire of Liberty,'" *Virginia Quarterly Review* 24 (1948): 538–54. Also see Brian Steele, *Thomas Jefferson and American Nationhood* (New York: Cambridge University Press, 2012), ch. 1.

11. Aditya Chakrabortty defined it as "the practice of using the levers of the state and of government to get difficult things done that otherwise wouldn't happen. The power to bang tables and knock heads together and face down opponents. The ability, in short, to govern." Aditya Chakrabortty, "Whatever Happened to Statecraft?" *Guardian* (London), June 25, 2011, http://www.guardian .co.uk/commentisfree/2011/jul/25/what-happened-to-statecraft, accessed January 19, 2013.

12. Leonard J. Sadosky, "Jefferson and International Relations," in Francis D. Cogliano, ed., *A Companion to Thomas Jefferson* (Oxford: Blackwell, 2012), 199–217. Also see Peter P. Hill, "The Early National Period, 1775–1815," in Robert D. Schulzinger, ed., *A Companion to American Foreign Relations* (Oxford: Blackwell, 2006), 48–63.

13. Robert W. Tucker and David C. Hendrickson, *Empire of Liberty: The State-craft of Thomas Jefferson* (New York: Oxford University Press, 1990), ix; Bradford Perkins, *The Creation of a Republican Empire, 1776–1865* (New York: Cambridge University Press, 1993), 111. For other historians who see Jefferson as an idealist, see Alexander DeConde, *This Affair of Louisiana* (New York: Scribners, 1976); Alexander DeConde, "Historians, the War for Independence, and the Persistence of the Exceptionalist Ideal," *International History Review* 5 (1983): 399–430; Doron Ben-Atar, *The Origins of Jeffersonian Commercial Policy and Diplomacy* (New York: St. Martin's Press, 1993). Most scholars who criticize Jefferson as an idealist tend to endorse the realist approach to international relations.

14. Walter LaFeber, "Jefferson and American Foreign Policy," in Peter S. Onuf, ed., *Jeffersonian Legacies* (Charlottesville: University Press of Virginia, 1993), 370–91, quotation 371. Lawrence S. Kaplan argued that Jefferson, although he employed radical rhetoric in discussing international relations, was most success-ful when he acted in a more traditional manner, respecting the conventional Euro-pean balance of power. He aptly describes Jefferson as the "idealist as realist." Lawrence S. Kaplan, *Entangling Alliances with None: American Foreign Policy in the Age of Jefferson* (Kent, OH: Kent State University Press, 1987). Also see Law-rence S. Kaplan, "Jefferson, the Napoleonic Wars and the Balance of Power," *WMQ*, 3rd ser., 14 (1957): 196–217. For other examples of Jefferson as a realist, see Mary P. Adams, "Jefferson's Reaction to the Treaty of San Ildefonso," *Journal of Southern History* 21 (1955): 173–88; Tim Matthewson, "Jefferson and Haiti," *Jour-nal of Southern History* 61 (1995): 209–48; James R. Sofka, "The Jeffersonian Idea of National Security: Commerce, the Atlantic Balance of Power, and the Barbary War, 1786–1805," *Diplomatic History* 21 (1997): 519–44.

15. Autobiography, *TJW*, 97.

16. TJ to Samuel Du Pont de Nemours, Jan. 18, 1802, *PTJ*, 36:391.

17. Jon Meacham, *Thomas Jefferson: The Art of Power* (New York: Random House, 2012), 351; 318–19.

One
According to the Judgment of a Good Man

1. *Journal of the House of Delegates of the Commonwealth of Virginia, 1779* (Richmond: Thomas White, 1827), 29. John Page to TJ, June 2, 1779, TJ to John Page, June 3, 1779, *PTJ*, 2:278, 279.

2. Isaac Jefferson, *Memoirs of a Monticello Slave*, ed. Rayford W. Logan (Char-lottesville: University of Virginia Press, 1951), 25; Marquis de Chastellux, *Travels in North America in the Years 1780, 1781, and 1782*, 2 vols., ed. and trans. Howard C. Rice (Chapel Hill: University of North Carolina Press, 1952), 1:390–91.

3. [Thomas Jefferson], *A Summary View of the Rights of British America* (Wil-liamsburg: n.p., 1774).

4. The most complete study of Jefferson's early life remains Malone, *Jefferson and His Time,* vol. 1, *Jefferson the Virginian* (Boston: Little, Brown, 1948). Also see Merrill D. Peterson, *Thomas Jefferson and the New Nation* (New York: Oxford University Press, 1970), chs. 1–2; R. B. Bernstein, *Thomas Jefferson* (New York: Oxford University Press, 2003), chs. 1–3; Jon Meacham, *Thomas Jefferson: The Art of Power* (New York: Random House, 2012), chs. 1–10.

5. Peterson, *Thomas Jefferson and the New Nation,* 172–75. It is worth observing that Jefferson initially shared the concerns of his fellow Virginians regarding executive power. In his 1776 draft constitution for Virginia (which was not adopted) he advocated creating a weak executive. See Jeremy D. Bailey, *Thomas Jefferson and Executive Power* (New York: Cambridge University Press, 2007), ch. 2; and Francis D. Cogliano, " 'The Whole Object of the Present Controversy': The Early Constitutionalism of Paine and Jefferson," in Peter S. Onuf and Simon P. Newman, eds., *Transatlantic Revolutionaries: Jefferson and Paine in America, Britain, and France* (Charlottesville: University of Virginia Press, 2013), 26–48.

6. John Ferling, *Almost a Miracle: The American Victory in the War of Independence* (New York: Oxford University Press, 2007), chs. 17–21; Ira D. Gruber, "Britain's Southern Strategy," in W. Robert Higgins, ed., *The Revolutionary War in the South: Power, Conflict and Leadership* (Durham: Duke University Press, 1979), 205–38. For the events surrounding Jefferson's governorship and the British invasions of Virginia, see John E. Selby, *The Revolution in Virginia, 1775–1783* (Williamsburg: Colonial Williamsburg Foundation, 1988); Michael Kranish, *Flight from Monticello: Thomas Jefferson at War* (New York: Oxford University Press, 2010); Peterson, *Thomas Jefferson and the New Nation,* ch. 4; and Malone, *Jefferson and His Time,* vol. 1, chs. 22–25 For Jefferson's accounts of these events, see "Notes and Documents Relating to the British Invasions in 1781," in *PTJ,* 4:256–78.

7. Henry Clinton, "Expedition to Portsmouth, Virginia, 1779," *WMQ,* 2nd ser., 12 (1932): 181–86; Ithiel Town, "A Detail of Some Particular Services Performed in America (Journal of Collier and Matthews's Invasion of Virginia)," *Virginia Historical Register and Literary Notebook* 4 (1851): 181–95; Selby, *Revolution in Virginia,* 204–10; Ferling, *Almost a Miracle,* 355; Kranish, *Flight from Monticello,* 114–19.

8. *Hening's Statutes at Large,* Oct 5, 1780, 10:331; L. Scott Philyaw, "A Slave for Every Soldier: The Strange History of Virginia's Forgotten Recruitment Act of 1 January 1781," *Virginia Magazine of History and Biography* 109 (2001): 367–86; Kranish, *Flight from Monticello,* 128.

9. TJ to Samuel Huntington, Sept. 14, 1780, *PTJ,* 3:647–48.

10. GW to TJ, Oct 10, 1780, *PTJ,* 3:26–30; Thomas Nelson to TJ, Oct. 21, 1780, *PTJ,* 4:54–55; James Innes to TJ, Oct 21, 1780, *PTJ,* 4:55–57; TJ to GW, Oct. 22, 1780, *PTJ,* 4:59–60; TJ to Samuel Huntington, Oct. 25, 1780, *PTJ,* 4:67–68; TJ to GW, Oct 25, 1780, *PTJ,* 4:68–69; TJ to Virginia Delegates in Congress, Oct 27, 1780, *PTJ,* 4:76–77; TJ to Samuel Huntington, Nov. 3, 1780, *PTJ,* 4:92; TJ to

Horatio Gates, Nov. 19, 1780, *PTJ*, 4:127; Alexander Leslie to George Germain, Nov. 27, 1780, in K. G. Davies, ed., *Documents of the American Revolution, 1770–1783*, 21 vols. (Dublin: Irish University Press, 1972–81), 18:235; Selby, *Revolution in Virginia*, 216–17; Kranish, *Flight from Monticello*, 134–38; Ferling, *Almost a Miracle*, 477.

11. GW to TJ, Dec. 9, 1780, *PTJ*, 4:195. Also see GW to TJ, Nov. 8, 1780, *PTJ*, 4:105; and GW to TJ, Dec. 27, 1780, *PTJ*, 4:241.

12. TJ to Edward Stevens, Nov. 10, 1780, *PTJ*, 4:111.

13. TJ to Samuel Huntington, Oct. 25, 1780, *PTJ*, 4:67–68.

14. Arnold's Invasion as Reported by Jefferson in the *Virginia Gazette*, Jan. 13, 1781, *PTJ*, 4:269–70. Also see TJ to GW, Jan. 10, 1781, *PTJ*, 4:333–35, which closely follows the account that appeared in the *Gazette*; TJ to the Speaker of the House of Delegates, March 1, 1781, *PTJ*, 5:35–36. Selby, *Revolution in Virginia*, 221–25; Kranish, *Fight from Monticello*, 159–99.

15. John Daly Burk, Skelton Jones, and Louis Hue Girardin, *The History of Virginia from Its First Settlement to the Present Day*, 4 vols. (Petersburg: Dickson and Pescud; M. W. Dunnavant, 1804–16), 4:456. John Daly Burk began the *History of Virginia* but he died before he could complete it. The history was continued by Skelton Jones and Louis Girardin. Girardin wrote vol. 4 (published by Dunnavant in 1816) with Jefferson's support.

16. Harry M. Ward and Harold E. Greer, *Richmond during the Revolution, 1775–83* (Charlottesville: University of Virginia Press, 1977), 53.

17. Deposition of James Currie, [Oct. 12, 1796], *PTJ*, 4:272.

18. TJ to Charles Lee, May 15, 1826, TJP.

19. John Graves Simcoe, *Simcoe's Military Journal: A History of the Operations of a Partisan Corps, called the Queen's Rangers, Commanded by Lieut. Col. J. G. Simcoe, during the War of the American Revolution* (New York: Bartlett and Welford, 1844), 159–65.

20. "List of the Losses Sustained by the Rebels, by the Detachments under Brigadier General Arnold and Lieut-Colonel Simcoe, at Westham and Richmond, in Virginia, Jan. 5, 1781," in Robert Beatson, *Naval and Military Memoirs of Great Britain from 1727 to 1783*, 6 vols. (London: Longman, Hurst, Rees, and Orme, 1804), 6:273.

21. Johann von Ewald, *Diary of the American War: A Hessian Journal*, ed. Joseph P. Dustin (New Haven: Yale University Press, 1979), 268.

22. TJ to Abner Nash, Jan. 16, 1781, *PTJ*, 4:381. Also see TJ to GW, Jan. 10, 1781, *PTJ*, 4:333–35; and TJ to George Weedon, Jan. 10, 1781, *PTJ*, 4:336. Benedict Arnold reported that he had captured or destroyed 31 cannons of various sizes as well as destroying carriages, shells, 2,200 small arms, thousands of cartridges, 330 barrels of gunpowder, and "all the public stores, houses, magazines of oats, &c. with the armouries, and workshops: a great number of other military stores, which could not be taken account of, and a large rope-walk with a quantity of cordage and sails in it." He noted that in the skirmishing around Richmond 7 British

soldiers and officers were killed and 32 wounded. "List of the Losses Sustained by the Rebels," 272–73.

23. TJ to Abner Nash, Jan. 16, 1781, *PTJ*, 4:381.

24. GW to TJ, Feb. 21, 1781, *PTJ*, 4:683–85; Marquis de Lafayette to TJ, Feb. 21, 1781, *PTJ*, 4:676.

25. Lafayette to TJ, March 3, 1781, *PTJ*, 5:51.

26. John Walker to TJ, March 8, 1781, *PTJ*, 5:101; TJ to the County Lieutenants of Prince George and Other Counties, March 1, 1781, *PTJ*, 5:32; TJ to County Lieutenants of Chesterfield and Dinwiddie, March 9, 1781, *PTJ*, 5:104.

27. TJ to Marquis de Lafayette, March 12, 1781, *PTJ*, 5:129.

28. TJ to GW, May 28, 1781, *PTJ*, 6:32–33; Diary of Arnold's Invasion and Notes on Subsequent Events in 1781, *PTJ*, 4:260; Benedict Arnold, "Arnold's Expedition to Richmond, Virginia, 1781," *WMQ*, 2nd ser., 12 (1932): 187–90; Samuel Graham, "Phillips' Expedition to Virginia, 1781," *WMQ*, 2nd ser., 12 (1932): 191–92; Peterson, *Thomas Jefferson and the New Nation*, 221–34; Kranish, *Flight from Monticello*, 231–63.

29. May 10, 1781, *Journal of the House of Delegates of the Commonwealth of Virginia, 1781* (Richmond: Thomas White, 1828), 3.

30. TJ to GW, May 28, 1781, *PTJ*, 6:33.

31. Diary of Arnold's Invasion and Notes on Subsequent Events in 1781, *PTJ*, 4:260.

32. Banastre Tarleton, *A History of the Campaigns of 1780 and 1781 in the Southern Provinces of North America* (Dublin: Colles, Exshaw, White, H. Whitestone, Burton, 1787), 304.

33. For Jefferson's account of these events, see Diary of Arnold's Invasion and Notes on Subsequent Events in 1781, *PTJ*, 4:258–68, quotation 265. Also see TJ to William Gordon, July 16, 1788, *PTJ*, 13:362–64. For Jouett's ride, see Kranish, *Fight from Monticello*, 275–83.

34. Diary of Arnold's Invasion and Notes on the Subsequent Events in 1781, *PTJ*, 4:265; Sarah N. Randolph, *The Domestic Life of Thomas Jefferson* (New York: Harper, 1871; repr. Charlottesville: University of Virginia Press, 1978), 55–56.

35. Deposition of Christopher Hudson respecting Tarleton's Raid in June 1781, July 26, 1805, *PTJ*, 4:277.

36. Randolph, *Domestic Life of Thomas Jefferson*, 56; Girardin, *History of Virginia*, 4:502; Diary of Arnold's Invasion and Notes on Subsequent Events in 1781, *PTJ*, 4:265–68. Approximately thirty of Jefferson's slaves fled or were liberated by the British during Cornwallis's campaign in Virginia. Most of these were at Elkhill, another of Jefferson's plantations, which Cornwallis occupied in early June, TJ to William Gordon, July 16, 1788, *PTJ*, 13:363.

37. TJ to William Gordon, July 16, 1788, *PTJ*, 13:362.

38. Carter's Mountain, now known as Montalto, is beside Monticello. Betsy Ambler to Mildred Smith, [June 1781], "An Old Virginia Correspondence," *Atlantic Monthly* 84 (July 1899): 537–39, quotation 538.

39. *Journal of the House of Delegates, 1781,* June 7, 1781, 10.

40. *Journal of the House of Delegates, 1781,* 15; John Beckley to TJ, June 12, 1781, *PTJ,* 6:88–90; Archibald Cary to TJ, June 19, 1781, *PTJ,* 6:96–97; Selby, *Revolution in Virginia,* 282–85.

41. TJ to George Nicholas, July 28, 1781, *PTJ,* 6:104–5.

42. George Nicholas to TJ, July 31, 1781, *PTJ,* 6:105–6.

43. Archibald Cary to TJ, June 19, 1781, *PTJ,* 6:96–97. For the (non) role of the council in the inquiry, see the editorial note to John Beckley to TJ, June 12, 1781, *PTJ,* 6:88–90.

44. Girardin, *History of Virginia,* 4: app. 12.

45. Charges Advanced by George Nicholas with Jefferson's Answers, [after July 31, 1781], *PTJ,* 6:106–9; *Journal of the House of Delegates,* Oct. 1781, 37, 42, 48; John Harvie to TJ, Nov. 27, 1781, *PTJ,* 6:133–34; Resolution of Thanks to Jefferson by the Virginia General Assembly, Dec. 12, 1781, *PTJ,* 6:135–37; *Journal of the House of Delegates, 1781,* Dec. 12, 1781, 37; Edmund Pendleton to JM, Dec. 31, 1781, in Robert A. Rutland et al., eds., *Papers of James Madison: Congressional Series,* 17 vols. (Chicago and Charlottesville: University of Chicago Press/University of Virginia Press, 1962–91), 3:347; *Pennsylvania Packet,* Jan. 19, 1782.

46. Diary of Arnold's Invasion and Notes on Subsequent Events in 1781, *PTJ,* 4:265.

47. Diary of Arnold's Invasion and Notes on Subsequent Events in 1781, *PTJ,* 4:267–68n13.

48. TJ, Autobiography, *TJW,* 45. I discuss Jefferson's efforts to assist Girardin in Francis D. Cogliano, *Thomas Jefferson: Reputation and Legacy* (Charlottesville: University of Virginia Press, 2006), 63–66. To a large extent historians have followed the interpretation of Girardin. Richard Bernstein argued, "Governor Jefferson had done as well responding to the crisis as anyone could expect." Bernstein feels that Jefferson erred in leaving the commonwealth without a governor between June 4 and 12 owing to his literal-minded approach to government. In her Pulitzer Prize–winning book on the Heming family, Annette Gordon-Reed concluded, "It is hard to know what Jefferson's critics at the time and later expected him to have done in that situation—engage Tarleton's troops in a single-handed, meaningless fight to the death (probably just his own) or allow himself (the governor) to be captured and held for ransom. Flight was the only prudent decision." R. B. Bernstein, *Thomas Jefferson* (New York: Oxford University Press, 2003), 46; Annette Gordon-Reed, *The Hemingses of Monticello: An American Family* (New York: W. W. Norton, 2008), 138. Also see Malone, *Jefferson and His Time,* 1:368.

49. George Nicholas, *A Letter from George Nicholas, of Kentucky, to His Friend, in Virginia* (Lexington, 1798), 28.

50. Henry S. Randall, *The Life of Thomas Jefferson,* 3 vols. (New York: Derby and Jackson, 1858), 1:348.

51. *Journal of the House of Delegates, 1781,* June 4, p. 10; May 29, pp. 5–6; Archibald Cary to TJ, June 19, 1781, *PTJ,* 6:96–97.

52. See Archibald Stuart to TJ, Sept. 8, 1818, as quoted in *PTJ*, 6:85n. Also see Henry Young to William Davies, June 9, 1781, *PTJ*, 6:84–85; Selby, *Revolution in Virginia*, 283.

53. Richard Henry Lee to the Virginia Delegates in Congress, June 12, 1781, *PTJ*, 6:91.

54. Robert A. Rutland, ed., *The Papers of George Mason, 1725–1792*, 3 vols. (Chapel Hill: University of North Carolina Press, 1970), 1:326, as quoted in Selby, *Revolution in Virginia*, 129.

55. The legislative records are incomplete for this period and no official record of the proposal appears in the *Journal of the House of Delegates*. A report from Staunton written on June 9 stated, "Two days ago Mr. Nicholas gave notice that he shou'd this day move to have a Dictator appointed. Genl. Washington and Genl. Greene are talk'd of." Henry Young to William Davies, June 9, 1781, *PTJ*, 6:84.

56. William Wirt, *Sketches of the Life and Character of Patrick Henry* (Philadelphia: James Webster, 1817), 231.

57. Girardin, *History of Virginia*, 4: app. 11–12. Also see Randall, *Life of Thomas Jefferson*, 1:350; and George Tucker, *The Life of Thomas Jefferson*, 2 vols. (Philadelphia: Carey, Lea and Blanchard, 1837), 1:150.

58. *TJW*, 252–55.

59. As the political scientist Jeremy Bailey has written, "Jefferson adhered to a strict interpretation of the Virginia Constitution, and when necessity demanded that he move outside his constitutional authority, Jefferson acted and then afterward sought legislative approval. By being both an advocate of executive action and a defender of the legislative process, the governor expanded his office without treading upon the legislature's duty to write the laws." Bailey, *Thomas Jefferson and Executive Power*, 45.

60. *TJW*, 254.

61. TJ to the First Magistrate of Each County, Jan. 20, 1781, *PTJ*, 4:415; TJ to the Speaker of the House of Delegates, March 1, 1781, *PTJ*, 5:33–37. On March 21 the Assembly passed an "Act to remedy the inconveniences arising from the interruption given to the execution of two acts passed at the last session of assembly, for recruiting this state's quota of troops to serve in the continental army, and for supplying the army with clothes, provisions and waggons." *PTJ*, 5:37n. Also see TJ to the Members of the Assembly, Jan. 23, 1781, *PTJ*, 4:433–34.

62. Constitution as adopted by the Convention, [June 29, 1776], *PTJ*, 1:381.

63. TJ to Steuben, Jan. 13, 1781, *PTJ*, 4:351–52; TJ to Steuben, Jan. 14, 1781, *PTJ*, 4:356; TJ to Samuel Huntington, Jan. 15, 1781, *PTJ*, 4:369–71; TJ to Thomas Nelson, Jan. 15, 1781, *PTJ*, 4:372; TJ to Thomas Nelson, Jan. 16, 1781, *PTJ*, 4:382; TJ to George Weedon, Jan. 16, 1781, *PTJ*, 4:384; TJ to Richard Claiborne, Jan. 18, 1781, *PTJ*, 4:393; TJ to Samuel Huntington, Jan. 17, 1781, *PTJ*, 4:386–91; TJ to John Walker, Jan. 18, 1781, *PTJ*, 4:400.

64. Proclamation Concerning Paroles, *PTJ*, 4:403–5; H. R. McIlwaine, ed., *Journals of the Council of State of Virginia: Vol. 2, October 6, 1777–November 30, 1781* (Richmond: Virginia State Library, 1932), 341–42.

65. *Journals of the Council of Virginia*, 344.

66. TJ to the Speaker of the House of Delegates, March 1, 1781, *PTJ*, 5:34; Girardin, *History of Virginia*, 4:491.

67. TJ to the Speaker of the House of Delegates, May 28, 1781, *PTJ*, 6:28–29; *Journal of the House of Delegates, 1781*, May 29, 5–6.

68. TJ to the Speaker of the House of Delegates, March 1, 1781, *PTJ*, 5:34.

69. TJ to Edmund Pendleton, Aug. 13, 1776, *PTJ*, 1:492.

70. *TJW*, 253.

71. *TJW*, 253–54.

72. Girardin, *History of Virginia*, 4: app. 12.

73. *TJW*, 243–46; Draft Constitution for Virginia, [May–June, 1783], *PTJ*, 6:294–308. See Bailey, *Thomas Jefferson and Executive Power*, 55–60.

74. James Barbour to TJ, Jan. 22, 1812, *PTJ:RS*, 4:415.

75. TJ to James Barbour, Jan. 22, 1812, *PTJ:RS*, 4:432, 433.

76. TJ to John B. Colvin, Sept. 20, 1810, *PTJ:RS*, 3:99, emphasis in original.

77. TJ to James Barbour, Jan. 22, 1812, *PTJ:RS*, 4:433–34.

78. Malone, *Jefferson and His Time*, 1:368; Julian P. Boyd, "Editorial Note," *PTJ*, 4:256.

79. Unaccountably he failed to take immediate action for twenty-four hours when he was confronted by news of Arnold's arrival in Virginia in January 1781. He would never again make such a mistake when confronted by a crisis.

Two
"To Compel the Pyratical States to Perpetual Peace"

1. Richard O'Bryen to TJ, Aug. 24, 1785, *PTJ*, 8:440–41; TJ to James Currie, Sept. 27, 1785, *PTJ*, 8:559; Matthew Irwin to George Washington, July 9, 1789, *PGW:PS*, 3:155–58; Worthington C. Ford, ed., *Journals of the Continental Congress*, 34 vols. (Washington, DC: Government Printing Office, 1904–37) (hereafter *JCC*), Dec. 28, 1785, 29:906; List of American Prisoners at Algiers, July 9, 1790, Dudley W. Knox, ed., *Naval Documents Related to the United States Wars with the Barbary Powers*, 6 vols. (Washington, DC: Government Printing Office, 1939–44), 1:1. O'Brien (c. 1758–1824, whose name is spelled variously as "O'Bryen" and "O'Brian") was the leader and spokesman of the captives and corresponded with Jefferson and other American government officials during their prolonged captivity. After his release he served as an American consul on the Barbary Coast.

2. For the Barbary States and their relations with the West, see John B. Wolf, *The Barbary Coast: Algiers under the Turks, 1500–1830* (New York: W. W. Norton, 1979); R. C. Anderson, *Naval Wars in the Levant, 1559–1853* (Princeton: Princeton

University Press, 1952); Robert C. Davis, *Christian Slaves, Muslim Masters: White Slavery in the Mediterranean, The Barbary Coast, and Italy, 1500–1800* (New York: Palgrave Macmillan, 2003); Seton Dearden, *A Nest of Corsairs: The Fighting Karamanlis of Tripoli* (London: John Murray, 1976); Godfrey Fisher, *Barbary Legend: War, Trade, and Piracy in North Africa, 1415–1830* (Oxford: Clarendon Press, 1957); Kola Folayan, *Tripoli during the Reign of Pasha Yusuf Karamanli* (Ife-Ife, Nigeria, 1979); G. N. Clark, "The Barbary Corsairs in the Seventeenth Century," *Cambridge Historical Journal* 8 (1944): 22–35.

3. In 1783 John Baker Holroyd, Earl of Sheffield, argued, "It is not probable the American States will have a very free trade in the Mediterranean; it will not be the interest of any of the great maritime powers to protect them there from the Barbary States. If they know their interests, they will not encourage the Americans to be carriers. That the Barbary States are advantageous to the maritime powers is certain. If they were suppressed, the little States of Italy, &c. would have much more of the carrying trade." Lord Sheffield, *Observations on the Commerce of the American States* (London: Debrett, 1783), 204–5. Richard O'Brien reported from Algiers in 1785, "They [the Algerines] have very little Idea of America and I believe the British Consuls used their influence in signifying to the Algerines the unjustness of our cause." Richard O'Bryen and Others to TJ, June 8, 1786, *PTJ,* 9:617–18.

4. For the capture of the *Betsey,* see the *Virginia Journal and Alexandria Advertiser,* Oct. 13, 1785; Giuseppe Chiappe to GW, July 18, 1789, *PGW:PS,* 3:229–32; Priscilla H. Roberts and James N. Tull, "Moroccan Sultan Sidi Muhammad Ibn Abdallah's Diplomatic Initiatives toward the United States, 1777–1786," *Proceedings of the American Philosophical Society* 143 (1999):233–65; Priscilla H. Roberts and Richard S. Roberts, *Thomas Barclay, 1728–1793: Consul in France, Diplomat in Barbary* (Bethlehem, PA: Lehigh University Press, 2008), 23–27; Frank Lambert, *The Barbary Wars: American Independence in the Atlantic World* (New York: Hill and Wang, 2005), 3–4.

5. For the death of Martha Jefferson, see Malone, *Jefferson and His Time,* 1:393–96; Andrew Burstein and Nancy Isenberg, *Madison and Jefferson* (New York: Random House, 2010), 92–94. For Jefferson's appointment to the Commission for Negotiating Commercial Treaties, see TJ to William Short, May 7, 1784, *PTJ,* 7:229; *JCC,* May 12, 1784, 27:372–73.

6. *The Notes on the State of Virginia* was published privately by Jefferson in France (in French) in 1785. After pirated editions began to appear in English he authorized the publication of an English-language edition in 1787. This was published in London by John Stockdale. Although Jefferson intended to publish a second expanded and corrected edition, he never did so. The 1787 Stockdale edition has been reprinted in Merrill D. Peterson's collection of Jefferson's writings (New York: Library of America, 1984), pp. 123–325. That edition is referenced below.

7. For Jefferson's understanding of history, see Francis D. Cogliano, *Thomas Jefferson: Reputation and Legacy* (Charlottesville: University of Virginia Press, 2006), ch. 1; H. Trevor Colbourn, "Thomas Jefferson's Use of the Past," *WMQ,*

3rd ser., 15 (1958): 56–70; and H. Trevor Colbourn, *The Lamp of Experience: Whig History and the Intellectual Origins of the American Revolution* (Chapel Hill: University of North Carolina Press, 1965), 217–21.

8. In 1778 he drafted a "Bill for the More General Diffusion of Knowledge" which called for the creation of a comprehensive system of state-funded education in Virginia. When the legislature failed to enact this legislation he included it in the *Notes on the State of Virginia* as a statement of value of education. A Bill for the More General Diffusion of Knowledge, *PTJ*, 2:526–35; *Notes on the State of Virginia, TJW*, 271–75. Jefferson held this view throughout his life. Nearly forty years after he wrote *Notes* he wrote, "I know no safe depositary of the ultimate powers of the society but the people themselves; and if we think them not enlightened enough to exercise their control with a wholesome discretion, the remedy is not to take it from them, but to inform their discretion by education. This is the true corrective of abuses of constitutional power." TJ to William C. Jarvis, Sept. 28, 1820, TJP.

9. *Notes on the State of Virginia, TJW*, 290–91. My understanding of Jefferson's political economy owes much to Drew R. McCoy's *The Elusive Republic: Political Economy in Jeffersonian America* (Chapel Hill: University of North Carolina Press, 1980).

10. *Notes on the State of Virginia, TJW*, 290, 291.

11. McCoy, *Elusive Republic*, 9–10.

12. TJ to George Washington, March 15, 1784, *PTJ*, 7:26.

13. *Notes on the State of Virginia, TJW*, 291.

14. Francis D. Cogliano, *Revolutionary America: A Political History, 1763–1815*, 2nd ed. (New York: Routledge, 2009), 32.

15. TJ to John Jay, Aug. 23, 1785, *PTJ*, 8:426–27.

16. Report on American Trade in the Mediterranean, Dec. 28, 1790, *PTJ*, 18:423. Jefferson prepared this report while serving as George Washington's secretary of state. Notes on the Commerce of the Northern States, [May–June 1784], *PTJ*, 7:344; John Adams to TJ, July 3, 1786, *PTJ*, 10:86–87.

17. TJ to James Monroe, Nov. 11, 1784, *PTJ*, 7:511–12.

18. *JCC*, Feb. 14, 1785, 28:65; March 11, 1785, 28:139–48; TJ to John Adams, July 28, 1785, *PTJ*, 8:315–17; TJ to John Adams, Aug. 17, 1785, *PTJ*, 8:400; Documents Pertaining to the Mission of Barclay and Lamb to the Barbary States, *PTJ*, 8:610–24; Ray W. Irwin, *The Diplomatic Relations of the United States with the Barbary Powers, 1776–1815* (Chapel Hill: University of North Carolina Press, 1931), ch. 3.

19. John Adams to TJ, Aug. 23, 1785, *PTJ*, 8:424. Also see, TJ to John Adams, Aug. 17, 1785, *PTJ*, 8:394–95. For Barclay, see Roberts and Roberts, *Thomas Barclay*.

20. Instructions, Oct. 2, 11, 1785, *PTJ*, 8:613–16; Irwin, *Diplomatic Relations*, 30. Jefferson based the draft treaty on Benjamin Franklin's notes.

21. Thomas Barclay to TJ, March 23, 1786, *PTJ*, 9:352–53. Also see TJ to William Carmichael, Nov. 4, 1785, *PTJ*, 9:14; TJ to John Jay, Jan. 27, 1786, *PTJ*, 9:234.

22. Thomas Barclay to the American Commissioners, Sept. 13, 1786, *PTJ*, 10:360–61.

23. For Barclay's account of the negotiations, see Thomas Barclay to the American Commissioners, Sept. 18, 1786, *PTJ*, 10:389–92, quotation 390. For the treaty, see Morocco Treaty, [June 28, 1786, and July 18, 1787], in *Naval Documents*, 1:6–9. Also see Irwin, *Diplomatic Relations*, 32–33. Per his instructions Barclay also provided detailed information on Morocco. In addition to the letters cited above also, see Thomas Barclay to the American Commissioners, Sept. 10, 1786, *PTJ*, 10:334–48.

24. Thomas Barclay to the American Commissioners, Sept. 13, 1786, *PTJ*, 10:361.

25. Irwin, *Diplomatic Relations*, 33–34; Roberts and Tull, "Sultan Sidi Muhammad Ibn Abdallah,"

26. TJ to John Adams, Sept. 24, 1785, *PTJ*, 8:543; TJ to William Carmichael, Nov. 4, 1785, *PTJ*, 9:14. For Lamb's recommendation to Jefferson, see Abiel Foster to TJ, March 26, 1785, *PTJ*, 8:60. According to Julian Boyd, Jay and Alexander Hamilton were behind Lamb's appointment. *PTJ*, 18:384–85.

27. Supplementary Instructions to John Lamb, Oct. 1, 11, 1785, *PTJ*, 8:616–17; TJ to Richard O'Bryen, Nov. 4, 1785, *PTJ*, 9:17.

28. Supplementary Instructions to John Lamb, Oct. 1, 11, 1785, *PTJ*, 8:616.

29. John Lamb to the American Commissioners, May 20, 1786, *PTJ*, 9:549–53; TJ to JA, May 11, 1786, *PTJ*, 9:506–7; P. R. Randall to the American Commissioners, May 14, 1786, *PTJ*, 9:525–36; Irwin, *Diplomatic Relations*, 38–39; Lambert, *Barbary Wars*, 60–61.

30. From the American captives to John Adams, Feb. 13, 1787, *The Diplomatic Correspondence of the United States, Sept. 10, 1783 to March 4, 1789*, 7 vols. (Washington, DC: Blair and Rives, 1837), 5:247–51. Also see Richard O'Bryen and Others to TJ, June 8, 1786, *PTJ*, 9:614–22.

31. John Lamb to TJ, March 29, 1786, *PTJ*, 9:364–65. For Randall's appointment, see John Adams to TJ, Oct. 2, 1785, *PTJ*, 8:572.

32. Richard O'Bryen and Others to TJ, June 8, 1786, *PTJ*, 9:614–22 quotations 619–20; William Carmichael to TJ, July 18, 1786, *PTJ*, 10:149; William Carmichael to TJ, Oct. 15, 1787, *PTJ*, 12:239. Carmichael in the latter letter describes Lamb as Logie's "Dupe." Carmichael reported that Logie "is given to Liquor, but even in his Cups is artful indeed. For Logie, see *PTJ*, 18:375. For Lamb's recall, see *JCC*, Sept. 26, 1786, 31:692.

33. John Adams to TJ, Jan. 25, 1787, *PTJ*, 11:64.

34. John Adams to John Jay, Feb. 16, 1786, *Diplomatic Correspondence of the United States*, 4:488.

35. John Adams to John Jay, Feb. 16, 1786, *Diplomatic Correspondence of the United States*, 4:488; John Adams to John Jay, Feb. 17, 1786, in Charles F. Adams, ed., *The Works of John Adams*, 10 vols. (Boston: Little, Brown, 1856), 8:372. These negotiations are treated in Irwin, *Diplomatic Relations*, 37–42.

36. John Adams to TJ, Feb. 17, 1786, *PTJ*, 9:285–86. Adams sent a less detailed account of the meeting to John Jay. John Adams to John Jay, Feb. 17, 1786, *Works of John Adams*, 8:372–73. For another account of the meeting, see Abigail Adams to Charles Storer, March 23, 1786, in L. H. Butterfield et al., eds. *Adams Family Correspondence*, 10 vols. to date (Cambridge: Harvard University Press, 1963–), 7:115.

37. John Adams to John Jay, Feb. 20, 1786, *Works of John Adams*, 8:374–46, quoting Abdurrahman in translation by Benamor.

38. John Adams to John Jay, Feb. 22, 1786, *Works of John Adams*, 8:379. To Richard Cranch, Adams wrote, "We must not be afraid of two hundred Thousand Pounds to procure Treaties with the Barbary Powers which will be worth two Millions." *Adams Family Correspondence*, 7:113.

39. John Adams to John Jay, Feb. 20, 1786, *Works of John Adams*, 8:376. Adams also reported, "The ambassador, who is known to many of the foreign ministers here, is universally well spoken of." John Adams to John Jay, Feb. 22, 1786, *Works of John Adams*, 8:377. John Adams to TJ, Feb. 21, 1786, *PTJ*, 9:295.

40. James A. Bear, Jr., and Lucia C. Stanton, eds., *Jefferson's Memorandum Books*, 2 vols. (Princeton: Princeton University Press, 1997), 1:613.

41. JA to TJ, Feb. 21, 1786, *PTJ*, 9:295; American Commissioners to John Jay, March 28, 1786, *PTJ*, 9:357–59.

42. TJ to William Carmichael, May 5, 1786, *PTJ*, 9:448.

43. *JCC*, May 26, 1786, 30:311–12; John Adams to John Jay, Jan. 9, 1787, *Diplomatic Correspondence of the United States*, 5:158; John Jay to TJ, *PTJ*, 11:130.

44. TJ to John Jay, May 23, 1786, *PTJ*, 9:567–68.

45. TJ to Elbridge Gerry, May 7, 1786, *PTJ*, 9:467. Also see TJ to James Monroe, May 10, 1786, *PTJ*, 9:500.

46. John Adams to TJ, July 3, 1786, *PTJ*, 10:86–87.

47. TJ to John Adams, July 11, 1786, *PTJ*, 10:123.

48. Ibid., 123–24.

49. Proposed Convention against the Barbary States, [before July 4, 1786], *PTJ*, 10:566–68. Also see TJ to James Monroe, Aug. 11, 1786, *PTJ*, 10:223–25. For a thorough examination of the background to this proposal, see Julian P. Boyd's editorial note "Jefferson's Proposed Concert of Powers against the Barbary States," *PTJ*, 10:560–66.

50. TJ, Autobiography, *TJW*, 57–61, quotation 59.

51. Ibid., 61.

52. Lafayette to TJ, March 6, 1786, *PTJ*, 9:318–19. For the revised version of Jefferson's proposal, see Proposed Confederation against the Barbary States, [ca. Oct. 1786], *PTJ*, 10:569–70. For Jefferson's relationship with Lafayette, see William H. Adams, *The Paris Years of Thomas Jefferson* (New Haven: Yale University Press, 1997), 9–13.

53. Lafayette to TJ, Oct. 23, 1786, *PTJ*, 10:486.

54. Lafayette to George Washington, Oct. 26, 1786, in Louis R. Gottschalk, ed., *Letters of Lafayette to Washington, 1777–1799* (New York: H. V. Hubbard,

1944; 2nd ed., Philadelphia: American Philosophical Society, 1976), 315; Louis R. Gottschalk, *Lafayette between the American Revolution and the French Revolution, 1783–1789* (Chicago: University of Chicago Press, 1950), 255; Lafayette to John Jay, Oct. 28, 1786, *Diplomatic Correspondence of the United States,* 1:319–20.

55. Julian P. Boyd writes, "By letting it appear that the idea was Lafayette's, Jefferson doubtless felt, with reason, that the chances of Congressional support for the requested authority would be greatly augmented. Thus it was that both Adams and Congress were intentionally kept in the dark as to the true origin of the proposed policy." *PTJ,* 10:564. Also see Boyd's editorial note *PTJ,* 18:378; Merrill D. Peterson, *Thomas Jefferson and the New Nation* (New York: Oxford University Press, 1970), 314.

56. John Jay to Congress, Feb. 15, 1787, *JCC,* 23:65. Jay's motives are examined in detail by Julian Boyd in *PTJ,* 18:382–98.

57. *JCC,* 33:419–20. Jefferson described Grayson as "lazy" in a letter to James Monroe. TJ to Monroe, Aug 11, 1786, *PTJ,* 10:225.

58. *JCC,* 33:451–53.

59. Report on the American Captives in Algiers, Dec. 28, 1790, *PTJ,* 18:430–36. For the negotiations with the Mathurins, also see TJ to John Adams, Jan. 11, 1787, *PTJ,* 11:35–36; TJ to John Jay, Feb. 1, 1787, *PTJ,* 11:101–2; TJ to John Jay, Aug. 12, 1788, *PTJ,* 13:500; TJ to John Jay, Sept. 5, 1788, *PTJ,* 13:569; Irwin, *Diplomatic Relations,* 44–46.

60. Extract of letter from Colonel David Humphreys to the Secretary of State, Nov. 28, 1795, Treaty of Peace and Amity with the Dey of Algiers, Sept. 5, 1795, *ASPFR,* 1:530–31; Irwin, *Diplomatic Relations,* 69–81.

61. Reports on Mediterranean Trade and Algerine Captives, *PTJ,* 18:369–445.

62. Report on the American Captives, Dec. 28, 1790, *PTJ,* 18:435.

63. Report on Mediterranean Trade, Dec. 28, 1790, *PTJ,* 18:425, 427, 428.

64. Senate Resolution on the Algerine Captives, Feb. 1, 1791, *PTJ,* 18:444.

Three
"Mr. Jefferson Is a Decided Republican"

1. John Trumbull to TJ, Sept. 22, 1789, *PTJ,* 15:467–69; TJ to Madame de Corny, Oct. 14, 1789, *PTJ,* 15:520; TJ to William Short, Oct. 23, 1789, *PTJ,* 15:527; TJ to Nathaniel Cutting, Nov. 21, 1789, *PTJ,* 15:551–52. List of Baggage Shipped by Jefferson from France, [c. Sept. 1, 1789], *PTJ,* 15:375–77. James A. Bear and Lucia C. Stanton, eds. *Jefferson's Memorandum Books,* 2 vols. (Princeton: Princeton University Press, 1997), 743–47. Also see Malone, *Jefferson and His Time,* 2:234–43; and Annette Gordon-Reed, *The Hemingses of Monticello* (New York: W. W. Norton, 2008), 385–90.

2. JM to TJ, May 27, 1789, *PTJ,* 15:153; TJ to JM, Aug. 28, 1789, *PTJ,* 15:369.

3. *Senate Executive Journal,* 1st Cong., 1st Sess., 1:32–33.

4. TJ to William Short, Dec. 14, 1789, *PTJ,* 16:27–28; TJ to GW, Dec. 15, 1789, *PTJ,* 16:35; GW to TJ, Jan. 21, 1790, *PTJ,* 16:117; TJ to GW, Feb. 14, 1790, *PTJ,*

16:184. For Jefferson's appointment and Madison's attempts to persuade him to accept the nomination, see Andrew Burstein and Nancy Isenberg, *Madison and Jefferson* (New York: Random House, 2010), 202–4.

5. Opinion on the Powers of the Senate Respecting Diplomatic Appointments, April 24, 1790, *PTJ*, 16:378.

6. *PTJ*, 16:381; Edgar S. Maclay, ed., *Journal of William Maclay* (New York: Appleton, 1890), 272.

7. John Rutledge, Jr., to TJ, May 6, 1790, *PTJ*, 16:414. Also see William Short to John Jay, May 11, 1790, *PTJ*, 16:425–27. William R. Manning, "The Nootka Sound Controversy," *American Historical Association: Annual Report, 1904,* 279–478; Stanley Elkins and Eric McKitrick, *The Age of Federalism* (New York: Oxford University Press, 1993), 212–15. Also see John M. Norris, "The Policy of the British Cabinet in the Nootka Crisis," *English Historical Review* 70 (1955): 562–80; Lennox Mills, "The Real Significance of the Nootka Sound Incident," *Canadian Historical Review* 6 (1925): 110–22. George Verne Blue, "Anglo-French Diplomacy during the Critical Period of the Nootka Controversy, 1790," *Oregon Historical Quarterly* 39 (1938): 163–79; Howard V. Evans, "The Nootka Sound Controversy in Anglo-French Diplomacy—1790," *Journal of Modern History* 46 (1974): 609–40.

8. Gouverneur Morris to GW, May 29, 1790, *PGW:PS*, 5:431–38; Beatrix Cary Davenport, ed., *A Diary of the French Revolution by Gouverneur Morris,* 2 vols. (Boston: Houghton Mifflin, 1939), 1:458–66; Elkins and McKitrick, *Age of Federalism*, 215–17. Also see the Duke of Leeds to Gouverneur Morris, April 28, 1790, in Douglas Brymner, ed., *Report on Canadian Archives 1890* (Ottawa: Brown Chamberlin, 1891), 129–30, and Phillip Ziesche, "Exporting American Revolutions: Gouverneur Morris, Thomas Jefferson, and the National Struggle for Rights in Revolutionary France," *JER* 26 (2006): 419–47.

9. Grenville to Lord Dorchester, May 6, 1790, *Report on Canadian Archives 1890,* 133.

10. Lord Dorchester to Major Beckwith, June 27, 1790, *Report on Canadian Archives 1890,* 143–44.

11. Donald Jackson and Dorothy Twohig, eds., *The Diaries of George Washington,* 6 vols. (Charlottesville: University of Virginia Press, 1976–9), 6:87–89.

12. Lord Dorchester to Lord Grenville, Sept. 25, 1790, *Report on Canadian Archives 1890,* 146, 148–49. Julian P. Boyd has identified Beckwith's Agent Number 1 as William Samuel Johnson, *PTJ*, 17:52.

13. Burstein and Isenberg, *Jefferson and Madison,* 267. Some scholars have been critical of Hamilton's interference in foreign policy. Most notably Julian P. Boyd, the editor of Jefferson's papers, has alleged that Hamilton betrayed the United States and acted as a British agent. See Julian P. Boyd, *Number 7: Alexander Hamilton's Secret Attempts to Control American Foreign Policy* (Princeton: Princeton University Press, 1964). Also see Boyd's lengthy editorial note "The War Crisis of 1790," most of which is dedicated to Hamilton's dealings with Beckwith, *PTJ*, 17:35–108. For interpretations more sympathetic to Hamilton, see John

Lamberton Harper, *American Machiavelli: Alexander Hamilton and the Origins of American Foreign Policy* (New York: Cambridge University Press, 2004), ch. 6; and Elkins and McKitrick, *Age of Federalism,* 222–23.

14. Introduction to the Anas, Feb. 4, 1818, TJP; Notes on a Conversation with George Washington, Oct. 1, 1792, *PTJ,* 24:433–36.

15. TJ to GW, July 12, 1790, *PTJ,* 17:108.

16. Outline of Policy Contingent on War, July 12, 1790, *PTJ,* 17:109.

17. Ibid.

18. Ibid.

19. Ibid., 17:110.

20. Ibid.

21. TJ to GW, Aug. 8, 1790, *PTJ,* 17:120–21; TJ to David Humphreys, Aug. 11, 1790, *PTJ,* 17:125–27. For the letters carried by Humphreys, see TJ to William Carmichael, enclosing Outline of Policy, Aug. 2, 1790, *PTJ,* 17:111–17; TJ to Luis Pinto de Souza, Aug 7, 1790, *PTJ,* 17:117–19.

22. Jon Kukla, *A Wilderness So Immense: The Louisiana Purchase and the Destiny of America* (New York: Alfred A. Knopf, 2003), 114. Also see Arthur P. Whitaker, "The Commerce of Louisiana and the Floridas at the End of the Eighteenth Century," *Hispanic AHR* 8 (1928): 190–203.

23. JM to Charles Pinckney, Nov. 27, 1802, *PJM:SS,* 4:147. In this letter Madison reported that $1,622,672 worth of produce from Kentucky and the Mississippi Territory had passed through New Orleans in 1801. He estimated that the trade from the whole west would be worth 50 percent more in 1802 as Kentucky's exports alone were valued at $591,432 for the first six months of the year.

24. TJ to William Carmichael, Aug. 2, 1790, *PTJ,* 17:111–12.

25. Jefferson's Outline Policy on the Mississippi Question, *PTJ,* 17:113.

26. Ibid., 113–14.

27. Ibid., 114–17. Jefferson also wrote to William Short, his former secretary, who was looking after American interests in France. He advised Short to approach Lafayette and the French government in the event of a British-Spanish war to press for France to enter the war and to support the American acquisition of a port at the mouth of the Mississippi: "France will be called into the war, as an ally, and not on any pretence of the quarrel being in any degree her own. She may reasonably require then that Spain should do every thing which depends on her to lessen the number of her enemies. She cannot doubt that we shall be of that number, if she does not yield our right to the common use of the Missisipi, [*sic*] and the means of using and securing it. You will observe we state in general the necessity, not only of our having a port near the mouth of the river (without which we could make no use of the navigation at all) but of its being so well separated from the territories of Spain and her jurisdiction, as not to engender daily disputes and broils between us. It is certain that if Spain were to retain any jurisdiction over our entrepot her officers [122] would abuse that jurisdiction, and our people would abuse their privileges in it. Both parties must foresee this, and that it will end in war. Hence

the necessity of a well defined separation. Nature has decided what shall be the geography of that in the end, whatever it might be in the beginning, by cutting off from the adjacent countries of Florida and Louisiana, and inclosing between two of it's channels, a long and narrow slip of land, called the island of New Orleans." TJ to William Short, Aug. 10, 1790, *PTJ*, 17:121–22. Also see GW to Lafayette, Aug. 11, 1790, *PGW:PS*, 6:233–35.

28. Queries from the President to the Members of the Cabinet, Aug. 27, 1790, *PTJ*, 17:128–9.

29. TJ to GW, Aug. 27, 1790, *PTJ*, 17:129–30. Two days later Jefferson supplemented this advice with further observations concerning the expedition of General Arthur St. Clair, then in preparation against the Indians in Ohio. Jefferson assessed the impact St. Clair's expedition might have on a possible British movement through the Northwest. He concluded St. Clair might be able to obstruct the progress of the British. TJ to GW, Aug. 29, 1790, *PTJ*, 17:131. St. Clair did not launch his expedition until the autumn of 1791. His army was decisively defeated by the Miami Indians on Nov. 4, 1791. Gordon S. Wood, *Empire of Liberty: A History of the Early Republic, 1789–1815* (New York: Oxford University Press, 2009), 129–30.

30. TJ to Thomas Mann Randolph, Jr., Aug. 29, 1790, *PTJ*, 17:474.

31. David Humphreys to GW, Oct. 31, 1790, *PGW:PS*, 6:596–99 Manning, "Nootka Sound Controversy," 453, 459; Elkins and McKitrick, *Age of Federalism*, 212–15; Blue, "Anglo-French Diplomacy"; Evans, "Nootka Sound Controversy."

32. See, for example, Notes of Cabinet Meeting on the Southern Indians and Spain, Oct. 31, 1792, *PTJ*, 24:547–50; TJ to William Carmichael and William Short, Nov. 3, 1792, *PTJ*, 24:565–67.

33. Samuel Flagg Bemis, *Pinckney's Treaty: A Study of America's Advantage from Europe's Distress, 1783–1800* (Baltimore: Johns Hopkins University Press, 1926); Raymond A. Young, "Pinckney's Treaty—A New Perspective," *Hispanic AHR* 43 (1963): 526–35; Malone, *Jefferson and His Time*, 4:239–61; James E. Lewis, *The American Union and the Problem of Neighborhood: The United States and the Collapse of the Spanish Empire, 1783–1829* (Chapel Hill: University of North Carolina Press, 1998), 25; J. C. A. Stagg, *Borderlines in Borderlands: James Madison and the Spanish-American Frontier, 1776–1821* (New Haven: Yale University Press, 2009), 37–8; Elkins and McKitrick, *Age of Federalism*, 439–40 .

34. TJ to JM, July 22, 1789, *PTJ*, 15:299–301; TJ to John Jay, July 23, 1789, *PTJ*, 15:301–2; Lafayette to TJ, [Aug. 25, 1789], *PTJ*, 15:354. For a lengthy summary of the events of the summer, see TJ to John Jay, Sept. 19, 1789, *PTJ*, 15:454–60. Also see Burstein and Isenberg, *Madison and Jefferson*, 193–95; William H. Adams, *The Paris Years of Thomas Jefferson* (New Haven: Yale University Press, 1997), ch. 8. For an account very critical of Jefferson's support for the French Revolution, see Conor Cruise O'Brien, *The Long Affair: Thomas Jefferson and the French Revolution* (Chicago: University of Chicago Press, 1998).

35. *New-York Journal*, Feb. 6, 1793; *Independent Chronicle* (Boston), Jan. 31, 1793. Simon P. Newman, *Parades and the Politics of the Street: Festive Culture in*

the Early American Republic (Philadelphia: University of Pennsylvania Press, 1997), 122–35.

36. Autobiography, *TJW*, 97. For the impact of the French Revolution on the United States, see Elkins and McKitrick, *Age of Federalism,* ch. 8; Wood, *Empire of Liberty,* ch. 5.

37. TJ to William Short, Jan. 3, 1793, *PTJ*, 25:14. For critical analysis of this letter, see Burstein and Isenberg, *Jefferson and Madison,* 255–57; O'Brien, *Long Affair,* 144–51.

38. Notes on Washington's Questions on Neutrality and the Alliance with France, [May 6, 1793], *PTJ*, 25:665. For Washington's queries, see George Washington to the Cabinet with Enclosure: Questions on Neutrality and the Alliance with France, April 18, 1793, *PTJ*, 25:568–70.

39. Cabinet Opinion on Washington's Questions on Neutrality and the Alliance with France, [April 19, 1793], *PTJ*, 25:570; Minutes of a Cabinet Meeting, [April 19, 1793], *PGW:PS*, 12:459.

40. TJ to JM, June 23, 1793, *PTJ*, 26:346; Neutrality Proclamation, [April 22, 1793], *PGW:PS*, 12:472–73; Elkins and McKitrick, *Age of Federalism,* 336–41. Also see Charles M. Thomas, *American Neutrality in 1793* (New York: Columbia University Press, 1931); Charles S. Hyneman, *The First American Neutrality: A Study of the American Understanding of Neutral Obligations during the Years 1792 to 1815* (Philadelphia: Porcupine Press, 1974).

41. Jefferson's Opinion on the Treaties with France, *PTJ*, 25:597–619, quotation 618. Also see Elkins and McKitrick, *Age of Federalism,* 339–40.

42. Alexander Hamilton and Henry Knox to GW, May 2, 1793, *PGW:PS*, 12:504; Opinion on French Treaty, Harold C. Syrett et al., eds., *Papers of Alexander Hamilton,* 27 vols. (New York: Columbia University Press, 1961–87), 14:367–96; TJ to James Monroe, May 5, 1793, *PTJ*, 25:661. For Hamilton's position, see Harper, *American Machiavelli,* 109–14.

43. Edmund Randolph to GW, May 6, 1793, *PGW:PS*, 12:534–47; TJ to James Monroe, May 5, 1793, *PTJ*, 25:661; Notes on Washington's Question on Neutrality and the Alliance with France, [May 6, 1793], *PTJ*, 25:665–66.

44. Gouverneur Morris to GW, Dec. 28, 1792, *PGW:PS*, 11:561–62; Gouverneur Morris to GW, Jan. 6, 1793, *PGW:PS*, 11:593.

45. Gouverneur Morris to GW, Dec. 28, 1792, *PGW:PS*, 11:561. Genet's older sister wrote a memoir of her time at the French court: Jeanne-Louise-Henriette Campan, *Mémoires sur la vie privée de Marie-Antoinette, reine de France et de Navarre* (Paris, 1822), published in English as G. F. Forstescue, ed., *Memoirs of Madame Campan on Marie Antoinette and her Court,* 2 vols. (Boston: J. B. Millet, 1909).

46. Gouverneur Morris to GW, Dec. 28, 1792, *PGW:PS*, 11:561–62. Meade Minnegerode, *Jefferson, Friend of France, 1793; The Career of Edmond Charles Genet, Minister Plenipotentiary from the French Republic to the United States* (New York: Putnam's, 1928); Harry Ammon, *The Genet Mission* (New York: W. W. Norton, 1973); Elkins and McKitrick, *Age of Federalism,* 330–31.

47. "Instructions to Genet," in Frederick Jackson Turner, ed., *Correspondence of the of the French Ministers to the United States, 1791–1797, Annual Report of the American Historical Association for 1903* (Washington, DC: Government Printing Office, 1904) (hereafter *CFM*), 201–11.

48. Genet to Minister of Foreign Affairs, April 16, 1793, *CFM*, 211–13.

49. Genet to Minister of Foreign Affairs, May 18, 1793, *CFM*, 214; *Aurora* (Philadelphia), May 14, 17, 20, 1793; Newman, *Parades and Politics of the Street*, 139–40.

50. Edmond Charles Genet to TJ, May 16, 1793, *PTJ*, 26:46–49, enclosed Letter of Credence quoted p. 49; TJ to JM, May 19, 1793, *PTJ*, 26:62.

51. Edmond Charles Genet to TJ, May 22, 1793, *PTJ*, 26:86–87; Edmond Charles Genet to TJ, May 23, 1793, *PTJ*, 26:98; Edmond Charles Genet to TJ, May 27, 1793, *PTJ*, 26:124–27. Genet's letter of May 27 was a response to TJ to Jean Baptise Ternant, May 15, 1793, *PTJ*, 26:42–44. Jefferson wrote to Ternant, who forwarded the letter to Genet in response to a series of memorials from the British minister in Philadelphia, George Hammond, in protest of the capture of British vessels by American-based privateers commissioned by Genet. Memorials of George Hammond, May 8, 1793, *PTJ*, 25:683–86. Also see Melvin H. Jackson, "The Consular Privateers: An Account of French Privateering in American Waters, April to August, 1793," *American Neptune* 22 (1962): 81–98.

52. Notes on the *Citoyen Genet* and Its Prizes, May 20, 1793, *PTJ*, 26:71–72; TJ to Henry Knox and Proposed Circular to the Governors of the States, May 21, 1793, *PTJ*, 26:75–76; Cabinet Memorandum on French Privateers, [June 1, 1793], *PTJ*, 26:155.

53. TJ to Edmond Charles Genet, June 11, 1793, *PTJ*, 26:252. For the background to this episode, see the collection of documents, "Jefferson and the American Debt to France," *PTJ*, 26:174–84.

54. Opinion on the Restoration of Prizes, May 16, 1793, *PTJ*, 26:50–51; Notes on the *Citoyen Genet* and its Prizes, May 20, 1793, *PTJ*, 26:71–72. While Jefferson offered the "moderate apology" immediately (TJ to George Hammond, May 15, 1793, *PTJ*, 26:38–40), for two weeks he did not inform the British minister that the United States would not return the prizes (TJ to George Hammond, June 5, 1793, *PTJ*, 26:197–9).

55. Alexander Hamilton's Draft Report on the American Debt to France, with Jefferson's Commentary, [June 5, 1793], *PTJ*, 26:177–78.

56. TJ to GW, June 6, 1793, *PTJ*, 26:179–80.

57. Genet to Minister of Foreign Affairs, Aug. 7, 1793, *CFM*, 245. Jefferson's comments to Genet echo Hamilton's comments to George Beckwith.

58. TJ to JM, May 27, 1793, *PTJ*, 26:132. Although Randolph normally supported Jefferson's positions and often voted with him on key issues, Jefferson felt that the attorney general was unreliable and frequently prevaricated on key issues.

59. TJ to GW, June 6, 1793, *PTJ*, 26:180, emphasis added.

60. Genet to Le Brun, May 31, 1793, *CFM*, 216; *National Gazette* (Philadelphia), June 5, 1793; *General Advertiser* (Philadelphia), June 4, 1793.

61. Genet to TJ, June 8, 1793, *PTJ*, 26:231–3; Genet to TJ June 14, 1793, *PTJ*, 26:281–4; Genet to TJ June 22, 1793, *PTJ*, 26:339–42.

62. TJ to Genet, June 17, 1793, *PTJ*, 26:299–300. Also see Cabinet Opinion of French Privateers, June 17, 1793, *PTJ*, 26:296.

63. Genet to Minister of Foreign Affairs, June 19, 1793, *CFM*, 217–18.

64. Notes of Cabinet Meeting and Conversations with Edmond Charles Genet, July 5, 1793, *PTJ*, 26:437–39, emphasis in original. For Genet's account of this conversation, see Genet to Minister of Foreign Affairs, July 25, 1793, *CFM*, 221. Genet's anonymously published addresses to the peoples of Louisiana and Canada can be found in *PTJ*, 26:773–74 and *PTJ*, 27:291–93. For the documentation concerning Genet's western intrigues, see "Correspondence of Clark and Genet," *American Historical Association: Annual Report, 1896* 1 (1897): 930–1107, and "Documents on the Relations of France and Louisiana, 1792–1795,"*AHR* 3 (1898): 490–516. Also see Frederick Jackson Turner, "Origin of Genet's Projected Attack on Louisiana and the Floridas," *AHR* 3 (1898): 650–71; Wesley J. Campbell, "The Origin of Citizen Genet's Projected Attack on Spanish Louisiana: A Case Study in Girondin Politics," *French Historical Studies* 33 (2010): 515–44; Elkins and McKitrick, *Age of Federalism,* 349–50; Malone, *Jefferson and His Time,* 3:104–9.

65. For the dispute over the *Little Democrat,* see Memorandum of a Conversation with Edmond Charles Genet, July 10, 1793, *PTJ*, 26:463–67; Memorandum to GW (with enclosures), July 11, 1793, *PTJ*, 26:476–80.

66. Memorandum of a Conversation with Emond Charles Genet, July 10, 1793, *PTJ*, 26:463–67.

67. GW to TJ, July 11, 1793, *PTJ*, 26:481, emphasis in original.

68. TJ to Genet and Hammond, July 12, 1793, *PTJ*, 26:487

69. Notes on Neutrality Questions, July 13, 1793, *PTJ*, 26:498–9; Notes of Cabinet Meeting on Neutrality, July 29, 1793, *PTJ*, 26:579–80; Notes on Treaties and Neutrality, July 29–30, 1793, *PTJ*, 26:581; Notes of Cabinet Meeting on Neutrality, Aug. 3, 1793, *PTJ*, 26:607–8; Rules on Neutrality, Aug. 3, 1793, *PTJ*, 26:608–9; Elkins and McKitrick, *Age of Federalism,* 352–53; Thomas, *American Neutrality,* 206–20; Hyneman, *First American Neutrality,* 118–27; Christopher J. Young, "Connecting the President and the People: Washington's Neutrality, Genet's Challenge and Hamilton's Fight for Public Support," *JER* 31 (2011): 435–66.

70. GW to TJ, July 11, 1793, *PTJ*, 26:481; Notes of a Cabinet Meeting on Edmond Charles Genet, July 23, 1793, *PTJ*, 26:553–56; GW to TJ, July 25, 1793, *PTJ*, 26:569; Memorandum of Conversations with Edmond Charles Genet, July 26, 1793, *PTJ*, 26:571–73.

71. Notes of Cabinet Meeting on Edmond Charles Genet, Aug. 1, 1793, *PTJ*, 26:598; Notes of Cabinet Meeting on Edmond Charles Genet, Aug. 2, 1793, *PTJ*, 26:601–3; TJ to JM, Aug. 11, 1793, *PTJ*, 26:649–51; Harper, *American Machiavelli,* 124–25; Malone, *Jefferson and His Time,* 3:122–31.

72. For the relevant documents, see "The Recall of Edmond Charles Genet," *PTJ*, 26:685–715, the text of Jefferson's letter to Morris, backdated to August 16 is pp. 697–711.

73. Elkins and McKitrick, *Age of Federalism*, 372–73.

74. TJ to GW, July 31, 1793, *PTJ*, 26:593.

75. Notes of a Conversation with George Washington, Aug. 6, 1793, *PTJ*, 26:627–30; TJ to GW, Dec. 31, 1793, *PTJ*, 27:656. For Jefferson's resignation, see Malone, *Jefferson and His Time*, 3:145–63.

Four
The Reign of the Witches

1. Horatio Gates to TJ, Jan. 5, 1794, *PTJ*, 28:6; TJ to Horatio Gates, Feb. 3, 1794, *PTJ*, 28:14.

2. TJ to John Wise, Feb. 12, 1798, *PTJ*, 30:98. Also see John Wise to TJ, Jan. 28, 1798, *PTJ*, 30:63–64.

3. Horatio Gates to TJ, Jan. 5, 1794, *PTJ*, 28:7.

4. Report on Commerce, Dec. 16, 1793, *PTJ*, 27:532–81, statistics 554. Jefferson drafted his report in response to Earl of Sheffield [John Baker Holroyd], *Observations on the Commerce of the American States* (London: Debrett, 1783). Sheffield argued that Britain should wage commercial war against the United States. Stanley Elkins and Eric McKitrick have demonstrated that the policies Sheffield advocated were not in force when Jefferson wrote his Report on Commerce. In fact, owing to the European war, the British advantage in the carrying trade had diminished (*Age of Federalism*, 378–82). Also see Merrill D. Peterson, "Thomas Jefferson and Commercial Policy, 1783–1793," *WMQ*, 3rd ser., 22 (1965): 584–610; Doron S. Ben-Atar, *The Origins of Jeffersonian Commercial Policy and Diplomacy* (New York: St. Martin's Press, 1993), 17–133.

5. *Annals of Congress*, 3rd Cong. 1st Sess., 155–57. Also see Andrew Burstein and Nancy Isenberg, *Madison and Jefferson* (New York: Random House, 2010), 281–82; Elkin and McKitrick, *Age of Federalism*, 384–86.

6. George Grenville to George Hammond, Jan. 10, 1794, in *IBM*, 47n10, 48.

7. GW to the House of Representatives and Senate, March 25, 1794, *PGW:PS*, 15:450–52; Fulwar Skipwith to Edmund Randolph, March 1, 7, 1794, *ASPFR*, 1:428, 429. For a list of the ships seized, see *The Philadelphia Gazette and Universal Daily Advertiser*, Sept. 1, 1794. Also see Joseph M. Fewster, "The Jay Treaty and British Ship Seizures: The Martinique Cases," *WMQ*, 3rd ser., 45 (1988): 426–52.

8. Wiley Sword, *President Washington's Indian War: The Struggle for the Old Northwest, 1790–1795* (Norman: University of Oklahoma Press, 1993).

9. George Clinton to GW, March 20, 1794, *PGW:PS*, 15:417–18. *Annals of Congress*, 3rd Cong., 1st Sess., 459.

10. *Annals of Congress*, 3rd Cong., 1st Sess., 376–78.

11. Instructions to Mr. Jay, May 6, 1794, *ASPFR*, 1:472–73; GW to the United States Senate, April 16, 1794, *PGW:PS*, 15:608–9; Alexander Hamilton to GW, March 28, 1796, in Harold C. Syrett, ed., *Papers of Alexander Hamilton*, 26 vols. (New York: Columbia University Press, 1961–79), 20:83–84.

12. For the negotiations, see John Jay to Alexander Hamilton, Sept. 11, 1794, *Papers of Alexander Hamilton*, 17:221–22; William Grenville to George Hammond, Aug. 8, 1794, *IBM*, 60–63; William Grenville to George Hammond, Oct. 2, 1794, *IBM*, 67–68. Also see Samuel Flagg Bemis, *Jay's Treaty: A Study in Commerce and Diplomacy*, rev. ed. (New Haven: Yale University Press, 1962); Jerald A. Combs, *The Jay Treaty: Political Battleground of the Founding Fathers* (Berkeley: University of California Press, 1970); Elkins and McKitrick, *Age of Federalism*, 406–15; John Lamberton Harper, *American Machiavelli: Alexander Hamilton and the Origins of U. S. Foreign Policy* (Cambridge: Cambridge University Press, 2004), chs. 10–11; George C. Herring, *From Colony to Superpower: U. S. Foreign Relations since 1776* (New York: Oxford University Press, 2008), 73–78; Bradford Perkins, *The First Rapprochement: England and the United States, 1795–1805* (Berkeley: University of California Press, 1967), 1–16.

13. *Annals of Congress*, 3rd Cong., 3rd Sess., 853–68; Elkins and McKitrick, *Age of Federalism*, 415–31.

14. TJ to James Monroe, Sept. 6, 1795, *PTJ*, 28:449. For the debate over the treaty, see Todd Estes, *The Jay Treaty Debate, Public Opinion, and the Evolution of Early American Political Culture* (Amherst: University of Massachusetts Press, 2006); and Burstein and Isenberg, *Madison and Jefferson*, 305–10. George C. Herring writes: "No other treaty in U.S. has aroused such hostile public reaction or provoked such passionate debate, even though, ironically, the Jay Treaty brought the United States important concessions and served its interests well." Herring, *Colony to Superpower*, 78. Notwithstanding its political and diplomatic cost, the Jay Treaty was economically beneficial for the United States. American trade with Britain flourished between 1795 and 1807. In the immediate aftermath of the treaty the value of U.S. shipping increased from $19.4 million in 1794 to $27 million in 1796. Elkins and McKitrick, *Age of Federalism*, 382.

15. TJ to Thomas Mann Randolph, Aug. 11, 1795, *PTJ*, 28:435; TJ to James Monroe, Sept. 6, 1795, *PTJ*, 28:449; TJ to Henry Tazewell, Sept. 13, 1795, *PTJ*, 28:466; TJ to Mann Page, Aug. 30, 1795, *PTJ*, 28:441.

16. Noble E. Cunningham, *The Jeffersonian Republicans: The Formation of a Party Organization* (Baton Rouge: Louisiana State University Press, 1957); Estes, *The Jay Treaty Debate;* Joanne Freeman, *Affairs of Honor: National Politics in the New Republic* (New Haven: Yale University Press, 2001); Jeffrey L. Pasley, *"The Tyranny of Printers": Newspaper Politics in the Early American Republic* (Charlottesville: University of Virginia Press, 2001).

17. TJ to Elbridge Gerry, May 13, 1797, *PTJ*, 29:362. For the election of 1796, see Malone, *Jefferson and His Time*, 3:273–94; Burstein and Isenberg, *Madison and Jefferson*, 306–19.

18. Elkins and McKitrick, *Age of Federalism,* 529.

19. TJ to Pierre Auguste Adet, Oct. 14, 1795, *PTJ,* 28:503–4. Michael F. Conlin, "The American Mission of Citizen Pierre-Auguste Adet: Revolutionary Chemistry and Diplomacy in the Early Republic," *Pennsylvania Magazine of History and Biography* 124 (2000): 489–520.

20. Adet to Minister of Foreign Affairs, June 9, 1796, *CFM,* 920.

21. Adet to the Minister of Foreign Affairs, Sept. 24, 1796, *CFM,* 948.

22. Oct. 27, 1796, *ASPFR,* 1:577–78; Elkins and McKitrick, *Age of Federalism,* 520–21; Malone, *Jefferson and His Time,* 3:286–87.

23. *ASPFR,* 1:579–83; Malone, *Jefferson and His Time,* 3:286–88; JM to TJ, Dec. 5, 1796, *PTJ,* 29:214. Also see Adet to Minister of Foreign Affairs, Nov. 22, 1796, *CFM,* 972.

24. Adet to Minister of Foreign Affairs, Dec. 31, 1796, *CFM,* 983.

25. TJ to Elbridge Gerry, May 13, 1797, *PTJ,* 29:363.

26. Ibid., 363–64.

27. Alexandrew DeConde, *The Quasi-War: Politics and Diplomacy of the Undeclared War with France, 1797–1801* (New York: Charles Scribner's, 1966), ch. 1; Elkins and McKitrick, *Age of Federalism,* 549–56; E. Wilson Lyon, "The Directory and the United States," *AHR* 43 (1938): 514–32; Aaron N. Coleman, "'A Second Bounaparty?' A Re-examination of Alexander Hamilton during the Franco-American Crisis, 1796–1801," *JER* 28 (2008): 183–214; Nathan Perl-Rosenthal, "Private Letters and Public Diplomacy: The Adams Network and the Quasi-War, 1797–1798," *JER* 31 (2011): 283–311.

28. TJ to Elbridge Gerry, June 21, 1797, *PTJ,* 29:448. Also see TJ to Thomas Pinckney, May 29, 1797, *PTJ,* 29:404–5.

29. TJ to Elbridge Gerry, June 21, 1797, *PTJ,* 29:448. Not everyone shared Jefferson's confidence in Gerry. Some Federalist senators voted against confirming his appointment. William Vans Murray, a former congressman who was serving as American minister in the Netherlands said that Gerry was "the least qualified to play a part in Paris, either among the men or the women. He is too virtuous for the last, too little acquainted with the world and with himself for the first." As quoted in John C. Miller, *The Federalist Era* (New York: Harper and Brothers, 1960), 206. In 1800 Murray succeeded Gerry in peace negotiations with France.

30. Elkins and McKitrick, *Age of Federalism,* 549–79; William Stinchcombe, *The X, Y, Z Affair* (Westport, CT: Greenwood Press, 1980).

31. For the X, Y, Z dispatches, see *ASPFR,* 2:157–82, 185–99. TJ to Mann Page, March 6, 1798, *PTJ,* 30:165–66.

32. TJ to JM, March 21, 1798, *PTJ,* 30:189–90; TJ to JM, March 29, 1798, *PTJ,* 30:227; TJ to Edmund Randolph, April 2, 1798, *PTJ,* 30:241–42. Also see TJ to James Monroe, March 8, 1798, *PTJ,* 30:168; TJ to JM, March 15, 1798, *PTJ,* 30:181.

33. *ASPFR,* 2:164–65.

34. TJ to JM, April 6, 1798, *PTJ,* 30:251. The X, Y, Z dispatches were published as *The Message of President of the United States, of 5th March 1798; with a*

Letter from our Envoys Extraordinary at Paris, with Other Documents (Philadelphia, 1798). Elkins and McKitrick, *Age of Federalism,* 581–90.

35. TJ to Thomas Mann Randolph, April 19, 1798, *PTJ,* 30:282–84; TJ to JM, April 26, 1798, *PTJ,* 30:299–301; *Senate Journal,* 2:460, 464, 469, 476–78; *Annals of Congress,* 5th Cong., 2nd Sess., 1384, 1725–72; *House of Representatives Journal,* 3:237, 287, 296–302, 361.

36. Miller, *Federalist Era,* 213; Bradford Perkins, *The Creation of a Republican Empire* (New York: Cambridge University Press, 1995), 105.

37. For the "Quasi-War" see DeConde, *The Quasi-War;* Elkins and McKitrick, *Age of Federalism,* ch. 14; Gardner Weld Allen, *Our Naval War with France* (Boston: Houghton Mifflin, 1909); Dudley W. Knox, ed., *Naval Documents Related to the Quasi-War between the United States and France,* 5 vols. (Washington, DC, 1935–38).

38. Elkins and McKitrick, *Age of Federalism,* ch. 18.

39. TJ to JM, April 26, 1798, *PTJ,* 30:299; *Annals of Congress,* 5th Cong., 2nd Sess., 1427, 1566–70, 1956. James Morton Smith, *Freedom's Fetters: The Alien and Sedition Acts and American Civil Liberties* (Ithaca: Cornell University Press, 1956); Wood, *Empire of Liberty,* 248–68; Elkins and McKitrick, *Age of Federalism,* 694–719; Douglas Bradburn, "A Clamor in the Public Mind: Opposition to the Alien and Sedition Acts," *WMQ,* 3rd ser., 65 (2008): 565–600.

40. *Philadelphia Gazette,* April 6, 1798.

41. TJ to James Lewis, Jr., May 9, 1798, *PTJ,* 30:340.

42. John Taylor to TJ, [before May 13, 1798], *PTJ,* 30:348.

43. TJ to John Taylor, June 4, 1798, *PTJ,* 30:388.

44. Ibid., 388–89.

45. Ibid., 389.

46. The Kentucky Resolutions of 1798, *PTJ,* 30:529–56. Quotations from Jefferson's Draft, [before Oct. 4, 1798], 536, 539.

47. For the Virginia Resolutions and Jefferson's and Madison's collaboration over these resolutions, see Wood, *Empire of Liberty,* 268–70; Elkins and McKitrick, *Age of Federalism,* 719–26; Burstein and Isenberg, *Madison and Jefferson,* 337–41; Malone, *Jefferson and His Time,* 3:395–409; Adrienne Koch and Harry Ammon, "The Virginia and Kentucky Resolutions: An Episode in Jefferson's and Madison's Defense of Civil Liberties," *WMQ,* 3rd ser., 5 (1948): 145–76.

48. Resolutions Adopted by the Kentucky General Assembly, *PTJ,* 30:550–56. Also see Wilson Cary Nicholas to TJ, Oct. 4, 1798, *PTJ,* 30:556; TJ to Wilson Cary Nicholas, Oct. 5, 1798, *PTJ,* 30:557. For popular opposition to the Alien and Sedition Acts in Kentucky, see Bradburn, "Clamor in the Public Mind."

49. Merrill D. Peterson, *The Jefferson Image in the American Mind* (New York: Oxford University Press, 1960), 297–300.

50. The best analyses of the Kentucky Resolutions and Jefferson's constitutional thinking are Jeremy D. Bailey, *Thomas Jefferson and Executive Power* (New York: Cambridge University Press, 2007), 94–99; David N. Mayer, *The Constitu-*

tional Thought of Thomas Jefferson (Charlottesville: University of Virginia Press, 1994), 201–7; and R. B. Bernstein, "Thomas Jefferson and Constitutionalism," in Francis D. Cogliano, ed., *A Companion to Thomas Jefferson* (Oxford: Wiley-Blackwell, 2012), 419–38.

51. TJ to John Taylor, Nov. 26, 1798, *PTJ*, 30:588, emphasis in original. Leonard W. Levy argued that the Kentucky Resolutions prove that Jefferson was more concerned about states' rights than civil liberties. Leonard W. Levy, *Jefferson and Civil Liberties: The Darker Side* (Cambridge: Harvard University Press, 1963), 46–56. I think this is a misreading of the situation. Jefferson looked to the states to *protect* civil liberties from what he saw as an increasingly tyrannical federal government.

52. TJ to JM, Aug. 23, 1799, *PTJ*, 31:173–74.

Five
"Chastise Their Insolence"

1. Margaret Bayard Smith, *The First Forty Years of Washington Society,* ed. Gaillard Hunt (New York: Frederick Ungar, 1906), 26; *Aurora* (Philadelphia), March 18, 1801; *National Intelligencer* (Washington), March 6, 1801; Merrill D. Peterson, *Thomas Jefferson and the New Nation* (New York: Oxford University Press, 1970), 653–55.

2. Smith, *First Forty Years of Washington Society,* 25, 26. For the evolution of Jefferson's address, see First Inaugural Address, *PTJ*, 33:134–52.

3. For the election of 1800, see Gordon S. Wood, *Empire of Liberty: A History of the Early Republic, 1789–1815* (New York: Oxford University Press, 2009), ch. 8; Joanne B. Freeman, "A Qualified Revolution: The Presidential Election of 1800," in Francis D. Cogliano, ed., *A Companion to Thomas Jefferson* (Oxford: Wiley Blackwell, 2012), 145–63; John Ferling, *Adams vs. Jefferson: The Tumultuous Election of 1800* (New York: Oxford University Press, 2004).

4. First Inaugural Address, March 4, 1801, *PTJ*, 33:149, 150, 151. For the inaugural address, see Malone, *Jefferson and His Time,* 4:17–28; Peterson, *Thomas Jefferson and the New Nation,* 653–60; Peter S. Onuf, *Jefferson's Empire: The Language of American Nationhood* (Charlottesville: University of Virginia Press, 2000), 80–108; and Peter S. Onuf, "Thomas Jefferson, Federalist," in Peter S. Onuf, *The Mind of Thomas Jefferson* (Charlottesville: University of Virginia Press, 2007), 83–98.

5. First Inaugural Address, March 4, 1801, *PTJ*, 33:149, 150.

6. *PTJ*, 33:149.

7. Act Pertaining to the Navy, March 27, 1794, in Dudley W. Knox, ed., *Naval Documents Related to the United States Wars with the Barbary Powers,* 6 vols. (Washington, DC: Government Printing Office, 1939–44), 1:69–70; Frank Lambert, *The Barbary Wars: American Independence in the Atlantic World* (New York: Hill and Wang, 2005), 77; Ray W. Irwin, *The Diplomatic Relations of the United*

States with the Barbary Powers, 1776–1816 (Chapel Hill: University of North Carolina Press, 1931), 78–80. Irwin (p. 80) estimates that the launch of the frigates saved American merchants more than $8.6 million in reduced insurance rates. By 1800 America commerce in the Mediterranean was worth more than $10 million annually, which was more than 20 percent of American foreign trade. Michael Kitzen, "Money Bags or Cannon Balls: The Origins of the Tripolitan War, 1795–1801," *JER* 16 (1996): 617.

8. Report of Committee to the United States Senate Concerning Appropriation for Treaty with Algiers, Jan. 16, 1797, *Naval Documents,* 1:192; Truce with Tunis, June 15, 1796, *Naval Documents,* 1:158–59; Effects Granted to Tunis by the United States, c. April 30, 1799, *Naval Documents,* 1:324; Lambert, *Barbary Wars,* 90–94; Irwin, *Diplomatic Relations,* 80–91.

9. Lambert, *Barbary Wars,* 93.

10. George Washington to James McHenry, July 13, 1796, George Washington Papers, Library of Congress.

11. Kola Folayan, *Tripoli during the Reign of Pasha Yusuf Karamanli* (Ife-Ife, Nigeria, 1979); Seton Dearden, *A Nest of Corsairs: The Fighting Karamanlis of Tripoli* (London: John Murray, 1976); Robert Greenhow, *History and Present Condition of Tripoli* (Richmond: T. H. White, 1835), 9–11; Michael Russell, *History and Present Condition of the Barbary States* (New York: Harper and Brothers, 1837), 253–55; Irwin, *Diplomatic Relations,* 4–5, 85; Lambert, *Barbary Wars,* 90–91, 125.

12. James L. Cathcart, *Tripoli: First War of the United States,* ed. J. B. Newkirk (La Porte, IN: Herald Print, 1901), 9–21. Also see James Leander Cathcart, *The Diplomatic Journal and Letter Book of James Leander Cathcart, 1788–1796* (Worcester, MA: American Antiquarian Society, 1955). Cathcart had been aboard the *Maria* when it as captured in 1785. He was held as a slave at Algiers for eleven years and became proficient in Arabic and Turkish. The Tripolitan-American treaty had been negotiated by another former captive, Richard O'Brien, captain of the *Dauphin,* who served in various diplomatic posts in Barbary after his release in 1796. The relationship between Cathcart and O'Brien was rancorous.

13. Extract of a letter from James Leander Cathcart to the Secretary of State, Apr. 18, 1800, *ASPFR,* 2:350.

14. Extract of a letter from James Leander Cathcart to the Secretary of State, May 12, 1800; translated extract from a letter of the Bashaw of Tripoli to the President of the United States, May 25, 1800; extract of a letter from James Leander Cathcart to the Secretary of State, May 27, 1800, *ASPFR,* 2:350, 351, 352.

15. Protest of James Carpenter, Master, and Ebenezer Smith, Mate, of the American Merchant Brig, *Catherine,* [Sept. 25, 1800], *Naval Documents,* 1:372–73; James L. Cathcart to Charles Lee, Oct. 18, 1800, *Naval Documents,* 1:382–84; Protest of James L. Cathcart, [Oct. 29, 1800], *Naval Documents* 1:391–97; William Eaton to James Madison, April 10, 1801, *PJM:SS,* 1:78–81; Cathcart, *Tripoli,* 182–83;

Charles W. Goldsborough, *The United States' Naval Chronicle* (Washington, DC, 1924), 188–89; Irwin, *Diplomatic Relations*, 96–97; Lambert, *Barbary Wars*, 101–2, 125–26.

16. William Eaton to JM, April 10, 1801, *PJM:SS*, 1:78; Circular issued by James L. Cathcart, [May 15, 1801], *Naval Documents*, 1:454–45; Richard O'Brien to JM, June 24, 1801, *PJM:SS*, 1:345–46. Michael Kitzen, "Money Bags or Cannon Balls," chronicles the deterioration of Tripolitan-American relations, arguing that the Adams administration neglected Tripoli, pushing Yusuf to declare war.

17. Levi Lincoln to William Eaton, March 21, 1801, quoted in *PTJ*, 34:246.

18. David Humphreys to JM, April 14, 1801, *PJM:SS*, 1:92; William Willis to JM, April 22, 1801, *PJM:SS*, 1:110; Richard O'Brien to JM, May 12, 1801, *PJM:SS*, 1:167.

19. Notes on a Cabinet Meeting, May 15, 1801, *PTJ*, 34:114. Also see Samuel Smith to TJ, May 4, 1801, *PTJ*, 34:31. When the cabinet considered the question one day after Pasha Yusuf declared war on the United States, it did so without knowing of Yusuf's action.

20. Samuel Smith to Richard Dale, May 20, 1801, *Naval Documents*, 1:467.

21. JM to William Eaton, May 20, 1801, *PJM:SS*, 1:199–201; Circular Letter to American Consuls, Mediterranean, May 21, 1801, *PJM:SS*, 1:209–10; Circular Letter to American Ministers, May 21, 1801, *PJM:SS*, 1:210–11; JM to James Leander Cathcart, May 21, 1801, *PJM:SS*, 1:211–12; JM to Richard O'Brien, May 21, 1801, *PJM:SS*, 1:212–15.

22. TJ to Yusuf Qaramanli, May 21, 1801, *PTJ*, 34:159.

23. TJ to William Cary Nicholas, June 11, 1801 *PTJ*, 34:309.

24. John Gavino to JM, July 4, 1801, *PJM:SS*, 1:379; Richard O'Brien to JM, July 22, 1801, *PJM:SS*, 1:457.

25. Copy of Lieutenant Andrew Sterret's Letter to Commodore Dale, Aug. 1, 1801, *Naval Documents*, 1:537; Richard Dale to John Gavino, Aug. 19, 1801, *Naval Documents*, 1:555; *National Intelligencer* (Washington), Nov.18, 1801; [Stephen C. Blydon], *History of the War [with] Tripoli* (Salem, 1806), 91–92.

26. The second session of the 6th Congress had sat for 107 days between November 17, 1800, and March 3, 1801. The first session of the 7th Congress did not begin until December 7, 1801.

27. Notes on a Cabinet Meeting, May 15, 1801, *PTJ*, 34:114. Also see Samuel Smith to TJ, May 4, 1801, *PTJ*, 34:31.

28. Annual Message to Congress, Dec, 8, 1801 *PTJ*, 36:52–67, Jefferson submitted the government's correspondence with its diplomats and with Yusuf Karamanli relative to the outbreak of hostilities with Tripoli explaining, "I communicate all material information on this subject, that in the exercise of the important function considered by the constitution to the legislature exclusively, their judgment may form itself on a knowledge and consideration of every circumstance of weight." The relevant documentation can be found at *ASPFR*, 2:347–61.

29. *Annals of Congress*, 7th Cong., 1st Sess., 325–26.

30. Act for the Protection of the Commerce and Seamen of the United States, against the Tripolitan Cruisers, Feb. 6, 1802 *Annals of Congress,* 7th Cong., 1st Sess., 1303–4. David A. Carson persuasively argues that Jefferson effectively managed Congress during the Tripolitan War concluding, "President Jefferson assumed control of Barbary relations before his first Congress even met, and he never relinquished that control while he remained in office." David A. Carson, "Jefferson, Congress, and the Question of Leadership in the Tripolitan War," *Virginia Magazine of History and Biography* 94 (1986): 409–24, quotation 424. Frank Lambert argues that the act "eliminated constitutional reservations and signalled America's determination to use its full force on the high seas" and "Congress gave the president full authority to take whatever offensive as well as defensive measures necessary to defeat Tripoli and protect American interests." Lambert, *Barbary Wars,* 132, 133.

31. Richard O'Brien to JM, July 22, 1801, *PJM:SS,* 1:457; JM to James Leander Cathcart, [Feb. 6, 1802], *PTJ:SS,* 2:448; Cabinet Notes, Jan. 18, 1802, *PTJ,* 36:394.

32. Richard O'Brien to the U.S. Consul at Leghorn, June 26, 1802, *Naval Documents,* 2:187.

33. Richard O'Brien to JM, Oct. 22, 1802, *PJM:SS,* 4:47.

34. TJ to Robert Smith, March 29, 1803, TJP.

35. JM to James L. Cathcart, April 9, 1803, *PJM:SS,* 4:494–95. Cathcart had alienated the government in Tripoli as well as his fellow American diplomats. (He had had a longstanding feud with Richard O'Brien.) He was recalled. In November 1803 Tobias Lear arrived in Algiers to replace O'Brien. Lear was empowered to negotiate with the pasha of Tripoli. Tobias Lear to JM, Aug. 3, 1803, *PJM:SS,* 5:277–78.

36. *Annals of Congress,* 7th Cong., 2nd Sess., 423, 1565.

37. Christopher McKee, *Edward Preble: A Naval Biography* (Annapolis: Naval Institute Press, 1972), 101–4. After his recall to the United States Morris was subject to a court of inquiry which examined his conduct. He was dismissed from the navy in May 1804. He published a defense of his actions, [Richard V. Morris], *A Defence of the Conduct of Commodore Morris* (New York, 1804).

38. Edward Preble to JM, Oct. 15, 1803, *PJM:SS,* 5:532; Edward Preble to Robert Smith, Oct. 5–17, *Naval Documents,* 3:139–43; Tobias Lear to JM, Oct. 18, 1803, *PJM:SS,* 5:540–49; McKee, *Edward Preble,* 139–72. TJ to Robert Smith, March 29, 1803, TJP.

39. William Bainbridge to Robert Smith, Nov. 1, 1803, *Naval Documents,* 3:171–73; James L. Cathcart to JM, Dec. 15, 1803, *PJM:SS,* 6:172. On June 29, 1805, Bainbridge and several of the *Philadelphia*'s crew testified before a court of inquiry into the capture of their ship held aboard the U.S.S. *President.* The court ruled that Bainbridge "acted with fortitude and conduct in the loss of his ship, the U States frigate *Philadelphia* on the 31st Oct. 1803, and that no degree of censure should attach itself to him from that event." Court Enquiring into the Loss of

the U.S. Frigate *Philadelphia,* June 29, 1805, *Naval Documents,* 3:189–94, quotation 194.

40. Edward Preble to Robert Smith, Feb. 3, 1804, *Naval Documents,* 3:384–86.

41. Edward Preble to Robert Smith, Feb. 19, 1804, *Naval Documents,* 3:413; Stephen Decatur to Edward Preble, [Feb. 16, 1804], *Naval Documents,* 3:414–15; Charles Stewart to Edward Preble, Feb. 19, 1804, *Naval Documents,* 3:415–16; Ralph Izard, Jr., to Mrs. Ralph Izard, Feb. 20, 1804, *Naval Documents,* 3:416–17. *Message from the President of the United States Accompanying Sundry Documents, Exhibiting a Statement of . . . the Destruction of the Frigate Philadelphia* (Washington, DC, 1804).

42. George Davis to JM, Dec. 28, 1803, *PJM:SS,* 6:238.

43. Richard O'Brien to JM, Dec. 16, 1803, *PJM:SS,* 6:179–80.

44. Robert Smith to Edward Preble, May 22, 1804, *Naval Documents,* 4:114–15. Smith assured Preble that Barron's appointment as commodore of the enlarged squadron was not a reflection on Preble's performance but rather a result of Barron's seniority.

45. *Annals of Congress,* 8th Cong., 1st Sess., 1204, 1212–24; 303.

46. Robert Smith to Samuel Barron, June 6, 1804, *Naval Documents* 4:152–3. Also see Circular Letter to American Consuls, Mediterranean, June 2, 1804, *PJM:SS,* 7:270–71.

47. JM to Thomas FitzSimons, April 13, 1804, *PJM:SS,* 7:38–39.

48. See Levett Harris to James Madison, Feb. 7, 1804, *PJM:SS,* 6:453–54.

49. TJ to JM, April 27, 1804, *PJM:SS,* 7:116–17.

50. JM to Levett Harris, June 26, 1804, *PJM:SS,* 7:374–35. Also see JM to Count Vorontsov, June 10, 1804, *PJM:SS,* 7:303–4.

51. TJ to JM, April 27, 1804, *PJM:SS,* 7:117.

52. Robert Smith to Samuel Barron, June 6, 1804, *Naval Documents,* 4:153.

53. William Eaton to JM, Sept. 5, 1801, *Naval Documents,* 1:569. James L. Cathcart to JM, July 2, 1801, *PJM:SS,* 3:370–71. Also see William Eaton to JM, May 25, 1802, *PJM:SS,* 3:260. For Eaton, see Charles Prentiss, ed., *The Life of the Late General William Eaton . . . Principally Collected from His Correspondence and Other Manuscripts* (Brookfield, MA, 1813), 184–242, and L. B. Wright, *The First Americans in North Africa: William Eaton's Struggle for a Vigorous Policy against the Barbary Pirates, 1799–1805* (Princeton: Princeton University Press, 1945).

54. JM to William Eaton, Aug. 22, 1802, *PJM:SS,* 3:505–6; JM to James L. Cathcart, Aug. 22, 1802, *PJM:SS,* 3:506.

55. JM to Tobias Lear, June 6, 1804, *PJM:SS,* 7:287–88.

56. Samuel Barron to William Eaton, March 22, 1805, *Naval Documents* 5:438–41.

57. Prentiss, ed., *Life of the Late General William Eaton,* 301–92; Treaty of Peace and Amity between the United States and Tripoli, [June 4, 1805], *Naval Documents,* 6:81–82. Also see Irwin, *Diplomatic Relations,* 147–48.

58. Annual Message to Congress, Dec. 3, 1805, *Annals of Congress*, 9th Cong., 1st Sess., 14.

59. *Annals of Congress*, 9th Cong., 2nd Sess., 693–776. Also see *Documents Respecting the Application of Hamet Caramalli, ex-Bashaw of Tripoli* (Washington, DC, 1806).

60. *Annals of Congress*, 9th Cong., 2nd Sess., 693–96. William Eaton was very critical of the treaty and what he believed was the betrayal of Hamet Karamanli by the United States. William Eaton to Robert Smith, Aug. 9, 1805, *Naval Documents*, 6:213–19.

61. Carson, "Jefferson, Congress and the Question of Leadership in the Tripolitan War," 422.

62. Charles Francis Adams, ed., *The Memoirs of John Quincy Adams*, 12 vols. (Philadelphia, 1874–77), 1:431–45. Adams reported that Republican senators sought to postpone the formal ratification of the accord because the 2½ percent tax that supported the Mediterranean Fund would expire three months after ratification. On March 3, 1807, Congress agreed to extend the 2½ percent tax on imports. *Annals of Congress*, 9th Cong., 2nd Sess., 1278–79.

63. Dumas Malone addresses the conflict in a mere five pages, *Jefferson and His Time*, 4:97–99, 262–63. Also see Peterson, *Thomas Jefferson and the New Nation*, 799. A notable exception is James R. Sofka, "The Jeffersonian Idea of National Security: Commerce, the Atlantic Balance of Power, and the Barbary War, 1786–1805," *Diplomatic History* 21 (1997): 519–44. Sofka argues that Jefferson's actions in Barbary were motivated by traditional Old World conceptions of maintaining a balance of power and that war was a necessary tool to achieve this. He writes, "Throughout his half-century political career Jefferson consistently argued that the paramount national interest of the United States was not a crusade for republican liberty or a struggle for political hegemony in the Western Hemisphere but rather the attainment and preservation of a respectable share of the transatlantic balance of trade and the protection of maritime rights" (p. 522). This view suggests that the promotion of trade and republican liberty were antithetical. The premise of this book is that Jefferson believed that trade was an essential means by which republican liberty was maintained. As such, protecting and promoting trade was essential to protect the American republic, and Jefferson acted accordingly. Since 2001 there has been a spate of books on the military aspects of the Tripolitan War. See A. B. C. Whipple, *To The Shores of Tripoli: The Birth of the U.S. Navy and Marines* (Annapolis: Naval Institute, 2001); Joseph Wheelan, *Jefferson's War: America's First War on Terror, 1801–1805* (New York: Carroll and Graf, 2003); Lambert, *Barbary Wars;* and Richard Zacks, *The Pirate Coast: Thomas Jefferson, the First Marines, and the Secret Mission of 1805* (New York: Hyperion, 2005). Whipple's account appeared before the September 11, 2001, attacks but was reprinted subsequently. The other titles were written in the aftermath of the attacks.

64. Robert W. Tucker and David C. Hendrickson, *Empire of Liberty: The State-craft of Thomas Jefferson* (New York: Oxford University Press, 1990), 295, 299.

Six
Empire of Liberty

1. *National Intelligencer* (Washington), July 4, 1803; Thomas Jefferson to Thomas Mann Randolph, Jr., July 5, 1803, TJP.

2. *National Intelligencer,* July 4, 1803.

3. TJ to George Rogers Clark, Jan. 1, 1780, *PTJ,* 3:258–259. Also see TJ to George Rogers Clark, Jan. 29, 1780, *PTJ,* 3:273–277; TJ to George Washington, Feb. 10, 1780, *PTJ,* 3:291–92; and George Washington to TJ, March 5, 1780, *PTJ,* 3:312, for correspondence related to the 1780 campaign. For a discussion of Jefferson's treatment by historians with respect to the use of force, see Francis D. Cogliano, *Thomas Jefferson: Reputation and Legacy* (Charlottesville: University of Virginia Press, 2006), ch. 8.

4. TJ to John Todd, Jan. 28, 1780, *PTJ,* 3:272. Jefferson echoed these views the next day in a letter to Clark. See TJ to George Rogers Clark, Jan. 29, 1780, *PTJ,* 3:276.

5. TJ to George Rogers Clark, Dec. 25, 1780, *PTJ,* 4:237, 237–38.

6. TJ to Archibald Stuart, Jan. 25, 1786, *PTJ,* 9:218.

7. TJ to George Washington, April 2, 1791, *PTJ,* 20:97.

8. TJ to James Monroe, Nov. 24, 1801, *PTJ,* 35:719. Jefferson's model for colonization through the migration of people and institutions had deep roots in the Anglo-American tradition. Christopher Tomlins has persuasively examined the ways in which English colonists and their American settlers used the law to displace Native Americans and enslave African Americans in order to preserve and protect their liberty. Christopher Tomlins, *Freedom Bound: Law, Labor, and Civic Identity in Colonizing English America, 1580–1865* (New York: Cambridge University Press, 2010).

9. Thomas Jefferson, Plan for Government of the Western Territory, 3 Feb.–23 April 1784, *PTJ,* 6:581–617. The most complete treatment of Jefferson's plan and its successors is Peter S. Onuf, *Statehood and Union: A History of the Northwest Ordinance* (Bloomington: Indiana University Press, 1987). Also see Robert F. Berkhofer, Jr., "Jefferson, the Ordinance of 1784, and the Origins of the American Territorial System," *WMQ,* 3rd ser., 29 (1972): 231–62, and Malone, *Jefferson and His Time,* 1:411–16.

10. For the differences between Jefferson's plan and the Northwest Ordinance of 1787, see Onuf, *Statehood and Union,* as well as Berkhofer, "Jefferson, the Ordinance of 1784," and Merrill Jensen, *The New Nation* (New York: Alfred A. Knopf, 1950), 354–59.

11. TJ to François D'Ivernois, Feb. 6, 1795, *PTJ,* 28:263. Soon after becoming president Jefferson wrote, "Montesquieu's doctrine that a republic can be preserved

only in a small territory [has been proved a falsehood]. the reverse is the truth. had our territory been even a third only of what it is we were gone. but while frenzy & delusion like an epidemic gained certain parts, the residue remained sound & untouched, and held on till their brethren could recover from the temporary delirium." TJ to Nathaniel Niles, March 22, 1801, *PTJ*, 33:403.

12. Thomas Jefferson, Second Inaugural Address, March 4, 1805, *TJW*, 518–23, quotation 519. This analysis is derived from Peter S. Onuf, *Jefferson's Empire: The Language of American Nationhood* (Charlottesville: University Press of Virginia, 2000). Onuf argues that Jefferson's conception of the United States as a federal union of autonomous republics was crucial to his understanding of the Constitution. This theme is developed by David C. Hendrickson who sees the Constitution as a diplomatic treaty binding thirteen rival states together. David C. Hendrickson, *Peace Pact: The Lost World of the American Founding* (Lawrence: University Press of Kansas, 2003).

13. Jefferson, Second Inaugural, *TJW*, 520.

14. Jefferson wrote about Native Americans in "Query VI" in *Notes on the State of Virginia*. Also, in an appendix in the *Notes* he included Chief Logan's oration on the massacre of his family at the beginning of Dunmore's War in 1774 as evidence of the power and quality of Native American oratory. This version of Logan's speech was a source of later controversy. It and Jefferson's ethnographic activities are discussed in Anthony F. C. Wallace, *Jefferson and the Indians: The Tragic Fate of the First Americans* (Cambridge: Harvard University Press, 1999). Also see Roger Kennedy, "Jefferson and the Indians," *Winterthur Portfolio* 27 (1992): 105–21; Reginald Horsman, "American Indian Policy in the Old Northwest, 1783–1812," *WMQ*, 3rd ser., 18 (1961): 35–53; Reginald Horsman, *Expansion and American Indian Policy, 1783–1812* (East Lansing: Michigan State University Press, 1967); Bernard Sheehan, *Seeds of Extinction: Jeffersonian Philanthropy and the American Indian* (Chapel Hill: University of North Carolina Press, 1973); Bernard W. Sheehan, "Paradise and the Noble Savage in Jeffersonian Thought," *WMQ*, 3rd ser., 26 (1969): 327–59.

15. For Jefferson's role in prohibiting slavery in the Northwest, see Berkhofer, "Jefferson, the Ordinance of 1784," 247–48.

16. Jefferson, *Notes on the State of Virginia, TJW*, 264. Peter S. Onuf has shown that Jefferson saw Africans and European Americans as distinct nations. The former had been unjustly captured and enslaved by the latter; as such they could never be incorporated into the nation of their captors. Onuf, *Jefferson's Empire*, chs. 1, 5. The literature on Jefferson and slavery and Jefferson as a slaveholder is immense. For an overview, see Cogliano, *Thomas Jefferson: Reputation and Legacy*, ch. 7. The most notable recent works are Annette Gordon-Reed, *The Hemingses of Monticello* (New York: W. W. Norton, 2008), and Lucia Stanton, *"Those Who Labor for My Happiness": Slavery at Thomas Jefferson's Monticello* (Charlottesville: University of Virginia Press, 2012). For the impact of the three-fifths clause

on Jefferson's political career, see Garry Wills, *"Negro President": Jefferson and the Slave Power* (Boston: Houghton Mifflin, 2003). Also see Paul Finkelman, "Jefferson and Slavery: Treason against the Hopes of the World," in Peter S. Onuf, ed., *Jeffersonian Legacies* (Charlottesville: University Press of Virginia, 1993), 181–221; Paul Finkelman, "Jefferson and Antislavery: The Myth Goes On," *Virginia Magazine of History and Biography* 102 (1994): 193–228; Robert McColley, *Slavery and Jeffersonian Virginia* (Urbana: University of Illinois Press, 1964); William Cohen, "Thomas Jefferson and the Problem of Slavery," *Journal of American History* 56 (1969): 503–26; John Chester Miller, *The Wolf by the Ears: Thomas Jefferson and Slavery* (New York: Free Press, 1977; repr. Charlottesville: University of Virginia Press and the Thomas Jefferson Memorial Foundation, 1991).

17. Jedidiah Morse, *The American Geography; or, A View of the Present Situation of the United States of America* (Elizabethtown, NJ: Shepard Kollock, 1789), 469; Thomas Hutchins, *An Historical Narrative and Topographical Description of Louisiana, and West-Florida* (Philadelphia: Robert Aitken, 1784), 94.

18. TJ to Robert Livingston, April 18, 1802, *PTJ*, 37:264.

19. *Notes on the State of Virginia, TJW*, 131; TJ to Archibald Stuart, Jan. 25, 1786, *PTJ*, 9:218.

20. Population figures from Historical Census Browser, University of Virginia GeoState Center, http://fisher.lib.virginia.edu/collections/stats/histcensus/. Ohio figures from: http://nodis.csuohio.edu/nodis/historic/pop_county18002000.pdf. Also see Jon Kukla, *A Wilderness So Immense: The Louisiana Purchase and the Destiny of America* (New York: Alfred A. Knopf, 2003), 112. TJ to Robert Livingston, April 18, 1802, *PTJ*, 37:263–67.

21. Kukla, *Wilderness So Immense*, 113, 378n27; John G. Clark, *New Orleans, 1718–1812: An Economic History* (Baton Rouge: Louisiana State University Press, 1970), 212.

22. Martin de Navarro, Political Reflections on the Present Condition of the Province of Louisiana, [New Orleans, c. 1785], original Archivo de Indias, Seville, Papeles procdedentes de las Isla de Cuba, Estados del Mississippi, no. 7. in James Alexander Robertson, ed., *Louisiana under the Rule of Spain, France, and the United States, 1785–1807*, 2 vols. (Cleveland: Arthur H. Clark, 1911), 1:235–62, quotations 247. Navarro's was not the only such report produced by a Spanish official in Louisiana. Several other officials produced perceptive analyses of the strategic threat to Louisiana posed by the United States. See, for example, Manuel Gayoso de Lemos, Political Conditions of the Province of Louisiana, Natchez, July 5, 1792, in Robertson, ed., *Louisiana under the Rule of Spain, France, and the United States*, 1:269–89; Baron de Carondelet, Military Report on Louisiana and West Florida, Nov. 24, 1794, *Louisiana under the Rule of Spain, France, and the United States*, 1:292–351. These called for the strengthening of Spain's defenses in Louisiana by building new fortifications, increasing the number of soldiers in the province, and encouraging increased settlement. These reports are consistent in

viewing the growing American population in the trans-Appalachian region as a threat to Louisiana and, ultimately, Mexico.

23. TJ to Archibald Stuart, Jan. 25, 1786, *PTJ*, 9:218.

24. Carondelet, Military Report, Nov. 24, 1794, 1:298.

25. Samuel Flagg Bemis, *Pinckney's Treaty: A Study of America's Advantage from Europe's Distress, 1783–1800* (Baltimore: Johns Hopkins University Press, 1926); Raymond A. Young, "Pinckney's Treaty—A New Perspective," *Hispanic AHR* 43 (1963): 526–35; Malone, *Jefferson and His Time,* 4:239–61.

26. For events in Saint Domingue, see Laurent DuBois, *Avengers of the New World: The Story of the Haitian Revolution* (Cambridge: Harvard University Press, 2004); Laurent DuBois, *A Colony of Citizens: Revolution and Slave Emancipation in the French Caribbean, 1787–1804* (Chapel Hill: University of North Carolina Press, 2004); David P. Geggus, ed., *The Impact of the Haitian Revolution in the Atlantic World* (Columbia: University of South Carolina Press, 2001); David P. Geggus and David B. Gaspar, eds., *A Turbulent Time: The French Revolution and the Greater Caribbean* (Bloomington: Indiana University Press, 1997). For Jefferson's response to these events, see Tim Matthewson, "Jefferson and Haiti," *Journal of Southern History* 12 (1995): 209–48. For the Treaty of San Ildefonso, see E. Wilson Lyon, *Louisiana in French Diplomacy* (Norman: University of Oklahoma Press, 1934); Arthur P. Whitaker, "The Retrocession of Louisiana in Spanish Policy," *AHR* 39 (1934): 454–76; Arthur P. Whitaker, *The Mississippi Question, 1795–1803: A Study in Trade, Politics, and Diplomacy* (New York: Appleton, 1934).

27. Rufus King to JM, March 29, 1801, *PJM:SS*, 1:55. Also see William Vans Murray to JM, May 20, 1801, *PJM:SS*, 1:206. TJ to James Monroe, May 26, 1801, *PTJ*, 34:185–86.

28. JM to Charles Pinckney, June 9, 1801, *PJM:SS*, 1:276; JM to Rufus King, July 24, 1801, *PJM:SS*, 1:470, JM to Robert Livingston, Sept. 28, 1801, *PJM:SS*, 2:144–45.

29. Robert Livingston to JM, Dec. 31, 1801, *PJM:SS*, 2:359; Robert Livingston to JM, Jan. 13, 1802, *PJM:SS*, 2:389; Robert Livingston to JM, Nov. 10, 1802, *PJM:SS*, 4:110–11. Also see George Dangerfield, *Chancellor Robert R. Livingston of New York, 1745–1813* (New York: Harcourt, Brace, 1960).

30. TJ to Robert Livingston, April 18, 1802, *PTJ*, 37:264–65.

31. TJ to Pierre Samuel du Pont de Nemours, April 25, 1802, *PTJ*, 37:332–34. Two of the leading historians of the subject believe that Jefferson wrote out of frustration in what was a private communication. See James E. Lewis, Jr., *The Louisiana Purchase: Jefferson's Noble Bargain?* (Charlottesville: Thomas Jefferson Foundation, 2003), 34–37; and Peter J. Kastor, ed., *The Louisiana Purchase: The Emergence of an American Nation* (Washington, DC: Congressional Quarterly Press, 2002), 161. By contrast, Dumas Malone ascribes great significance to this letter. He writes, "The major significance of this letter in history arises chiefly from the fact that, better perhaps than any single source, it reveals his contemplation of a diplomatic revolution. It provides striking illustration of his flexibility

with respect to diplomatic means in pursuit of ends which were constant. The fixed goal in this case, the sin qua non, was the free navigation of the Mississippi." Malone, *Jefferson and His Time*, 4:255. For the various preparations Jefferson made, see TJ to Henry Dearborn, Hints on the subject of Indian Boundaries suggested for consideration, Dec. 29, 1802, TJP; and Mary P. Adams, "Jefferson's Reaction to the Treaty of San Ildefonso," *Journal of Southern History* 21 (1955): 173–88; Malone, *Jefferson and His Time*, 4:270.

32. E. Wilson Lyon reviewed the relevant Spanish documentation, "The Closing of the Port of New Orleans," *AHR* 37 (1932): 280–83. Also see Lewis, *Louisiana Purchase*, 42–43.

33. William C. C. Claiborne to JM, Oct. 29, 1802, *PJM:SS*, 4:67; Memorial of the Kentucky Legislature, Dec. 1, 1802, *PJM:SS*, 4:179, n1; Edward Thornton to Lord Hawkesbury, Jan. 3, 1803, in Robertson, ed., *Louisiana under the Rule of Spain, France, and the United States*, 2:15; *Gazette of the United States* (Philadelphia), Dec. 31, 1802.

34. Malone, *Jefferson and His Time*, 4:265–70.

35. Ebenezer Mattoon to Thomas Dwight, Jan. 12, 1803, Dwight-Howard Papers, Massachusetts Historical Society; "Pericles" [Hamilton], for the *Evening Post*, Feb. 8, 1803, in Harold C. Syrett, ed., *The Papers of Alexander Hamilton*, 27 vols. (New York: Columbia University Press, 1961–87), 26:83. Resolutions of James Ross, *Annals of Congress*, 7th Cong., 2nd Sess., 95–96. The full debate over Ross's resolutions can be found on pp. 83–96, 105–256. Also see *Speeches of Mr. Ross and Mr. Morris Delivered in the Senate of the United States, Thursday the 24th of February, 1803* (Philadelphia: Bronson and Chauncey, 1803); *Gazette of the United States* (Philadelphia), Feb. 22, 1803.

36. JM to Robert Livingston, Jan. 18, 1803, *PJM:SS*, 4:259–60.

37. For a view on these events affected the French, see the memoir by Napoleon's finance minister, François de Barbé-Marbois, *The History of Louisiana, Particularly of the Session of that Colony to the United States of America* (Philadelphia: Carey and Lea, 1830), 249–62. It was Marbois who as a young diplomat in Philadelphia had sent Jefferson the queries that inspired him to write *Notes on the State of Virginia*.

38. Marbois, *History of Louisiana*, quotation 274–75. For Marbois's account of Napoleon's deliberations, see 263–74; for negotiations with Monroe and Livingston, 278–310. For other accounts, see Robert R. Livingston to JM, April 11, 1803, *PJM:SS*, 4:500–502; Robert R. Livingston to JM, April 13, 1803, *PJM:SS*, 4:512–13; Robert R. Livingston and James Monroe to JM, May 13, 1803, *PJM:SS*, 4:601–6; James Monroe to JM, May 14, 1803, *PJM:SS*, 4:610–11. Also see Charles J. Ingersoll, *Recollections, Historical, Political, Biographical and Social* (Philadelphia: Lippincott, 1861), 356–72, by a young Philadelphia lawyer who visited Livingston during the negotiations.

39. TJ, Draft Amendments to the Constitution, [July 1803], TJP, repr. in Kastor, ed., *Louisiana Purchase*, 193–94; Levi Lincoln to TJ, Jan. 10, 1803, TJP;

Albert Gallatin to TJ, Jan. 13, 1803, TJP; TJ to Gallatin, [Jan. 13, 1803], TJP; TJ to
JM Aug. 18, 1803, *PJM:SS,* 5:323; TJ to JM, Aug. 25, 1803; James Morton Smith,
ed., *The Republic of Letters: The Correspondence between Thomas Jefferson and
James Madison, 1776–1826,* 3 vols. (New York: W.W. Norton, 1995); TJ to John
Breckinridge, Aug. 18, 1803, TJP.

40. Robert Livingston to TJ, June 2, 1803, TJP.

41. This left Jefferson open to charges of hypocrisy since he had previously adhered to strict construction in opposing Alexander Hamilton's fiscal policies during the early 1790s. For the immediate constitutional implications of the Louisiana
Purchase, see Jeremy D. Bailey, *Thomas Jefferson and Executive Power* (New
York: Cambridge University Press, 2007), ch. 7; Everett Somerville Brown, *Constitutional History of the Louisiana Purchase* (Berkeley: University of California
Press, 1920); Sanford Levinson, "The Louisiana Purchase as Seminal Constitutional Event," in Kastor, ed., *Louisiana Purchase,* 105–16; Lewis, *Louisiana Purchase,* 69–73; Malone, *Jefferson and His Time,* 4:311–33, 348–63.

42. [Alexander Hamilton], "Purchase of Louisiana," July 5, 1803, *Hamilton
Papers,* 26:129–33; Josiah Dwight to Thomas Dwight, Aug. 16, 1803, Dwight-
Howard Papers, Massachusetts Historical Society. For press coverage of the Loui-
siana Purchase, see Jerry W. Knudson, *Jefferson and the Press: Crucible of Liberty*
(Columbia: University of South Carolina Press, 2006), ch. 6; and Betty Houchin
Winfield, "Public Perception and Public Events: The Louisiana Purchase and the
American Partisan Press," in Kastor, ed., *Louisiana Purchase,* 38–50.

43. *Journal of the Executive Proceedings of the Senate of the United States of
America,* 1:456; *Annals of Congress,* 8th Cong., 1st Sess., 497–515, 545–51, app.
1245; *Statutes at Large,* 8th Cong., 1st Sess., 2:245.

44. JM to William C. C. Claiborne, Oct. 31, 1803, *PJM:SS,* 5:589–92, quotation
591–92. Also see Clarence E. Carter, ed., *The Territorial Papers of the United States,*
vol. 9: *The Territory of Orleans, 1803–1812* (Washington, DC: Government Printing
Office, 1940), 91–94. This volume is indispensable for the study of Louisiana from
the time the United States took possession of the territory until it was admitted as a
state in 1812. Laussat wrote a revealing memoir, which offers his perspective on these
events: Pierre-Clément de Laussat, *Memoirs of My Life* (Baton Rouge: Louisiana
State University Press, 2003). Also see Malone, *Jefferson and His Time,* 4:333–47.

45. Governor Claiborne and James Wilkinson to the Secretary of State, Feb. 7,
1804, including Enclosure: Deposition of George W. Morgan, Jan. 28, 1804,
Carter, *Territorial Papers,* 9:177–82, quotations 178, 181.

46. Isaac Briggs to TJ, Jan. 2, 1804, Carter, *Territorial Papers,* 9:146–48. For the
local response to the new American governmental presence, see Jay Gitlin, "Children of Empire or Concitoyens? Louisiana's French Inhabitants," in Kastor, ed.,
Louisiana Purchase, 23–37; and Peter J. Kastor, "'Motives of Peculiar Urgency': Local Diplomacy in Louisiana, 1803–1821," *WMQ,* 3rd ser., 58 (2001): 819–48.

47. TJ to John Breckinridge, Nov. 24, 1803, TJP; TJ, [Draft Bill, ca. Nov. 24,
1803], TJP.

48. The most thorough account of the debate over the Breckinridge Bill can be found in Everett S. Brown, ed., "The Senate Debate on the Breckinridge Bill for the Government of Louisiana, 1804," *AHR* 22 (1917): 340–64.

49. Thomas Dwight to John Williams, Jan. 28, 1804, Dwight Howard Papers, Massachusetts Historical Society. *National Intelligencer* (Washington), Jan. 30, 1804.

50. Richard R. Stenberg, "The Boundaries of the Louisiana Purchase," *Hispanic AHR* 14 (1934): 32–64; Reginald Horsman, "The Dimensions of an Empire for Liberty: Expansion and Republicanism, 1775–1825," *JER* 9 (1989): 1–20; J. C. A. Stagg, *Borderlines in Borderlands: James Madison and the Spanish-American Frontier, 1776–1821* (New Haven: Yale University Press, 2009), 136–37, 144, 265n11.

51. Christian B. Keller, "Philanthropy Betrayed: Thomas Jefferson, the Louisiana Purchase, and the Origins of Federal Indian Removal Policy," *Proceedings of the American Philosophical Society* 144 (2000): 39–66; Peter J. Kastor, "Dehahuit and the Question of Change in North America," in Kastor, ed., *Louisiana Purchase,* 74–89; Wallace, *Jefferson and the Indians;* and Sheehan, *Seeds of Extinction.*

52. Briggs to TJ, Jan. 2, 1804, Carter, *Territorial Papers,* 9:148. Briggs quoted Ovid's *Metamorphoses,* book 1, lines 758–59.

53. John Craig Hammond, *Slavery, Freedom, and Expansion in the Early American West* (Charlottesville: University of Virginia Press, 2007), ch. 3; John Craig Hammond, " 'They Are Very Much Interested in Obtaining an Unlimited Slavery': Rethinking the Expansion of Slavery in the Louisiana Purchase Territories," *JER* 23 (2003): 353–80; Adam Rothman, *Slave Country: American Expansion and the Origins of the Deep South* (Cambridge: Harvard University Press, 2005), 26–34; and Jed Handelsman Shugerman, "The Louisiana Purchase and South Carolina's Reopening of the Slave Trade in 1803," *JER* 22 (2002): 263–90. Also see Robert F. Bonner, "Empire of Liberty, Empire of Slavery: The Louisiana Territories and the Fate of American Bondage," in Kastor, ed., *Louisiana Purchase,* 129–38.

54. For the controversies among historians regarding Jefferson's handling of the Mississippi crisis and the resulting Louisiana Purchase, see Cogliano, *Thomas Jefferson: Reputation and Legacy,* ch. 8.

55. Robert W. Tucker and David C. Hendrickson, *Empire of Liberty: The Statecraft of Thomas Jefferson* (New York: Oxford University Press, 1990), 14, 145.

Seven
"They Expect the President to Act"

1. Depositions of Upton Bruce, July 18, 1807, and William McNair, July 17, 1807, *ASPFR,* 3:13. Also see the Deposition of Sarah Lewis, July 17, 1807, *ASPFR,* 3:13–14.

2. Deposition of William McNair, July 17, 1807, *ASPFR*, 3:13. Also see Max Grivno, *Gleanings of Freedom: Free and Slave Labor along the Mason-Dixon Line, 1790–1860* (Champaign: University of Illinois Press, 2011), 61–63; T. Stephen Whitham, *The Price of Freedom: Slavery and Manumission in Baltimore and Early National Maryland* (Lexington: University Press of Kentucky, 1997). It was not uncommon in the eighteenth century for owners to give their slaves classical names. Perhaps Romulus Ware changed his name in response to the association between classical names and enslavement.

3. W. Jeffrey Bolster, *Black Jacks: African American Seamen in the Age of Sail* (Cambridge: Harvard University Press, 1998).

4. As a neutral power Americans supplied both French and far more numerous British vessels during the war. British warships frequently put into American ports for supplies.

5. John Hamilton to Stephen Decatur, March 6, 1807, *ASPFR*, 3:16–17; James Barron to Robert Smith, April 7, 1807, *ASPFR*, 3:17–18.

6. Admiral George Cranfield Berkeley to the respective captains and commanders, June 1, 1807, *ASPFR*, 3:12.

7. Jefferson and Ware shared an important bond—their lives were shaped by interracial families that spanned the boundary between slavery and freedom. Ware was the mixed-race son of an enslaved mother and a free father who was allowed to escape bondage and live as a free man. Jefferson engaged in a prolonged relationship with a mixed-race enslaved woman, Sally Hemings (who was his deceased wife's half-sister). They had at least six children, two of whom, a son Beverly and a daughter Harriet, were allowed to leave Monticello and live as free people in 1822. Their escape from slavery parallels that of Romulus/William Ware. See Annette Gordon-Reed, *The Hemingses of Monticello: An American Family* (New York: W. W. Norton, 2008).

8. For trade figures, see Francis D. Cogliano, *Revolutionary America, 1763–1815: A Political History,* 2nd ed. (New York: Routledge, 2009), 236; Bradford Perkins, *The Creation of a Republican Empire, 1776–1815* (New York: Cambridge University Press, 1993), 92; George C. Herring, *From Colony to Superpower: U.S. Foreign Relations since 1776* (New York: Oxford University Press, 2008), 114–16.

9. JM to Elbridge Gerry, Feb. 17, 1804, *PJM:SS,* 6:489–90.

10. TJ to Thomas Lomax, Jan. 11, 1806, TJP.

11. Albert Gallatin to TJ, April 16, 1807, in Henry Adams, ed., *The Writings of Albert Gallatin,* 3 vols. (Philadelphia: Lippincott, 1879), 1:336; Denver Brunsman, *The Evil Necessity: British Naval Impressment in the Eighteenth-Century Atlantic World* (Charlottesville: University of Virginia Press, 2013); James F. Zimmerman, *Impressment of American Seamen* (New York: Columbia University Press, 1925); *Observations on the Impressment of American Seamen by the Officers of Ships of War and Vessels Commissioned by and Acting under the Authority of Great Britain* (Baltimore: Dobbin and Murphy, 1806); [U.S. Department of State], *Copies and Extracts of Documents on the Subject of British Impressments of American Seamen*

(London: Longman, 1812); Anthony Steel, "Impressment in the Monroe-Pinkney Negotiation, 1806–1807,"*AHR* 57 (1952): 352–69; Bradford Perkins, *Prologue to War: England and the United States, 1805–1812* (Berkeley: University of California Press, 1961), 84–95; Wood, *Empire of Liberty,* 641–49; Perkins, *Creation of a Republican Empire,* 121–22. For the political and diplomatic importance of impressment, as well as free trade, in the United States, see Paul A. Gilje, "'Free Trade and Sailors' Rights': The Rhetoric of the War of 1812," *JER* 30 (2010): 1–23.

12. Anthony Merry to JM, June 24, 1804, *PJM:SS,* 7:357–60, n3 p. 359.

13. Anthony Merry to JM, June 28, 1804, *PJM:SS,* 7:383; JM to Anthony Merry, July 3, 1804, *PJM:SS,* 7:413. For Merry, see Anthony Steel, "Anthony Merry and the Anglo-American Dispute about Impressment," *Cambridge Historical Journal* 9 (1949): 331–51.

14. JM to Anthony Merry, July 23, 1804, *PJM:SS,* 7:505–6; Anthony Merry to JM, Aug. 15, 1804, *PJM:SS,* 7:601–8, quotation 604; James Monroe to JM, Sept. 8, 1804, *PJM:SS,* 8:25–31, quotation 29. Also see DeWitt Clinton to JM, June 19, 1804, *PJM:SS,* 7:332–33; Anthony Merry to JM, Sept. 6, 1804, *PJM:SS,* 8:22–23. For William Bradley, see Janet D. Hine, "Bradley, William (1757–1833)," in Douglas H. Pike et al., eds., *Australian Dictionary of Biography,* 12 vols. (Melbourne: Melbourne University Press, 1966). Australian National University, http://adb.anu.edu.au/biography/bradley-william-1820/text2085, accessed December 30, 2012.

15. James Monroe to JM, Dec. [14], 1803, *PJM:SS,* 6:171n3.

16. Harrowby quoted in James Monroe to JM, Sept. 8, 1804, *PJM:SS,* 8:25–31, quotation 29; JM to James Monroe, Jan. 5, 1804, *PJM:SS,* 6:292–93.

17. George Erving to JM, Sept. 1, 1804, *PJM:SS,* 8:10.

18. Between June 1797 and September 1801, 2,059 sailors impressed from American vessels claimed American citizenship. David Lenox to JM, Sept. 15, 1801, *PJM:SS,* 2:115–16. Brunsman, *Evil Necessity,* 247; Zimmerman, *Impressment,* 256; Perkins, *Prologue to War,* 91. These figures do not account for the thousands of Britons removed from American vessels. The United States government periodically sought to quantify and identify citizens who had been forced into British service. Monroe's 1812 estimate was based on the applications for relief made to American diplomatic officers. See James Maury to JM, March 24, 1803, *PJM:SS,* 4:451; Robert W. Fox to JM, May 14, 1803, *PJM:SS,* 4:615; William Savage to JM, June 25, 1803, *PJM:SS,* 5:124; Impressment of American Seamen, Dec. 5, 1803, *ASPFR,* 2:593–95; JM to the Speaker of the House of Representatives, Jan. 19, 1805, *PJM:SS,* 8:486–87; *Letter from the Secretary of State Accompanying Statements and Abstracts Relative to the Number of American Seamen Who Have Been Impressed or Detained On Board of the Ships of War of any Foreign Nation . . . 23d January, 1805* (Washington, DC: William Duane, 1805); [James Madison], American Seamen Impressed, March 5, 1806, *ASPFR,* 2:776–98; and Great Britain— Impressed American Seamen, March 2, 1808, *ASPFR,* 3:36–45.

19. JM to Rufus King, July 24, 1801, *PJM:SS*, 1:468.

20. JM to James Monroe, Dec. 26, 1803, *PTJ:SS*, 6:212. Madison first mentioned this plan to Monroe in a letter on October 10. It seems likely that the cabinet discussed and refined it throughout the autumn of 1803. JM to James Monroe, Oct. 10, 1803, *PTJ:SS*, 5:504–5.

21. JM to James Monroe, Jan. 5, 1804, *PJM:SS*, 6:282–308, quotations 283, 306.

22. James Monroe to JM, Feb 25, 1804, *PJM:SS*, 6:511.

23. James Monroe to JM, June 3, 1804, *PJM:SS*, 7:278. Harrowby became foreign secretary on May 14, 1804.

24. James Monroe to JM, Aug. 7, 1804, *PJM:SS*, 7:569–73; James Monroe to JM, Sept. 8, 1804, *PJM:SS*, 8:25–31; James Monroe to JM, Oct. 3, 1804, *PJM:SS*, 8:109–13.

25. James Monroe to JM, Oct. 18, 1805, in S. M. Hamilton, ed., *The Writings of James Monroe*, 7 vols. (New York: G. P. Putnam's Sons, 1898–1903), 4:352–65; Bradford Perkins, "Sir William Scott and the *Essex*," *WMQ*, 3rd ser., 13 (1956): 169–83; Perkins, *Prologue to War*, 77–82; James Stephen, *War in Disguise; or, the Frauds of Neutral Flags* (London: Whittingham, 1805).

26. Report by James Monroe, July 6, 1812, *ASPFR*, 3:584; Exhibit of Captures by the Belligerent Powers of Property Insured . . . in Philadelphia, [Dec. 1805], *ASPFR*, 2:742–45.

27. Report by James Monroe, July 6, 1812, *ASPFR*, 3:584. All told, according to Monroe's figures, between 1803 and 1812 the British seized 917 American ships compared to 558 vessels taken by the French. Wood, *Empire of Liberty*, 645–46; Perkins, *Creation of a Republican Empire*, 119–21. Charles James Fox became foreign secretary on February 7, 1807.

28. Perkins, *Prologue to War*, 73.

29. TJ Special Message on Neutral Commerce, Jan. 17, 1806, *ASPFR*, 2:727, 730–34. The petitions appear in *ASPFR*, 2:737–73. Also see *Memorial of the Inhabitants of the Town of Salem* (Washington, DC: A. and G. Way, 1806); *Memorial of the Merchants of the Town of Boston* (Washington, DC: A .and G. Way, 1806); Protest of Boston Merchants, *New-York Evening Post*, Feb. 7, 1806.

30. [James Madison], *An Examination of the British Doctrine, Which Subjects to Capture a Neutral Trade, Not in Time of Peace* (Philadephia, n.p., 1806).

31. For Jefferson's thinking on the importance of economic coercion, see Burton Spivak, *Jefferson's English Crisis: Commerce, Embargo, and the Republican Revolution* (Charlottesville: University Press of Virginia, 1979), ch. 1; Doron Ben-Atar, *The Origins of Jeffersonian Commercial Policy and Diplomacy* (New York: Macmillan, 1993).

32. For the debate on the Non-Importation Act, see *Annals of Congress*, 9th Cong., 1st Sess., 851–78, Randolph quotation 851. For the passage of the act, see *Annals of Congress*, 9th Cong., 1st Sess., 240, 877–78, 1259–60.

33. TJ to James Monroe, May 4, 1806, *WTJ*, 10:262.

34. Charles James Fox to Anthony Merry, April 7, 1806, in Bernard Mayo, ed., *Instructions to the British Ministers to the United States, 1791–1812* (Washington, DC: Government Printing Office, 1941), 221.

35. [William Pinkney], Memorial of the Merchants of Baltimore, Jan. 21, 1806, *ASPFR*, 2:750–56; William Pinkney to TJ, March 13, 1806, TJP. *Senate Executive Journal,* 9th Cong., 1st Sess., April 19, 1806, April 21, 1806, 2:35. For Pinkney, see Henry Wheaton, *Some Account of the Life, Writings, and Speeches of William Pinkney* (New York: J. W. Palmer, 1826), and William Pinkney, *The Life of William Pinkney* (New York: Appleton, 1853).

36. JM to James Monroe and Thomas Pinkney, May 17, 1806, *ASPFR*, 3:119–24.

37. TJ to James Monroe, May 4, 1806, *WTJ*, 10:263.

38. TJ to Jacob Crowninshield, May 13, 1806, *WTJ*, 10:266. For the *Leander* incident and the response to it, see *New-York Evening Post,* April 26, 1805; Thomas Barclay to Anthony Merry, April 27, 1806, George L. Rives, ed., *Selections from the Correspondence of Thomas Barclay* (New York: Harper Bros, 1894), 232–33; Cabinet Notes, May 1, 1806, *WTJ*, 1:397–98; Henry Whitby Proclamation, May 3, 1806, *WTJ*, 10:256–59; Proclamation Concerning 'Cambrian' etc., Dec. 20, 1806, *WTJ*, 10:325–27. Bradford Perkins, *Prologue to War,* 107–8, is critical of Jefferson's response to the *Leander* incident, arguing that Jefferson and Madison might have taken stronger action had the United States possessed stronger naval force. "As it was," Perkins writes, "they felt forced to fall back upon those favorite weapons of Jeffersonian diplomacy, a proclamation and a protest. . . . Then Jefferson and Madison sat back to wait, hoping that they had satisfied the minimum demands of American anger and that the British government would offer atonement for Whitby's action" (p. 107). This interpretation supposes that war with Britain should have been a viable option in 1806 and was an appropriate response to the accidental killing of James Pierce. It fails to take account of Jefferson's willingness to exploit Pierce's death to improve the American position in the forthcoming Monroe-Pinkney negotiations.

39. TJ to James Monroe, Oct. 26, 1806, *WTJ*, 10:296–97. For the negotiations, see James Monroe and William Pinkney to JM, Nov. 11, 1806, *ASPFR*, 3:137–40; Monroe and Pinkney to JM, Jan. 3, 1807, *ASPFR*, 3:142–47; Monroe and Pinkney to JM, April 22, 1807, *ASPFR*, 3:160–61. Also see Perkins, *Prologue to War,* 101–39; Donald R. Hickey, "The Monroe-Pinkney Treaty of 1806: A Reappraisal," *WMQ,* 3rd ser., 44 (1987): 65–88.

40. Henry Richard, Lord Holland, *Memoirs of the Whig Party during My Time,* 2 vols. (London: Longman, 1852–54), 2:100–101.

41. William Lord Grenville to Lord Holland, Oct. 30, 1806, in Walter Fitzpatrick, ed., *Report of the Manuscripts of J. B. Fortescue, Esq. Preserved at Dropmore,* 10 vols. (London: Historical Manuscripts Commission, 1892–1927), 8:410.

42. Holland, *Memoirs of the Whig Party,* 2:102.

43. James Monroe and William Pinkney to JM, Sept. 11, 1806, *ASPFR*, 3:133–35; James Monroe to JM, Feb. 28, 1808, *ASPFR*, 3:174. Also see Anthony Steel,

"Impressment in the Monroe-Pinkney Negotiations, 1806–1807," *AHR* 57 (1952), 352–69. An informal agreement according to these terms would still allow the British to impress sailors from American vessels in British and British-controlled ports.

44. Note of British Negotiators, Nov. 8, 1806, *ASPFR*, 3:140.

45. For the text of the Monroe-Pinkney Treaty, see *ASPFR*, 3:147–51. Also see James Monroe and William Pinkney to JM, Jan. 3, 1807, *ASPFR*, 3:142–47.

46. TJ to Congress, Dec. 3, 1806, *Annals of Congress,* 9th Cong., 2nd Sess., 16. The legislation to delay the implementation of the Non-Importation Act was approved on December 19, 1806. *Annals of Congress,* 9th Cong., 2nd Sess., 1250. For the optimistic report that Jefferson received requesting the delay, see Report on British Negotiations, Nov. 27, 1806, TJP.

47. *ASPFR*, 3:151–52.

48. TJ to JM, Feb. 1, 1807, in James Morton Smith, ed., *The Republic of Letters: The Correspondence between Thomas Jefferson and James Madison, 1776–1826,* 3 vols. (New York: W. W. Norton, 1995), 3:1464.

49. Notes of Cabinet Meeting, Feb. 2, 1807, *WTJ*, 1:406–8. Madison informed Monroe and Pinkney of the Jefferson's decision on February 3. *ASPFR*, 3:153–56.

50. JM to Monroe and Pinkney, Feb. 3, 1807, *ASPFR*, 3:153–56. Jefferson himself followed this with a letter to Monroe to explain his reasoning and to assure Monroe that his rejection of the treaty was not a rejection of Monroe's diplomatic efforts. TJ to James Monroe, March 21, 1807, *WTJ*, 10:374–77. Also see Jefferson's letters to Robert Livingston of March 24 (*WTJ*, 10:377) and Levi Lincoln of March 25 (*WTJ*, 10:377–78). Jefferson also consulted beyond the cabinet, seeking the views of prominent merchants. See Spivak, *Jefferson's English Crisis,* 61–67.

51. Perkins, *Prologue to War,* 139; Perkins, *Creation of a Republican Empire,* 125; Donald R. Hickey, *The War of 1812: A Forgotten Conflict* (Urbana: University of Illinois Press, 1989), 16; Malone, *Jefferson and His Time,* 5:403. Also see Hickey, "Monroe-Pinkney Treaty."

52. As quoted in Malone, *Jefferson and His Time,* 6:405.

53. JM to James Monroe and William Pinkney, May 20, 1807, *ASPFR*, 3:173.

54. For extensive documentation on the *Chesapeake-Leopard* affair, see *ASPFR,* 3:6–24, quotations 22, 20. For the incident, see Spencer C. Tucker and Frank T. Reuter, *Injured Honor: The* Chesapeake-Leopard *Affair, June 22, 1807* (Annapolis: Naval Institute Press, 1996); Ian W. Toll, *Six Frigates: The Epic Story of the Founding of the U.S. Navy* (New York: W. W. Norton, 2006), 288–313.

55. James Barron to Robert Smith, June 23, 1807, *ASPFR*, 3:18; also see the statements of the *Chesapeake*'s officers and the ship's logbook *ASPFR*, 3:19–20.

56. TJ to William Duane, July 20, 1807, *WTJ*, 10:471; Samuel Smith to JM, June 30, 1807, TJP; *Virginia Argus* (Richmond), July 1, 1807. For the immediate response to the attack on the *Chesapeake,* see the *Virginia Argus* (Richmond), June 27, 1807; *Norfolk Gazette and Public Ledger,* June 29, 1807. Also see Edwin M. Gaines, "The *Chesapeake* Affair: Virginians Mobilize to Defend National Honor,"

Virginia Magazine of History and Biography 64 (1956): 131–42; Robert E. Cray, Jr., "Remembering the U.S.S. *Chesapeake:* The Politics of Maritime Death and Imprisonment," *JER* 25 (2005): 445–74.

57. James Barron to Robert Smith, June 23, 1807, *ASPFR,* 3:18.

58. Samuel Smith to TJ, June 30, 1807, TJP.

59. TJ to Albert Gallatin, June 25, 1807, *WTJ,* 10:432; TJ to Henry Dearborn, June 25, 1807, TJP.

60. Notes of Cabinet Meeting, July 2, 1807, *WTJ,* 10:410.

61. Albert Gallatin to Hannah Gallatin, July 10, 1807, in Henry Adams, *The Life of Albert Gallatin* (Philadelphia: Lippincott, 1880), 357. Jefferson used almost identical language in writing to his son-in-law, Congressman John Wayles Eppes on July 12: "Reason & the usage of civilized nations require that we should give them an opportunity of disavowal & reparation." TJ to John W. Eppes, July 12, 1807, *WTJ,* 10:457.

62. Proclamation of the President of the United States, July 2, 1807, *ASPFR,* 3:23–24. Andrew Burstein and Nancy Isenberg argue that Madison was responsible for the harshest wording of the proclamation: "lawless & bloody purpose," "uncontrouled abuses," "injuries & irritations." Andrew Burstein and Nancy Isenberg, *Madison and Jefferson* (New York: Random House, 2010), 447. For the draft proclamation Thomas Jefferson, July 2, 1807, Proclamation and [Madison's] Draft on Armed Vessels, TJP. Madison wrote to Monroe in London on July 6, 1807, *ASPFR,* 3:183–85.

63. TJ to William H. Cabell, June 29, 1807, *WTJ,* 10:433; Notes of Cabinet Meeting, July 4, 1807, *WTJ,* 10:411; Albert Gallatin to Hannah Gallatin, July 10, 1807, in Adams, *Life of Albert Gallatin,* 358.

64. Quotation, Toll, *Six Frigates,* 300. Also see Stephen Decatur to Robert Smith, July 4, 1807, *ASPFR,* 3:21; Notes of Cabinet Meeting, July 7, 1807, *WTJ,* 10:410. Also see Gaines, "*Chesapeake* Affair."

65. TJ to Henry Dearborn, July 7, 1807, *WTJ,* 10:449–50. New York's vulnerability was a major concern of the government during the *Chesapeake* crisis. On June 30 Senator Smith of Maryland urged Jefferson to "show the people of that great and important city that you will protect them & their property." Samuel Smith to JM, June 30, 1807, TJP. Albert Gallatin wrote on July 10: "I have, in a national point of view, but one subject of considerable uneasiness, and that is New York, which is now entirely defenceless, and from its situation nearly indefensible." Albert Gallatin to Hannah Gallatin, July 10, 1807, in Adams, *Life of Albert Gallatin,* 358.

66. See, for example, TJ to Officers and Various Militia, July 8, 1807; TJ to Norfolk, Virginia, Master of Vessels, July 8, 1807; TJ to John Saunders, July 8, 1807; TJ to John Page, July 9, 1807; TJ to Thomas Appleton, July 9, 1807; TJ to James Bowdoin, July 10, 1807, TJP.

67. From the attack on *Chesapeake* until the end of July 1807 Cabell wrote to Jefferson on June 25, July 6, 8, 10, 15, 19, 20, 21. Jefferson wrote to Cabell on June 29

and July 16, 19, 24, 27, and 31. Also see TJ to Thomas Mathews, July 8, 1807, TJP. Also see Gaines, *"Chesapeake* Affair" and Malone, *Jefferson and His Time,* 5:432–34.

68. TJ to Henry Dearborn July [17], 1807, *WTJ,* 10:467–8; Notes of Cabinet Meeting, July 26, 1807, *WTJ,* 10:411–15.

69. TJ to John Page, July 17, 1807, *WTJ,* 10:470.

70. As quoted in Boyd Hilton, *A Mad, Bad, and Dangerous People? England, 1783–1846* (Oxford: Clarendon Press, 2006), 211.

71. *The Trial of John Wilson, Alias Jenkin Ratford, for Mutiny, Desertion and Contempt* (Boston: Snelling and Simons, 1807).

72. George Canning to James Monroe, Aug. 3, 1807, *ASPFR,* 3:188; George Canning to James Monroe, Sept. 23, 1807, *ASPFR,* 3:200; Proclamation of George III, Oct. 16, 1807, *ASPFR,* 3:25–26. The deserters taken from the *Chesapeake* were court-martialed.

73. Paul L. Ford provides side-by-side versions of the various drafts of the address as well as Gallatin's detailed feedback on the address. See *WTJ,* 10:503–27.

74. TJ to William H. Cabell, Nov. 1, 1807, TJP.

75. Ibid. On October 31 the cabinet discussed the disposition of the navy's gunboats assigning seventeen to New York, three to Norfolk, fifteen to Charleston, and eight to New Orleans. Notes of Cabinet Meeting, [Oct.] 31, 1807, *WTJ,* 1:418. For the debate over and appropriation of the funding for the gunboats, see *Annals of Congress,* 10th Cong., 1st Sess., 32–33, 985–1000, 1061–62, 1065–1170.

76. Confidential Message, Dec. 7, 1807, *WTJ,* 10:528–9.

77. Special Message on Commercial Depredations, Dec. 18, 1807, *WTJ,* 10:530–31. For the adoption of the Embargo Act, see *Annals of Congress,* 10th Cong., 1st Sess., 50–51, 1216–28.

78. TJ to William H. Cabell, June 29, 1807, *WTJ,* 10:433.

79. Economic statistics from Cogliano, *Revolutionary America,* 241–42. For the embargo, see Ben-Atar, *Origins of Jeffersonian Commercial Policy;* Spivak, *Jefferson's English Crisis,* ch. 4; Richard Mannix, "Gallatin, Jefferson, and the Embargo of 1808," *Diplomatic History* 3 (1979): 151–72; Perkins, *Prologue to War,* 140–83; Spivak, *Jefferson's English Crisis,* ch. 4; Tucker and Hendrickson, *Empire of Liberty,* 204–28; Louis M. Sears, *Jefferson and the Embargo* (Durham: Duke University Press, 1927); Malone, *Jefferson and His Time,* 5:469–90; Burstein and Isenberg, *Madison and Jefferson,* 450–57; James Duncan Phillips, "Jefferson's 'Wicked Tyrannical Embargo,'" *New England Quarterly* 18 (1945): 466–78; Jeffrey A. Frankel, "The 1807–1809 Embargo against Great Britain," *Journal of Economic History* 42 (1982): 291–308; Douglas Lamar Jones, "'The Caprice of Juries': The Enforcement of the Jeffersonian Embargo in Massachusetts," *American Journal of Legal History* 24 (1980): 307–30; Christopher Ward, "The Commerce of East Florida during the Embargo, 1806–1812: The Role of Amelia Island," *Florida Historical Quarterly* 68 (1989): 160–79 .

80. *Annals of Congress*, 10th Cong., 2nd Sess., 1172–1350; Reginald C. Stuart, "James Madison and the Militants: Republican Disunity and Replacing the Embargo," *Diplomatic History* 6 (1982): 145–68;

81. TJ to William Cabell, March 13, 1808; TJ to JM, March 11, 1808, *Republic of Letters*, 3:1514–15.

82. Wood, *Empire of Liberty*, 649; Robert W. Tucker and David C. Hendrickson, *Empire of Liberty: The Statecraft of Thomas Jefferson* (New York: Oxford University Press, 1990), 178, 179.

83. TJ to Thomas Mann Randolph, Nov. 30, 1807, TJP; *Anti-Monarchist, and Republican Watch-man* (Edgefield, SC), Dec. 14, 1808, as quoted in Burstein and Isenberg, *Madison and Jefferson*, 728n53. Herring, *From Colony to Superpower*, 119.

84. Herring, *From Colony to Superpower*, 120.

85. Cray, "Remembering the U.S.S. *Chesapeake*," 472–73.

86. J. C. A. Stagg et al., eds., *Papers of James Madison:Presidential Series*, 7 vols. to date (Charlottesville: University of Virginia Press, 1984–), 4:432–33.

Conclusion
"Ne Plus Ultra"

1. J. C. A. Stagg et al., eds., *Papers of James Madison: Presidential Series*, 7 vols. to date (Charlottesville: University of Virginia Press, 1984–), 1:117–19, 125–26; Bradford Perkins, *Prologue to War: England and the United States, 1805–1812* (Berkeley: University of California Press, 1961), 211–13.

2. TJ to JM, April 27, 1809, *PTJ:RS*, 1:168–69.

3. Richard Kluger, *Seizing Destiny: How America Grew from Sea to Shining Sea* (New York: Alfred A. Knopf, 2007); Walter Nugent, *Habits of Empire: A History of American Expansion* (New York: Alfred A, Knopf, 2008).

Index